Opening Doors to the World

Opening Doors to the World

A New Trade Agenda for the Middle East

Edited by Raed Safadi

The American University in Cairo Press

International Development Research Centre

in association with the
Economic Research Forum
for the Arab Countries, Iran and Turkey

Published in the Arab countries, Iran and Turkey by
The American University in Cairo Press
113 Sharia Kasr el Aini
Cairo, Egypt

Dar el Kutub No. 7444/98
ISBN 977 424 496 6

Published in North America and Europe by the
International Development Research Centre
P.O. Box 8500, Ottawa, Ontario
Canada K1G 3H9

ISBN 0 88936 877 5

Designed and typeset by the
Economic Research Forum for the Arab Countries, Iran and Turkey

Canadian Cataloguing in Publication Data

Main entry under title :

Opening doors to the world : a new trade agenda for the Middle East

Co-published by the American University in Cairo Press.
ISBN 0-88936-877-5

1. Middle East — Commerce.
2. Africa, North — Commerce.
3. Free trade.
4. International trade.
I. Safadi, Raed, 1958–
II. International Development Research Centre (Canada).
III. Title: A new trade agenda for the Middle East.

HC415.15063 1998   382'.0956   C98-980336-8

Printed in Egypt

Contents

Foreword

The Economic Research Forum for the Arab Countries, Iran and Turkey (ERF) is an independent, nonprofit networking institution based in Cairo. Its mandate is to promote and fund quality research on policy-relevant topics – to inform decision-makers and the economics research community in the Middle East and North Africa region – and to enrich the dialogue between North and South, and among countries of the South. The ERF is equally committed to contributing to capacity-building among younger researchers in the region.

This volume is the second to be published by the ERF in association with the American University in Cairo Press, as part of its efforts to disseminate the findings of ongoing research on the region. The first volume, Economic Transition in the Middle East, addressed the questions posed by the processes of globalization, deregulation, privatization, and institutional reform, paying particular attention to country-specific cases. This book brings together a number of papers on the different aspects of trade liberalization and the implications for Middle East and North Africa countries of joining the World Trade Organization (WTO) and the Free Trade Agreements with Europe. Contributions are by some of the most prominent international and regional specialists on trade; they range from providing a historical perspective, as countries first began to adapt their trade system to the WTO and EuroMed challenges, to addressing key issues such as export prospects, trade in financial services and catching up with Eastern Europe. It is hoped that the broad range of contributions will add to the on-going debate on what constitutes the best trade practices for the region in the coming years.

This book could not have been produced without the efforts of a number of people. Distinguished trade economist Raed Safadi selected and edited the papers, as well as commissioned some of the contributions. The ERF's Publications Director Gillian Potter helped to finalize the manuscript and to reproduce it in camera-ready form; Maureen Moynihan followed up on administrative matters with great efficiency; Pauline Wickham from the American University in Cairo Press also provided invaluable advice and support throughout the production process. The ERF is grateful to all of these individuals for their efforts in making this book possible.

Heba Handoussa
Managing Director
Economic Research Forum for the Arab Countries, Iran and Turkey

Part I
Trading into the 21st Century

The Evolving Agenda for Trade
in a Globalizing World

Introduction

The increasing globalization of economic activity has intensified policy inter-action in traditional areas of multilateral economic cooperation. The most obvious manifestations of this have involved governments in continuing efforts to remove tariff and non-tariff barriers to trade, to extend the coverage of liberalization efforts in such areas as government procurement and agri-culture, and to sharpen trade rules, including those relating to matters like safeguards, subsidies and countervailing duties, and antidumping. In addition, closer economic integration among nation states has "internationalized" a range of policy domains that previously were either simply neglected, or con-sidered an exclusively national preserve, or else were subject only to comity-like coordination and consultation arrangements. As a result, major multilat-eral initiatives have led to negotiations, and in some instances agreements, in new areas such as trade in services, the protection of intellectual property rights, and investment. Other issues, such as competition policy and labor rights, have been proposed by some governments as matters ripe for interna-tional negotiation. This chapter attempts to identify what pressures for increased policy commitments at the international level mean in practice in the area of trade.

The deepening and broadening of the international economic agenda has influenced governments' approaches and priorities with respect to policy in at least two significant ways. First, a number of new policy areas that have either found their way onto the international agenda, or are under discussion, are not necessarily about trade per se, but rather are treated as "trade-related" matters. This is most obvious in the case of intellectual property rights, labor standards and environmental issues. In these areas, an organic link may exist between the issues at hand and trade policy, but it may also be the case that the trade policy dimension is concerned primarily with the question of enforcement. In other words, the link between policies in such areas as those mentioned above and trade policy may reside fundamentally in the notion that the threat of denial of trade benefits offers an effective means of enforcing unrelated poli-cy obligations. The practical implication of this tendency for bodies like the World Trade Organization is that subjects brought within the institution's purview will not necessarily relate to traditional areas of concern. This is but one reflection of how closer economic integration among nations triggers broad-based policy responses from governments.

More generally, governments have demonstrated increasing concern with a broad range of policy-related determinants of competitiveness. The globalization of economic activity has nurtured a growing interest in the numerous ways in which the conditions of market access may be influenced. Perhaps the area where this concern is most noticeable is in standard-setting and domestic regulation more generally. Sensitivity to the reality that regulations can be manipulated to tilt the conditions of competition in favor of a subset of economic actors, together with the realization that sharply divergent preferences in such matters as environmental quality and social policy are increasingly crucial determinants of competitive advantage, have increased pressures for harmonization in many policy areas. Such harmonization may be negotiated, or may come about through de facto competition among regulatory systems. Whichever approach dominates, the imperative felt by governments to ensure that their economic constituencies are not placed at a disadvantage through sharply different approaches to policy intervention can be a source of significant friction at the international level. Managing this friction is one of today's most pressing challenges for policy-makers.

Second, globalization and a growing attachment to regionalism seem to have coexisted in a manner which might seem contradictory at first sight. At the same time as barriers to integrated economic activity on a global scale appear to be disintegrating, so does governments' fascination seem to grow with intensified cooperation bounded by a localized or regional focus. If the phenomenon of growing interdependence is apparent not only in respect of relations with near neighbors, why limit the policy response to this subset of players? The risk of too narrow a policy focus is that the economic benefits of globalization may be compromised through regional integration arrangements that discriminate against outsiders. On the other hand, it is probable that a regional approach has been preferred more because of the greater ease of managing a complex set of relations among a limited number of like-minded countries than because governments have wished to discriminate. To the extent that this is the case, the risk is not great that the prominence of geographically-bound policy responses to international economic integration will frustrate natural tendencies towards globalization. Nevertheless, the danger that regionalism could become a splintering and destructive force cannot be ignored, and should remain uppermost in the minds of policy-makers.

In the remainder of this chapter, attention will be focused on particular issues that appear to be among the most significant in defining the evolving agenda for trade, investment and finance. The next three sections deal with, respectively, trade in services, intellectual property rights and technical standards and regulatory reform. Finally, the last section offers some concluding remarks.

Trade in Services

Background

It took more than four decades after the birth of GATT (the General Agreement on Tariffs and Trade) for the subject of trade in services to find its way onto the multilateral negotiating agenda. By about the latter half of the 1970s, the absence of rules and multilateral commitments on trade in services was beginning to be seen as a significant systemic gap. Awareness was growing of the importance of services-related activities in the world economy. The process of globalization probably accelerated the pace at which this perception became generalized, on account of the fundamental importance of a number of services sectors in international trade – most notably, transport, telecommunications and financial services.

The production of services was increasingly seen as an independent activity, worthy of explicit multilateral attention. Prior to this, international trade had been seen largely through the prism of trade in goods. Services were altogether subsidiary, either in the sense of being embodied in goods, or as secondary activities undertaken in the cause of facilitating the supply and commerce of goods. Also missing from this perception of what was important in the world economy was the role of investment. Investment was treated largely as a matter of domestic policy concern. The notion that investment and trade are merely different means of gaining access to markets, to be treated in a complementary fashion rather than as substitutes, is also a rather recent phenomenon.

Technological advances have also played a key role in bringing trade in services to the forefront of policy makers' concerns. Advances in transport and information technologies have contributed to a rapid expansion of services trade. Many international transactions, which previously would have been considered prohibitively expensive, have now become commonplace because of the ease with which people can move and communicate electronically across national boundaries. These trends are reflected in the fact that trade in services has grown faster than trade in goods for well over a decade. While services exports accounted for some 16 percent of world exports in 1980, the share had risen to over 20 percent in the early 1990s. Annual average growth in services exports was approximately 8 percent from 1980 to 1992, compared to some 5 percent for merchandise exports.

Salient Characteristics of Services

It is arguable that some of the features of services and the nature of services transactions have contributed to the relative neglect of services in policy discourse. It is useful to consider briefly a number of the differences between goods and services, as these are at least part of the explanation as to why the General Agreement on Trade in Services (GATS) is different in a number of important respects from the GATT.

Invisibility, Measurement and Data

The intangible or invisible nature of services has made the measurement of them difficult, and resulted in significant lacunae in the existing information base on services transactions at both the national and international levels. For the most part, production and investment data on services are scarce, and it is virtually impossible to make international comparisons, even on a cross-sectional basis. National input-output tables are the most detailed source of production data on services, since they help to isolate services transactions which otherwise stay hidden as goods production, but few countries maintain recent and significantly disaggregated input-output matrices. Data on investment are frequently not sufficiently disaggregated for it to be possible to derive reliable information on trends in investment, and this problem is even more acute at the international level. By contrast, data on international trade in services have been collected on a systematic basis for many years in balance-of-payments statistics. But the statistics are highly aggregated, concentrating primarily on transport and travel, and only providing a limited picture. The International Monetary Fund, however, has recently introduced more disaggregation in balance-of-payments data.

Another problem in the sphere of data is known as the "disembodiment" or "splintering" question. Increased specialization has resulted in services activities being broken off from goods production. A manufacturer, for example, may in the past have maintained all advertising activities in-house, with the consequence that the production of advertising services would simply be counted as an input into the production of manufactured goods. If this manufacturer subsequently purchases advertising services from an agency specialized in producing these services, then national statistics will record this same element of production as services production and not goods production.

Thus, disembodiment via specialization may create the impression that services production is increasing relative to goods production, when in effect some of this perceived shift is the result of structural change within the economy. Another factor which may give rise to an exaggerated picture of growth in the relative importance of services is simply that measurement techniques have improved over time. Thus, what data are available measure a growing component of services activities in total production at least in part because the hardest part of measurement is being done better. Notwithstanding these sources of bias, however, it is clear that demand for services does rise relative to demand for goods as income grows, and that services-related activities are therefore bound to become a greater source of interest from a policy perspective.

Simultaneity in Production and Consumption, and Physical Proximity

A feature of most services is that they cannot be produced and then stored for later consumption. Production and consumption are simultaneous. This is clearly an additional source of measurement difficulty, and also gives rise to a greater tendency for "customization" or product differentiation, such that it can be misleading to assume that unit prices can be identified for homogenous output. Even the question of what represents a unit of production may be open to debate.

Simultaneity in production and consumption also carry the implication that producers and consumers often need to be in the same location in order for a transaction to take place. The classic example of haircutting services makes this point clear, given the obvious impossibility of supplying haircutting services at a distance. There are, however, some services transactions that may occur over distance, on account of the possibility that they can be transmitted electronically. Moreover, one class of services – transport services – is intrinsically about bridging distance, so the question of physical proximity does not arise. The immediate policy implication of the importance of physical proximity in services trade is that liberalization cannot be discussed solely in the traditional terms of cross-border trade. It is also necessary to consider commercial presence, or investment. A further point to note is that even if physical presence is not a technical prerequisite of consummating transactions in services, it is in the nature of many service products that suppliers will want to be in close proximity to their customers.

As discussed below, the significance of investment in trade in services is reflected in GATS, and is what makes GATS into an agreement about both cross-border trade and investment. It might also be argued that the prominence of investment issues in trade in services has contributed to a growing awareness of the need to deal with investment questions as an integral part of the international economic policy agenda.

A Detour: Investment in the GATT Context

If rules on investment had already existed in GATT, it is possible that investment in both goods and services would have been treated together, and so would trade in goods and services. This was, the pattern that emerged in NAFTA (North American Free Trade Agreement), for example, an agreement that was negotiated from a clean slate. The differential treatment of goods and services within the WTO (the World Trade Organization) framework raises questions of coherence that will have to be addressed in due time, not least because of the asymmetries between rules on goods and services that this model has produced.

The issue of investment was taken up in the GATT context in the Uruguay Round (UR), eventually leading to the Agreement on Trade-Related Investment Measures (TRIMS). But the TRIMS Agreement is very limited in scope. Some industrial countries, most notably the United States, had pressed for a far-reaching mandate to negotiate about investment in the broad sense. Many developing countries were unwilling to engage in such an exercise at that time. They believed that it would challenge a basic tenet of their development policy, which saw the careful management of investment flows as indispensable to appropriate, balanced growth.

Investment policy, involving a mix of controls and incentives, has traditionally been used by many countries as a tool for promoting specific objectives, such as technology transfer, industrialization, regional development and export expansion. Some of these objectives, like regional development, have also been pursued through investment incentives in industrial countries. The emphasis of the Uruguay Round TRIMS exercise, however, was mostly on trade-related investment conditionality. The subsidy aspect of investment policy was addressed in the Agreement on Subsidies and Countervailing Measures, where regional subsidies are defined as non-actionable, provided they are granted in the context of an overall regional development program, are non-specific to an enterprise or industry, and do not result in serious adverse effects to the industry of another party.

Moreover, the ability to condition and control investment flows has traditionally been considered necessary to avoid monopolistic abuses by transnational corporations. Seen from this perspective, multilateral efforts to liberalize investment threatened to weaken the ability of countries to pursue active development policies. Opposition to a broad-based negotiation on investment in the UR was strong enough, given the disposition of interests and priorities in other areas (especially intellectual property rights and trade in services), for agreement to be reached on a narrow negotiating mandate for TRIMS. The negotiating mandate simply called for an examination of the operation of GATT articles related to the trade restrictive and distorting effects of investment measures, following which "negotiations should elaborate, as appropriate, further provisions that may be necessary to avoid such adverse effects on trade." The use of the phrase "as appropriate," along with the conditional tense, left open the possibility that governments might agree to nothing at all.

However, the UR TRIMS agreement only reaffirmed existing GATT rules on national treatment (Article III) and on the prohibition of quantitative restrictions (Article XI). An illustrative list of TRIMS identified two measures as being inconsistent with GATT's national treatment provisions and three as constituting illegal quantitative restrictions. The first category included local content requirements and trade balancing requirements. The TRIMS identified as quantitative restrictions included trade balancing requirements (also Article III-inconsistent), foreign exchange balancing requirements, and domestic sales requirements.[1] The agreement requires that WTO-inconsistent TRIMS must be phased out, and that no new WTO-inconsistent TRIMS are to be introduced during the phase-out period.[2] Industrial countries must complete the phase-out within two years, developing countries within five years, and least-developed countries within seven years. These transition periods may be extended for developing and least-developed countries under certain circumstances. All TRIMS subject to the phase-out requirement had to be notified to the WTO.

The Role of Regulation

Given the invisible character of services, the normal requirement for production and consumption to occur simultaneously, and the general lack of information about services transactions within the economy, it is unsurprising that regulation is a prominent feature of services activities. Governments are much more heavily involved in regulation in services sectors than they typically are in goods sectors. Two aspects of regulation in services may be usefully distinguished.

First, in contrast to goods sectors, interventions are more often of a quantitative nature rather than price-based. The preference for administrative interventions of a quantitative character may be understandable in view of the difficulties of identification and measurement that plague the services sector. But from an efficiency perspective, price-based interventions are likely to prove better in many cases. A policy challenge in the services field, therefore, is to find ways of improving the information base so that greater reliance can be placed upon fiscal policy in the future to achieve regulatory objectives. It is noteworthy in this context that the GATS has very little to say about price-related measures, basing almost all its rules dealing with access to markets upon quantity-based interventions.

Second, the impossibility of storing most services, or of distancing production and consumption in a temporal sense, means that much regulation is of an ex ante variety. In other words, instead of focusing on output, regulatory interventions need to occur on the input side. This means regulating suppliers rather than products. Regulators can hardly be expected to wait upon the consequences of a surgical intervention, for example, before judging whether the person performing it is capable of doing so.

One implication of the regulatory focus on the supply side is that much regulation, at least in the first instance, is about authorization to enter the market, rather than performance in the market. This automatically translates into a greater preponderance of regulatory interventions, since product regulation does not necessarily involve conformity assessment with respect to every single unit of production, whereas if services need to be regulated, this cannot be achieved on the supply side via sampling. All service suppliers will have to submit to whatever procedures are required. From a policy perspective, this means that progress in liberalization of trade in services is highly dependent on progress in the field of regulatory reform.

The General Agreement on Trade in Services (GATS)

Scope and Structure

Governments exercised caution when they negotiated the GATS, providing themselves with ample scope to condition their multilateral commitments. Two aspects of the GATS that need to be distinguished are the part that establishes a framework of rules governing trade in services, and the part that sets out the specific sectoral commitments undertaken by Members. The latter are inscribed in schedules appended to the Agreement. Only some of the provisions of the GATS framework agreement relate to the universe of trade in services, as defined under the agreement, while others are restricted to those service activities subject to scheduled sectoral commitments.

Several provisions clearly reflect the pervasiveness of regulations in many service sectors, and the intent to prevent the protectionist abuse of such regulations. The specific schedules indicate which service sectors each signatory has been willing to subject to non-general obligations under GATS. The schedules also provide for qualifications to the national treatment and market access commitments that otherwise apply to sectoral commitments. Finally, a series of annexes and decisions elaborate on commitments and exceptions with respect to different rules and sectors, and also establish a work program, including further sectoral negotiations.

The obligations and disciplines set out in the GATS framework include rules on most-favored nations (MFNs) treatment, transparency, increasing participation of developing countries, economic integration, domestic regulation, recognition, monopolies and exclusive service suppliers, business practices, emergency safeguards, payments and transfers, balance-of-payments restrictions, government procurement, general and security exceptions, and subsidies.

The scope of the agreement, the definition of trade in services, and sectoral coverage are laid out in Part I of GATS. The Agreement applies to all measures taken by Members that affect trade in services. Trade in services is defined in terms of four modes of supply. The first mode involves the cross-border (arms-length or long-distance) supply of a service from one jurisdiction to another. This mode of delivery is analogous to international trade in goods, in that a product crosses a frontier. Many different kinds of electronic information flow occur across national borders. The second mode of supply requires the movement of consumers to the jurisdiction of suppliers.[3] Tourism is a good example of this mode, involving the movement of (mobile) tourists to (immobile) tourist facilities in another country.

The third mode of supply is through the commercial presence of a supplier in the jurisdiction where the consumers are located (abstracting from export sales). This is the investment mode, referred to above. An important point to note about the investment mode is that it involves two distinct components. The first relates to the authorization to invest, or in other words to the setting up of business in another Member's territory. The second deals with post-establishment operations, or in other words with actually doing business. Both these aspects are covered by GATS. The idea of including commercial presence in GATS was initially opposed by many developing countries. They argued that commitments on service transactions under this mode of supply were tantamount to a surrogate obligation on foreign direct investment, and they expressed unwillingness to tie in their investment regimes in this manner.

Finally, the fourth mode entails the movement of natural persons from one jurisdiction to another. This is the mode under which the sensitive issue of the movement of labor is addressed. The Agreement makes it clear that provisions on movement of natural persons do not address issues relating to access to the employment market, nor measures regarding citizenship, residence or employment on a permanent basis. The fourth mode relates both to independent service suppliers and to employees of juridical persons supplying services. Just as with the commercial presence mode, the GATS covered both the right to establish a presence and the right to do business under the fourth mode.

The conceptual approach underlying these modes was first developed in the academic literature as a heuristic device to explain the nature of international transactions in services. Differentiation by modes of supply later formed the basis on which governments defined market access commitments under GATS, permitting a choice to be made from among alternative modes. The use of modal distinctions is a reflection of the manner in which liberalization is defined under the Agreement, and the possibility of applying different policy regimes to different modes of supply is a potential source of economic distortion. It may also be argued that the absence of symmetry in the policy conditions affecting the different modes imposes limitations on the reach of liberalization. Despite early reservations about commercial presence, a tendency is discernible for scheduled commitments to be concentrated in the commercial presence mode. In some cases, this may be because countries have attempted to use the GATS as an instrument for encouraging foreign direct investment. In others, it reflects the desire to avoid "regulatory competition" between different jurisdictions. Furthermore, where regulatory control is considered important, as in prudential controls in banking, for example, governments find it easier to impose and enforce regulations in their own territories.

A second feature of the definition of services covered by GATS is the exclusion of services supplied in the exercise of governmental authority. The definition of a service supplied in the exercise of governmental authority is "any service which is supplied neither on a commercial basis, nor in competition with one or more service suppliers" (Article 1:3(c)). The intention of this provision is to permit governments to exclude basic infrastructural and social services which they supply their populations on an exclusive basis from the purview of the Agreement.

The most important general obligations in GATS are the MFN principle articulated in Article II and the publication and supply of information aspects of the transparency provisions in Article III. The MFN clause states that:

> With respect to any measure covered by this Agreement, each Member shall accord immediately and unconditionally to services and service suppliers of any other Member treatment no less favorable than that it accords to like services and service suppliers of any other country.

Note that the MFN principle refers to both services and service suppliers, reflecting the fact that the GATS is both an investment and a trade agreement. Article II of GATS also provides the possibility that Members may maintain MFN-inconsistent measures as long as they are scheduled in the Annex on Article II Exemptions. Exemptions from MFN could only be registered prior to the entry into force of the Agreement, and cannot be supplemented. Moreover, they are subject to periodic review and are in principle meant to be maintained for no longer than ten years.

The MFN exemption provisions reflected the concern of some larger countries that by granting MFN access to their markets, they would be losing the opportunity to exchange their relatively open access for further liberalization in other markets. In other words, these countries were arguing that "free riding" would occur in the absence of an effective instrument to ensure reciprocity. The issue was raised most explicitly in the telecommunications and financial service negotiations. Some 60 countries took MFN exemptions, affecting most significantly the audio-visual, financial, basic telecommunications, and transport services sectors. The MFN exemption in the financial services sector was suspended pending the outcome of post-UR negotiations. MFN provisions did not apply either to basic telecommunications and maritime services (except where specific scheduled commitments have been undertaken) pending completion of negotiations in these areas. Audio-visual MFN exemptions reflect European concerns about the cultural reach of US entertainment products, and are justified in terms of arguments about defending the national heritage. The European Union (EU) not only exercised its right to insist on an MFN exclusion, but also failed to make any specific commitments in this sector.

A fundamental feature of GATS is the principle of progressive liberalization (Part IV). It reflects the reality that governments were neither willing nor able simply to open up their services markets to international competition from one day to the next. Progressive liberalization implies a gradual approach, and the structure of the GATS accommodates such gradualism. Members have already committed themselves to enter into successive rounds of negotiations aimed at achieving higher levels of liberalization. The first such negotiation is to take place at the turn of the century. A question to consider, however, is whether the GATS does indeed offer a vehicle for achieving trade liberalization, or whether its structure is such as to allow governments to support a putatively market-opening instrument while in practice holding off liberalization into the indefinite future. In other words, has a proper balance been struck between gradualism and the gradual attainment of ever higher levels of liberalization?

In considering this question, it is useful to examine certain structural features of GATS which, it could be argued, are important in determining the pace of liberalization. Two of them relate to the discussion so far, and others are dealt with later in relation to scheduled commitments. First, there is the question of the scope of application of the provisions of GATS. Under the existing structure, few obligations in GATS apply unless a sector and the associated modes of delivery have been made subject to specific commitments in the schedule of a Member. As noted above, the MFN principle in Article II and the transparency commitments in Article III are the main general obligations of the agreement. In addition, certain provisions dealing with recognition of qualifications (Article VII), monopolies and exclusive suppliers (Article VIII), and business practices (Article IX) are of general application. The most important gaps in general application, which have the effect of reducing the reach of GATS, are those relating to domestic regulation, market access and national treatment.

The intensity of regulation in services, as well as the fact that the GATS deals with both investment and trade, makes the GATS provisions on domestic regulation a crucial element of the Agreement. To the extent that the disciplines on regulations laid out in Article VI do not apply to unscheduled activities and sectors, the disciplinary impact of GATS is correspondingly limited. Moreover, only the bare bones of rules on regulations have so far been established. These are based primarily on the notion of necessity, such that any regulatory interventions relating to qualification requirements and procedures, technical standards and licensing requirements should not constitute unnecessary barriers to trade in services. Regulatory interventions must also be non-discriminatory and based on objective and transparent criteria. Licensing procedures must not in themselves create a restriction on the supply of a service.

In light of the acknowledged inadequacy of these provisions in terms of their generality, paragraph 4 of Article VI calls for a work program to develop further the GATS provisions on domestic regulation. In addition, the Decision on Professional Services calls for recommendations for the elaboration of multilateral disciplines in the accountancy sector. Governments might consider whether regulatory disciplines should cover all sectors, and the work program could provide an opportunity for extending regulatory disciplines beyond specific commitments in schedules, to all services covered by GATS.

A second structural issue relates to the difference between a "positive" and a "negative" list approach to scheduling specific commitments under GATS. A positive list approach to sectoral coverage requires that Members list the sectors in which they are willing to undertake commitments, and any sector or activity not so listed in a Member's schedule is not subject to specific commitments. The GATS has adopted a positive list approach to scheduling sectors. A negative list approach, by contrast, requires that Members list those sectors or activities in respect of which they are unwilling to assume commitments, leaving all other sectors covered by implication.

Three arguments are advanced as to why a negative list approach may foster greater liberalization than a positive list approach. First, it is argued that with a negative list greater transparency is assured, since the true coverage of the Agreement would be readily revealed. On the other hand, given that all governments know what services are included in the established sectoral nomenclature under GATS, the validity of the transparency argument would seem to depend on whether adequate transparency provisions per se are in place, rather than upon the choice of means to indicate sectoral coverage.

The second argument is that by forcing governments to list sectors in which they are unwilling to accept commitments, a greater pro-liberalization dynamic will be created, as long lists might cause embarrassment. It is not altogether clear, however, why governments should be more embarrassed by long negative lists than by short positive ones. The third argument is probably the most powerful in favor of a negative list approach. It is that with a negative list, new sectors would automatically be covered by GATS disciplines, unless explicit action were taken to exclude them. As technology moves fast in many service sectors, this is a significant consideration, and may help explain the reluctance of governments to adopt a negative list approach.

Schedules of Specific Commitments

Articles XVI, XVII and XVIII are the core of the Agreement as far as specific commitments are concerned. Article XVI deals with market access, which is defined in a very specific manner. Having established that signatories will accord services and service suppliers treatment at least as favorable as that provided for in the schedules, the Article goes on to define six types of market access restrictions that will not be adopted in respect of sectors where market access commitments are undertaken unless there is a specification to the contrary in the schedule of specific commitments. In other words, disciplines on market access impediments will apply to scheduled commitments unless a reservation is registered to the contrary. This is a negative list approach nested in the overall positive list approach of the GATS schedules. The six impediments or limitations on access are defined as: a) limitations on the number of suppliers; b) limitations on the total value of service transactions or assets; c) limitations on the total number of service operations or on the total quantity of service output; d) limitations on the total number of natural persons that may be employed; e) measures which restrict or require specific types of legal entity or joint venture; and f) limitations on the participation of foreign capital. Article XVI limitations are exhaustive, in the sense that these are the only limitations on market access that Members are permitted to inscribe in their schedules.

It should be noted that items (a) to (d) of Article XVI are expressed in terms of quantitative market access limitations – the number of suppliers, the value of transactions or assets, the number of operations or quantity of output, or the number of natural persons that may be employed. In considering the overall GATS objective of progressive liberalization, a question is whether it would be more appropriate to express these limitations in terms of price measures rather than quantitative limitations. Access limitations could be imposed on foreign suppliers through fiscal measures, and perhaps even subjected to periodic negotiations aimed at reducing such limitations. If this approach were adopted, governments may then want to consider whether the framework agreement contained enough provisions for applying quantitative restraints on services trade under particular circumstances. A structural change of this nature would almost certainly imply a greater degree of liberalization than the existing arrangements. It is questionable, however, whether governments would be willing, in the foreseeable future, to move in this direction.

Article XVII contains the national treatment provision of the agreement. The approach here is very similar to that of market access, with national treatment applicable only to scheduled commitments, and only then if reservations are not made to the contrary. National treatment is defined in the traditional GATT manner, as treatment no less favorable than that accorded to domestic homologues, in this case services and service suppliers. Article XVII recognizes, however, that the attainment of national treatment may involve treatment that is not formally equivalent, and that formally equivalent treatment may not yield a non-discriminatory outcome either. A significant difference between national treatment in GATT and in GATS is that in the former case, national treatment is established as a principle to be applied across the board,[4] whereas in the latter case, national treatment has been given negotiating currency – it is something to be granted, denied or qualified, depending on the sector and signatory concerned.

One reason why governments may have been unwilling to see national treatment play the same role in GATS as in GATT, or the role that MFN plays in GATS as a general principle, is that under the commercial presence and movement of natural persons modes in GATS (Modes 3 and 4), full national treatment is equivalent to free trade – it would guarantee unlimited investment rights for foreign service suppliers. While governments were willing to guarantee this treatment in some sectors where they made scheduled commitments unencumbered by national treatment limitations, this was clearly not true across the board. In these circumstances, if national treatment had been an inviolate principle not subject to conditioning, it is probable that even less would have been incorporated in the schedules than what is there at present.

An intermediate approach to using the national treatment rule as a more effective instrument of liberalization would be to impose limitations on the nature of permissible departures from national treatment. At present, any kind of departure is permitted, provided the limitation is entered in the schedule against the relevant sectoral commitment. The nature of departures from national treatment could be defined, with an emphasis on price-based measures, and these measures could also be subject to progressive reductions in the context of negotiations aimed at greater liberalization. Once again, it is an open question whether governments would be willing to embark on a structural change of this nature.

Article XVIII offers the possibility for signatories to negotiate additional commitments not dealt with under the market access and national treatment provisions of Article XVI and Article XVII. These commitments could apply to such matters as qualifications, standards and licensing, and would be inscribed in Members' schedules. Limited use was made of this option in the UR negotiations. The most important aspect of Article XVIII measures is that they must express commitments favoring more open access, and not additional market barriers.

As noted at the beginning of this chapter, any analysis of GATS or trade in services more generally suffers from an acute shortage of reliable data. In the case of specific commitments, no statistical base exists from which to estimate the value in trade or welfare terms of what countries have bound. The only alternative is to undertake a frequency count of commitments. Such a procedure ignores the relative importance of different service activities, and takes no account of the implications of market access and national treatment limitations inscribed in the schedules.

On the basis of a frequency count, industrial countries on average made commitments on 64 percent of all service activities, while the comparable figures for transition and developing economies were 52 percent and 16 percent respectively. It is important to note that these averages conceal significant variance among countries within the groupings. This is especially true of the developing countries, of whom a number made commitments more far-reaching than suggested by the average. For various reasons, commitments were more sparse in the audiovisual sector, basic telecommunications and transportation. When these are excluded from the reckoning, the shares increase to 82 percent (industrial countries), 66 percent (transition economy countries), and 19 percent (developing countries). Only five participants made more than 100 commitments out of the population of 149 possible sectoral commitments, based on the highly aggregated sectoral nomenclature developed for the negotiations (Austria, European Union, Japan, Switzerland, United States). At the other extreme, 28 countries made less than ten commitments.

Clearly, considerable scope exists for increasing the level of obligations accepted by governments without undertaking the kinds of adjustments to the structure of the Agreement discussed above. Action could be taken on several fronts. First, governments could reduce and eventually eliminate all exemptions to the MFN principle. As already noted, a presumption exists in GATS that this ought to occur over time. Second, governments could include more sectors and activities in their schedules of specific commitments. Third, they could reduce and eliminate the market access and national treatment limitations that they have inscribed in their schedules. It has been suggested that the limitations which have been inscribed reflect the status quo in terms of policies applying at the time the commitments were made, and that in this sense, the GATS has yielded little so far by way of trade liberalization. Fourth, governments could eliminate the gap that is sometimes maintained between the actual policies they apply in practice and the level of commitments they undertake in GATS. By aligning GATS commitments with policies actually in place, governments would be providing greater market security and ultimately a more liberal trading environment, pending the attainment of additional trade liberalization which could be scheduled.

Future Work Program

A good place to start would be the post-UR work program, which took up several issues on which agreement proved impossible within the time frame of the negotiations. In some areas dealing with sectoral negotiations, the program was a "rescue" operation, designed to prevent the withdrawal of market access offers or the adoption of a discriminatory approach at the sectoral level. The work program also contains the mandate on domestic regulation referred to earlier, and negotiating mandates for emergency safeguards, government procurement and subsidies, which were all areas where it proved impossible to conclude within the time frame of the UR.

Sectoral negotiations that were left over from the UR involved financial services, movement of natural persons, basic telecommunications and maritime transport. An interim agreement on financial services, securing further market access and national treatment commitments in the areas of banking, securities trading and insurance, was accepted by some 30 countries in mid-1995, excluding the United States. The fact that the United States is not part of this agreement is the reason why the negotiations will be resumed at the end of 1997, in the hope of securing further liberalization, fuller geographical participation and a longer-lasting arrangement.

The negotiations on movement of natural persons were also completed in mid-1995. Most countries had made commitments on the movement of natural persons in the UR, but nearly all of them were narrow, limited to intra-corporate transferees, and then only to personnel at the managerial level. A few schedules, notably those of Canada and the United States, also contained limited commitments in respect of independent professional service suppliers. Movement of labor is a sensitive issue for all governments, and it is noteworthy that even those countries pressing for better access for different categories of natural persons, such as India and the Philippines, were unwilling to offer much themselves. The post-UR negotiations on movement of natural persons brought very little by way of improvements in the schedules of offers, again reflecting the unwillingness of governments to forego control over what is universally seen as a sensitive policy area.

As with financial services, the negotiations in basic telecommunications were prolonged beyond the end of the UR against a background of the risk that major participants, on the basis of their dissatisfaction with the overall package on offer, would schedule limited commitments and seek reciprocity-based exchanges of market access on a discriminatory basis. It became clear before the end of the negotiations that significant liberalization was unattainable within the time frame of the Round. While a few countries (such as the United States, the United Kingdom, Australia, New Zealand, Sweden, Chile and Mexico) had already opened up their telecommunications sectors, or were in the process of doing so, others (most notably the EU) were still deciding what to do.

A worldwide trend toward liberalization in the telecommunications sector is clearly discernible. Globalization of economic activity has increased the importance of telecommunications as a production input, making firms much more sensitive to competitive disadvantages arising from poor or costly services. This has mobilized powerful private sector constituencies in many countries that are pushing governments to liberalize and to eliminate or dilute telecommunications monopolies. The extended negotiations in this sector were due to be completed on 30 April 1996, but it proved impossible to meet this deadline. Governments have agreed to freeze their best offers until a one-month period ending on 15 January 1997, at which time efforts will be made to consolidate high quality liberalization commitments from as many countries as possible. The results of these negotiations are scheduled to enter into force at the beginning of 1998.

Despite the efforts of negotiators on maritime transport services, it became obvious towards the end of 1993 that it would be impossible to reach a broad-based agreement on maritime services. A decision was therefore taken to prolong the negotiations. A number of countries have traditionally maintained restrictive shipping regimes. The United States, for example, prohibits foreign participation in cabotage.[5] Cabotage is widely restricted in other countries as well, and indeed, was excluded from the negotiations. Liner conferences have played a prominent role in EU shipping arrangements in various parts of the world. By contrast, the Nordic countries, some EU nations, a number of Asian countries, and others maintain relatively open maritime regimes. When maritime services were initially placed on the negotiating table, the United States opposed the move, seeking the explicit exclusion of the sector from GATS coverage. With the decision taken by the United States not to participate in the maritime negotiations, an agreement was made to carry forward the exercise into the new round of negotiations already scheduled for the year 2000.

Turning to those aspects of the post-UR work program dealing with rules, Article X of GATS consists of a negotiating mandate on emergency safeguard measures. A safeguard provision would allow a signatory to withdraw benefits contingent upon some occurrence or development adversely affecting domestic production. The absence of safeguard measures at the outset would have presented governments with greater difficulty had they not been given scope through other means to avoid the application of GATS disciplines in sensitive areas.[6] On the other hand, some might argue that safeguard provisions are now needed in order to allow governments to extend their specific commitments into new areas. Article X provides three years in which to negotiate appropriate provisions. The mandate indicates that negotiations on emergency safeguard measures will be based on the principle of non-discrimination.

Article XIII deals with government procurement, which is defined as the purchase of services for governmental purposes and not with a view to commercial resale or use in the supply of services for commercial sale. Procurement is exempted from market access and national treatment provisions (Articles XVI and XVII), as well as from the MFN rule in Article II. This exemption in GATS is similar to what is found in GATT, although in the latter case the exemption applies to national treatment but not the MFN principle. Article XIII of GATS calls for negotiations on government procurement within two years. The existing government procurement agreement under the WTO, which was first negotiated in the Tokyo Round (1973-79), is one of the few agreements with membership restricted to less than the full complement of WTO signatories.[7] Indeed, only twenty-two countries have committed themselves to procurement disciplines, in part because of rigidities perceived by governments to exist in the present agreement, but also on account of a natural reluctance by governments to forego this particular source of patronage.[8] The existing agreement covers both goods and services, so the question arises as to how this agreement would relate to any provisions on procurement developed under the GATS. Among the factors being considered in the discussions currently taking place are the role of transparency and national treatment in procurement, and the nature of complaints and dispute settlement procedures that might be contemplated in any future agreement.

Article XV deals with subsidies but has no substantive provisions. The Article contains general GATT-like language recognizing that subsidies may distort trade, but also that they may play an important role in development. Negotiations are called for with a view to establishing subsidy disciplines and examining the case for countervailing remedies. It is noteworthy that Members have already accepted subsidy disciplines to the extent that they have made national treatment commitments in their schedules of specific commitments. The undertaking in such a case is not to discriminate against foreign services or service suppliers in granting any subsidy. The inability to discriminate in this way is likely in itself to impose a significant subsidy discipline. Unlike the negotiations foreseen for safeguards and government procurement, no time frame is set for these negotiations. Pending their outcome, signatories are entitled to request consultations when they consider that adverse effects result from the subsidies of other parties, and such requests are to be accorded sympathetic consideration.

Intellectual Property Rights

Background

The Agreement on Trade-Related Intellectual Property Rights (TRIPS) was one of the most far-reaching results of the UR. The TRIPS Agreement is by no means the first international effort to establish rules for the protection of intellectual property rights – indeed, it rests heavily on previous agreements such as the Paris Convention, the Berne Convention, the Rome Convention, and the Treaty on Intellectual Property in Respect of Integrated Circuits. At the same time, however, the TRIPS Agreement goes much further than this earlier patchwork, creating a seamless network of minimum uniform standards of protection for a wide range of intellectual property on a near-universal basis.

The pressure for strengthened rules for protecting intellectual property (IP) rights that emerged from the late 1970s onwards was a natural outgrowth both of globalization and of the increasing role of knowledge and technology as determinants of international competitiveness. Firms seeking to produce research and technology-intensive goods and services in diverse locations around the world, as well as those wishing to serve diverse markets for such products through trade, clamored increasingly for higher levels of IP protection. Without this, the owners of intellectual property argued that they would be unable to recoup investments made in fostering creativity, accumulating knowledge and developing new technologies.

Four particular aspects of the TRIPS Agreement deserve emphasis in the context of intensified economic linkages among nations. First, the TRIPS

Agreement covers a broad range of intellectual property rights, including patents, trademarks and copyright. These are covered more comprehensively – that is, in greater depth and detail – than in any previous international agreements. Second, the TRIPS Agreement has been subscribed to by all WTO Members. This means that most countries, with the notable exceptions of China and Russia, are subject to the disciplines of the Agreement. When China and Russia become members of the WTO, as they are expected to do in due course, they will also be required to subscribe to the TRIPS Agreement. No scope exists for securing departures or exemptions from the rules in accession negotiations.

Third, the TRIPS Agreement is a prime example of how an area of law and policy has been designated "trade-related", when it might be argued that the protection of IP rights has little to do with trade per se. On the other hand, the protection of IP rights does have much to do with the conditions of competition in markets. Whatever view is taken of the degree to which IP rights are linked to trade, the fact of placing the TRIPS Agreement squarely within a multilateral trade agreement has significant implications for the manner in which IP rights are protected. In particular, the WTO's integrated dispute settlement system creates the conditions under which non-compliance with IP-related commitments may be addressed with reference to a broad range of trade policy commitments. What this means in practice is that significant leverage has been created well beyond the domain of intellectual property rights, such that refusal to abide by the TRIPS Agreement can trigger retaliatory action in any number of trade areas. This possibility undoubtedly expands the number of countries favorably disposed towards making serious efforts to implement the TRIPS Agreement in full measure.

Fourth, the TRIPS Agreement is a reflection of the recent trend in international rule-making towards a greater concern with the manner in which international obligations will be fulfilled. Thus, instead of considering it sufficient for governments to undertake certain specified commitments, with the understanding that the manner in which these commitments will be carried out is a matter for individual governments, pressure has grown for such commitments to be accompanied by supplementary undertakings as to the way in which they will be given force. In the TRIPS Agreement, governments have not only subscribed to a set of substantive IP protection standards, but have also signed on to a series of domestic enforcement commitments. This is a reflection both of heightened economic integration, giving rise to interest in a wider set of policy areas, and of the increased complexity of international rule-making that inevitably comes with an agenda that has expanded into many more detailed and varied areas of policy.

A vigorous debate occurred during the UR negotiations on IP rights, which at least in the early stages of the negotiations, tended to divide countries along North-South lines. It is only a mild simplification to distinguish the protagonists in this discussion into those that were significant generators and exporters of intellectual property (usually OECD countries) and those that were not (typically non-OECD countries). As expected, the first group was determined to ensure that foreign governments would provide high standards of IP protection regardless of the ownership of IP rights. Such rights, it was argued, were essential if the necessary investments were to be made so that creativity, inventions and technological innovations would be supplied in socially desirable quantities. The initial position of the second group was somewhat hostile to IP protection, seeing it either as a pretext for denying developing countries access to modern technology and know-how, or as a questionable means of increasing reverse resource transfers via the abuse of monopoly positions and payments for access to intellectual property.

As the UR progressed, however, developing country attitudes softened considerably. Several factors explain this change of heart, thus opening the way for the TRIPS Agreement, which is the most comprehensive and far-reaching IP agreement ever negotiated. Two of these factors are worthy of mention in the present context. First, a significant reason why net importers of IP became less negative to the idea of providing stronger guarantees of IP protection was the realization that the absence of adequate protection may well inhibit foreign investment in high technology sectors. The argument was that in choosing an investment location, a prospective foreign investor would be significantly influenced by differences in IP protection standards and in the perceived ability of the host government to enforce them. In other words, insisting on higher levels of IP protection could not simply be dismissed as a ruse to extract additional resources from poor countries.

A second reason for a more accommodating view towards a strong IP regime on the part of net importers of intellectual property, and in particular among the more advanced non-OECD countries, was that producers in their countries were increasingly developing creative and technological bases which relied for their prosperity on adequate IP protection. Inadequate IP protection in other countries would reduce the scope for competing successfully in foreign markets and diminish export opportunities. Such concerns are typified, for example, by the entertainment industry in India and the computer software industry in many of the more advanced non-OECD countries.

Principal Features of the TRIPS Agreement

The TRIPS Agreement is one of the three pillars of the WTO system. The other two comprise trade in goods – the traditional area of GATT concern – and the General Agreement on Trade in Services, which was negotiated in the UR. All three pillars are unified as constituent parts of the Marrakech Agreement Establishing the World Trade Organization (the WTO Agreement). Apart from common provisions relating to such matters as joint decision-making, amendments, non-application of the Agreement between parties, and a range of institutional provisions, the most important unifying thread of the three pillars is the dispute settlement system. The system operates with respect to the entire Organization, both in terms of procedure, and in terms of remedies. What this means in practice is that compensatory adjustments may, under certain conditions, be made in any area of the WTO in the event that a Member is found in breach of a WTO obligation.

The TRIPS Agreement covers seven areas of intellectual property. These are copyright and related rights (rights of performers, producers of sound recordings and broadcasting organizations), trademarks, geographical indications including appellations of origin, industrial designs, patents including the protection of new varieties of plants, layout- designs of integrated circuits, and undisclosed information including trade secrets. In each of these areas, the Agreement establishes minimum standards of protection, provisions relating to the domestic enforcement of IP rights, and provisions concerning international dispute settlement.

A noteworthy feature of the TRIPS Agreement is that it only sets minimum standards. In other words, it does not prevent governments from establishing higher standards, provided that these do not infringe upon the Agreement, including with respect to its rules regarding non-discrimination. Thus, harmonization is not an objective of the Agreement, except in the narrow sense of establishing a benchmark below which commitments cannot fall. A general issue facing all international rule-making endeavors is whether harmonization is a desirable or attainable objective. In the field of IP, governments interested in establishing rules did not insist on harmonization, largely in recognition of the reality that harmonized provisions would be constrained to the level attained through the minimum standards, and that it would be neither realistic nor desirable to prevent governments from imposing more rigorous requirements to the extent that they did not undermine the TRIPS Agreement. It is worth noting, nevertheless, that the standards contained in the TRIPS Agreement are broadly similar to those in existence in many industrialized countries.

Like the rest of the WTO, the principles of most-favored nation (MFN) and national treatment form a vital part of the base upon which the Agreement is structured. These principles apply not only to the standards of protection themselves, but also to the use of IP rights, their acquisition, scope, maintenance and enforcement. In other words, they apply to all obligations under the Agreement. Certain exceptions have been "grandfathered", however, in relation to national treatment and MFN, where such exceptions existed in earlier international agreements on intellectual property rights.

Article 8 of the TRIPS Agreement contains provisions on technology transfer to which a number of non-OECD Members attach importance. One of these provisions allows Members to adopt any necessary measures to promote technological development,[9] provided that such measures are consistent with the Agreement. Article 8 also acknowledges that measures may be needed to prevent the abuse of intellectual property rights by right holders or the resort to practices which unreasonably restrain trade or adversely affect the international transfer of technology. Again, any such measures must be consistent with the Agreement.

The TRIPS Agreement is cognizant of a possible tension between the monopolistic effects of granting exclusive rights through law to a particular economic agent and the general objective of promoting competition. Thus, paragraph 1 of Article 40 of the agreement states that:

> Members agree that some licensing practices or conditions pertaining to intellectual property rights which restrain competition may have adverse effects on trade and may impede the transfer and dissemination of technology.

The Agreement also states that Members may adopt licensing practices or conditions that might in particular cases constitute an abuse of intellectual property rights. But the right is also recognized to take appropriate measures to prevent or control abuses of intellectual property rights that have an adverse effect on competition in the relevant market. The Agreement further provides that a Member seeking to take action against abusive practices involving the companies of another Member may enter into consultations with that other Member in order to seek cooperation through the supply of publicly available non-confidential information.

In recognition of the fact that many countries, especially developing countries, would have to make significant changes to existing laws, and in some cases introduce entirely new ones, it was agreed that certain transitional periods should be permitted before Members would be in full conformity with their obligations. Broadly, industrial countries were given one year to implement the Agreement, while developing countries were given five years, and the least-developed countries eleven years. However, all Members were required to apply the MFN and national treatment obligations of the

Agreement with effect from one year from the entry into force of the Agreement.

Prior to the UR, provisions relating to "special and differential treatment" for developing countries were often such as to provide substantively different obligations for developing countries. It is noteworthy that the tendency to vary the actual content of rules in the name of fostering development or avoiding the imposition of an undue burden on poor countries has diminished sharply in recent years. The bulk of special provisions for developing countries agreed to in the UR were of an exclusively temporal nature, simply allowing developing countries a longer time period to come into full conformity with their new obligations. The TRIPS Agreement is no exception in this regard.

Standards of Protection

With respect to each of the seven areas of intellectual property listed above, the Agreement defines the subject matter to be protected, the rights to be conferred and the duration of the protection. With the exception of moral rights under the Berne Convention, the substantive provisions of the Paris Convention and the Berne Convention are incorporated in the TRIPS Agreement by cross reference to the original instruments. This is the starting point upon which the TRIPS Agreement then builds.

Copyright and Related Rights

While considering the Berne Convention generally adequate, the Agreement does add a few provisions. One is to designate and protect computer programs as literary works. Another is to protect data bases, even if they contain information not protected by copyright, provided a data base can be considered an intellectual creation. The Agreement grants exclusive rental rights to authors of computer programs, and in certain circumstances does the same for the creators of cinemagraphic works.

Performers, producers of phonograms and broadcasting organizations are all granted specified protection. Performers can prevent recording of their performances on a phonogram and the reproduction of such recordings. Producers of phonograms are assured exclusive rights over the reproduction and rental of their phonograms. Broadcasting organizations have similar rights to prevent unauthorized recording, reproduction of recordings and dissemination with respect to broadcasts, although such rights may reside with the copyright owner rather than the broadcasting organization. As for the term of protection, if this is not calculated on the basis of the life of a natural person, then it must be at least fifty years.

Trademarks

Any sign or combination of signs that distinguishes a good or a service must be eligible for registration as a trademark, provided that it is visually perceptible. Where signs do not inherently distinguish the relevant good or service, the authorization to register a trademark may be attainable on the basis of distinctiveness through use. Owners of registered trademarks have the exclusive right to prevent third parties from using identical or similar signs for any goods or services which are identical or similar where such use may cause confusion. Trademarks must be registered for at least seven years, and registration is renewable indefinitely.

A trademark can be canceled if it is not used for an uninterrupted period of three years, unless some valid reason exists for why it has not been used. Government-imposed measures, such as import restrictions, could be considered valid reasons for non-use. If another person uses a trademark with the approval of its owner, this shall be recognized as use. The use of a trademark should not be unjustifiably encumbered by any special requirements, such as use with another trademark or use in another form that inhibits the effectiveness of the trademark. The compulsory licensing of trademarks is not permitted, and the owner of a registered trademark has full rights to transfer the trademark in question, with or without the business with which it is associated.

Geographical Indications

Geographical indications are defined as indications identifying a good as originating in a particular locality where a given quality, reputation or other characteristic of the good in question is attributable to its geographical origin. Geographical indications are protected against any designation or presentation that misleads the public as to the true origin of a good, or which constitutes an unfair means of competition. Additional protection is provided, however, in the case of wines and spirits, where neither the effects of misleading the public nor of interfering with competition are applied as tests in determining whether a geographical indication is being misused. Certain exceptions to the above provisions are contemplated, the most significant of which is designed to accommodate a situation in which a geographical indication has already become a generic term. If a Member avails itself of these exceptions, it must at the same time show willingness to enter into negotiations aimed at increasing the protection of geographical indications.

Industrial Designs

Protection must be provided for industrial designs that are new or original. In order to be new or original, they must differ significantly from known designs or combinations thereof, and the designs must not be dictated essentially by technical or functional considerations. In the case of textiles designs, which tend to be of commercial value for short periods of time, Members must ensure that requirements for securing protection are not overly burdensome or costly. The protection of designs prevents them from being made, sold or imported without the design owner's consent. Limited exceptions to these provisions may be granted, provided they do not conflict unreasonably with the legitimate interests of the owner of a protected design. Protection for industrial designs is granted for a minimum period of ten years.

Patents

Patent protection is to be available for any invention, whether a product or a process, in all new fields of technology involving an inventive step and capable of industrial application. Patents must be available without discrimination as to the place of invention, the field of technology and whether products are imported or locally produced. Exclusions from patentability are permitted if commercial exploitation of the patent may pose a threat to ordre public or morality, including to protect human, animal or plant life or health, or to avoid serious prejudice to the environment. Additional areas where exclusion may be permitted are in respect of diagnostic, therapeutic and surgical methods for the treatment of humans or animals, plants and animals other than micro-organisms, and essentially biological processes for the production of plants or animals other than micro-biological processes. If plant varieties are excluded from patentability, an effective sui generis system of protection must be employed.

Where the subject matter of a patent is a product, a patent owner has the right to prevent third parties from making, using, offering for sale, selling, or importing the product in question for such purposes. Similarly, patented processes may not be used, nor may products obtained directly from the process in question be used, offered for sale, sold or imported for such purpose. Thus, it may be noted that process protection extends to products obtained directly using the protected process. Patent owners have full rights to assign or transfer by succession a patent, as well as to license the use of a patent by a third party.

Compulsory licensing or government use are anticipated without the authorization of the patent holder. But the right to force the working of a patent in this manner is heavily conditioned in a number of different ways. A prospective user must have made previous unsuccessful attempts to obtain authorization from the patent holder on reasonable commercial terms, although this requirement can be waived in a national emergency. The scope and duration of a compulsory license or use must be limited to the specific purpose for which authorization is granted, and the use must be non-exclusive, non-assignable, and authorized predominantly for supplying the domestic market. Right holders must be adequately compensated, and decisions relating to the compulsory allocation of patent rights must be subject to judicial or independent review by a higher body. The authorities may waive certain of the above requirements in order to remedy a practice found through a judicial process to be anti-competitive. The minimum term of patent protection under the TRIPS Agreement is 20 years from the date of filing.

Layout-Designs of Integrated Circuits

The provisions for protecting layout-designs (topographies) of integrated circuits are based on the 1989 Treaty on Intellectual Property in Respect of Integrated Circuits. In addition, the TRIPS Agreement provides that protected layout-designs and products incorporating protected layout-designs may not be imported, sold or otherwise distributed for commercial purposes without the authorization of the right holder. In order to address the concerns that made the above-mentioned Treaty unacceptable to many governments, the Agreement added a number of provisions. These included the understanding that persons unknowingly using or selling integrated circuits (which may or may not be incorporated in products) containing unlawfully reproduced layout-designs would not be liable for this action prior to their being informed of the situation. Also, most of the conditions dealing with compulsory licensing of patents apply in the event of non-voluntary licensing or government use of a layout-design. Layout-designs are protected for a minimum of ten years.

Undisclosed Information

Undisclosed information, relating to trade secrets or know-how had not been subject to protection under any international agreement prior to the TRIPS Agreement. The protection granted relates to secret information with a commercial value that derives from the fact that it is secret and has been maintained so. Persons in control of undisclosed information must have the right to prevent such information from being disclosed, acquired or used in a manner contrary to honest commercial practice. The Agreement also deals with undisclosed test data relating to governmental approval procedures for pharmaceuticals and agricultural chemicals.

Enforcement of Intellectual Property Rights

The introduction of explicit provisions on enforcement was a novel feature of the TRIPS Agreement, in that such provisions had not been developed before in international agreements dealing with the protection of intellectual property rights. As noted earlier, this was also a more general innovation from the perspective of multilateral rule-making. The basic idea behind insistence upon international obligations relating to enforcement provisions is a simple one – substantive standards can be rendered meaningless if the necessary mechanisms for enforcement are not in place and if no way exists of ensuring that such mechanisms are used as required. The provisions in the TRIPS Agreement on enforcement attempt to address both of these concerns, that is, the existence of the necessary enforcement mechanisms and their use. Thus, the obligations that the Agreement establishes in relation to enforcement, address both the substance of procedures and remedies and the practical working of these procedures and remedies.

The enforcement provisions in the TRIPS Agreement seek to guarantee both that the owners of intellectual property rights can fully exercise those rights, and that procedures associated with the use of IP rights are not abused in a fashion that transforms them into barriers to legitimate trade. An important point to make about the first of these objectives is that what the rules actually do is to underwrite the right of action of private right holders. Governments have agreed to guarantee these rights as a matter of international commitment. The Agreement attempts to accommodate significant differences in national approaches to these matters, while at the same time embodying a sufficient degree of specificity to impose real disciplines. Enforcement provisions are targeted at infringing activity in general, for which civil judicial procedures and remedies are contemplated, as well as at counterfeiting and piracy (relating to serious trademark and copyright infringements respectively), in respect of which criminal procedures and border measures are foreseen.

General obligations in relation to enforcement stipulate that remedies must be available both to prevent infringements and to deter further infringements. Enforcement procedures must be fair and equitable, and must not be unnecessarily complicated or costly, or entail unreasonable time-limits or unwarranted delays. Parties to a proceeding are entitled to judicial review of legal aspects of final administrative decisions, and at least the legal aspects of initial judicial decisions on the merits of a case, but not to review of acquittals in criminal cases. The Agreement states that no obligation is created to put in place a judicial system for enforcement of IP rights distinct from that for the enforcement of law in general, nor is there any obligation created with respect to the distribution of resources for enforcement of the law in favor of IP law.

Civil judicial procedures must exist to enforce all rights in the TRIPS Agreement, and certain basic features of the procedures are stipulated. Available remedies linked to civil judicial procedures must include injunctions, damages and in some circumstances the forfeiture or disposal of infringing goods. Members must also provide for provisional measures that may be taken to prevent infringing activity from occurring and to preserve evidence. Provisional measures may be required in certain circumstances without the right of a prior hearing for the affected party. Measures are also established to safeguard against the abuse of provisional action.

While the preferred method of dealing with IP infringements is at the source of the problem, the TRIPS Agreement does provide for border measures. These are particularly relevant in the case of counterfeiting and piracy, but border measures may also be applied in appropriate circumstances in respect of infringements of other IP rights. Border measures basically entail a procedure by which a right holder can request the customs authorities, upon production of sufficient evidence, to prevent the goods in question from entering into circulation. The Agreement also spells out conditions for ensuring that border measures do not become a barrier to legitimate trade. These include the posting of a security by right owners seeking the detention of goods, and indemnification in the case of wrongful detention. Criminal procedures apply to willful counterfeiting and piracy on a commercial scale. Penalties must be sufficient to act as an effective deterrent.

Dispute Settlement

Previous international agreements on the protection of intellectual property rights did not provide any mechanism for governments to seek redress in the event of alleged non-compliance by another party. The WTO dispute settlement machinery provides such recourse both with respect to infringements of substantive standards of IP protection, and domestic enforcement commitments. The WTO dispute settlement procedures are significantly stronger than those that existed under the GATT. Most notably, procedural time limits have been established for every stage of the process, and losing parties to a dispute can no longer delay or block the adoption of dispute panel decisions. Given the more binding and automatic nature of the WTO juridical process, an Appellate Body has also been established, so that losing parties have the opportunity to appeal panel decisions. The decisions of the Appellate Body are final.

As noted earlier, an aggrieved Member may be authorized to withdraw commitments in respect to a Member that fails to comply with a dispute settlement panel finding and recommendation. Where such retaliation is not deemed practical or effective in the same policy area as that in which a recommendation for remedial action has been made, the retaliation may be applied in any other area of policy covered by WTO disciplines. Both the increased automaticity of the system and the enhanced scope for retaliation are illustrative of how governments have tried to increase international accountability through legal due process in a world of intensified dependency. One of the effects of these changes in the dispute settlement system is to create a situation in which refusal by a government to comply with its international obligations would be much more visible than in the past. It is no longer so easy to obfuscate and procrastinate in ways which might be tantamount to non-compliance, but which were never openly identified as such. Under the new arrangements, the stakes are much higher, since unwillingness to abide by the rules is in open view, and is therefore more easily perceived as systemic failure.

Technical Standards and Regulatory Reform

Background

The rationale and appropriate role of regulatory intervention has become a central concern in international economic policy-making. Until comparatively recently, governments considered both the objectives of regulation and the nature of interventions deployed to meet regulatory objectives largely a matter of domestic policy, interference with which was a threat to national sovereignty. The idea that regulation can be treated as the exclusive prerogative of individual governments is no longer tenable, if it ever was, and there is growing pressure for governments to find ways of accommodating one another with respect to a wide range of domestic regulatory policies.

This is apparent at both the multilateral and regional levels, and it touches upon virtually all countries in some measure. In the GATT/WTO context, several agreements address regulatory issues in increasingly detailed, explicit and intrusive ways. This trend has become particularly marked following the UR. In the Round, the Agreement on Technical Barriers to Trade (TBT) was reformed, and entirely new agreements that were negotiated include the GATS, the TRIPS Agreement, and the Agreement on the Application of Sanitary and Phytosanitary Measures (SPS). All these agreements deal in significant ways with domestic regulatory interventions. Moreover, the UR results, embodied in the Marrakech Agreement establishing the World Trade Organization and the Annexes to that Agreement and the associated ministerial decisions, declarations and understandings are a "single undertaking" to which all WTO Members subscribe.

This is in sharp contrast to the pre-UR situation, when governments could pick and choose in relation to a range of agreements and associated commitments. In the case of the TBT Agreement, for example, only 46 countries were signatories of the precursor to the present Agreement, the Tokyo Round TBT Code. Now some 120 countries subscribe to the strengthened UR TBT Agreement. According to one estimate, this expanded membership represents an increase of approximately US$ 182 billion in imports subject to new international discipline, representing an increase of 17.5 percent in coverage compared to the Tokyo Round Code.

The WTO Agreements embody the international commitments that are of most relevance to the great majority of countries, especially non-OECD countries. Although their contents are discussed below, it is perhaps worth noting how the one significant WTO Agreement dealing with regulation that was not introduced for the first time in the UR – the TBT Agreement – has changed as a result of the negotiations. The significant point about all these changes is that they strengthen the degree of international accountability to which governments have submitted their regulatory regimes. This is indicative of the direction that globalization and growing interdependence is inevitably taking nations.

The first major point to note about the new TBT Agreement is that it was extended to product-related production and process methods (PPMs) for the first time. This means that the disciplines of the Agreement relate not only to products per se, but also to those aspects of product characteristics that may be attributable to the way in which a product is produced or processed. Second, under the pre-UR Agreement national treatment applied only to product testing and certification programs in the field of conformity assessment. The new Agreement extends the non-discrimination principle to all aspects of conformity assessment, including registration, inspection, laboratory accreditation, and quality system registration programs. Third, governments were previously only required to take such "reasonable measures" as may be available to them in order to ensure compliance with the rules of the TBT Agreement by local government bodies and non-governmental bodies. Under the new Agreement, they are required to accept full responsibility for the observation of all relevant provisions by such bodies, and also to formulate and implement measures and mechanisms in support of observance of relevant provisions by subsidiary bodies. Similar provisions are written into the SPS Agreement (Article 13).

Regulation has also been the subject of attention in regional arrangements such as NAFTA, ANZCERTA, ASEAN, APEC and MERCOSUR.[10] Bilateral cooperation has led to the negotiation or establishment of various understandings and arrangements relating to regulatory policy, for example, between the EU and the United States, the EU and Australia, the EU and Canada, the United States and Australia, the United States and New Zealand, and the United States and Japan. The integration process of the European Communities is the most far-reaching of all experiences with international cooperation in the domain of domestic regulation.

The pressure for international cooperation in matters of regulation is a natural outgrowth of globalization, and of the deeper level of economic integration inevitably implied by increased international economic interdependency. Moreover, the removal of traditional barriers to trade and investment in many countries has made regulatory interventions a far more crucial determinant of the conditions of competition in markets and of the ability of foreign suppliers of goods and services to secure effective market access outside the confines of national boundaries. Traditional trade and investment barriers can often be understood in relatively straightforward terms as interventions by governments to accord advantages to domestic suppliers over foreign ones – in other words to provide economic protection. Any international agenda designed to address protection is also uncomplicated, since it essentially entails the single objective of approximating, if not attaining, unimpeded market access.

But the objectives of domestic regulation are altogether more diverse and often more complex. Regulatory interventions may be designed to deal with poorly functioning markets or they may pursue non-market objectives. Because regulatory reform cannot simply be equated with liberalization, the possibility of conflicting policy objectives is ever present. Thus, for example, the attainment of a given social objective may not be compatible with unrestrained market access. But at the same time, it is very well known that the putative pursuit of legitimate regulatory objectives can easily cloak a protectionist intent. Regulations can be used to undo or neutralize market access commitments undertaken in other policy domains, such as tariff reductions, the removal of quantitative import restrictions, or the opening up of the investment regime. The policy challenge, therefore, is to safeguard the right of governments to pursue legitimate public policy objectives without using the regulatory interventions involved as an illegitimate means of frustrating economic liberalization or undermining pre-existing market access commitments.

Policy discussions about regulation and regulatory reform rest on a broad and generally vague notion of the nature and circumstance of regulatory interventions. In these general terms, however, it may be said that regulation seeks to intervene in decisions and circumstances surrounding market entry, product attributes, production methods, and market transactions. The central objective of regulatory reform is to attain efficiency in the nature and form of regulatory intervention, both in the sense of attaining the "least-cost" or "least-disruptive" method of intervention, as well as minimizing undesirable side-effects from such interventions. Regulatory reform, therefore, may cover a wide variety of policies. These can range from structural approaches such as privatization to positive rules about deregulation per se or about standard-setting and standards-related procedures.

In broad terms, there are two distinct elements in the rationale for regulatory intervention. One is to do with the failure of markets to function properly on account of structural impediments of one kind or another, usually attributable to the behavior of economic agents in the market concerned, or on account of market failure in the sense of externalities. The second rationale concerns the pursuit by governments of social goals that markets simply cannot address. Those shortcomings of the market mechanism that reside in structural impediments to competition are the subject matter of competition or antitrust policy. They result from the ability of actors in the market to use a dominant position to override market forces and determine outcomes in a manner advantageous to their own narrow interests.

The appropriate policy response to anti-competitive behavior depends to a degree upon the source of the market distortion. Sometimes it may be other policies of governments that give rise to the problem, in which case the solution may well be to change those policies rather than to introduce an additional layer of regulation. In other circumstances, the need may well be present for a regulatory intervention to eliminate the source of market power. Some regulatory interventions of this nature may be ex post in the sense of correcting observed anti-competitive behavior, while others may already be written into laws proscribing certain kinds of behavior.

The other kind of market failure alluded to above arises when the calculus of private costs and benefits diverges from the calculus of social costs and .benefits, giving rise to externalities, or to a situation in which private economic agents in the market behave in ways that are optimal from their perspective, but suboptimal in a social sense. This could arise, for example, when resource inputs are not priced to reflect their true scarcity value because of a lack of well-defined property rights over the resources. In this case, scarce resources will be priced too low, so that producers use them in a manner and at a rate that does not reflect their true value to society. In many instances like the example just cited, a price-based intervention, such as a tax, would be the most appropriate means of bringing private and social returns into alignment. In other cases, such as the production of a toxic emission considered to pose an unacceptable risk at any level above zero, a regulatory intervention prohibiting the offending production process would be called for.

The distinction between price and non-price interventions is important to make in the present context, not so much because of the efficiency consideration underlying the choice of instrument (in the first example above, a government might have chosen the less efficient policy of restricting access to the scarce resource quantitatively instead of through influencing the price), but rather because the policy debate seems to have separated tax and subsidy policy from administrative or other kinds of regulatory intervention. While this may be useful in clarifying the issues at hand, it should be borne in mind that analytically, all these different interventions are part of the same continuum of government actions that affect access to markets and the conditions of competition in those markets.

The second rationale for regulation mentioned above, that of the pursuit by governments of social goals not attended to by markets, is closely linked to the idea of market failures that generate externalities. But in this case, a market-related remedy may not be an option because the public policy objective which needs to be addressed is simply too far removed from the array of market signals to which producers and consumers respond. Regulatory interventions to protect moral values, for example, could only be achieved by a specific intervention targeted to that objective. A similar argument might apply in relation to an income distribution objective.

Before considering the various ways in which international cooperation might be secured in matters of domestic regulation, it is perhaps worth highlighting one fundamental distinction that underlies the entire debate. This is the distinction between seeking to influence the objectives of public policy, and setting the rules about how to achieve those public policy objectives. The "models" of international cooperation relating to domestic regulatory regimes discussed below contain elements of these two aspects of regulation in sharply differing degrees. At one extreme, the objectives of public policy are considered sacrosanct, and the entire focus of rule-making efforts is on the manner in which these objectives are to be met. At the other extreme, countries might be so similar that they are willing to agree jointly upon the objectives of any intervention.

Similar contrasts, although not necessarily at the outer limits of the spectrum, are to be found in international agreements. The GATT/ WTO, for example, has generally been fastidious in avoiding rules that impinge upon the objectives of public policy – governments for the most part, but not in all circumstances, retain full sovereignty with respect to what they claim to be the social or public policy objectives of their regulatory interventions. Other agreements, on the other hand, more readily give rise to accountability in terms of regulatory objectives. This can happen partly through commitments to regulatory harmonization, and partly through "regulatory competition" induced by mutual recognition arrangements.

Alternative Approaches to International Cooperation in the Field of Domestic Regulation

Four different approaches to regulatory cooperation at the international level are discussed below. They are not mutually exclusive in terms of the regulatory mix that might be chosen by governments. The principle distinguishing feature between these different approaches is the extent to which they impose international regulatory commitments on governments, or lead to convergence. The four approaches are, first, what has been described as "policed decentralization,"[11] which amounts' to a set of international rules about the conduct of regulatory policies. Second, there is harmonization, where governments agree to harmonize defined aspects of their regulatory regimes, most notably the substantive content of regulations. Third, international enforcement commitments do not involve efforts to harmonize anything, but do entail the establishment of an internationally justifiable obligation to enforce national regulations. Finally, mutual recognition agreements do not seek to harmonize regulations either, but they may well lead in that direction over time.

Policed Decentralization

Policed decentralization describes an arrangement whereby governments operate their regulatory regimes independently, including in respect of the possibility of divergent regulatory objectives and substantive regulations, but subject to certain commitments relating to the operation of the regulatory regime. Such commitments might include non-discrimination, the obligation to give reasons for regulating and the means of doing so, transparency, and the use of the least-trade restrictive interventions. Non-discrimination refers to national treatment and by extension, the MFN principle. The commitment not to discriminate is a powerful discipline, especially in the national treatment sense, since it precludes the possibility of setting regulations in a fashion designed to disadvantage foreign suppliers or foreign products. Matters do not always turn out to be simple, however, because formally non-discriminatory interventions may still have discriminatory effects in practice, depending on the design of the substantive obligation, or the design of the procedures associated with its implementation.

The idea behind making governments accountable in the sense of explaining the objectives of a regulatory intervention is that if the authorities know they will be obliged to explain why they are intervening, they will be less likely to deploy regulatory interventions for protectionist purposes. The reasons for embracing the principle of transparency are self-evident. A question, however, is precisely what aspects of regulation-setting or implementation should be subject to transparency requirements. Clearly, publication of rules and regulations is a basic requirement. In addition, governments may have the obligation to consult, both on the substantive content of regulations prior to their implementation and on all matters of implementation. The commitment to use the least-trade restrictive intervention to achieve a public policy objective is also a powerful discipline. It means that regulations must not inflict any unnecessary barriers to trade, although the consequence of a regulation complying with this requirement could, depending on the regulatory objective, still have the practical effect of limiting trade.

The approach of policed decentralization bears a close resemblance to many international rules dealing with regulation. The primary hallmark of this model of international cooperation is that it maximizes the flexibility of governments, particularly with respect to the objectives of regulatory interventions, although less so with respect to the manner of achieving them. Moreover, even where international commitments go further than this, these principles frequently form the basis upon which more far-reaching commitments are built. The WTO rules constitute the most significant set of international commitments in the field of regulation for most countries, especially non-OECD countries. They are based largely, but not exclusively on the policed decentralization approach.

Thus, the TBT Agreement does not define regulatory objectives. It refers in its Article 2 to "legitimate" objectives, but only provides an illustrative list of what objectives might be legitimate. Included in this list are national security requirements, the prevention of deceptive practices, and protection of human health or safety, animal or plant life or health, or the environment. These are all unexceptionable public policy goals, but reliance on a non-exhaustive illustrative list in the Agreement means that governments remain free to use regulations to pursue other objectives, provided they are prepared to defend them as legitimate. The approach in GATS is very similar, where in Article VI it only refers to a single objective, that of ensuring the quality of a service. The SPS Agreement, on the other hand, because it is more narrowly focused, is able to specify the single and exclusive objective of protecting human, animal or plant life or health (Article 2:1).

Turning to the question of non-discrimination, the TBT Agreement, which applies to all industrial and agricultural products, is firmly rooted in the principle of non-discrimination, via the national treatment commitment in Article

III:4 of the GATT. The latter provision states that:

> Members agree that some licensing practices or conditions pertaining to intellectual property rights which restrain competition may have adverse effects on trade and may impede the transfer and dissemination of technology.

Article 2:1 of the TBT Agreement itself states that products imported from the territory of any Member "shall be accorded treatment no less favorable than that accorded to like products of national origin and to like products originating in any other country." This phraseology captures both the national treatment and the MFN principles. The SPS Agreement requires that sanitary and phytosanitary measures do not "unjustifiably discriminate between Members where identical or similar conditions prevail, including between their own territory and that of other Members." (Article 2:3). Again, the wording addresses both MFN and national treatment.

The GATS national treatment provision is more elaborate than those mentioned above. It reads:

> 1. In the sectors inscribed in its Schedule, and subject to any conditions and qualifications set out therein, each Member shall accord to services and service suppliers of any other Member, in respect of all measures affecting the supply of services, treatment no less favorable than that it accords to its own like services and service suppliers.
> 2. A Member may meet the requirement of paragraph 1 by according to services and service suppliers of any other Member, either formally identical treatment or formally different treatment to that it accords to its own like services or service suppliers.
> 3. Formally identical or formally different treatment shall be considered to be less favorable if it modifies the conditions of competition in favor of services or service suppliers of the Member compared to like services or service suppliers of any other Member.

The wording of the first paragraph covers MFN as well as national treatment. The GATS provisions address two situations in which a problem may arise: i) identical treatment may be discriminatory, thus calling for formally different treatment; ii) different treatment may be discriminatory, thus calling for formally identical treatment or for modified different treatment. This elaboration, which requires that whatever the treatment accorded is, it must not modify the conditions of competition in a manner less favorable to services or service suppliers of foreign origin, reflects earlier GATT case law.[12]

In sum, the national treatment requirement is a minimum standard. This means that countries are not obliged to apply to imports of goods or services, or to service suppliers, the regulations they apply to their domestic analogues. In other words, nothing in the WTO prevents governments from discriminating against domestic goods, services or service suppliers. In addition, the national treatment provision is not outcome-oriented, but rather opportunity-oriented. For a regulation to be non-discriminatory, it must not change competitive opportunities in a market.

From a regulatory perspective, then, the substantive details or procedures associated with a regulation do not have to be identical, as long as any differences do not modify the conditions of competition in the relevant market. At the same time, regulations cannot be designed so that although they impose identical requirements upon domestic and foreign suppliers, they do not afford the same competitive opportunities to foreigners. An example of a regulation according identical treatment to foreign and domestic suppliers that would most likely be considered discriminatory would be a requirement that all lawyers wishing to practice in a particular country would have had to have received their formal legal training in that country.

An obligation to give reasons for a regulatory intervention is somewhat related to transparency requirements. The basic idea is that if the regulatory authorities are obliged to explain their regulatory policies, this would have the effect of deterring protectionist subterfuge. The strength and effectiveness of such a requirement would depend upon what it aimed at. Such accountability could relate to regulatory objectives, to the substantive design of a regulation, or to a procedure associated with the enforcement of a regulatory requirement, including conformity assessment.

The WTO agreements dealing with regulation do not contain explicit requirements of this nature. However, both the TBT Agreement (Article 2) and the SPS Agreement (Annex B) require that Members should be given adequate time to comment in writing about any intended new or modified regulatory intervention, where such an intervention is not substantially based upon international norms or practice. Moreover, there is an obligation to consult upon request in relation to the written comments, and to take the comments and the results of any discussion into account when formulating the final content of the regulation. The GATS does not contain comparable provisions, but Members have committed themselves to develop any necessary disciplines in the regulatory field to replace the very general provisions that currently exist in Article VI:4.

As for transparency requirements more generally, WTO Members are required to publish all laws, regulations, judicial decisions, and administrative rulings of general application insofar as these pertain to the subject matter of the relevant agreements. Publication should occur before implementation, except in particular circumstances of urgency. In addition, the TBT and SPS Agreements and the GATS require the establishment of inquiry points to which any requests for information by other Members may be addressed. Wide-ranging notification requirements are also written into all the relevant WTO agreements that touch upon regulatory matters. In general, it may be said that transparency requirements, designed to raise the degree of accountability of national governments at the international level, offer a valuable means of influencing national policy while at the same time avoiding the more intrusive nature of approaches involving harmonization and mutual recognition.

As noted earlier, the requirement that regulatory interventions must not constitute unnecessary barriers to trade is another effective means of controlling the misuse of regulations to provide protection to domestic interests in a relatively non-intrusive manner. The necessity test may not always be straightforward to interpret in specific cases where disputes arise, but it nevertheless creates a strong presumption that adverse trade effects will be minimized. The necessity test is explicit in the TBT Agreement (Article 2.2), the SPS Agreement (Article 5), and in GATS (Article VI:4). In line with the generally conservative approach of these agreements towards judgment about the objectives of regulatory interventions, the necessity test applies only to the design and procedural features of regulations.

Harmonization

Even the most casual empirical observation reveals that approaches to regulatory policy and the content of regulations differ significantly from country to country. In considering the case for harmonization as a mode of international cooperation in the area of regulatory policy, it may be useful in the first instance to consider why regulatory objectives may differ among countries. Firstly, income levels are a key determinant of the content of standards because of the effect of income on preferences, as well as differences in the ability to afford the "quality of life" goals underlying many regulatory interventions. Moreover, even if standards are formally quite similar regardless of significant differences in income, there are often important differences in the degree to which standards are enforced in practice. This should be borne in mind by those interests seeking to impose standards on governments for whom the implementation of such standards is of no interest, or at least not a matter of priority. In addition, there are likely to be differences in tastes among different societies, independently of income differentials, which may also militate against harmonization.

Second, standards may differ because of different geographical conditions. In some cases, these translate into local differences which do not present any significant difficulty in terms of relations among countries, nor any interest in harmonization. It is hard to imagine, for example, that a building code in a tropical country that does not set insulation standards for houses would be a source of contention, despite the fact that insulation is a significant element of building costs in temperate climates.

As soon as trade enters the picture, however, differences in production or process standards may generate friction, even if a solid rationale exists for differing standards. In the field of environmental policy, for example, emission standards may well be set in line with a judgment regarding the absorptive capacity of the surrounding environment. For example, authorities responsible for geographical areas with low population density and little polluting activity are likely to see less need to attain high emission control standards than the authorities responsible for an already highly industrialized and polluted center of production. Such differences in standards will bear on relative costs faced by producers in the two locations competing for the same market, and they can be a source of pressure for harmonization. While the case for harmonization would be hard to sustain on environmental grounds, there may nevertheless be grounds for legitimate concern about the abuse of this diversity to gain an illegitimate trade advantage. This kind of concern is analogous, but diametrically opposite, to that underlying the necessity test. The point is that regulations concealing an illegitimate trade objective could be either too weak or too strong.

In practice, it is no easy matter to set differentials in standards precisely to reflect the objective conditions that warrant such differences. An alternative to harmonization that avoids this problem is the establishment of minimum standards. A minimum standards approach may help to bridge wide gaps in national preferences while at the same time eliminating the risk of egregious standard-setting practices aimed at securing an illegitimate advantage. As noted earlier, the WTO has tended to shy away from establishing the substantive content of standards, even of the minimum variety. But in the TRIPS Agreement, minimum standards are established in relation to the substantive content of intellectual property rights. The TRIPS Agreement also contains an element of harmonization in the domestic enforcement procedures that are established to ensure that private right holders can exercise their rights through domestic judicial procedures. But the harmonization element of these obligations is relatively light, since it focuses primarily on the existence of an appropriate institutional setting and on a number of procedural obligations.

While arguments based on the desirability of diversity and the inappropriateness of imposing a straightjacket of uniformity in dissimilar conditions may be persuasive in some circumstances, there are also important reasons why a harmonized approach may be attractive. First, a corollary of the consensus implicit in the establishment of an international standard is the existence of less scope for the protectionist capture of regulatory interventions. In other words, harmonization automatically reduces the scope for abuse and a potential source of contention in international economic relations. Second, regulatory heterogeneity can carry real economic costs for foreign products and producers. These costs may include the requirement to submit to more than one conformity assessment procedure,[13] additional uncertainty as to the stability of regulatory regimes, higher information costs for producers, and the loss of scale economies in production if differences in standards are sufficiently far-reaching to lead to significant differentiation of products or production processes.

The WTO Agreements dealing with regulatory matters are generally cautious when it comes to harmonization, seeking to tread an intermediate path and avoiding any direct involvement in standard-setting activities. Article 2:4 of the TBT Agreement states that:

> Where technical regulations are required and relevant international standards exist or their completion is imminent, Members shall use them, or the relevant parts of them, as a basis for their technical regulations except when such international standards or relevant parts would be an ineffective or inappropriate means for the fulfillment of the legitimate objectives pursued, for instance because of fundamental climatic or geographical factors or fundamental technological problems.

The Agreement establishes a rebuttable presumption that whenever a standard is adopted or applied in accordance with relevant international standards, it does not constitute an unnecessary barrier to trade. The Agreement also calls upon Members to play as full a part as possible in the preparation of standards in appropriate international standardizing bodies.

The SPS Agreement adopts a similar approach, requiring Members to base their SPS measures on international standards, guidelines and recommendations when these exist (Article 3), and establishing that such standards conform to the Agreement in the sense of meeting the necessity criterion. The Agreement allows Members to establish standards that are higher than those existing internationally, provided they can be justified scientifically and respond to an appropriate assessment of risk. Members are also required to participate in the work of relevant international standardization bodies, including the Codex Alimentarius Commission, the International Office of Epizootics, and organizations operating within the framework of the International Plant Protection Convention.

Thus, both of the main WTO agreements dealing specifically with standards encourage harmonization while at the same time avoiding involvement in standard-setting. Clearly, this is only possible by cross-reference to bodies that do set standards, and implicit in the work of such bodies is consideration of the trade-off between the lower transactions costs associated with uniformity and the weight to be attached to objectively different conditions obtaining in different countries. The TBT Agreement in particular does, however, provide a basis to challenge the trade-off implicitly settled upon in the formulation of an international standard by recognizing that governments may have valid reasons for departing from international standards.

The GATS approach to the harmonization objective is conservative, consisting in the relatively weak requirement of taking account of international standards of relevant international organizations in ensuring that licensing and qualification requirements and technical standards do not constitute unnecessary barriers to trade in services. However, a recent noteworthy development in the direction of regulatory harmonization is the establishment of a common set of regulatory principles in the basic telecommunications sector. In the context of negotiations on liberalization of trade in basic telecommunications services carried over from the UR, some 30 governments have provisionally agreed[14] to incorporate a common set of regulatory principles in their schedules of specific commitments.

The reason for doing this is that despite the widespread trend towards the removal of monopoly privileges in the sector, strong elements of natural monopoly are likely to persist, through ownership and control of telecommunications networks by dominant suppliers in the market. This market dominance potentially renders the liberalization commitments of governments meaningless in terms of real access to markets. The common regulatory principles establish WTO-enforceable commitments by governments to impose interconnection obligations upon major suppliers and they also embody a number of competitive safeguards against abuse of market dominance. These provisions are remarkable for how far they go, considering the traditional reluctance of governments to harmonize the substantive content of regulations in a WTO context. Although only 30 countries or so are likely to assume these commitments, they are MFN-based, which means that any WTO Member can raise a non-compliance challenge. One explanation for why it was possible to move so far in this direction in a GATS negotiation is perhaps that the subject matter was sufficiently specific for governments to be assured of a requisite degree of reciprocity and for there to be little uncertainty as to any future implications of the commitments. Moreover, in some respects the common regulatory principles are stated at a sufficient level of generality to permit flexibility on detail at the national level.

International Enforcement

Another approach to cooperation in regulatory matters entails the acceptance of an international commitment to enforce domestic regulations. In other words, governments promise one another to enforce their respective regulatory regimes and submit to the possibility of an international challenge through dispute settlement in the event of lax enforcement. This approach does not involve harmonization, and is perhaps best suited to situations where governments are comfortable with the content of diverse regulatory regimes because the diversity is not considered excessive, but less comfortable with the degree of assiduity applied to the enforcement of such regimes.

Examples of international agreements based on this approach are not numerous, but elements of it may be found, for example, in the TRIPS Agreement. Here, governments have made explicit enforcement commitments, but they have been supplemented by certain provisions relating to the underlying enforcement regimes and procedures, as well as by the fact that they apply to internationally agreed' minimum substantive standards. Nevertheless, a right of international action has been created on grounds of a failure to respect domestic enforcement procedures, and these procedures have not been fully harmonized.

A purer example of the international enforcement model is the 1994 North American Agreement on Labor Cooperation (NAALC). This is a supplementary agreement negotiated in the context of the North American Free Trade Agreement. In essence, the NAALC sets up cooperative machinery in matters of labor policy, the centerpiece of which is the right of a NAFTA Member to challenge another Member through NAFTA-based dispute settlement machinery in the event that the latter party is considered to be failing to enforce its own labor laws. Remedies in the face of non-compliance with a dispute finding include monetary penalties, and ultimately, retaliation through trade restrictions.

Mutual Recognition

Mutual recognition could be characterized as a market-based approach to harmonization, insofar as the regulatory competition implicit in mutual recognition may be expected to lead over time to a narrowing of differences among national regulatory regimes. This convergence process, if permitted to occur, is likely to be most pronounced and rapid in circumstances where regulations are a significant determinant of competitiveness. It is precisely this implication of regulatory competition that provokes governments to worry about mutual recognition as an assault on sovereignty, as well as about such consequences as the much vaunted "race to the bottom" in standard-setting.

Mutual recognition, or for that matter unilateral recognition, is most likely to be promoted where national regulatory regimes are already similar – a situation most prevalent among countries at comparable income and development levels. This is why mutual recognition has not occurred on an across-the-board basis, and is not likely to in any foreseeable future. Yet many international agreements, including under WTO auspices, actively promote mutual recognition because of its attractiveness as a mechanism for facilitating trade and eliminating any possibility of regulatory manipulation for protectionist purposes. But permitting the establishment of mutual recognition agreements (MRAs) with restricted membership raises a serious prospect of MFN-inconsistency. Some would even argue that MRAs amount simply to conditional MFN, with all the actual and potential discriminatory implications of such an outcome. On the other hand, it may also be argued that open-ended MRAs based on objective, pre-announced conditions of participation are MFN-consistent, insofar as they do not set out to discriminate against any party, nor prescribe the ab initio exclusion of any particular countries.

The most extensive experience with mutual recognition is that of the EU, which is built on a far-reaching process of constructing a single market. It has taken many years for the EU to reach its present stage of integration in the regulatory field. Apart from certain standards-related regulation defined at the Community level, the EU's regulatory policies are a combination of judicial mutual recognition,[15] and regulatory mutual recognition. These approaches are supported by a commitment to the principle of free movement of goods, services and factors of production within the EU and by the principles of subsidiarity and proportionality. At the political level, reliance on qualified majority voting (subject to exceptions) reinforces the integrating effects of a regulatory regime relying on mutual recognition. One lesson from the EU experience is that mutual recognition arrangements are not simple to attain, and may often require complicated negotiations. The recent experience of the United States and the EU in attempting to craft a mutual recognition agreement has confirmed how complicated such negotiations can be, even when restricted to conformity assessment procedures in relation to a selected group of agreed products.

The relevant WTO agreements in this area are supportive of recognition, whether unilateral or mutual, but they do not create strong obligations in this respect. The TBT Agreement encourages recognition both in relation to the substantive content of regulations and conformity assessment procedures. In relation to standards, Article 2.7 states that:

> Members shall give positive consideration to accepting as equivalent technical regulations of other Members, even if these regulations differ from their own, provided they are satisfied that these regulations adequately fulfill the objectives of their own regulations.

In a sense, this requirement does not entail "mutual" recognition, since Members are enjoined to make their own independent judgments as to whether they can accept the standards of others as equivalent to their own. In practice, however, pressures for reciprocity reduce the likelihood that governments would make favorable equivalence judgments in the absence of reciprocal treatment. The approach with respect to mutual recognition of conformity assessment procedures is very similar. Article 6:1 requires that Members shall "ensure, whenever possible, that results of conformity assessment procedures of other Members are accepted, even when those procedures differ from their own, provided they are satisfied that those procedures offer an assurance of conformity with applicable technical regulations or standards equivalent to their own procedures." The TBT Agreement also explicitly enjoins Members to show willingness to enter into negotiations for the conclusion of mutual recognition agreements with respect to conformity assessment procedures (Article 6:3).

The GATS provisions on recognition are more elaborate. Article VII:1 of GATS states that for the purpose of meeting standards or criteria in relation to the authorization, licensing or certification of services suppliers, Members "may recognize the education or experience obtained, requirements met, or licenses or certifications granted in a particular country." The paragraph goes on to say that "[S]uch recognition, which may be achieved through harmonization or otherwise, may be based upon an agreement or arrangement with the country concerned or may be accorded autonomously." The text of Article VII then states that:

> 2. A Member that is a party to an agreement or arrangement of the type referred to in paragraph 1, whether existing or future, shall afford adequate opportunity for other interested Members to negotiate their accession to such an agreement or arrangement or to negotiate comparable ones with it. Where a Member accords recognition autonomously, it shall afford adequate opportunity for any other Member to demonstrate that education, experience, licenses, or certifications obtained or requirements met in the other Member's territory should be recognized.
> 3. A Member shall not accord recognition in a manner which would constitute a means of discrimination between countries in the application of its standards or criteria for the authorization, licensing or certification of services suppliers, or a disguised restriction on trade in services.

Paragraph 5 of Article VII requires that wherever appropriate, multilaterally agreed criteria should be used in the area of recognition. Members are further directed to work in cooperation with "relevant intergovernmental and non-governmental organizations towards the establishment and adoption of common international standards and criteria for recognition and common international standards for the practice of relevant services trades and professions." In addition, paragraph 4 of Article VII requires that all existing recognition measures be notified to GATS, and that any new negotiations concerning recognition and any new or modified arrangements relating to recognition must also be notified.

Like the TBT Agreement, the GATS does not seek to dictate the pace in relation to recognition, but seems at the same time to espouse recognition as a valid instrument of trade facilitation. One reason for the more elaborate GATS provisions is that they pay particular attention to the risks of unwarranted discrimination inherent in recognition arrangements that are less than universal. This tension between the attractiveness of recognition agreements and the specter of unjustified discrimination is a theme that will likely become more prominent in years to come.

Concluding Remarks

The past quarter-century has seen much progress in strengthening the processes of international consultation and negotiation about global issues. Completion of the Tokyo and URs of trade negotiation led to broad-based tariff reductions and the easing of some of the important non-tariff barriers. The establishment of the WTO in 1995 has greatly strengthened the permanent institutional mechanisms for the discussion of trade issues and the resolution of disputes. A larger number of countries, including the majority of ERF countries (the Arab countries, Iran and Turkey) increasingly accept the importance of trade as a engine of development. During the seven years following the launch of the UR in 1986, over 60 developing countries unilaterally lowered their barriers to imports and 26 have since joined GATT/WTO. Thus, membership has grown from 88 in 1985 to 130 today.[16] Moreover, both China and Russia as major players outside the WTO have defined their policies and programs to gain acceptance into the WTO.

With the progressive reduction in external trade barriers, further promotion of competition depends critically on the reform of "behind-the-border" barriers–notably, domestic regulation, restrictions on service sector activities, government procurement and subsidies. The further integration of economies facilitated by the removal of these barriers is sometimes referred to as "deep integration" in contrast to the "shallow integration" permitted by removal of border trade barriers. Along with progress on the traditional agenda of tariff cuts, the UR built up momentum to tackle these issues – witness the reform of the Agreement on Technical Barriers to Trade (TBT), plus three new agreements: the General Agreement on Trade in Services (GATS), the Agreement on Trade-related Aspects of Intellectual Property Rights (TRIPS) and the Agreement on the Application of Sanitary and Phytosanitary Measures (SPS). Some of the unresolved sectoral issues left over from the UR are now being tackled or are scheduled for negotiation in the next few years.

Regional groupings, notably the EU, have worked to harmonize national regulatory frameworks in the interests of improved efficiency and closer integration of partner economies. Convergence of domestic laws and regulations can come about through either negotiation or de facto competition among regulatory systems. Either way, however, governments still face pressures to preserve if not enhance the competitive positions of their business and labor interests. Their efforts to fulfill these expectations will continue as a significant cause of friction at the international level and managing it will remain a pressing challenge for international trade-related policy.

Although the starting point for advancing the global agenda of trade liberalization may look auspicious, the problems are getting much tougher and more complex. The remaining barriers comprise a mix of hard core protection of vital national interests such as farming, and other measures supported by powerful lobbies or local monopolies such as anti-dumping measures. Protection from competition through anti-dumping measures or other means usually proves very expensive and is often ineffective in preserving jobs and companies. Repeal of anti-dumping legislation is unlikely, however, even in a long term horizon as it enjoys widespread political support. The most practical approach towards lessening its threat (or making it less prone to capture by special interests) may be to introduce a stronger voice for the national interest via a greater involvement of competition policy agencies in decisions made in this area.

Although contingency protection (such as anti-dumping measures) and hard-core trade restrictions remain important, the "along-the-border" impediments to trade generally are diminishing. Of greater concern are so-called "behind the frontier" regulations and administrative practices that powerfully impede certain types of trade. Many regulations reduce or eliminate domestic competition and some aim directly at foreign competition. Well-known examples include "buy local" public procurement, monopoly concessions granted to local companies (often public companies) through bans on the entry of other potential players (power, postal services, telecommunications, tobacco and alcoholic beverage sales are examples commonly found in the OECD countries), and the regulation of professional services that mandate local presence, require local professional qualifications, restrict the establishment of foreign firms, or require payment of services according to standardized fees.

Large benefits can be achieved by stimulating more competition in domestic markets through regulatory reform, including deregulation. Changing the rules to facilitate new local entrants is a part of the process, but in markets dominated by large players international competition plays a vital role. Indeed, a strong complementarity between competition policy and trade and investment policy has become increasingly recognized as a key element in the new trade agenda. The growing interest in competition law and practice at the international level in part reflects these concerns: thus chapter 15 of the North American Free Trade Agreement (NAFTA) explicitly recognized the importance of competition policy, and Mexico took steps prior to implementation of the Agreement to create a competition law. Competition policies however, tend to have a rather limited scope and many competition-inhibiting policies (for instance public procurement rules) tend to fall outside the jurisdiction of the competition authority. The strengthening of competition policy and international agreements or understandings relating to it likely will remain high on the policy agenda.

Other interactions occur between trade policy and the regulatory environment. Domestic regulations can, intentionally or not, undo or neutralize commitments undertaken in other policy domains, including trade liberalization. Divergent preferences in domestic policy areas such as environmental quality and social policy lead to different regulations and financial charges which have an impact on competitive advantage. Sometimes, as in the discussion of intellectual property rights and environmental issues, the trade policy dimension is associated primarily with the enforcement of agreements, as the threat of denial of trade benefits may appear to offer an effective means of securing other policy objectives. Thus, at a time when many of the traditional arguments for protection have been largely discounted (on practical grounds, if not in theory), other kinds of justification are replacing them. In these cases, however, the traditional argument is stood on its head: the threat of trade sanctions is a powerful weapon precisely because the benefits of trade are so valuable. The fear is that tougher trade restraints could emerge as a by-product of new domestic policy objectives.

Notes

1   Other TRIMS identified in the Uruguay Round discussions, but not mentioned in the illustrative list annexed to the TRIMS agreement, include manufacturing requirements, export performance requirements, product mandating requirements,

manufacturing limitations, technology transfer requirements, licensing requirements, remittance restrictions, and local equity requirements. The TRIMS agreement would have needed to go further than reiterating the established interpreta-
tions of GATT Article III and Article XI in order to cover most of these measures.
A notable omission of the TRIMS agreement, however, was its silence on export
performance requirements (EPRs). EPRs are analogous to local requirements on
the import side, and strongly resemble export subsidies, which are prohibited on
manufactured goods under the WTO.

2   It is provided, however, that existing TRIMS may be imposed on new enterprises
during the phase-out period if this is considered necessary in order not to place
existing enterprises subject to the same measures at a disadvantage.

3   Both a service supplier and a service consumer could, of course, move to a third
jurisdiction. Under GATS, this would be treated as two separate transactions from
the point of view of the host country.

4   Exceptions to national treatment under GATT exist in respect of subsidies and
government procurement.

5   The Jones Act requires that US coastal trade should be conducted by US-owned,
US-built and US-manned vessels.

6   Scope for restricting the application of GATS to particular activities or disciplines
resides in the choice of whether to accept market access commitments with respect
to particular sectors and sub-sectors, or particular modes of supply, and whether to
impose limitations on market access or national treatment in respect of scheduled
commitments.

7   This is one of the so-called plurilateral agreements, for which membership is
optional and must be separately negotiated. The other plurilateral agreements are
the Agreement on Trade in Civil Aircraft, the International Dairy Agreement and
the International Bovine Meat Agreement.

8   The signatories of the Government Procurement Agreement are: Canada, the 15
Member States of the EU, Israel, Japan, Korea, Norway, Korea, Switzerland, and
the United States.

9   Reference is made in the same context to the protection of public health and nutrition, and to the public interest in sectors of vital importance to socio-economic and
technological development.

10 North American Free Trade Agreement (NAFTA), Australia-New Zealand Closer
Economic Relations Trade Agreement (ANZCERTA), Association of South East
Asian Nations (ASEAN), Asia-Pacific Economic Cooperation Forum (APEC),
Common Market formed by Argentina, Brazil, Paraguay, Uruguay (MERCO-
SUR).

11 This expression is attributable to Sykes. See Alan O. Sykes, (1996), "Strategies for
Increasing Market Access Under Regulatory Heterogeneity," Unpublished paper
prepared as a contribution to the OECD Trade Committee brainstorming on
"International Contestability of Markets: Economic Perspectives," (Paris,
February 1996).

12 The report of the GATT panel on "United States - Section 337 of the Tariff Act of
1933."

13 There could be duplication in conformity assessment procedures with harmonized
standards as well, but a double compliance requirement would seem less likely in
a situation where the degree of international cooperation was already sufficient to
permit harmonization of standards.

14 The basic telecommunications negotiations under GATS were finalized in
February 1997.

15 Judicial mutual recognition is an integrating force that took hold in the EU with

respect to non-SHEC products (products not regulated on grounds of safety, health, environment or consumer protection objectives) following the 1979 Cassis de Dijon Decision of the European Court of Justice, which in essence required that if free circulation of a product was permitted in one Member State, then the same should be permitted in others.

16 Since the launching of the Uruguay Round in 1986, Egypt, Morocco, Tunisia and Turkey have unilaterally lowered their barriers to imports, mainly in conjunction with a reorientation of domestic policies. Morocco, Tunisia, Bahrain, the UAE and Qatar have since joined the GATT; Algeria, Jordan and Saudi Arabia are now in the process of acceding, while other countries in the region have expressed interest in GATT membership and have so far held observer status in the GATT (Iran).

Opening Up and Distribution in the Middle East and North Africa: The Poor, the Unemployed and the Public Sector*

Introduction

The process of opening up an economy to international trade and capital is both a desirable and precarious activity. No economy has achieved sustained, rapid growth in wages and employment without making use of international markets. Yet, at the point of opening up, fear has too often been the dominant collective emotion, whether of specific groups or of the whole populace, fed by anticipation of job losses or wage declines. Nowhere is this apparent paradox more evident – and more relevant – than in the group of Middle Eastern and North African economies. Until the early 1980s, almost all of these countries pursued employment strategies that were dependent on growth in public sector employment coupled with substantial expansion of education for public sector jobs, with the boom and bust in employment closely linked to the oil cycle. This strategy is now bankrupt: in most countries public sector wages have stagnated or fallen and unemployment has risen; in some others, returns to education have significantly declined. One group has already started to follow the first path (including Morocco, Tunisia and Turkey) while another (notably Algeria, Egypt, Syria and Yemen) remains stuck on the second. Some, notably Jordan, fall in between. On the other hand, the West Bank and Gaza have an extreme form of the employment problems more as a result of the political and economic environment in which they have been operating, than as a result of internal policy choices. No country has yet completed the transition. An employment malaise is present everywhere in the region.

In this chapter we review the links between long-run growth patterns, the process of opening up of economies and its impact on different socio-economic groups. We mainly focus on the middle-income Arab countries that have been reviewed more thoroughly elsewhere by the authors,[1] but we also refer to Turkey. We discuss the overall effects on income distribution, and in particular we explore stylized effects on three groups: the poor or near-poor, the unemployed and public sector workers.

* The authors wish to thank Ismail Serageldine and the participants of the ERF trade conference in Istanbul, Turkey for their comments.

The chapter explores the following three themes:
- the historical pattern of development and the implicit social contract brought dividends to all until the end of the oil boom. This strategy is now bankrupt and is a potential disaster for poverty and employment in the long run;
- much of the region is, or has been, on a knife's edge between two options: opening to trade combined with public sector reform; and hanging on to the old path and social contract. Political risks are attached to both paths, since both involve losers, but the first path can lead to robust employment growth, the maintenance of reasonably equal income distribution and poverty reduction, at least in the medium term. Hanging on to the old path is likely to lead to sharpened distributional conflicts, and further loss of social cohesion;
- sequencing of policy reforms matters: probably the best sequence is to open first, and undertake employment-reducing public sector reforms afterwards. But interactions are key – throughout the reform period, some fiscal adjustments are indispensable in order to cushion reforms and buy off permanent losers, while failure to follow opening with deep public sector reform can lead to a fragile and unstable position. Restructuring public employment is central to public sector reform.

The chapter is organized as follows. The first section outlines the key facts on employment, unemployment and poverty in the region. The second relates these aspects to interactions between growth, openness, and education, and describes the actual historical pattern of development in the region. The third section sets the international stage in relation to the domestic plight many countries are in. The fourth discusses the consequences of opening up of economies for different groups, and the fifth looks briefly at the issues associated with the sequencing of public sector and trade reforms from an employment perspective.

Unemployment, Poverty and the Public Sector – Some Stylized Facts

The region is struggling with a deep-rooted employment problem. This has manifested itself with the following symptoms: high unemployment, stagnant or falling wages, high public sector employment, and (in some) low or falling returns to education, in part linked to wage compression in the public sector. Despite a generally dismal employment situation, poverty is relatively low for the income level, a reflection of relatively equal income distribution. There is, of course, substantial diversity: in general the group of reforming countries (especially Morocco, Tunisia and Turkey) have begun to work their way out of some of these difficulties; while those caught in the old growth path, whether due to policy or politics, are suffering worsening problems. And there have been large changes over time, reflecting the booms or busts that have mirrored the oil cycle. We will frequently come back both to the diversity and the boom and bust cycle, but it remains useful to start by characterizing the inherited situation in terms of five stylized facts.

High unemployment. Unemployment has risen enormously and is now higher than in any other region of the world (Figure 1). On average 15 percent of the regional labor force is unemployed. In Algeria, Jordan, Tunisia, the West Bank and Gaza and Lebanon, unemployment rates exceed 15 percent; in Egypt, Morocco, Turkey and Yemen unemployment is 12-14 percent of the labor force, and only in Syria is recorded unemployment less than 10 percent (Figure 2).

In most countries, the unemployed are predominantly first-time job seekers, reflecting the fast rise in labor supply as baby-boomers enter the labor market.[2] But the proportion of young workers among the unemployed is especially large in Egypt and Syria (at about 80 percent) where first time entrants have to line up in order to get increasingly scarce jobs. However, in Jordan, Morocco and Tunisia, reforms have shaken up previously protected industries, and over half of the unemployed have lost a previous job.

Figure 1: Unemployment Rate by Region, 1993

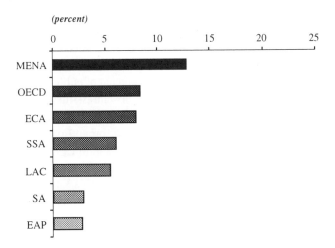

Source: Filmer (1995).
Key: MENA: Middle East & North Africa; ECA: Europe & Central Asia; SSA: Sub-Saharan Africa; LAC: Latin America & the Caribbean; SA: South Asia; EAP: East Asia & the Pacific.
Notes: The regional unemployment rates are weighted averages for a sample of countries within the region where the weights are the shares in the working age population in 1995. For MENA region the sample comprises Jordan, Tunisia, Yemen, Syria, Algeria, Morocco, Iran, and Egypt.

Figure 2: Unemployment Rates in the Middle East & North Africa, 1993

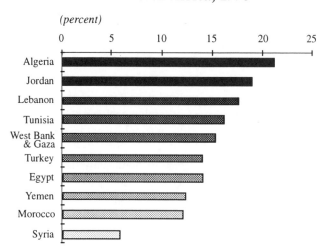

(percent)

Sources: Algeria: World Bank, 1994a; Egypt, 1991 Labor Force Survey; Jordan, World Bank, 1994b; Lebanon, Issa, 1993; Morocco, World Bank, 1994c; Syria, Louis, 1993; Tunisia, World Bank, 1995d; West Bank & Gaza, World Bank, 1994f; Yemen, Seif, 1993. Turkey, Filmer, 1995.

In the countries where public employment is large, unemployment is high among the kind of workers that are over-represented in public service. In Egypt, Jordan, and Syria, the share of young workers with secondary education among the unemployed is abnormally large at between 40 and 60 percent (Table 1). In Egypt, workers with more than a secondary education represent 26 percent of the labor force but they hold 60 percent of public sector jobs and make-up about 60 percent of the unemployed; in contrast, they constitute only about 20 percent of private non-agricultural sector employment. This pattern is also prevalent among women where they are disproportionately employed in the public sector, as in Egypt, Jordan, and Tunisia. In Egypt 71 percent of women with university degrees work for the state, and their chances of being unemployed are about 5 times larger than for men. This kind of unemployment tends to have long duration, young workers lining up until jobs in the public sector open up.

Falling wages. The wages in the formal sector declined in most countries in the mid to the late 1980s and have stagnated since. In manufacturing, for which data exist for most countries,[3] wage growth during the 1970s was comparable to that of East Asia, Latin America, and Eastern Europe. But while wage growth continued in East Asia in the 1980s, they fell in other regions, with particularly sharp declines in the Arab countries, by some 30 percent on average.[4] This reflects the tail end of the oil-based boom and bust cycle and the failure to achieve sustainable growth in labor demand for other sources.

There is again significant diversity in experiences. The sharpest recent declines have been in those countries that have felt the full brunt of the international oil cycle and its spillovers, and have not yet undertaken, or completed, reforms, such as Egypt and Jordan. Morocco had a more moderate decline in wages. Turkey experienced falling wages during much of the 1980s as part of its stabilization and restructuring strategy, but then witnessed a sharp real wage increase in the early 1990s.

Table 1: Unemployment Structure in the Middle East and North Africa

							First time job seekers as %of total unemployed	Young entrants (25 yrs & less) as % of total unemployment	Those with at least secondary education as %of unemployed
		Unemployment Rate* (%)							
	Year	Total	Men	Women	Rural	Urban			
Country (1)	(2)	(3)	(4)	(5)	(6)	(7)	(8)	(9)	(10)
Algeria	1991	21.0	22.0	17.0	na	na	na	40.0	31.3
Egypt	1991	10.6	6.3	27.8	8.8	13.1	76.6	78.4	57.0
Iran	1991	9.1	11.1	9.5	24.4	12.4	10.2	na	33.3
Jordan	1991	18.8	na	na	na	na	37.2	58.0	53.0
Morocco	1991	12.1	11.6	13.0	5.6	20.6	45.6	41.0	24.9
Syria	1991	5.7	na	na	na	na	78.0	68.0	45.0
Tunisia	1993	16.1	14.7	21.9	14.8	15.6	42.7	54.5	31.0
WBG	1993	15.3	8.4	2.7	na	na	na	na	na
Yemen	1992	12.3	14.0	6.0	11.4	16.3	32.0	na	18.0

Sources: Algeria: World Bank, 1994f; Morocco: 1191 LSMS; Tunisia: World Bank, 1995a; Jordan: World Bank, 1994e; Egypt, 1991 Labor Force Survey; West Bank and Gaza (WBG): 1991 Labor Force Survey; Syria: Louis, 1993; Yemen: Seif, 1993.
Note: na: not available
* The definition of unemployment in some cases is not consistent with that of the International Labor Organization (ILO).

High public sector employment. The public sector is a big employer in the region, probably employing a higher fraction of the workforce in any region outside the centrally planned states. The share of the labor force employed in the public sector is commonly between 30-40 percent (Figure 3). Central government employment varies between nearly 20 percent in Morocco and Tunisia to 40 percent in Jordan. In all countries, central governments are larger than the average for middle income countries;[5] indeed, they are larger than in rich OECD countries (18 percent).[6] Public enterprises employment is also high in several countries. It is highest in socialist Algeria (31 percent of the labor force), followed at a distance by Egypt and Tunisia (around 10 percent). In the OECD and Latin America, the comparable figure is only 5 percent.

While the public sector has been large in the numbers of employees, it has been increasingly poor in the wages offered. In the post-oil bust/post-stabilization period, the typical response of public sectors has been to keep expanding employment but to squeeze wages.[7] The syndrome of the large, but poor state is now widespread, but again particularly severe amongst those hard-hit by shocks and stuck in the old path. In Egypt government wages fell 50 percent between 1980 and 1992, but government employment rose 80 percent, almost entirely by 1990.[8]

Figure 3: Government Wages and Employment

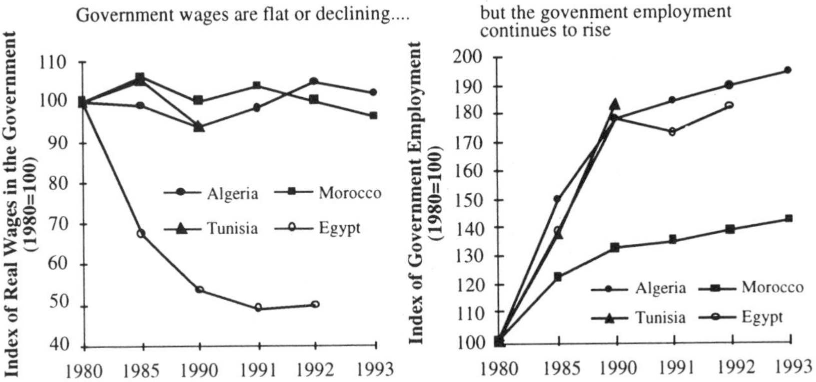

Low returns to education. Low and falling returns to education is a feature of some economies – though here there is a relatively sharp contrast between those stuck, for various reasons, and the early-reforming group. Returns to education are low in Jordan and Egypt, and barely exist in the West Bank and Gaza, but are much higher in Morocco and Turkey – comparable to an East Asian economy such as Thailand (Figure 4).

Where the public sector is large, it has an important influence on overall wage structures. While public sector wages have fallen across the region, they have tended to remain higher than in the private sector for the average public servant. In Morocco and Tunisia, wages are higher in the public sector at all skill levels.[9] In Egypt and Jordan cash wages are now smaller in the public sector, but recent studies show that once the value of all benefits are taken into account, the wage differential between the public and private sectors are about 20-40 for the average public servant.[10] Civil service pay tends to be more sensitive to seniority than the private sector, less sensitive to performance, and less dispersed across skill levels than private wages. As a result, women, older workers, and workers with medium levels of education tend to earn higher wages compared to what they would command in the private sector. The general effect is to distort the structure of wages and the returns to education. The one exception is that for women lower differences in public employment may reflect the benefits of a public sector working against norms of discrimination in many societies.[11]

Figure 4: Returns to Eduction for Men

(Wage with schooling/wage with no schooling)

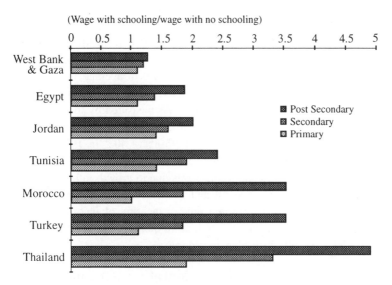

In Egypt, there is evidence of public sector wage compression over time. For other countries there is evidence of compression not over time, but by comparing wage differentials among private and public sectors. In the public sector, the ratio of skilled/unskilled is smaller than in the private sector, while the difference for unskilled is smaller.[12]

Relatively low poverty and equal income distribution. Poverty levels, unlike unemployment, are low by international standards. Using a conservative poverty line of $30 per person per month,[13] the estimated average poverty for six countries in the region where information was available (Algeria, Egypt, Iran, Jordan, Morocco and Tunisia) was 6 percent in 1990 compared with 28 percent in Latin America, despite only slightly lower average income there.[14] This reflects the relatively low degree of income inequality in the region – much less than in the case of Latin America or the more unequal East Asian societies, such as Malaysia, but still more unequal than the former centrally planned countries, such as Hungary. This relative equality of income and spending probably reflects a combination of relatively equal asset distribution and substantial private transfers between households.

In most countries, the typical poor is a rural household with little or no land. Jordan is an exception, with private employees in urban areas accounting for a high fraction of the poor. Elsewhere, urban poverty, while relatively low, is highest amongst low-skilled workers in the informal sector. In all countries, poverty is strongly correlated with lack of education, and with large households with few bread-earners. Although some of the unemployed are poor, most of the poor cannot afford to remain unemployed.

Changes in poverty have generally reflected the overall economic cycle. Where average incomes rose between 1985 and 1990, as in Algeria, Morocco and Tunisia, poverty fell; where incomes fell, as in Iran and Jordan, poverty rose. In Egypt poverty rose despite a small rise in average incomes. This reflected an aggravation in inequality. There have also been changes in inequality in Morocco, Tunisia and Jordan. As measured by the Gini coefficient, inequality has risen slightly in Morocco (39.1 in 1985 up to 39.6 in 1991), fallen in Tunisia (from 43.5 in 1975-85 to 40.2 in 1990), and has increased in Jordan (36.2 in 1986 to 43.3 in 1992). Thus, a lot of the reduction in poverty in Morocco and Tunisia was due to growth rather than redistribution effects (which were small and positive for Tunisia and small and negative for Morocco). At the same time, a measure of income dispersion (household income ratio of the top to bottom quintile) has risen in the three countries and especially in Jordan and Morocco.[15]

Openness, Labor Demand and Education: Alternative Growth Dynamics

The previous section has examined five stylized facts: high unemployment, falling or stagnant wages, high public employment, low returns to education (for some), and relatively modest poverty incidence. In this section we seek to relate these to patterns of development. Some may see pressures on employment as a typical consequence of a market-oriented growth path and an increasingly integrated world economy – this is after all the subject of intense debates in industrial countries. We first sketch a scenario of a virtuous long-run cycle in which openness can lead to highly favorable employment outcomes. We then describe the key features of the very different actual patterns of growth pursued in much of the region that help to explain the stylized facts. We come in a subsequent section to issues of transition.

A Virtuous Long-run Cycle

The fast growing East Asian economies exemplify a pattern of growth in which educational expansion, investment and openness interacted to produce huge, sustained increases in labor incomes, large reductions in poverty and generally some lessening in income differentials (though country experiences vary). The gains have been astonishing: as a group, they have enjoyed a growth rates of 170 percent in industrial wage and 400 percent in employment between 1970 and 1990. Three relevant lessons can be distilled from these experiences.

First, growth in labor incomes are essentially driven by increases in labor productivity. In this, the East Asian stars excelled. Rising labor productivity is determined by three factors: (1) capital accumulation (that raises the ratio of physical capital to labor); (2) expansion in skills (that raises the ratio of human capital to workers); and (3) the effectiveness with which these factors are combined (including gains from structural shifts, better use of resources and from technological change). There is some debate about what proportion of the better performance of East Asia is attributable to each of the three determinants. All observers agree that capital deepening was key, and that skills' development mattered. Some think this is the whole story, others are of the view that in the East Asian economies, the residual, or total factor productivity growth, also grew significantly faster.[16] We do not need to take a strong position on this issue since what matters is that workers were able to reap the gains from accumulation and technological change in the conditions prevailing in the fast-growing East Asian countries.

Second, openness was important in sustaining both labor demand and labor productivity growth by freeing growth in production of non-food tradable goods, especially in manufactures, from the constraints of domestic demand, and encouraging productivity-increasing structural change. These were made possible through the movement of workers from lower to higher productivity activities (at a broad level, agriculture to manufacturing and services) and through the induced productivity growth within subsectors encouraged by international trade. There were large movements of labor out of agriculture and into secondary and tertiary activities, complemented by rising labor productivity in agriculture. The balance of distribution between the two latter sectors depended largely on the countries' comparative advantage in trade. In resource-poor countries such as Korea, a high fraction of workers went into manufacturing, while in resource-rich ones, such as Indonesia and Malaysia, more went into services, though labor-intensive manufacturing activities remained an important source of employment growth.

Third, there was a changing but blissful equilibrium between growth in demand for skills and expansion in education systems, both of which contributed to rising average productivity and underpinned the steady structural shift in production and trade. All the successful East Asian countries invested heavily in basic education – often in the decade or so prior to rapid growth, so that when growth took off, it did so in parallel with quite fast increases in the skills of the workforce. This supported the initial shift into labor-intensive manufacturing activities, for which basic education is usually a prerequisite, which was then followed by a steady move into more skill-intensive activities that countries such as Korea, Hong Kong, and Malaysia have passed through.

Capital-deepening is obviously a blessing for labor productivity but only when the capital is combined effectively with labor and skills put to good use. But behind these developments were also a set of relationships between growth, openness and skills. Growth itself typically leads to rising demands for skills – induced by the structural transformation of production from agriculture to industry and services. The effects of openness are more complex. We return to this below, but it is worth thinking broadly in terms of two factors, both of which can be observed in the East Asian context. First, there are the effects of trade on the international division of labor, and consequently the internal structure of demand for labor of different types of skills. Broadly speaking, a Hechsker-Ohlin view of the world, in which countries trade in line with their factor endowments holds. This is reflected in the strong correlation between the structure of trade and the ratio of skills to land in a country – the higher the ratio, the more a country exports manufactures.[17] As skills-to-land ratios rise, countries increase their exports of manufactures – the typical trajectory of most East Asian countries, though how much manufactured products are exported at any one point in time also depends on how resource-intensive they are. Second, however, opening up an economy can by itself induce the demand for skills upgrading. Analysis of firm behavior in Taiwan, China and Malaysia shows that export-oriented firms, especially in the more technologically advanced sectors, also train their workers much more – this provides evidence of higher demands for skills.[18] We return to these relations below when we discuss the process of opening up.

Finally, the fast-growing East Asian countries have low open unemployment rates. This is the result of two factors. First, steadily rising labor demand and growing wages absorbed a growing labor force, and meant that new cohorts did not enter the market with expectations of jobs that were not met. Second, labor market dualism was relatively low by international standards – wages of those in "good" jobs, primarily in the formal sector of manufacturing and services, did earn more than other workers (even after adjusting for skill differentials), but the gaps were kept relatively low, most importantly by the market test of openness and relatively small public sectors.[19]

The Arab Path: from Boom to Bust

As the stylized facts vividly show, the countries in the Middle East and North Africa region did not sustain the blissful paths for labor as did most East Asian economies. We now turn to the relationships between their development paths and the adverse labor conditions of the 1980s and 1990s. However, at this stage we postpone the examination of the initial impact of reforms for those countries – especially for Morocco, Tunisia and Turkey.

During the 1960s and 1970s, the Arab economies were among the fastest growing in the world. The young states advocated modernity and "the big push." They invested heavily in large infrastructure projects, built state industries and erected protective walls to nurture them during infancy, and sought shared growth and social mobility by encouraging education and initiating nationalization and land reforms. Fueled by the regional oil boom, average growth per worker was about 3 percent a year during the period 1965-80 – not far below that of East Asia. As in East Asia, rising urbanization was a common feature of this growth path.

For the working population, this growth path brought large benefits. These originated from two aspects of the development pattern, where the public sector played a key role: policies that promoted the modern sector, especially through expansion of millions of jobs in government services and protected public enterprises; and vigorous expansion in publicly-funded education, at all levels. This was to a large extent financed by proceeds from oil sales. And since oil was concentrated in only some of the states, it had an important international dimension, with economies with high ratios of labor to oil reserves – notably Jordan, Egypt, the West Bank and Gaza, and Yemen getting access to the jobs and resources to underwrite this strategy through a mixture of workers migrating to the oil centers, and oil money flowing in (in the form of grants and remittances). The labor-surplus economies exported workers directly rather than moving into labor-intensive manufactures. In a comparable fashion, large numbers of Turkish workers went to Germany.

The old social contract kept labor demand high, especially for educated workers, through policies that protected and promoted the modern sector. Food and consumption subsidies were also broad, bringing benefits to the middle classes and the poor. Unskilled workers reaped gains from domestic and international construction booms. And there was the promise of social mobility through education and public employment.[20]

When oil prices collapsed in the mid-1980s, the sources of employment growth disappeared. The combination of declining public sector revenues, fast-rising labor supply, rapid urbanization, and large gains in education have rendered the old social contract unaffordable. Since the second part of the

1980s, growth performance has been dismal (Figure 5). Labor productivity has stagnated in the non-oil producing countries and has fallen by more than 4 percent a year in the oil producing countries. The slow-down in the demand for labor in Europe, and later in the Gulf region have depressed labor markets in the labor-exporting countries. At the peak in the mid-1980s, there were over 5 million Arab workers in the Gulf, and perhaps half as many migrants from the Maghreb working in Europe. This exodus accounted for 10 percent of the labor-exporting countries' labor force on average (much more for Jordan, Lebanon, the West Bank and Gaza, and Yemen), boosted wages at home, and generated large remittances.[21]

Figure 5: Annual Growth in GDP per Worker in MENA and Other Regions

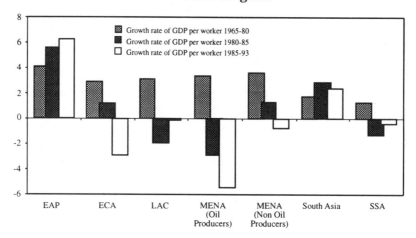

Annual GDP Growth per Worker in the MENA Region

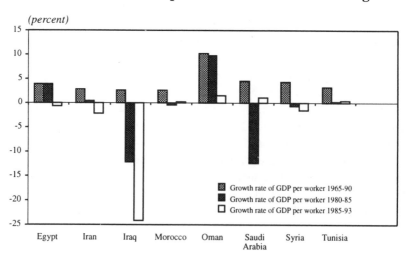

Regional and European labor markets stopped growing in the mid-1980s. Employment opportunities in the oil-rich economies declined dramatically in the wake of the Gulf war in 1991, hitting Jordanian, Palestinian, and Yemeni workers hard. In Jordan, returnees (about 10 percent of the labor force) crowded out young entrants to the labor market.[22] Although returning workers had invested part of their savings thereby increasing labor demand and reducing the effect of the shock, this effect was only temporary. In the West Bank and Gaza, the return of highly educated Palestinians from the Gulf led to a crash in the wages of skilled labor, pushing returns to education nearly to zero.[23] More recently, many Palestinian workers were hit by the reduced access to the Israeli labor market. In 1992, about a third of the labor force (mostly unskilled workers) worked in Israel. In 1995, less than 10 percent received work permits. In Yemen, returnees represented about 13 percent of the labor force; unemployment soared and remained high as civil war broke out.[24] In Lebanon, unemployment among the population displaced by the war has been estimated to be twice the national average.[25]

At the same time the public sector, which was the main employer of skilled workers in many of the countries of the region, was under pressure. The limits of state-led growth were recognized in the region as early as the 1970s. But the massive external assistance received during the 1970s and early 1980s allowed the system to continue for an extra decade or so. With the oil bust, private demand for labor slumped, and public sectors increased their hiring initially, financing their rising deficits with financial repression and external borrowing. In Algeria, hiring grew at 10 percent a year after 1985 when private demand stumbled.[26] Half the new jobs created in Tunisia between 1982 and 1989 were in the public sector.[27] The experiences of Egypt and Jordan were similar. Public hiring accelerated and then stalled with the fiscal crisis and stabilization programs of the late 1980s.

The private sector continued to generate new jobs until the mid-1980s as rising incomes led to increased demand for labor in the services sector. The construction industry alone employed more than 10 percent of the labor force in most countries of the region, and up to 20 percent in the Gulf.[28] Protected private industries became large employers in Jordan, Morocco, and Tunisia. More recently, the rising scarcity of capital inflows, coupled with some measures of financial liberalization wreaked havoc on firms accustomed to two decades of cheap foreign exchange. Old firms in import-substitution sectors are now struggling and are a weak source of employment growth.

Overall, the old path and the associated social contract quite effectively delivered expanding employment opportunities and reduced poverty for a while. Public employment and protected industrialization can be a source of economic and employment growth for a given period of time (recall the rapid growth of many Latin America economies in the 1960s and 1970s). When there is a massive positive resource shock, it can be sustained for much longer. In particular, the oil revenues were able to bankroll the cycle of public employment growth and provision of education for entry into public sector jobs. But the oil boom basically hid the underlying problems of an unsustainable growth and employment strategy. When boom turned to bust, not only did past sources of employment growth – both national and international – disappear, but the unproductive nature of many of the jobs created became a distressing and problematic heritage for the future.

Why has unemployment stayed so high? As in Europe, only more so, large scale unemployment emerged because of the adverse effects of the bust – the dynamics of falling labor demand and continued rapid growth in supply. It has persisted because of the deep-rooted expectations of the young – especially the educated young now in abundant rather than scarce supply, that a secondary education was the pathway to a "good," modern-sector job, and the capacity and willingness of families (especially non-poor ones) to support the unemployed. The old social contract is still present, if increasingly fragile, and within this contract, it is the state that is expected to deliver jobs, especially to the educated.[29]

With rising unemployment many governments responded, as noted above, with continued expansion of public employment – most dramatically in Algeria since the late 1980s. But since macroeconomic difficulties prevented increases in spending, such expansion took place amid stagnant or declining wages, further contributing to the phenomenon of a large pool of unproductive labor in the public sector, with little output contribution and a negative influence on public savings. Unlike some Sub-Saharan African countries (such as Tanzania), in most cases the process of wage decline has not been drastic enough so as to put public sector wages below those prevailing in the private sector – especially when non-cash benefits and greater security are accounted for (in Egypt for instance).[30] But this employment strategy tends to perpetuate dualism, and adds to the future adjustment problems created by a large, poor state sector.

All three groups – public sector workers, the unemployed and the poor – suffered when boom turned to bust, and the lack of viability of the old growth path and contract became exposed. With declining resources, the specter of distributional conflict is now rising. Old forms of largesse – notably food subsidies – have often been cut drastically, in direct competition with the public sector wage bill. Food subsidies were typically cut more than the salaries of the elite.[31] In Egypt, food subsidies fell by 5 percent of GDP between 1989 and 1993. The public sector wage bill fell by only 0.4 percent of GDP over the same period. Food subsidies were virtually abolished in Jordan between 1990 and 1992, but the public sector wage bill kept rising, reaching 7 percent of GDP in 1993 (excluding military and public enterprises), an all time high. In Morocco, food subsidies were cut from 5.5 to 0.5 percent of GDP between 1981 and 1993. The wage bill rose from 11.1 to 14.3 percent of GDP over the same period. Only in Tunisia were food subsidies (and other social sectors) protected and made better targeted, falling from 3 to 2 percent of GDP in recent years (public sector wage bill remains constant since 1986).

Sooner or later, change had to come. Countries such as Egypt and Syria appear to be in a fragile state of paralysis. Meanwhile rising international integration is both creating opportunities and sharpening competition.

A World of Rising Competition

The world is becoming increasingly competitive as more and more countries open their borders to trade, as the capital markets are becoming increasingly international, and as the costs of transport and communication have fallen sharply.[32] The Middle Eastern and North African economies were traditionally highly integrated with the rest of the world via the oil market, and with each other via the labor market. There was quite a high degree of official capital movement from oil-rich to oil-poor countries, but probably the deepest form of integration for most was via capital flight to Zurich, London and elsewhere.

However, with the partial exceptions of Turkey and then Morocco and Tunisia, deep integration through open trading has been limited within the region. In the international environment of the 1990s, failure to effectively integrate production structures through trade will impart high long-run costs. This means lost opportunities now, but more importantly countries that fail to integrate risk getting increasingly left behind. Much of the Arab world and Sub-Saharan Africa are facing this risk. We will quickly survey the three channels of integration for the region – via international migration, capital and trade – in order to provide the context for the opening up faced by the regional economies.

International migration, as we have seen, was an integral part of the de facto growth and employment strategy of the past few decades, from countries with large populations relative to their oil reserves to oil-rich economies, to Europe and, for Palestinians, to Israel. Migration was a powerful source of labor demand, with important second round effects via the spending of foreign-earned income, that had a powerful effect on the bottom half of the income distribution.[33]

This source of employment creation has now largely disappeared, and it is its negative linkage effects that are now more important. Palestinians lost jobs in the Gulf, exacerbating labor problems in Jordan, the West Bank and Gaza, though these were hidden for a while (apart from the collapse of skill differentials noted above) by the spending of the repatriated savings of returning migrants. When Israel cut the employment of migrant Palestinian, labor difficulties turned into something closer to a labor crisis in the West Bank and Gaza. Yemen has also suffered a severe return migration shock. In addition, labor market problems in Egypt and Syria are spilling over into Lebanon and Jordan.

Capital flows matter as much or more than migration flows for employment outcomes. Workers need productive capital to raise their productivity, while movements of financial capital have a powerful immediate effect on macroeconomic activity, wages and employment. When capital flew out of the region in the 1980s, workers were left behind to pick up the bill. As with Latin America – only more so – capital controls proved feeble in preventing private outward capital flight when the going got rough. It is now estimated that privately-owned foreign assets are equivalent to some 90 percent of GDP, more than any other region in the world. They represent a large tax on past growth, but also an opportunity for the future if internal policies are rectified to allow for their repatriation. Some of the potential has already been seen in the significant repatriation of capital that occurred in Egypt in the early 1990s seduced by a combination of opening of the capital account, and the euphoria that flowed from the dual impulses of optimism over peace and the new-found international delight in "emerging" markets.[34]

Capital flows into Egypt in the early part of the 1990s did benefit workers – overall economic activity was higher than it would have been in their absence and this helped the national labor market. But capital is fickle and, to a first degree, cannot be controlled, as the experience with capital flight in the 1980s has vividly revealed. The only way to permanently attract capital that will help create sustainable jobs and raise productivity is by putting in place a sound political and economic environment for domestic investment. What happens to the progress toward Arab-Israeli peace will be a contributing factor to the willingness of both domestic and foreign capital to commit to the region and thus to job creation – the closer a country is to Israel, the more important this aspect is (that is, it is mildly important for Morocco, but obviously vitally so for the West Bank and Gaza). Economic policy has little or no influence over peace. But it has strong implications on the expectations over profits and the perceived policy risks of investing. Workers, far from being in conflict with capital, have an interest in promoting economic reforms that provide the macroeconomic conditions and the economic environment where capital is more secure, but eschew special incentives (whether via tax deals, special protection or kickbacks) that essentially are taxes on the local populace.

Of the three channels of international integration, trade is probably the most important one in the long run. Trade is however the least exploited sector in the region (with the partial exceptions of the countries noted above). Meanwhile, the world is in the midst of a profound opening. Economic reform is leading the entry into world product markets of huge pools of labor in South and East Asia, the former COMECON bloc and Latin America. The Uruguay Round Agreements (UR) will lead to some further liberalization and opening of markets, especially with respect to labor-intensive manufactures and agriculture (albeit modest), and, perhaps more importantly, helping to lock-in on a multilateral basis the ongoing regional process of liberalization.

The direct effects of the Uruguay Round on the Arab world are modest and in some cases negative, with a net loss of $3 billion.[35] Two particular aspects of the UR are of particular concern to the region: the dismantling of the Multifiber Arrangement (MFA), that will lead to lower prices of textiles, and the partial liberalization of agriculture and gradual removal of agricultural subsidies, that will lead to higher prices of foods. Since the region exports textiles and imports food, it will suffer negative terms of trade effects overall, but farmers would enjoy gains in their terms of trade (assuming international price increases were passed on to them). In the long run, once the migration effects have been factored in, the consequences are negligible for agricultural and unskilled workers, and slightly negative for skilled workers. If there is closer association with the European Union, however, there are much larger gains for farmers and, in the long run – after allowing for the effects on rural-urban migration – small increases in agricultural and unskilled wages of some 3 percent may occur together with a small loss for skilled workers, owing to the effects of integration.

However, the above estimates of the effects of integration do not take into account the more important consequences of opening up. As noted in the brief review of the East Asian experience, it was not the terms of trade effects that led to the extraordinary long run growth. Rather, long-run growth was stimulated by the engagement in international markets – together with sound domestic economic policies – which created an environment conducive to the growth of labor-intensive activities, structural shifts in employment and overall productivity growth. The key lies in the inter-relationship between openness and the internal growth dynamics. In this area, even Morocco and Tunisia have lagged behind East Asian competitors, especially in productivity growth.[36] It is noteworthy, however, that Turkey with the longest and deepest period of engagement in international markets, plus greater progress in policy aspects of integration with Europe, has a performance in productivity growth that rivals Indonesia and Malaysia.

While an increasingly integrated world economy increases opportunities, it also raises the stakes. Weak domestic conditions, in terms of politics, macroeconomics or the microeconomic and business environment, will lead to paltry capital investments and vulnerability to destabilizing international capital flows. Many countries within the region risk being left out of the global process of integration. And while there will always be some place in the international division of labor, the real benefits come from getting on to a path of rapid productivity growth and effective use of national skills. The next decade may even represent an opportunity for the region to open up its economies, especially with respect to Europe, before the full force of competition from Asia comes to bear on them with the removal of the MFA early in the next century.

The Process of Opening Up and Labor

We have argued that the employment strategy that has defined the old path of public sector expansion and education for public sector jobs is now bankrupt, and that the need to open up to a more integrated world is becoming ever more urgent. Some countries – notably Algeria, Egypt and Syria – are in a fragile state of paralysis, in need of new economic opportunities to tackle persistent poverty and unemployment but fearful of the adverse effects of opening up on inefficient and unproductive current employment structures, especially in the government and public enterprise sectors. Others – Morocco, Tunisia and Turkey – are beginning to break out of this vicious cycle and have embraced the strategy of opening up as a means to do so. But they remain in the midst of the transition and fears over unemployment remain, as does large public sector employment.

While the gains for workers from East Asian style exploitation of opportunities in the international markets may provide compelling support for such an approach in the long run, most politicians are more concerned with short term gains. It is thus the transitional effects of opening up that are likely to be of dominant concern. Opening up involves changes in the pattern of demand for different products, with indirect effects on the pattern of demand for different categories of labor. It also involves an acceleration of the normal process of creation and destruction of jobs. It is useful to divide the effects into two: the effects on public sector employment – for which the question of destruction of unviable jobs is key; and those on the overall structure of labor demand for skilled and unskilled workers.

The effects on public employment are analytically easy to trace and practically harsh. Protected state enterprises that are engaged in tradable activities which are subject to the brutal winds of international competition, are likely to close or contract, in either case shedding labor. Both government employment and enterprise employment in services (utilities, for example) are shielded from the direct effects of competition, but there will be heightened pressure from the need for fiscal probity and higher quality services to raise productivity, layoff surplus labor and bring wage scales in line with the private sector. We saw above that among the stylized facts about public employment are first that it is too large (that is, there is surplus, unproductive labor), and second that wages are generally not significantly out of line with the private sector on average, but that wage differentials are sometimes out of line.

So the effects on public employment are likely to be negative. The key issue in designing a new strategy concerns the implications of opening up on the level and structure of private sector labor demand. We discuss this here, including the relationship between medium-term effects and the timing of job losses. In the next section we briefly turn to the implications for managing the joint process of opening up and public sector reform.

The dominant popular view in rich countries is that opening up an economy leads to job losses, especially amongst unskilled workers, and causes rising income inequalities (in the United States) and persistent unemployment (in Europe). While few observers would deny that trade with low-wage countries is a source of some job losses, the weight of the evidence in fact suggests that such trade contributes only part, and probably a small part, to the employment problem in rich countries. In Europe, technological change, slow supply responses in the creation of skills, and the functioning of labor markets play a much larger role.[37]

Fears of job losses are also common in low and middle income countries. It is however important to distinguish between two processes: the effect of opening up on the level and structure of labor demand once changes have worked their way through the system; and the likely acceleration of the process of creation and destruction of jobs that a change in incentives will bring. For the Arab countries – and to some extent for Turkey – the accelerated destruction of unproductive jobs is essentially the same as the public sector employment issue, while we are, for the time being, trying to focus on the lasting effects on the structure of labor demand.

The traditional view of economists is that opening up in poorer countries would be unambiguously good for unskilled labor.[38] This was based on both theory and evidence. Poorer countries that opened up would be expected to trade and produce more in activities that intensively used their more abundant factors of production. Natural resources and land matter in this context – and we gave evidence above on the role of relative land availability in influencing trade patterns. There are then two reasons why unskilled labor would be expected to benefit from opening up in labor-abundant poorer countries: across labor categories, unskilled labor is abundant relative to richer countries; and for land-rich countries, expansion in agriculture involves higher demand for unskilled labor that is complementary to land. The situation is different for oil-rich countries, since oil production is capital and skill-intensive, and most labor is in services activities. These countries are unlikely to export labor-intensive agricultural or manufactured goods.

Evidence for the view that opening up increases the relative demand for unskilled labor comes from data on the higher unskilled-labor content of exports compared with (protected) import substitutes in many countries, and from the observed narrowing of wage differentials over time in export-oriented economies – especially the four Asian "tigers": Hong Kong, Korea, Singapore and Taiwan, China.[39] Evidence of actual changes over time is probably more compelling for a government contemplating opening up its economy. Unfortunately, previous research on these countries has generally failed to take into account either the shifts in relative supply of different categories of labor (and, as noted above, all of the economies were enjoying the fruits of previous educational expansion) or the changes in labor market institutions. Moreover, more recent evidence, especially from studies of Latin American countries, show widening differentials that broadly accompanied the process of opening up – notably in Chile and Mexico, and also in Costa Rica and Colombia.[40] Attempts in some of these studies to control for effects of changes in the relative supply of skilled workers (in all cases there was an increase in the relative supply of skilled workers), confirm a shift in relative demand away from unskilled and toward skilled workers.

How might the process of opening up an economy lead to shifts in demand against the unskilled, when on the face of it, these are the abundant factor? The theory and evidence are still being disentangled – most of the empirical work that found widening wage differentials is recent.[41] There are three possible explanations that offer promise:

First, widening wage differentials is a phenomenon that has occurred in middle income countries whose relative shares of factors of production fall in-between rich and poor countries and which are experiencing the effects of a relatively substantial increase in the international supply of goods, which are intensive in their use of unskilled-labor as a result of opening up to trade of Asian labor-intensive countries such as China, Indonesia and Bangladesh and India. China's exports to the European Union have risen from 2.3 percent of the ECU's total imports in 1985 to 4.9 percent in 1991. By one measure the relative price of labor-intensive manufactures has fallen by 20 percent between the mid-1980s and early 1990s.

Second, openness releases the market for skills from essentially domestic constraints. Closed economies that invest heavily in education might run into significant relative price changes that affect skilled labor as a result of an increase in the supply of educated workers. The evidence of compressed wage differentials in Arab countries that remained closed and suffered stagnant modern sector job growth is consistent with this. For open economies, the price of educated labor is going to be more strongly influenced by international trade, while unskilled wages may continue to be held down by large supplies of labor in low-productivity agriculture.[42]

Third, some categories of exports – or features of exporting – may demand more skilled workers. It has often been argued that modern sector manufacturing requires at least basic education, in contrast to agriculture and informal sector services. This could be important for exports in which high quality is of importance. The same may apply to high-value agricultural production for rich country markets.[43]

What do the above explanation mean for the regional economies? There is little time series' evidence on skill differentials, but it is striking to note that the three economies that have initiated the process of opening up – Morocco, Tunisia and Turkey – have higher returns to skills, but still not unusually high differentials by international standards. Those that are stuck in their old development strategy have unusually compressed differentials. This raises questions on whether the return to education is going to be high enough to justify household investment in schooling. Opening up may restore differentials in countries that have suffered significant compression. Beyond this, since most of the oil-poor economies in the region fall around the middle of the international income and wage levels, the effects of opening up on relative demand for skilled and unskilled labor are ambiguous. Much will depend on agriculture, to the extent there are potential exporters of agricultural goods (that tend to be more unskilled intensive). This is, of course, of particular importance to the poor who mainly rely on income from unskilled labor on farms. Finally, we should re-emphasize that the net effects during the transition will also depend on the dynamics of creation and destruction of jobs, especially the timing of destruction of old protected jobs.

The experiences of Morocco and Tunisia, the early trade reformers of the region, illustrate well both the opportunities and difficulties ahead. Both countries started to liberalize their trade regime in the early 1980s. Quantitative restrictions were virtually eliminated in Morocco and their coverage reduced in Tunisia; maximum tariffs were reduced from 165 to 45 percent in Morocco and from 235 to 45 percent in Tunisia. Since then, foreign investment has boomed, reaching $975 million in Morocco in 1993, and $600 million in Tunisia in 1994, with subcontracting business for European firms (especially in textiles and clothing) taking off.

Textiles and clothing exports increased at a rate of 15 percent a year in Morocco and 12 percent in Tunisia between 1985 and 1991. Labor demand rose fast: in Morocco, total employment rose by about 5 percent a year in urban areas during 1984-1994; manufacturing employment rose at 10 percent; employment in the manufacturing export sector rose at a rate of 20 percent.[44] But while employment expanded fast, measured average wages and productivity did not rise. The most plausible explanation is that this was due to compositional effects with the relative expansion of lower-wage jobs. The manufacturing sector was small and protected in the past, it used capital intensively and employed skilled workers at high wages – these subsectors have been stagnant. The new jobs created in manufacturing exports were instead labor intensive and lower-wage. It is precisely this adjustment that allowed employment to grow so fast in these sectors. In contrast, both wages and employment expanded slowly in firms producing for the internal market, although recently, the demand for skilled workers has started to rise.

The experience of Tunisia further illustrates structural change.[45] An analysis of changes in employment between 1984 and 1993 that decomposes job creation into within-sector productivity growth and structural shifts in employment and growth, finds that almost all sectors (except "other services") enjoyed productivity increases, but there was net employment expansion as a consequence of growth in output and structural shifts. Rising within-sector productivity was particularly important in agriculture – the major low-productivity sector – and likely to be a major source of labor income growth for the poor. These changes accommodated, at rising average productivity, a large increase in female labor force participation between the ages of 20 and 44 (there is an offsetting effect for the youth with increased time spent on education).

In reforming Morocco and Tunisia, the net effects on income inequality have been small. The demand for skilled workers has fallen in the protected industries, but has started to rise in the export industries as a result of attempts to increase competitiveness with better technologies and management. In other words, trade reforms may have led to a reduction in income inequality; however, rising demand for skilled and surplus workers have pushed inequality back up.

Let us return to the three groups in the population that we started with:

The poor. The poor are likely to gain from opening up, especially from the twin process of accelerated transfer of labor from agriculture to labor-intensive manufacturing and productivity increases within agriculture. Where there are terms of trade gains to farmers, the opening up process will also be poverty-reducing. The expansion in the demand for unskilled work was a key aspect in the dramatic fall in poverty experienced in both Morocco and Tunisia. It accommodated the rise in female labor participation in both societies, and it allowed rural workers and those in the construction sector to get more productive higher wage jobs. While average wages in manufacturing were stagnant or falling in Morocco, the new jobs that were being created tended to tighten the labor market for poorer workers – those who got these jobs experienced significant increases in their wages.

Public sector workers. The effects on public sector employment are likely to be negative, so those that are laid-off will almost certainly suffer, at least temporarily. When shifts in private sector demand take place, the wage differentials in the public sector may be restored, benefiting the more productive public sector workers.

The unemployed. The net effects on the unemployed will reflect different phenomena. Some will gain from more dynamic job creation in new activities; there will also be a temporary rise in unemployment, to the extent inefficient activities become unprotected and governmental employment reforms take place. Both, total unemployment and that of the educated young are still high in Morocco and Tunisia, in part because of labor market rigidities in the modern sector, but also because of the persistence of expectations and support mechanisms referred to in the previous section. However, both countries have a much higher proportion of laid off workers in the pool of unemployed. In 1991, Morocco had an unemployment rate of 12 percent, of which 55 percent had previously worked and 25 percent had secondary education. By contrast Egypt had only slightly lower unemployment rate of 11 percent, but of the unemployed, only 23 percent had ever worked and 57 percent had secondary education.

The international and regional evidence suggest that opening up can solve two long-run problems, it can both be good for unskilled labor demand and restore excessively compressed education differentials. However, the demand will be for productive, not unproductive skills, and during the transition it is highly likely to be also associated with job losses for some of the educated now in "bad" jobs. The transition period will also adversely affect the relatively old who do not have productive or flexible skills, and the educated young who have grown up with now incorrect expectations of public sector job opportunities. Expectations can change – especially if governments undertake credible reforms in both areas: opening up and public hiring policies. But there is likely to be a case for transfers in order to deal with permanent and temporary losers.

Sequencing and the Problem of Large but Poor States

There are two reasons for being concerned with the design of public sector reforms and their sequencing in the context of opening up an economy. First, there is a large pool of public sector employees who correctly feel vulnerable: opening up will destroy many public sector jobs and some incumbents may not have the kind of education or the flexibility to benefit from future rises in demand for productive skilled workers. These workers are likely to suffer permanent welfare losses (and even those with "good", flexible skills, may suffer temporary welfare losses) and are unlikely to vote for opening up. Second, at both the macroeconomic and microeconomic levels, the reform of the public sector is a prerequisite to achieving the potential gains from opening up – and especially the dramatic gains from jumping onto dynamic development paths as exemplified by the experiences of the East Asian economies. Macroeconomics matter even more after opening up, because fiscal imprudence is swiftly punished in a world of mobile capital. Micro reforms count because they in the end determine the macroeconomic public sector position, via the effects of wage and public enterprise policy, and because of supply side effects on efficiency of production, most of all in the education sector.

In the past, the overwhelming role the state has played as an employer has distracted it from focusing enough attention on the core issues of macroeconomic stability, infrastructure, fiscal justice, or education. What is less recognized is that it has also reduced the ability of reformers to pursue trade liberalization. From a distributional point of view, opening can lead to increased fiscal pressures on the state. Old forms of public employment in inefficient public enterprise activities are turned into open losses and while aggregate fiscal imbalances become much less tolerable in an open economy. It is true that most of the region's economies have undertaken major fiscal adjustments prior to or in conjunction with trade reform; but the structural reforms of the public sector have been relatively neglected: privatizing or closing inefficient public enterprises, restructuring the state-sponsored education systems, laying off of surplus government workers, and developing rational pay; none of these measures have figured in the core of the fiscal changes, even in the leading reformers.

With large numbers of public employees who have suffered real wage declines, macroeconomic stability is at the permanent mercy of wage increases. The public sector wage bill (excluding public enterprises) ranges from

10 percent of GDP in Egypt to 15 percent in Morocco. In most countries, the fiscal deficit would rise by 2 to 5 percentage points of GDP if public sector employees manage to regain the losses they have sustained in the second part of the 1980s. This is precisely what initiated a financial crisis in Lebanon in 1991, and in Turkey in 1994, ending in both cases with large devaluations and huge losses for workers. The credibility of the reform program is undermined by this fiscal fragility.

The fear of fiscal instability is also taxing the reform agenda. In the countries with large public enterprises, such as Algeria, Egypt, Syria, and Tunisia, measures to increase competition through, inter alia the liberalization of prices, investments, or trade will increase the losses of the public enterprises and ultimately enlarge fiscal deficits. Financial market reforms also hurt those public enterprises with traditionally large capital to labor ratios and high debts to the banking system. Morocco and Tunisia have, like most countries in Latin America, promoted import substitution by protecting private industry. Trade liberalization has hurt the financial sector. In contrast, many countries of the Mashrek (Egypt, Jordan, Yemen, and Syria) have instead built state industries; for these countries, trade reforms hurt both the financial sector and the fiscal accounts.

The most advanced country in terms of trade success, Turkey, vividly illustrates the fragility of opening up without deep public sector reform. In Turkey, income inequality deteriorated following the implementation of the reforms of the early 1980s: the state cut price support for agriculture and initiated simultaneously financial liberalization; profits became a much larger share of income; and labor was repressed. By 1989, political liberalization and the resumption of competitive politics led labor to become more active and wages rose sharply under union pressure. But because the problems of a large public sector were not resolved during the reform period, wage pressure led to larger fiscal deficits, inflation, and a foreign exchange crisis in 1993 that ended up eroding away most of labor's previous gains. Turkey's experience exemplifies how distributional conflicts, centered on public sector involvement in the economy, can jeopardize the process of opening up that is potentially a source of rapid employment and productivity growth.

Is the answer to reform public sectors first? Did the early reformers, who (largely) opened up first and then faced the public sector problems, get it wrong? The answer to both question is probably not. A scenario of public sector reform first (or even simultaneously) implies public employment declines, as well as welfare losses amongst a key base of political support, prior to reaping any of the gains from opening up. As noted throughout this chapter, such a sequencing of reforms will likely lead to increased distributional conflicts – and thus increase credibility-thwarting uncertainty. It also increases the probability that public sector employees might lose and unemployment rise in the critical early period of reform. There would be some hope that the poor would be gaining from opening up, but the poor tend to be a weak base of support. Of course, while initiating early on general employment-reducing public sector reforms may not be advisable, other complementary reforms do make sense and are desirable as soon as possible: removal of job guarantees for graduates (explicit or implicit) to try and break the expectation of "good" (but actually "bad") public sector jobs; and deep educational reform to create the preconditions for flexible and market-oriented educational institutions.

The following sequence would seem to make sense for large-but-poor states:

First, partially open up, "easy" fiscal adjustment, continued partial protection for public employment, and selected public sector reforms (for example, education), and design of transfers for both temporary and permanent losers. Second, once some growth in employment has started, deep public sector reform should be initiated and complemented by selected expansion of non-employment related public spending, including transfers to losers, and selected public services to marginalized groups in the population.

Conclusion

Most Arab countries pursued an employment strategy that worked while the oil revenues were booming but collapsed when they fell. Some employment cycles were unavoidable, given that no one had anticipated the scale of the oil cycle (if they did they could have smoothed the use of revenues). But the pattern of growth chosen by most Arab countries (and to some extent by Turkey until the 1980s) was a disaster for employment, leaving the characteristic syndrome of high unemployment and high public employment, in large, but increasingly poor states. Past educational expansion contributed more to frustrated expectations of getting "good" public sector jobs than to a dynamic of productivity growth that characterized open economies.

Now the political and social situation is fragile. Governments can choose to open up their economies or can struggle to maintain the current fragile state. There are political risks to both courses. The poor are the most robust potential beneficiaries, but least influential. Unemployment effects in transition are ambiguous.

The political necessity and the political risks associated with opening up an economy are clear. It is the only way to get on to a labor-demanding path and to attract stable capital flows; but there will be some permanent and some temporary losers especially among public sector workers. Employment-reducing reforms of the public sector are unlikely and probably not advisable prior to a growth dynamic taking off, yet failure to reform could lead opening up to end in a blaze of either fiscal crisis or growth-reducing fiscal repression of economic and social services. This implies that some gradualism may be important, provided the forces of conservatism do not undercut reform. The dynamics between opening up and public sector employment matter; some opening up of trade may be necessary to even start on a blissful path. We argue for starting with opening up, followed by reforms of the public sector and compensation for losers.

Countries such as Morocco, Tunisia, Turkey and most recently Jordan, have started on this path, but failure to deal with the critical second stage of public sector reform will jeopardize the chances for growth. Those countries that have not started reforms face a tougher situation. Algeria, Egypt and Syria are confronting a bigger challenge. Currently public sector elites are holding on, but this is becoming an ever-more desperate, and ultimately self-defeating act.

Notes

1 See World Bank 1995b.
2 The working age population grew at over 3 percent per annum in the past thirty years, the fastest of any region in the world. See World Bank, 1995e.
3 The data are available from UNIDO (United Nations Industrial Development Organization).
4 World Bank, 1995f.
5 For example, Turkey and Greece: 10 percent; Spain and Portugal: 15 percent.
6 Organization for Economic Cooperation and Development.
7 Said, 1995.
8 Handoussa, 1992.
9 World Bank 1995c, Zouarri-Bouattour 1994.
10 Assaad, 1995.
11 See also World Bank, 1995b for the case of Jordan.
12 Said, 1995.
13 More precisely, this is a cutoff of $30 for average monthly per capita consumption in terms of 1985 purchasing power parity dollars. While a figure of $30 per month is a useful yardstick for international comparisons, most observers of the region would probably use a higher cutoff for absolute poverty. Using a cutoff of $50 per month for per capita consumption raises the head count ratio for poverty to 18 percent for the six countries in 1990, ranging from 7 percent in Algeria, to 24 percent in Egypt and 36 percent in Jordan.
14 van Eeghen, 1995.
15 Jordan: 6.0 to 8.3 between 1986 and 1992; Morocco: 4.0 to 7.0 between 1985 and 1991; Tunisia: 7.0 to 7.85 between 1985 and 1990. See van Eeghen, 1995.
16 Compare, for example, *The East Asia Miracle* (1993), with Alwyn Young 1993.
17 Wood, 1994.

18 See Tan, Hong and Batra, 1995.
19 See World Bank, 1995g.
20 Richards, 1995.
21 Up to 10 percent of GNP in Morocco, 12 percent in Egypt, 18 percent in Jordan, 22 percent in Yemen, and 30 percent in the West Bank and Gaza.
22 Pissarides, 1993.
23 Angrist, 1992.
24 Seif, 1993.
25 Issa, 1993.
26 Bernard, 1991.
27 Zouari-Bouatour, 1994.
28 Al-Qudsi et al, 1993.
29 Richards, 1995
30 See Assaad, 1994.
31 van Eeghen, 1995.
32 See *World Bank World Development Report, 1995*, chapter 7.
33 Although the poor tend to be under-represented amongst migrants, who generally have some education and resources to move, the indirect effects via tightening the labor market, private transfers and second-round spending impacts, undoubtedly contributed to poverty reduction
34 Diwan and Squire, 1993.
35 This is based on the analysis in Diwan, Yang and Wang, 1995, that uses an aggregation for the Arab countries, and does not include Turkey.
36 World Bank, 1995f.
37 Wood, 1994; Lawrence and Slaughter, 1993.
38 In addition to the dynamic effects of getting on to a productivity and investment enhancing growth path emphasized above.
39 See especially Krueger for the first category of evidence, and Wood for a survey of the latter.
40 See Robbins, Gindling and Robbins, Revenga and Montenegro, Hanson and Harrison
41 See Wood 1995 for a survey and discussion.
42 See Pissarides, 1995.
43 See Robbins 1995 for this argument.
44 World Bank, 1994b.
45 See Zouari-Bouattour, 1994.

References

Al-Qudsi, Sulayman, Ragui Assaad, Radwan Shaban. 1993. "Labor Markets in the Arab Countries: A Survey." Paper presented at the First Annual Conference on Development Economics, June 4-6. Cairo, Egypt.

Angrist, Joshua D. 1992. "Wages and Employment in the West Bank and the Gaza Strip: 1981-1990." Maurice Falk Institute for Economic Research in Israel. Discussion Paper No. 92.02.

Assaad, Ragui. 1993. "The Employment Crisis in Egypt: Trends and Issues." Humphrey Institute of Public Affairs, University of Minnesota.

____. 1994. "The Effects of Public Sector Hiring and Compensation Policies on the Egyptian Labor Market." Humphrey Institute of Public Affairs, University of Minnesota.

____. 1994b. "The Effects of Public Sector Hiring and Compensation Policies on the

Egyptian Labor Market." *The World Bank Economic Review*. Forthcoming.

Bernard, Chantal. 1991. "Le Marche du Travail Urbain en Algerie." Discussion Paper DP/34/1991, Institut International D'etudes Sociales.

Currie, Janet, and Ann Harrison. 1994. "Trade Reform and Labor Market Adjustment in Morocco." Paper presented at Labor Markets Workshop at the World Bank, July 6-8. Washington, D.C.

Diwan, Ishac, and Lyn Squire. 1992. "Economic and Social Development in the Middle East and North Africa." World Bank Discussion Paper No. 3. Middle East and North Africa Region.

___. 1993. "Public Debts and Private Assets: External Finance in a Peaceful Middle East." *Middle East Journal*, Vol. 49, No.1: 69-88.

Diwan, Ishac, Chang-Po Yang and Zhi Wang. 1995. "The Arab Economies, the Uruguayan Round Predicament, and the European Union Wildcard." The World Bank. Mimeo

Feenstra, Robert C., and Gordon Hanson. 1994. "Foreign Investment, Outsourcing and Relative Wages." University of California, Davis. Mimeo. October.

Hanson, G.H. and A. Harrison. 1995. "Trade, Technology and Wage Inequality." Columbia Graduate School of Business Series Paper.

Handoussa, Heba. 1992. "The Burden of Public Sector Employment and Remuneration: The Case of Egypt." Paper presented at the American University, Cairo, Egypt.

International Labor Office. 1986. *Economically Active Population: 1995-2025*. Geneva: ILO.

International Monetary Fund. 1994a. *Algeria: Recent Economic Developments*. Washington D.C.: IMF.

___. 1994b. *Morocco: Review of Adjustment Experience*. Washington D.C.: IMF.

Issa, Najib. 1993. "Unemployment and Reconstruction in Lebanon." Paper presented at the Experts Meetings on Unemployment in the ESCWA Countries, Amman. (In Arabic.)

Karshenas, Massoud. 1994. "Structural Adjustment and Employment in the Middle East and North Africa." SOAS, University of London.

Krueger, A. O. 1983. *Trade and Employment in Developing Countries: 3 Synthesis and Conclusions*. Chicago: University of Chicago Press.

Lawrence, Robert, and Matthew Slaughter. 1993. "Trade and U.S. Wages: Great Sucking Sound or Small Hiccup?". Faculty Research Series (R93-16), Kennedy School of Government, Harvard University.

Louis, Michael. 1993. "Employment and Unemployment in Syria." Paper presented at the Experts Meetings on Unemployment in the ESCWA Countries, Amman. (In Arabic)

Moghadam, V.M. 1994. "Women in the Textiles and Garments Industry in the Middle East and North Africa." World Institute for Development Economics Research of the United Nations University.

Ozar, Semsa. 1994. "Patterns and Trends in the Female Labour Force Participation: Some Reflections on the Middle East." Bogazici University, Istanbul.

Pissarides, Christopher A. 1993. "Labor Markets in the Middle East and North Africa." World Bank Discussion Paper No. 5. Middle East and North Africa Region.

___. 1995. "Trade and the Return to Human Capital in Developing Countries." The *World Bank Economic Review*. Forthcoming.

Revenga, A. 1995. "Employment and Wage Effects of Trade Liberalization: The Case of Mexican Manufacturing." World Bank Working Papers on Education and Labor Markets.

Richards, Alan. 1995. "Is Unemployment a Bourgeois Luxury? The Case of the Arab

World." UCSC Department of Economics Working Paper No. 313. University of California, Santa Cruz, January.

Robbins, Donald. 1994. "Worsening Relative Wage Dispersion in Chile During Trade Liberalization and Its Causes: Is Supply at Fault?". Harvard Institute for International Development Series Paper.

___. 1995. "Trade, Trade Liberalization, and Inequality in Latin America and East Asia. Synthesis of Seven Country Studies." *The World Bank Economic Review*. Forthcoming.

Sachs, J., and H. Schatz. 1994. "Trade and Jobs in U.S. Manufacturing." Brookings Papers on Economic Activity, Spring

Said, Mona. 1994. "Public Sector Employment and Labor Markets in Arab Countries: Recent Developments and Policy Implications." International Monetary Fund.

Seif, Abdallah. 1993. "Returning Migration and Unemployment in Yemen." Paper Presented at the Experts Meetings on Unemployment in the ESCWA Countries, Amman. (In Arabic)

Shaban, Radwan A. 1993. "Palestinian Labor Mobility." *International Labor Review*. Vol. 134, No. 5-6.

Tan, Hong, and Geeta Batra. 1995. "Explaining Wage Differentials: The Role of Employer Investment in Technology." *The World Bank Economic Review*. Forthcoming.

Tansel, Aysit. 1992. "Wage Employment, Earnings and Returns to Schooling for Men and Women in Turkey." Yale University Economic Growth Center Discussion Paper No. 661.

van Eeghen, Wilhem. 1995. "Poverty in the Middle East and North Africa." The World Bank. Mimeo.

Wood, Adrian. 1994. *North-South Trade, Employment and Inequality: Changing Fortunes in a Skill-Driven World*. Oxford: Clarendon Press.

___. 1995. "Does Trade Reduce Wage Inequality In Developing Countries?". Institute of Development Studies, University of Sussex. *The World Bank Economic Review*. Forthcoming.

World Bank. 1993. *The East Asia Miracle: Economic Growth and Public Policy*. New York: Oxford University Press.

___. 1994a. "Hashemite Kingdom of Jordan: Poverty Assessment." World Bank Report No. 12675-JO, Vol. 2, Population and Human Resources Operations Division, Middle East and North Africa Region.

___. 1994b. "Kingdom of Morocco – Republic of Tunisia Export Growth: Determinants and Prospects." World Bank Report No. 12947-MN. Country Operations Division, Middle East and North Africa Region.

___. 1994c. "Kingdom of Morocco: Poverty, Adjustment, & Growth." World Bank Report No. 11918-MOR, Middle East and North Africa Region.

___. 1994d. "The Democratic and Popular Republic of Algeria Country Economic Memorandum: The Transition to a Market Economy." Country Operations Division, Middle East and North Africa Region.

___. 1995a. "Egypt: Structural Adjustment and Labor Market Reforms". Country Operations Division, Middle East and North Africa Region.

___. 1995b. "Jordan: Women and the Labor Force." Country Operations Division, Middle East and North Africa Region.

___. 1995c. "Kingdom of Morocco: Country Economic Memorandum Towards Higher Growth and Employment." Report No. 14155 MOR., Vol. 2,-Annexes Country Operation Division, Middle East and North Africa Region.

___. 1995d. "Republic of Tunisia: Growth, Policies and Poverty Alleviation." World

Bank Report No. 13993-TUN, Country Operations Division, Middle East and North Africa Region.

___. 1995e. "Workers in an Integrating World." *World Development Report 1995.*

___. 1995f. "Will Arab Workers Prosper or Be Left Out in the Twenty-First Century?". Supplement to the *World Development Report:1995*

___. 1995g. "Involving Workers in East Asian Growth." Supplement to the *World Development Report 1995.*

Young, Alwyn. 1993. "Lessons from the East Asian NICs: A Contrarian View."National Bureau of Economic Research Working Paper. Cambridge, MA: NBER.

Zaytoun, Mohaya A. 1991. "Earnings and the Cost of Living: An Analysis of Recent Developments in the Egyptian Economy" in Heba Handoussa and Gillian Potter (eds.), *Employment and Structural Adjustment: Egypt in the 1990s.* Cairo: American University in Cairo Press

Zouari-Bouattur, Salma. 1994. "Evolution du Marche du Travail Tunisien 1983-1993." Universite de Sfax, Tunisia.

Export Prospects of Middle Eastern Countries: A Post-Uruguay Round Analysis

Introduction: The Importance of the Uruguay Round

Major changes have recently occurred in external markets that can have important implications for the export prospects of the Middle-Eastern (ME) countries.[1] The North American Free Trade Agreement (NAFTA) liberalized barriers to the intra-trade of Canada, Mexico and the United States while further integration efforts continue in Europe. The Uruguay Round Agreements will also have a major impact on international trading conditions. Among the Round's achievements are an average 40 percent reduction in industrial countries' most-favored-nation (MFN) tariffs, agreement on a phase-out of the Multifiber Arrangements restrictions, nontariff barriers (NTBs) on agricultural products were converted to tariffs and then lowered, "voluntary" export restraints (VERs) were abolished, and progress was made toward the liberalization of barriers to trade in services.

While many of these developments have positive implications for ME countries, there could be some negative aspects. Regional integration initiatives like NAFTA or the European Union (EU) provide member countries preferential access to each others markets which may allow them to displace non-members' exports. This raises the question of whether a significant amount of ME exports may be diverted and in which product sectors could this occur? Similarly, the Uruguay Round's reduction of MFN tariffs may have negative implications since these cuts will lower (or eliminate) the preference margins some ME countries receive under the Generalized System of Preferences (GSP) programs or EU regional schemes.[2] The phase-out of the Multifiber Arrangement, tariffication of agricultural NTBs, and the liberalization of services trade seemingly have positive implications for the Middle-East if these countries can compete with producers in other regions. To help illustrate the implications of such developments, this chapter provides a series of Appendix "boxes" which discuss the potential effects on a specific Middle-East country – Egypt).

Recognizing that improved export opportunities can make a positive contribution to economic growth in the region, and also help reinforce the peace process, this chapter attempts to quantify the effects of the Uruguay Round on ME countries' exports, and also to determine how their trade might be affected by regional arrangements in Europe and North America. The magnitude and composition of intra-trade within the Middle East region is analyzed, and an attempt is made to generate information relating to future prospects. To provide an introduction, trends in the level, composition and direction of ME exports are analyzed. Measures such as the "revealed" comparative advantage, trade intensity, and export similarity indices are employed to help assess ME export opportunities (and constraints) both within and outside the region.

Trends in the Level and Composition of Regional Exports

Any assessment of the importance of external developments would be facilitated by identifying the current major markets for Middle East exports. Table 1 provides relevant information by showing the direction (value) and share of ME exports to different destinations, that is, all Organization for Economic Cooperation and Development (OECD) countries, OECD countries in Europe, North America and several other regional country groups (Box 1 provides more detailed information on the direction of Egypt's exports). These figures clearly show the current importance of OECD markets for all ME exports; yet, three different trade patterns exist. First, countries like Cyprus, Iran, Libya, Syria and Turkey are primarily dependent on OECD European markets and they may be negatively affected by integration efforts like the extension of the EU. On the other hand, Oman, Qatar, Saudi Arabia and the United Arab Emirates (UAE) have a larger share of exports destined for North America and Japan so these countries seemingly would be more concerned with the effects of NAFTA on their trade. Third, several ME countries rely on non-OECD markets. Over 60 percent of Bahrain, Jordan, Lebanon, and Oman's exports go to developing countries, most of which are in the region or in Asia.[3]

Table 1 compares the direction of ME countries' exports with that for all developing countries combined (see the memo item). Overall, little difference is observed between the two groups' trade shares (64 percent of ME exports are destined to OECD markets as opposed to 63 percent for all developing countries combined). However, the Middle East does have a greater dependence on OECD Europe and Japan (49.7 versus 31.5 percent) while the share of exports going to OECD North America is 16 points below average. For the region as a whole, these data accent the potential importance of changes in European market access conditions.

Table 1: The Geographic Destination of Middle East Countries' Exports

Exporting Country (Year)	World ($million)	OECD Markets (Percent of total Exports)	of which: Europe	North America	Japan	Others	Other Countries	of which: Europe	Asia	Americas
Bahrain (91)	3,578.0	16.4	2.4	2.5	11.2	0.3	83.6	3.2	81.0	1.9
Cyprus (91)	975.2	67.1	63.3	1.6	0.4	1.8	32.9	--	18.3	2.8
Egypt (90)	2,582.0	58.1	41.2	8.1	3.1	5.7	41.9	14.7	17.8	0.3
Iran, Islamic Rep. of(91)	15,762.3	68.1	50.0	1.9	16.1	0.1	31.9	3.4	16.9	6.5
Israel(91)	11,890.8	78.7	39.8	31.0	6.1	1.8	21.3	0.9	9.8	2.4
Jordan(91)	878.9	5.5	3.1	0.4	1.8	0.2	94.5	3.8	67.8	0.4
Kuwait (90)	8,148.6	51.1	24.0	7.0	19.1	1.0	42.9	0.5	33.3	2.0
Lebanon (86)	517.0	31.6	22.9	8.3	0.2	0.2	68.4	4.6	60.3	1.0
Libyan Arab Jamahiriya (87)	8,502.7	84.5	84.5	--	--	--	16.3	4.5	10.1	2.2
Oman (89)	3,932.9	39.8	2.0	2.8	34.6	0.4	60.2	--	52.9	3.8
Qatar (91)	3,176.7	73.7	18.0	5.9	49.7	0.1	26.3	--	22.8	2.2
Saudi Arabia (91)	44,062.0	62.0	21.1	24.2	15.8	0.9	38.0	0.7	27.9	2.7
Syria (91)	3,295.0	61.4	60.0	1.4	--	--	38.6	13.5	19.8	--
Turkey (91)	13,603.0	65.9	57.9	6.1	1.9	--	34.1	6.6	12.2	--
United Arab Emirates (88)	11,873.0	64.2	10.9	6.0	46.4	0.9	35.8	1.0	24.5	5.8
All MIDDLE EAST COUNTRIES	132,777.6	63.2	33.6	13.2	15.7	0.7	36.4	2.6	24.2	2.9
MEMO ITEM:										
ALL DEVELOPING COUNTRIES	708,949.0	63.1	23.7	29.5	7.8	2.1	36.9	3.1	24.1	3.9

Source: Statistics compiled from UN Conference on Trade and Development(UNCTAD), Handbook of International Trade and Development Statistics, 1993 or directly from the United Nations Statistical Office Series D Trade Tapes.

Alexander Yeats

Table 2: The Product Composition of Middle East Countries' Global Exports

Exporting Country (Year)	Total Exports ($ million)	All Foods	Agricultural Materials	Fuels	Ores and Metals	All Manufactures	Select Commodity Groups Textiles and Clothing	Chemicals	Transport and Machinery
Bahrain (90)	3,415.2	0.6	--	76.9	11.0	11.4	--	0.5	2.0
Cyprus (89)	793.0	37.7	0.9	1.8	0.7	59.0	29.5	7.6	4.7
Egypt (90)	2,582.0	9.3	6.2	46.9	4.0	32.4	35.4	3.3	3.3
Iran, Islamic Rep. (90)	14,409.4	2.5	0.9	92.5	0.3	3.7	--	--	0.1
Israel (91)	11,890.8	7.6	2.6	0.6	1.6	87.5	7.6	14.0	27.3
Jordan (91)	878.9	16.0	0.5	--	37.9	45.7	3.7	29.6	1.3
Kuwait (89)	11,476.5	1.1	0.4	84.1	0.5	13.7	0.7	1.0	2.4
Lebanon (89)	410.0	3.0	27.5	0.2	55.8	13.0	--	0.5	0.4
Libyan Arab Jamahiriya (87)	8,502.7	--	--	97.8	--	2.1	--	1.9	--
Oman (89)	3,932.9	2.2	--	88.9	1.4	5.7	0.3	0.2	5.4
Qatar (89)	2,609.7	--	--	70.0	--	17.4	--	13.0	0.4
Saudi Arabia (90)	44,062.0	0.5	0.3	89.7	0.6	8.1	--	4.4	1.7
Syria (90)	4,061.6	11.6	3.8	40.5	1.4	42.6	--	10.8	0.2
Turkey (90)	12,959.3	22.4	3.0	2.3	4.3	67.9	39.0	5.9	8.2
United Arab Emirates (88)	11,873.0	1.9	0.1	84.5	1.4	11.5	--	0.7	4.3
ALL MIDDLE EAST	133,857.0	4.5	1.1	68.7	1.8	23.1	5.4	4.5	4.7
MEMO ITEM:									
ALL DEVELOPING COUNTRIES	708,947.0	11.6	3.1	26.1	4.2	54.0	13.1	4.2	19.8

Source: United Nations Series D Trade Tapes. Import statistics as reported (c.i.f.) by the OECD countries. Product groups are defined as follows: All foods and feeds (SITC 0+1+22+4); Agricultural materials (2-22-27-28); mineral fuels (3); ores minerals and nonferrous metals (27+28+68); all manufactures (5 to 8 less 68); yarns, textiles and clothing (26+65+84); chemicals (5); transport and machinery (7).

Table 2 provides information on the product composition of each Middle East country's exports as well as that for the region as a whole. Mineral fuels are by far the largest product group accounting for approximately 68 percent of all regional exports. This is more than two and one half times higher than energy products' share in the exports of all developing countries combined (see the memo item). The value of fuel exports ($82.3 billion) is about $53 billion higher than the second largest product group (manufactures – which accounts for 24 percent of regional exports). Several countries, including Iran, Libya, Oman, Saudi Arabia and the UAE have developed only a limited capacity for exports of manufactures and are almost totally dependent on mineral fuels which account for at least 80 percent of their exports. This export concentration of some ME countries in fuels is an obvious factor limiting the opportunities fro developing mutually beneficial intra-regional trade.

Table 2 shows that the exports of Turkey, Israel and Cyprus, and to a lesser extent those of Jordan and Syria are more heavily concentrated in manufactures than other middle-Eastern countries (68 percent of Turkey's exports are manufactured goods and the share of these goods in Israel's exports is 88 percent). Countries not specializing in energy products probably hold the key to increased regional trade opportunities since they can accommodate oil exports from other ME countries.[4] Increased opportunities for intra-regional trade may also occur in foodstuffs, the third largest ME export group (12 percent of total exports), with Cyprus, Jordan, Syria and Turkey being important net food importers.

The data in Table 2 provide preliminary evidence that some ME countries may not be strongly affected by changes in foreign trade barriers (particularly those in the OECD). Agricultural raw materials, fuels, ores and nonferrous metals generally are imported duty free, or face relatively low OECD tariffs and nontariff barriers. These items account for about 70 percent of all regional exports and over 90 percent of the exports of Iran, Libya, Oman and Saudi Arabia. The exporters of manufactured and food products (Cyprus, Israel, Jordan, Syria and Turkey) have the potential to be more affected by developments relating to the Uruguay Round, European integration or NAFTA.

The fact that OECD markets constitute the most important outlets for ME exports (see Table 1) raises the question of how the relative importance of individual countries differs in this exchange. The top half of Table 3 shows the value, share, and growth rates for individual regional country's total exports to the OECD markets for selected years from 1970 to 1992, while the lower half excludes fuels. The relative importance of ME countries changes markedly depending on whether petroleum is included or not. Israel and Turkey are by far the largest regional non-oil exporters, accounting for over $20 billion, or

Table 3: The Share of Individual Countries in Total and Non-Oil Exports to the OECD, Selected Years from 1970 to 1992

Product Group/Exporter	Value of Regional Exports to the OECD (US$million)				Share of Regional Exports to the OECD(%)				Growth Rate	
	1970	1980	1986	1992	1970	1980	1986	1992	1970-92	1980-92
ALL GOODS	11,207.5	157,363.6	60,229.0	107,192.7	100.0	100.0	100.0	100.0	11	-3
Bahrain	153.9	799.3	558.1	651.7	1.4	0.5	0.9	0.6	7	-2
Cyprus	98.3	451.4	344.6	583.8	0.9	0.3	0.6	0.5	8	2
Egypt	333.0	4,470.9	2,237.3	3,898.3	3.0	2.8	3.7	3.6	12	-1
Iran, Islamic Rep.of	2,131.3	10,781.0	5,637.0	10,925.9	19.0	6.9	9.4	10.2	8	--
Israel	579.0	4,049.4	5,937.2	10,022.6	5.2	2.6	9.9	9.4	14	8
Jordan	2.0	90.0	214.8	172.3	--	0.1	0.4	0.2	22	6
Kuwait	1,750.7	9,899.0	4,067.6	2,510.4	15.6	6.3	6.8	2.3	2	-11
Lebanon	100.1	164.3	158.2	205.5	0.9	0.1	0.3	0.2	3	2
Libyan Arab Jamahiriya	2,469.1	19,795.3	6,070.6	9,801.7	22.0	12.6	10.1	9.1	6	-6
Oman	457.7	2,810.6	1,828.0	2,359.4	4.1	1.8	3.0	2.2	8	-1
Qatar	393.8	4,546.0	1,645.9	2,329.8	3.5	2.9	2.7	2.2	8	-5
Saudi Arabia	2,005.9	77,827.4	19,171.7	37,520.2	17.9	49.5	31.8	35.0	14	-6
Syria	133.5	1,439.6	523.7	2,103.8	1.2	0.9	0.9	2.0	13	3
Turkey	493.4	1,903.9	4,586.6	10,673.6	4.4	1.2	7.6	10.0	15	15
United Arab Emirates	105.8	18,335.4	7,247.5	13,433.7	0.9	11.7	12.0	12.5	25	-2
NON-ENERGY GOODS	1,804.1	9,927.2	14,577.9	28,763.7	100.0	100.0	100.0	100.0	13	9
Bahrain	10.1	111.9	267.8	383.8	0.6	1.1	1.8	1.3	18	11
Cyprus	98.3	439.0	344.6	582.1	5.4	4.4	2.4	2.0	8	2
Egypt	187.4	747.3	759.3	1,469.2	10.4	7.5	5.2	5.1	10	6
Iran,Islamic Rep.of	248.9	878.9	760.4	1,406.0	13.8	8.9	5.2	4.9	8	4
Israel	553.6	3,916.7	5,856.1	9,917.4	30.7	39.5	40.2	34.5	14	8
Jordan	2.0	90.0	188.7	172.3	0.7	1.1	0.9	0.4	22	6
Kuwait	12.8	110.8	125.2	115.6	0.1	0.9	1.3	0.6	11	2
Lebanon	60.6	164.3	158.2	205.2	3.4	1.7	1.1	0.7	6	2
Libyan Arab Jamahiriya	8.5	138.0	129.4	186.0	0.5	1.4	0.9	0.6	15	3
Oman	30.3	73.3	151.7	283.0	1.7	0.7	1.0	1.0	11	12
Qatar	2.4	21.5	51.1	118.9	0.1	0.2	0.4	0.4	19	15
Saudi Arabia	19.3	695.5	1,293.7	1,998.3	1.1	7.0	8.9	6.9	23	9
Syria	61.5	110.7	113.9	263.7	3.4	1.1	0.8	0.9	7	7
Turkey	487.1	1,886.9	4,035.6	10,454.8	27.0	19.0	27.7	36.3	15	15
United Arab Emirates	21.4	542.3	342.4	1,2074	1.2	5.5	2.3	4.2	20	7

Source: OECD countries import statistics as reported in the UN COMTRADE: Data Base

70 percent of ME shipments to the OECD. These countries' free trade area (FTA) agreements with the EU are certainly a factor accounting for their performance – Israel also has FTA agreements with the European free trade areas (EFTAs) and the United States. However, once petroleum products are excluded the relative importance of individual countries changes dramatically – Saudi Arabia alone accounts for 36 percent of all regional exports to the OECD markets, while Iran and the UAE add a further 23 percent. Table 3 also shows that the shares of some energy exporting countries have experienced sizable changes since the early 1970s. Saudi Arabia's share increased by about 15 percentage points (to over one-third of the region's total exports) while Iran and Libya's shares fell by 13 and 15 points, respectively.

What non-energy products are regional countries exporting to the OECD markets, and how has the composition of these exports changed? Table 4 lists the 30 largest non-oil products ME countries currently export. The table also shows the shares of these goods for selected years back to 1970. One three-digit SITC item (nonfur clothing) now accounts for over one-fifth of all 1992 exports. This product has also had one of the highest growth rates over the last decade. The Uruguay Round achieved major liberalization in the trade of textiles and clothing products (see further below) which could further increase ME export opportunities provided that these products are cost competitive. Other products in Table 4 that previously faced relatively high European and North American trade barriers which were lowered in the Round include: fresh and preserved fruit and vegetables, and textile fabrics.

An interesting point relating to Table 4 is that one-third of the products listed actually experienced declining market shares over the full 1970-1992 period – a development which is, in part, associated with the major expansion of clothing exports. Cotton experienced the largest overall reduction (a fall of about 16 percentage points), but the shares of other agricultural products like fresh fruit and nuts, fresh vegetables, tobacco, and dried fruit also experienced important reductions. There is evidence (Laird and Yeats, 1990) that rising protection in European markets (and subsidized OECD agricultural exports) was an important constraint to the growth of agricultural exports.

There are at least three reasons why one should attempt to identify "dynamic" (fastest growing) exports from amongst those that presently may not constitute a large share of ME exports. First, if current above average growth rates continue for an extended period, the affected items may become an important part of a country's export earnings. Second, it could be important to determine if the dynamic products have different production characteristics than traditional exports. If they are (say) significantly more capital intensive, one would want to determine the reason and whether export

Table 4: Middle Eastern Countries' Thirty Largest Three-Digit Non-Energy Product Exports to OECD Countries, 1992

Description (SITC)	Value of Exports ($ million)				Percent of Total Exports (%)			
	1970	1980	1986	1992	1970	1980	1986	1942
Clothing not of Fur (841)	43.5	413.4	1,620.9	6,064.9	4.2	2.4	11.1	12.1
Pearls and Precious Stones (667)	139.2	1,174.0	1,771.6	2,817.7	7.7	11.8	12.2	9.8
Fresh Fruit and Nuts (051)	258.8	904.9	919.2	1,231.3	14.3	9.1	6.3	4.3
Organic Chemicals (512)	6.3	205.6	736.1	1,103.3	0.3	2.1	5.0	3.8
Floor Coverings (657)	125.5	676.5	474.3	856.4	7.0	6.8	3.3	3.0
Telecommunications Equipment (724)	5.7	58.3	136.4	839.3	0.3	0.6	0.9	2.9
Gold and Silver Jewelry (897)	1.4	123.7	278.9	582.1	0.1	1.2	1.9	2.0
Aluminum (684)	0.4	148.6	442.5	568.1	--	1.5	3.0	2.0
Fruit Preserved (053)	38.2	178.4	259.6	554.2	2.1	1.8	1.8	1.9
Textile Yarn and Thread (651)	44.5	344.9	499.4	552.4	2.5	3.5	3.4	1.9
Scientific Instruments (861)	3.4	57.6	141.1	531.3	0.2	0.6	1.0	1.8
Plastic Materials (581)	3.3	48.1	357.7	526.3	0.2	0.5	2.5	1.8
Non-Electric Machinery (719)	6.5	89.0	161.8	499.6	0.4	0.9	1.1	1.7
Non-Electric Power Machinery (711)	13.1	276.7	324.0	498.4	0.7	2.8	2.2	1.7
Fresh Vegetables (054)	63.5	232.8	220.1	467.6	3.5	2.3	1.5	1.6
Office Machinery (714)	2.4	33.2	143.7	439.4	0.1	0.3	1.0	1.5
Tobacco Unmanufactured (121)	74.6	204.8	314.1	431.7	4.1	2.1	2.2	1.5
Electrical Machines (729)	4.7	98.5	272.9	358.5	0.3	1.0	1.9	1.2
Dried Fruit (052)	35.1	195.2	183.6	345.7	1.9	2.0	1.3	1.2
Textile Products, nes (656)	0.7	59.2	113.0	333.0	--	0.6	0.8	1.2
Manufactured Fertilizers (561)	16.6	122.2	283.2	315.6	0.9	1.2	1.9	1.1
Woven Textiles Non -Cotton (653)	7.4	21.4	41.4	302.7	0.4	0.2	0.3	1.1
Crude Vegetable Materials (292)	30.7	209.5	218.4	301.9	1.7	2.1	1.5	1.0
Cotton Fabrics Woven (652)	13.2	54.7	126.8	267.2	0.7	0.6	0.9	0.9
Other Crude Minerals (276)	21.5	166.6	202.8	246.3	1.2	1.7	1.4	0.9
Cotton (263)	292.3	565.6	461.8	241.3	16.2	5.7	3.2	0.8
Electric Power Machinery (722)	2.1	39.5	77.0	239.4	0.1	0.4	0.5	0.8
Electrical Distributing Machinery (723)	0.1	5.9	32.6	236.9	--	0.1	0.2	0.8
Rubber Articles, nes (629)	10.1	52.5	76.4	215.0	0.6	0.5	0.5	0.7
Road Motor Vehicles and Parts (732)	1.5	22.2	46.3	204.6	0.1	0.2	0.3	0.7
TOTAL OF ABOVE PRODUCTS	1,266.4	6,783.4	10,937.6	22,172.0	70.2	68.3	75.0	77.1

Source: United Nations Series D.Trade Tapes. The above statistics exclude aircraft and special transactions recorded in SITC 931.

opportunities exist in other related goods. Third, there is an obvious interest in ensuring that foreign trade barriers are not imposed on these items, or that existing restrictions are removed. Table 5 lists the 30 fastest growing three-digit exports from the region over the period 1986-92 (1988-92 growth rates are also shown) and identifies the major ME supplier along with its regional trade share. Table 6 provides similar information for Egypt's dynamic and declining products.

Two-thirds of the ME dynamic products listed in Table 5 are manufactured goods. Several of these items require locally available natural resource-based production inputs (that is, manufactures such as cement and products; clay and refractory materials), and many of these items are above average in labor intensity in comparison to all manufactured goods. This raises the question of whether other similar types of exports could be developed on the basis of further processing of domestically-available natural resources? Petroleum-based chemical and plastic industries may be one such suitable sector for further export development given the availability of crude petroleum in many ME countries.[5] The fact that these plants require sizable capital investments could make multi-country regional investment in jointly owned plants to process and refine petroleum an attractive option.

It is somewhat surprising that two of the fastest growing products over 1986-1992 (barley and rice) are foodstuffs – although barley exports fell sharply from 1988 levels. Wheat meal, unmilled wheat, and milk and cream also recorded growth rates that are well above average.[6] The fact that one-sixth of the dynamic products are foodstuffs, coupled with the Uruguay Round's tariffication and reduction of nontariff barriers on agricultural trade, provide solid grounds to focus attention on the possibility to further develop agricultural export opportunities. Increased agricultural exports should assume special importance for Egypt, and several other ME countries, since, inter alia, this could alleviate the situation of the rural poor.[7] Specifically, studies by the International Labor Office (ILO) show that developing countries may use (on average) up to 30 times as much labor per unit of agricultural output as some developed countries. The ILO studies also conclude that the linkage and multiplier employment creation effects in the agricultural sector of developing countries are among the largest (with textiles) of all industry groups. These findings imply that an expansion of agricultural exports could make a significant contribution to alleviating the basic social and employment situation in developing countries (Lydall, 1985).

One troubling aspect associated with Table 5 is that two countries (Turkey and Israel) are the major suppliers for most of the ME dynamic products. In only 9 of the 30 products do other countries register a presence – often with

Table 5: Dynamic Products in Middle East Countries' Exports to OECD Markets

Product(STTC)	Major 1992 Supplies (share)	OECD Imports ($000)			Growth Rate	
		1986	1988	1992	1988-92	1986-92
Barley Unmilled(043)	Cyprus(100)	18.6	5,633.7	1,534.9	-28	109
Rice(042)	Egypt(88)	115.1	3,235.8	6,062.3	17	94
Cement and Bulding Products(661)	Turkey(89)	7,708.2	42,472.8	150,721.8	37	64
Lead(685)	Lebanon(48), Israel(27)	90.8	1,678.2	1,397.2	-4	58
Clay and Refractory Products(662)	Turkey(88)	4,740.4	13,263.9	62,029.4	47	54
Domestic Electrical Equipment(725)	Turkey(83)	5,905.6	82,513.6	73,264.5	-3	52
Leather(611)	Saudi Arabia(66)	2,734.8	11,502.2	30,354.7	26	49
Plumbing and Heating Equipment(812)	Turkey(85)	8,451.1	21,736.1	73,978.8	36	44
Wire Products(693)	Turkey(86)	4,320.8	8,359.0	34,496.7	43	41
Woven Textiles Non-Cotton(653)	Turkey(74), Israel(21)	41,421.2	162,818.0	302,697.6	17	39
Electrical Distributing Machines(723)	Turkey(86)	32,646.4	20,717.2	236,913.0	84	39
Natural Abrasives(275)	Israel(60), Turkey(39)	4,920.7	26,550.6	34,625.0	7	38
Silk(261)	Turkey(100)	105.0	1,464.3	718.5	-16	38
Special Textile Products(655)	Israel(61), Turkey(36)	11,315.8	29,013.7	75,066.7	27	37
Leather Manufactures(612)	Turkey(75)	982.8	3,495.4	6,571.2	18	37
Wood in the Rough(242)	Turkey(94)	1,057.0	580.5	6,721.1	84	36
Telecommunications Equipment(724)	Israel(54), Turkey(26)	136,379.9	353,722.6	839,290.7	24	35
Iron and Steel Castings(679)	Turkey(84)	1,211.2	3,203.1	7,469.3	24	35
Zoo Animals and Pets(941)	Turkey(48), Egypt(33)	766.5	2,421.2	4,726.3	18	35
Radioactive Materials(515)	Israel(92)	237.5	570.5	1,393.8	25	34
Wood Shaped(243)	Turkey(93)	1,687.5	1,729.2	9,767.5	54	34
Iron and Steel Wire(677)	Turkey(87)	327.7	5,418.0	1,882.4	-23	34
Non-Alcoholic Beverages(111)	Cyprus(35), Turkey(32)	1,189.8	3,770.1	6,283.1	14	32
Wheat Meal or Flour(046)	Turkey(38), Lebanon(34)	143.3	498.9	677.9	8	30
Road Motor Vehicles and Parts(732)	Turkey(70), Israel(13)	46,253.0	91,420.1	204,645.4	22	29
Base Metal Household Equipment(697)	Turkey(83)	11,753.0	20,578.0	50,718.4	25	28
Wheat Unmilled(041)	Saudi Arabia(96)	3,652.2	61,955.2	15,850.5	-29	28
Soaps and Cleansing Preparations(554)	Israel(58), Turkey(32)	2,789.4	2,907.1	12,012.1	43	28
Milk and Cream(022)	Israel(50), Saudi Arabia(13)	416.5	400.1	1,454.3	38	27
Iron and Steel Forms(672)	Turkey(80), Egypt(9)	17,784.6	149,733.8	73,519.7	-16	27

Source: United Nations Series D Trade Tapes. To be included in the above tabulations OECD imports of the product had to total at least $500,000 in 1992.

either Turkey or Israel. This suggests that the recent rapid growth of exports from the region has been highly concentrated, and that most countries are not participating in the associated benefits. Egypt appears as a primary supplier for only three dynamic products (rice, zoo animals and pets, and iron and steel forms) while Iran, Syria and the smaller regional countries fail to appear on the list for any product.

Table 6 shows the dynamic products in Egypt's exports over 1980-82 to 1990-92 along with those products where exports declined. (Box 3 provides information on Egypt's largest export products for comparison). For the most part, Egypt's dynamic products differ from those of the region as only cement, leather manufactures, and plumbing equipment also appear on the list of ME fast growing exports. However, a common point is that manufactured goods also are predominant in Egypt's fastest growing exports (15 out of 21 dynamic products are manufactures). Four of Egypt's manufactures exports: iron and steel shapes; glassware; miscellaneous chemicals; and plastic articles maintained a 50 percent compound annual growth rate over the decade.

Five food products (fresh meat and fish, cereal preparations, cheese and miscellaneous food are among Egypt's fastest growing exports and the total trade in these items surpassed $42 million annually in 1990-92. Given the major trade barriers these products face in OECD markets Egypt's exports were directed almost exclusively to other developing countries. For example, over 94 percent of Egypt's 1992 exports of fresh meat (SITC 011) went to Kuwait, Saudi Arabia and Qatar while over 50 percent of the exports of cereal preparations went to Russia and Saudi Arabia. Russia received about one-third of Egypt's exports of miscellaneous food preparation (SITC 099) while about 28 percent of these shipments went to Jordan, Kuwait and Saudi Arabia. Italy was the major destination for Egypt's fresh fish exports (SITC 031) absorbing 65 percent of total shipments.

Eleven of Egypt's "declining" products recorded negative growth rates with crude and refined petroleum accounting for almost half of this groups' total exports. The decline is largely the result of weakness in crude petroleum prices which fell by about 50 percent on average over the 1980-82 to 1990-92 period. The fall in cotton exports, which accounted for 6 percent of the declining products' exports, can be attributed to the increased utilization of cotton by the local textile and garment industry and the fact that Egyptian cotton became less competitively priced over the period.

Trends in Intra-Regional Trade

A major problem one faces in trying to analyze trends in intra-regional trade is that some countries have gaps in their import and export statistics reported to the United Nations. Egypt, Turkey, Israel and several other countries are exceptions since they provided the UN with complete trade data from the early 1960s to 1992. Conversely, Lebanon and Iran have not reported trade data to the United Nations since 1977 and 1988 is the most recent year for which Bahrain's data are available. Major gaps in data (missing years) exist in Oman, Qatar, Saudi Arabia and the UAE's trade statistics. As such, partner country statistics must be used to derive estimates of intra-regional trade trends.[8] This procedure is employed in the preparation of Table 7 which shows the value and share of each country's 1970, 1980 and 1990 intra-regional trade along with compound annual growth rates. The notes to Table 7 provide information on how these data were derived.

Intra-regional exports are estimated to have been $8.3 billion in 1990 – down by approximately 45 percent from their value of a decade earlier. The overall decline is largely due to a sharp decline in intra-regional shipments of crude oil for refining, lower petroleum prices and the importance of energy products in regional intra-trade (see Table 8). Five countries, namely, Jordan, Saudi Arabia, Syria, Turkey and the UAE account for the bulk of this exchange, that is, over 60 percent of intra-trade. In contrast, Bahrain, Israel, Lebanon and Qatar have a combined share of about 8 percent. Egypt's share of intra-regional exports is under 5 percent, with petroleum exports to Israel accounting for a large portion of this exchange. Box 4 provides details on Egypt's largest three-digit SITC regional exports.

How important is intra-regional trade in the total exports of these ME countries? Taking the statistics in Table 7 as a share of the total export values for ME countries given in Table 1 shows intra-trade accounts for only about 7 to 8 percent of all exports. These figures may appear low at first, but a key point is that ME countries as a group only absorb about 3 to 4 percent of global exports. As such, ME countries have a higher than average propensity to trade with each other. For several countries, the intra-regional trade shares are considerably higher than the group's average. Between 13 to 16 percent of all Egypt and Turkey's exports are destined to the region as do over 50 percent of all Cyprus' exports (mainly to Turkey).

What products are of primary importance in intra-regional trade? Table 8 shows the 20 largest three-digit SITC products traded along with the estimated value and share of this exchange. Although their shares have been very volatile – due mainly to price changes – crude and refined petroleum products accounted for approximately one-third of intra-regional trade in 1990 – down from their 80 percent share in 1980. The petroleum price changes and their impact on product shares conceal to some extent the impressive growth that has occurred in the intra- regional exports of fruit, vegetables and live animals (that is, items which are now three of the five largest export products).

Table 6: Dynamic and Declining Products in Egypt's Exports: 1980-82 to 1990-92

Description(STTC)	1980-82 Average Exports		1990-92 Average Exports		Compound Growth Rate
	Value ($000)	Share of Total	Value ($000)	Share of Total	
DYNAMIC PRODUCTS					
Iron and Steel Shapes (673)	181	--	32,573	1.2	68.1
Glassware (665)	52	--	6,768	0.2	62.7
Chemicals, nes (599)	203	--	21,185	0.8	59.2
Articles of Plastic (893)	125	--	7,860	0.3	51.4
Plumbing and Lighting Equipment (812)	167	--	9,453	0.3	49.7
Meat Fresh and Frozen (011)	226	--	12,504	0.4	49.4
Cereal Preparations (048)	100	--	4,220	0.1	45.5
Rubber Articles (629)	59	--	2,491	0.1	45.3
Iron and Steel Tubes (678)	286	--	10,546	0.4	43.4
Stone, Sand and Gravel (273)	130	--	3,857	0.1	40.3
Leather Manufactures (612)	206	--	5,892	0.2	39.9
Cheese and Curd (024)	150	--	3,863	0.1	38.4
Food Preparations, nes (099)	484	--	10,897	0.4	36.5
Manufactured Fertilizers (561)	1,165	--	25,544	0.9	36.2
Structures and Parts (691)	252	--	4,973	0.2	34.7
Inorganic Chemicals (514)	58	--	989	0.0	32.7
Furniture (821)	2,702	0.1	40,974	1.5	31.2
Metal Manufactures, nes (698)	581	--	8,600	0.3	30.9
Wood Manufactures, nes (632)	268	--	3,686	0.1	30.0
Fresh Fish (031)	870	--	11,478	0.4	29.4
Cement/BuildingProds. (661)	310	--	3,534	0.1	27.6
DECLINING PRODUCTS					
Live Animals (011)	21,347	0.7	17,256	0.6	-2.1
Petroleum Products (332)	264,736	8.6	212,159	7.5	-2.2
Oil Seeds and Nuts (221)	7,787	0.3	5,832	0.2	-2.8
Essential Oils (551)	10,982	0.4	7,928	0.3	-3.2
Preserved Fruit (053)	6,795	0.2	3,720	0.1	-5.8
Sugar and Honey (061)	18,370	0.6	9,751	0.3	-6.1
Crude Petroleum (331)	1,746,086	56.7	818,362	29.1	-7.3
Tobacco Manufactures (122)	2,498	0.1	923	--	-9.5
Cotton (263)	431,453	14.0	130,811	4.6	-11.2
Crude Fertilizers (271)	2,349	0.1	513	--	-14.1
Non-Ferrous Metal Scrap (284)	25,368	0.8	586	--	-31.4

Source: Author's calculations from United Nations Series D COMTRADE Statistics.

Table 7: The Share of Individual Countries in Total Intra-Regional Exports, Selected Years from 1970 to 1992

Product Group/Exporter	Value of Intra-Regional Exports (US$ million)			Share of All Intra-Regional Exports (%)			Growth Rate	
	1970	1980	1990	1970	1980	1990	1970-90	1980-90
ALL GOODS	3,399.9	16,708.7	8,879.1	100.0	100.0	100.0	4.9	-6.1
Bahrain	242.2	3,808.5	231.7	7.1	22.8	2.6	-0.2	-24.4
Cyprus	109.1	551.7	94.4	3.2	3.3	1.1	-0.7	-16.1
Egypt	34.0	269.0	387.4	1.0	1.6	4.4	12.9	3.7
Iran, Islamic Rep. of	2,454.8	851.3	734.6	72.2	5.1	8.3	-5.8	-1.4
Israel	30.3	69.1	128.1	0.9	0.4	1.4	7.5	6.4
Jordan	29.8	419.4	208.6	0.0	2.5	2.3	10.2	-6.7
Kuwait	49.1	1,402.1	139.8	1.4	8.4	1.6	5.4	-20.5
Lebanon	222.0	742.2	263.1	6.5	4.4	3.0	0.8	-9.9
Libyan Arab Jamahiriya	7.3	783.1	636.1	0.2	4.7	7.2	25.0	-2.2
Oman	0.1	3,748.3	279.3	--	22.4	3.1	48.7	-22.9
Qatar	18.5	116.7	260.3	0.5	0.7	2.9	14.1	8.4
Saudi Arabia	143.9	3,264.3	1,609.2	4.2	19.5	18.1	12.8	-6.8
Syria	2.4	103.2	866.4	0.1	0.6	9.8	34.2	23.7
Turkey	47.8	493.3	1,923.8	1.4	3.0	21.7	20.3	14.6
United Arab Emirates	8.6	75.5	116.3	0.3	0.5	12.6	27.5	30.9

Source: United Nations COMTRADE records.

Methodological Notes

1990 – Countries failing to report trade statistics for 1990 include: Bahrain; Iran; Lebanon; Qatar and the UAE. Regional partner country statistics for Iran, Lebanon and the UAE were employed to estimate these countries exports. The above tabulations will, therefore, not include these nations' intra-trade. Also, 1988 trade statistics were used in the above for Bahrain and 1991 data for Qatar. Partner country statistics were used to estimate Saudi Arabia's exports to the region. In 1990 Cyprus did not report exports to Turkey.

1980 – Countries failing to report trade data for 1980 include: Iran, Lebanon, Qatar and the UAE. Partner country data were used to estimate Iran and Lebanon's exports. The above tabulations employ 1979 trade statistics for Qatar and the UAE.

1970 – Partner country data were used to estimate UAE exports. The above tabulations are based on 1974 trade data for Saudi Arabia and Syria, 1972 data for Qatar, and 1975 data for Oman.

Characteristics of Regional Trade

Several statistical indices can provide useful insights concerning internation-al trade trends. One such measure – the "trade intensity" index has been used to determine whether the value of trade between two countries is greater or smaller than what would be expected on the basis of their importance in world trade. For example, Table 1 showed that approximately 40 percent of Egypt's exports go to the European Union. Is this above or below what would be pro-jected on the basis of the two partner's relative size in global trade? Is Egypt's trade with other regional countries, about 14 percent of total exports, higher or lower than might be expected? Identification of bilateral combinations where trade is well below expected levels may often help focus attempts to identify and remove important trade barriers.

Table 9 shows 1992 "trade intensity" indices between selected individual ME countries (for which UN data were available) and various trading part-ners. The index may range between zero and infinity and has a relatively sim-ple interpretation.[9] Values below unity indicate that the trade between two countries is lower than expected, while values above unity indicate it is rela-tively larger. A point to note is that, on average, ME countries absorb about 3 to 4 percent of global exports. Therefore, any country that had a higher share of total exports going to the middle-East could be thought of as having an above average tendency to trade with the region.

.Table 9 suggests that most regional trade flows are not consistently lower than what should be expected, while the exchange with Europe is larger in the case of Cyprus, Libya and Turkey. For example, Table 9 indicates that the share of Egypt's exports to the region are about four times larger than what might be expected while the trade intensity indices for Syria, Oman and Jordan are even higher. Where does intra-regional trade originate and where does it go? As previously noted (see Table 7) this question is not easily answered since there are major gaps in some ME countries' official trade sta-tistics. However, employing partner country trade data will allow one to pro-duce some estimates.[10] Of course, this approach does not work in situations where a partner country has not reported its data – as in the case of Iran-Lebanon, UAE, and other countries.

Table 10 relies on the available information to construct a 1990 matrix of the origins and destinations of regional intra-trade. As previously indicated, Turkey plays a key role in this exchange. It accounts for 22 percent of all exports to the region and also serves as the destination of 26 percent of all other regional countries' exports. These figures understate Turkey's impor-tance somewhat since, for political reasons, Cyprus is not reporting exports to Turkey in its official statistics. Saudi Arabia and the UAE combined account

Table 8: Middle Eastern Countries' Twenty Largest Three-Digit Intra-Regional Exports, 1970, 1980 and 1990

Description(SITC)	Value of Exports($000)			Percent of Total Exports (%)		
	1970	1980	1990	1970	1980	1990
Crude Petroleum (331)	31,684	2,051,579	1,886,796	0.93	12.28	21.25
Petroleum Products (332)	29,051	963,226	424,976	0.86	5.76	4.79
Fresh Fruit and Nuts (051)	20,727	48,472	331,344	0.61	0.29	3.73
Fresh Vegetables (054)	18,887	46,829	288,776	0.56	0.28	3.25
Live Animals (001)	32,845	19,021	283,055	0.96	0.11	3.19
Plastic Materials (581)	1,867	7,352	279,824	0.06	0.04	3.15
Iron and Steel Shapes (673)	3,239	64,125	255,721	1.09	1.38	2.88
Aluminum (684)	1,605	16,789	143,153	0.05	0.10	1.61
Non-Fur Clothing (841)	8,274	92,921	137,907	0.24	0.56	1.55
Articles of Paper (642)	902	7,133	95,222	0.03	0.04	1.07
Fixed Vegetable Oils (421)	2,563	1,411	93,289	0.08	0.01	0.05
Electrical Distributing Machinery (723)	1,562	7,778	85,611	0.05	0.05	0.96
Textile Yarn and Thread (651)	4,283	543	84,181	0.13	–	0.95
Machines Non-Electric, nes (719)	12,039	39,853	83,418	0.35	0.24	0.94
Road Motor Vehicles (732)	34,194	149,107	82,060	1.01	0.89	0.92
Natural Gas (341)	934	88,500	81,831	0.03	0.53	0.92
Gold, Silverware and Jewelry (897)	2,608	26,234	79,358	0.08	0.16	0.89
Copper (682)	207	1,954	72,775	0.01	0.01	0.82
Soaps and Cleaning Preparations (554)	1,441	10,985	70,879	0.04	0.07	0.80
Medicinal Products (541)	3,198	3,526	69,672	0.06	0.02	0.78

Source: United Nations Series D Trade Tapes. Data are based on import statistics of the regional countries. Information on Iran, Bahrain and Lebanon's imports are missing from the 1990 data. The 1980 statistics do not include Lebanon and Iran while UAE data are not included in the 1970 totals. See the notes to Table 7 for details on how the totals were compiled.

Table 9: "Trade Intensity" Indices for Selected
Middle Eastern Countries'1990 Exports

Exporter	Partner Country All OECD Countries	European Union	North America	Japan	Middle East Region
Cyprus	0.90	1.44	0.10	0.07	4.52
Egypt	0.71	0.92	0.49	0.51	4.19
Israel	1.07	0.85	1.66	1.38	0.31
Jordan	0.12	0.08	0.03	0.40	6.00
Libya	1.21	2.04	--	--	1.32
Oman	0.25	0.25	0.21	0.40	17.27
Saudi Arabia	0.36	--	1.40	--	--
Syria	0.63	1.00	0.05	0.01	5.84
Turkey	0.93	1.29	0.44	0.35	4.07

Source: Computed from trade data extracted from United Nations Series D Trade Tapes.

for about one-third of intra-regional exports and about 28 percent of all imports. Saudi Arabian exports to Turkey (mostly crude oil) constitute the single largest bilateral trade flow (about three quarters of a billion dollars) followed by UAE's exports to Oman and Libya's exports to Turkey which, combined, are over one billion dollars.

What are the factors that limit further trading opportunities among ME countries? Trade barriers are clearly an important factor as an UNCTAD (1987) study showed that average tariffs in Syria, Turkey and Libya ranged between 27 to 34 percent and actually reached 100 percent in Iran. In addition, many of the ME countries trade regimes were ridden by nontariff barriers. Over 70 percent (by value) of Turkey's imports encountered some form of nontariff measure while this ratio was 99 percent in the case of Iran. In addition, there is also evidence that transport links within the region can be an important constraint to increased trade as most established liner conference routes follow a North-South pattern. Another factor that may limit opportunities for intra-trade relates to the fact that the trade profiles of some ME countries are so similar, and this applies particularly to the oil exporting countries.

The "revealed" comparative advantage (RCA) index can provide some rough indication as to where opportunities for expanded intra-trade may exist. Countries with different revealed comparative advantage profiles should have more opportunities to trade than those whose RCA indices are similar. The revealed comparative advantage (RCA) of country i for product j is measured by the item's share in the country's exports relative to its share in world trade.[11] The index (RCA_{ij}) has a simple interpretation. If it takes a value of less than unity (which indicates that the share of product j in i's exports is less than the

Table 10. The Origin and Destination of Middle Eastern Countries' 1990 Intra-Regional Trade (Values in $000)

Exporter	Bahrain	Cyprus	Egypt	Iran	Israel	Jordan	Kuwait	Lebanon	Libya	Oman	Qatar	Saudi Arabia	Syria	Turkey	UAE
Bahrain	--	254	1.38	108	0	11,088	9,792	12	0	5,995	6.530	107,036	2	4,932	65,857
Cyprus	2,645	--	19,113	188	4,011	4,447	4,865	13,050	6,861	2,598	2.764	22,315	1,158	9,186	10,715
Egypt	1,520	11,160	--	4,139	167,652	15,728	11,396	9,228	43,550	14,521	4.192	76,579	11,682	16,069	0
Iran	7,316	2,571	0	--	0	2,508	10,937	na	2,778	55	14.235	178	32,579	492,399	169,073
Israel	0	33,286	6,366	0	--	--	0	0	0	0	0	0	0	88,438	0
Jordan	8,529	769	15,992	1,359	0	--	16,646	13,303	6,286	1,224	6.375	70,482	12,670	22,755	32,300
Kuwait	8,220	129	5,459	3,133	0	10,984	--	2,574	--	4,082	1.520	74,142	426	1,145	28,062
Lebanon	11,311	9,725	14,563	na	0	16,619	17,558	--	19,962	354	10.903	85,332	16,802	6,284	53,605
Libya	0	1,442	78,645	13,823	0	791	27	11,241	--	0	20	370	9,827	506,589	13,310
Oman	4,177	178	583	17,423	0	199	944	525	122	0	4.331	33,578	13	21	213,574
Qatar	6,664	0	49	40,414	0	5,454	19,258	259	0	12,972	--	61,842	99	445	122,308
Saudi Arabia	67,550	12,360	76,340	na	0	119,901	160,838	88,155	4,649	58,153	10.903	--	32,829	723,628	414,777
Syria	6,247	6,515	47,671	13,582	0	24,487	12,377	266,135	15,998	574	29.706	270,463	--	113,588	58,984
Turkey	3,532	154,841	160,104	495,483	45,504	80,870	92,208	50,666	220,541	4,545	6.115	338,427	194,494	--	75,426
UAE	50,561	793	0	na	0	4,531	43,549	na	5,117	580,291	73.522	161,266	4,261	192,511	--
MEMO ITEM															
Regional Trade															
Exports															
Value ($mill.)	211.7	103.9	387.4	734.6	128.1	208.7	139.8	263.0	636.1	275.7	269.8	1,770.1	866.3	1,922.8	1,116.4
Percent (%)	2.3	1.2	4.3	8.1	1.4	2.3	1.5	2.9	7.0	3.1	3.0	19.6	9.6	21.3	12.4
Imports															
Value ($mill.)	178.3	234.0	424.0	589.7	217.2	297.5	400.4	455.1	325.9	685.4	171.1	1,302.0	316.8	2,178.0	1,258.0
Percent (%)	2.0	2.6	4.7	6.5	2.4	3.3	4.4	5.0	3.6	7.6	1.9	14.4	3.5	24.1	13.9

Source: Computed from trade data extracted from United Nations Series D Trade Tapes.
Country Notes: Qatar - Regional exports as reported by Qatar for 1991 since no data are available for 1990.
Bahrain - Regional exports reported for 1988 which is the last year available.
Saudi Arabia, Lebanon, UAE and Iran - Reported 1990 imports by Cyprus, Egypt, Israel, Jordan, Libya, Oman, Saudi Arabia, Syria and Turkey, plus 1988 imports by Bahrain and 1991 imports of Qatar. Exports of Cyprus to Turkey are based on Turkey's reported imports from Cyprus.

Table 11: Middle Eastern Countries Revealed Comparative Advantage in Broad Product Groups: 1970, 1980, 1992

Exporter	Year	Foods & Feeds	Beverges & Tobacco	Crude Materials	Refined Fuels	Animal & Vegetable Oil	Chemicals	Manufactures by Material	Machinery & Transport	Misc. Manufactures
					RCA Indices for Processd Products Clarified by Major SITC Groups					
Bahrain	1970	0.00	0.01	0.00	27.93	0.03	0.17	0.05	0.03	0.03
	1980	0.02	0.00	0.00	11.72	0.00	0.01	0.29	0.08	0.25
	1992	0.01	0.02	0.08	18.43	0.07	0.54	1.21	0.17	0.53
Cyprus	1970	6.80	18.12	0.04	0.01	2.53	0.11	1.49	0.23	0.82
	1980	3.20	3.22	0.06	0.42	0.41	0.20	0.51	1.19	2.17
	1992	2.41	7.22	0.26	1.70	1.25	0.68	0.65	0.30	2.68
Egypt	1970	3.23	0.38	0.21	0.13	0.55	0.72	2.22	0.13	1.07
	1980	2.20	0.38	0.31	4.57	0.11	0.25	1.69	0.25	0.50
	1992	1.07	0.10	0.00	9.06	0.00	0.62	1.75	0.34	0.87
Iran	1970	2.26	0.01	0.00	16.19	0.00	0.12	1.22	0.04	0.09
	1980	1.42	0.02	0.00	9.22	0.00	0.17	1.04	0.02	0.06
	1992	6.62	0.02	0.08	11.04	0.00	0.11	2.58	0.09	0.15
Israel	1970	5.61	0.29	0.38	1.05	0.08	1.09	1.74	0.19	1.14
	1980	4.17	0.19	0.21	0.51	0.01	1.26	1.95	0.30	1.05
	1992	2.62	0.11	0.25	0.44	0.01	1.32	2.10	0.49	0.88
Jordan	1970	1.42	5.85	0.05	19.39	0.01	0.76	0.11	0.26	0.22
	1980	2.66	2.80	0.27	0.07	0.12	1.85	1.37	0.59	1.00
	1987	0.15	0.39	0.00	0.00	0.00	4.95	0.85	0.37	0.47
Lebanon	1970	2.99	0.04	0.15	0.76	0.29	0.08	1.13	0.35	2.96
	1980	2.15	0.19	0.03	0.02	0.53	1.11	1.46	0.43	2.23
	1992	2.90	3.73	0.02	0.08	0.03	0.32	1.38	0.30	2.54

Table 11: Continued

Exporter	Year	Foods & Feeds	Beverges & Tobacco	Crude Materials	Refined Fuels	Animal & Vegetabls Oil	Chemicals	Manufactures by Material	Machinery & Transport	Misc. Manufactures
						RCA Indices for Processd Products Clarified by Major SITC Groups				
Libya	1970	0.61	0.18	0.00	7.94	0.00	0.09	0.38	1.35	0.62
	1980	0.13	0.00	0.00	11.75	0.00	0.85	0.01	0.07	0.02
	1992	0.01	0.00	0.01	26.94	0.00	1.34	0.25	0.06	0.01
Oman	1970	0.22	0.01	0.00	0.00	0.09	0.04	3.18	0.06	0.03
	1980	0.34	0.06	0.00	2.71	0.00	0.02	0.08	1.84	0.58
	1992	0.25	0.00	0.00	13.59	0.00	0.18	0.37	0.64	1.29
Qatar	1970	0.41	0.00	0.00	0.20	0.44	4.81	0.31	0.74	0.76
	1980	0.03	0.00	0.00	1.03	0.00	2.58	2.09	0.18	0.10
	1992	0.01	0.00	0.05	15.89	0.20	3.02	0.25	0.07	0.63
Saudi Arabia	1970	0.32	0.00	0.00	25.14	0.00	0.48	0.01	0.20	0.07
	1980	0.27	0.01	0.01	10.11	0.00	0.18	0.07	0.51	0.14
	1992	0.15	0.00	0.16	19.59	0.01	2.26	0.23	0.23	0.17
Syria	1970	9.81	0.02	0.06	0.64	0.01	0.18	1.41	0.11	2.71
	1980	2.01	0.00	0.10	10.00	0.00	0.04	0.31	0.16	0.69
	1992	2.32	0.01	0.03	22.10	0.00	0.06	0.45	0.06	1.17
Turkey	1970	19.47	0.87	0.26	0.40	1.18	0.86	1.36	0.14	0.57
	1980	17.51	0.52	0.34	0.24	0.24	0.30	2.01	0.11	1.06
	1992	5.10	0.10	0.38	0.70	0.24	0.31	1.44	0.24	2.57
UAE	1970	0.23	0.02	0.04	0.02	0.82	0.17	2.76	0.29	0.21
	1980	0.85	0.06	0.00	2.65	0.12	0.30	2.08	0.37	0.61
	1992	0.57	3.28	0.38	10.27	0.06	0.57	1.01	0.39	1.20

Source: Author's calculations from United Nations Series D COMTRADE Statistics.

corresponding world trade share) this implies that the country has a revealed comparative disadvantage in the product. Similarly, if the index exceeds unity, then the country is said to have a revealed comparative advantage in the item. Table 11 reports the RCA indices for Egypt and other regional countries of products classified in 9 broad product groups. In order to determine how RCA patterns were changing separate indices were calculated for 1970, 1980 and 1992.

Table 11 reveals that Egypt has a strong comparative advantage in the production and export of refined petroleum products (RCA = 9.06 – that is, the share of these goods in Egypt's exports is nine times their share in world trade) and in manufactured goods classified in SITC 6 ("Manufactures Classified by Material"). The latter are generally composed of relatively labor-intensive products that use materials like leather, fibers, wood, or paper as production inputs. Egypt also registers a RCA slightly above unity in processed foods. However, the sharp decline in the index over the period 1970-1990 suggests that comparative advantage in this area is being lost. As expected, Egypt's RCA index is low for the highly capital-intensive machinery and transport group (SITC 7) and is actually zero for processed crude materials (in SITC 2) and animal and vegetable oils (SITC 4). The latter is somewhat surprising since in 1992 Egypt exported some $5.4 million in raw flax, $2 million in oilseeds, and $600 thousand in bovine hides – all items that could have been further processed. Trade barrier escalation in OECD markets is often cited as an important factor constraining the domestic processing of these types of primary commodities in Egypt and other developing countries.[12]

Of the 14 regional countries, 10 show a strong revealed comparative advantage for the refined petroleum products group (those not having a comparative advantage in this sector are Israel, Jordan, Lebanon and Turkey). Several countries have an RCA index over 15 for energy products (Bahrain, Libya, Qatar, Saudi Arabia and Syria) while the index is over 9 for all other countries except Cyprus. An important point to note is that most of these petroleum exporting countries have a very limited comparative advantage outside this one sector. For example, Libya, Qatar and Saudi Arabia only have RCAs above unity in refined fuels and chemicals (many of the latter utilize crude petroleum inputs). The potential for increased intra-regional trade appears to be limited by the narrow range of products these countries can produce under internationally-competitive conditions.

Opportunities for increased intra-regional trade appear greatest between the "energy exporters" and countries like Turkey, Israel and Lebanon that have relatively high RCAs in various types of manufactured goods and processed foodstuffs (note that Syria and Iran also have strong RCAs for foods).

Table 12: Average Pre-Uruguay Round Tariffs and Nontariff Measures Facing Middle East Exports to the European Union, Japan and the United States

	European Union		Japan		United States	
	All Products	All Non-Oil Goods	All Products	All Non-Oil Goods	All Products	All Non-Oil Goods
1992 Value of Exports ($million)	39,604.9	12,015.5	27,986.5	1,698.2	18,167.7	5,975.0
Bahrain	172.9	148.1	304.1	63.2	71.2	68.9
Cyprus	433.2	431.7	2.1	2.1	11.7	11.7
Egypt	2,893.4	923.9	91.0	33.9	465.6	223.2
Iran	6,649.1	537.9	2,604.5	82.6	0.8	0.8
Israel	3,731.3	3,671.8	694.6	694.6	3,902.3	3,880.6
Jordan	88.2	88.2	24.1	24.1	18.6	18.6
Lebanon	96.8	96.5	2.2	2.2	28.5	28.5
Libya	7,021.0	152.2	0.7	0.7	--	--
Oman	165.7	165.7	1,962.4	5.1	207.3	97.2
Qatar	55.8	24.2	2,175.5	9.6	75.9	71.5
Saudi Arabia	11,150.4	1,063.5	10,181.1	303.5	11,285.7	183.2
Syria	1,225.1	144.8	8.5	8.5	45.8	12.4
Turkey	4,208.4	4,018.1	202.2	202.2	1,183.4	1,155.4
UAE	1,713.7	549.0	9,733.3	265.9	871.0	222.9
Average Tariff (%)						
Bahrain	0.4	1.2	3.0	0.5	1.1	2.7
Cyprus	0.8	0.8	0.7	0.0	6.9	4.5
Egypt	3.9	4.0	9.9	9.9	7.9	7.9
Iran	0.6	1.3	2.0	0.7	4.6	8.9
Israel	0.1	0.4	3.3	0.4	2.0	2.0
Jordan	2.0	2.0	0.3	0.3	0.1	0.1
Lebanon	0.2	0.2	1.1	1.1	3.7	3.7
Libya	3.0	3.0	1.9	1.9	--	--
Oman	0.0	0.0	0.6	0.6	1.5	7.5
Qatar	0.9	2.4	3.6	0.6	2.0	3.4
Saudi Arabia	0.1	0.3	3.5	0.0	0.6	2.8
Syria	0.0	0.2	3.1	0.0	0.5	4.0
Turkey	0.5	0.4	0.2	2.6	6.3	8.3
UAE	0.4	2.6	2.5	0.0	2.5	9.6

Table 12: Continued

	European Union		Japan		United States	
	All Products	All Non-Oil Goods	All Products	All Non-Oil Goods	All Products	All Non-Oil Goods
NTB Coverage Ratio (%)	3.4	10.5	0.2	2.0	6.2	11.0
Bahrain	0.3	0.3	0.0	0.0	0.0	0.0
Cyprus	16.2	16.5	6.4	6.4	0.7	0.7
Egypt	13.2	31.1	0.0	0.0	17.6	36.2
Iran	0.2	1.2	0.0	0.0	0.0	0.0
Israel	5.9	6.0	1.0	1.0	0.4	0.6
Jordan	1.2	1.2	14.9	14.9	1.2	1.2
Lebanon	1.5	1.5	0.0	0.0	0.2	0.2
Libya	0.0	0.0	0.0	0.0	--	--
Oman	2.8	7.6	0.1	11.9	0.0	0.0
Qatar	0.2	1.0	1.4	76.5	0.0	0.0
Saudi Arabia	0.9	7.2	0.0	0.0	5.8	39.0
Syria	0.0	0.2	0.0	0.0	0.0	0.0
Turkey	13.5	14.2	6.7	7.3	24.4	32.4
UAE	0.1	0.6	0.0	0.0	10.4	47.2

Note: *For the EU, Japan and the United States combined the average trade weighted tariff on all exports is 1.4 percent, while the tariff on all non-oil goods is two percent. The average NTM trade coverage ratio for all goods is 2.9 percent, while the ratio for all non-oil goods is 9.3 percent.*

OECD Trade Barriers: Effects of the Uruguay Round

The Uruguay Round (UR) marks the eighth time since 1947 that General Agreement on Tariffs and Trade (GATT) members negotiated a reduction of trade barriers in a multilateral framework and, potentially, it could have important implications for ME exports.[13] Unlike previous negotiations, the Uruguay Round (UR) focused on a far broader range of trade-related issues (see Finger and Olechowski, 1987). Its accomplishments included: (i) reductions in tariffs and nontariff measures (NTMs), including in the previously excluded agricultural sectors and (largely excluded) textiles and clothing; (ii) extension of multilateral rules to trade in services, trade-related intellectual property rights, and trade-related investment measures; (iii) reform of some GATT rules such as those on subsidies, countervailing duties, antidumping actions, and safeguards; and (iv) institutional reforms relating to dispute settlement and the functioning of the GATT system.

Middle Eastern countries have tended to view the UR negotiations on tariffs and NTMs with a certain degree of apprehension. Israel, for example, has duty free access to the US, EU and EFTA markets as a result of previously negotiated FTAs. Similarly, Turkey and Lebanon have established FTAs that provide for duty free access for most goods exported to Europe. Countries like Egypt, Cyprus, Iran and Jordan receive important OECD trade preferences on some products under the Generalized System of Preferences (GSP) that allow them to be imported under zero duties or at tariffs below MFN rates. The reduction in MFN tariffs will reduce regional countries' preference margins and may cause some of their exports to be displaced. A key question is whether the overall ME gains from the Round will exceed, or fall short of, expected losses.

The Round's Impact on Tariffs

Table 12 shows the 1992 value of exports and average pre-UR tariff rates facing regional exporters in the EU, Japan and United States both in total and for all non-oil exports. The tariffs shown in the table are "applied" duties in that they reflect the average of the MFN, GSP or FTA tariff actually paid by the exporter. Finally, the lower third of the table shows the share (that is, coverage ratio) of each regional country's exports that encounter nontariff measures.[14]

The general impression one gets from Table 12 is that average pre-Uruguay tariffs facing middle-Eastern countries were generally low in Europe and Japan (with one or two exceptions) and higher in the United States. In the EU, duties on all non-oil goods average about 1.2 percent although they reach 4 percent for non-oil exports from Cyprus. Factors accounting for the relatively

Table 13: The Estimated Effects of the Uruguay Round on MFN Tariff Barriers

Product Group	Tariff Rate Pre-Uruguay	Post-Uruguay	Tariff Change Absolute Reduction	Percentage Reduction
ALL INDUSTRIAL PRODUCTS[1]	6.4	4.0	-2.4	38
Industrial Tropical Products	4.2	1.9	-2.3	55
Natural Resource Products	53.2	2.0	-1.2	38
Manufactures of:[2]				
Leather	6.7	5.4	-1.3	19
Rubber	5.3	3.4	-1.9	36
Wood	5.0	2.1	-2.9	58
Paper	4.8	1.6	-3.2	67
Textiles & Clothing	15.2	11.4	-3.8	25
Metals	5.4	2.6	-2.8	52
Chemicals	6.7	3.0	-3.7	55
Minerals	4.7	2.9	-1.8	38
Food & Agricultural Products[3]				
Cocoa Products	4.5	2.5	-2.0	44
Tobacco	17.3	11.2	-6.1	35
Coffee, Tea and Sugar	9.4	6.4	-3.0	32
Fruits and Vegetables	8.6	5.6	-3.0	35
Oilseeds, Fats and Oils	1.7	1.1	-0.6	35
Grains	6.6	4.5	-2.1	32
Dairy Products	15.8	11.9	-3.9	25
Spices. Flowers and Plants	2.2	1.1	-1.1	50
ALL NON- ENERGY ITEMS[4]	6.5	3.9	-2.6	40

[1] *Defined by GATT to include eleven industrial categories (fish and products: wood, pulp, paper and furniture; textiles and clothing; leather, rubber, footwear, travel goods; metals; chemicals and photographic supplies; transport equipment; non-electric machinery; electric machinery; mineral products and precious metals; manufactured article n.e.s.), nonagricultural tropical products (plaiting products, rubber and tropical wood, jute and hard fibers), and natural resource based products. The latter include: fish and fish products; forestry and forestry products; and non-ferrous metals and minerals. Tariff information from GATT(1993) Table 14.*

[2] *Based on GATT (1993) Table 15 and Appendix Table 5. The tariffs shown above are averages for the semi-manufactures and manufactures components of the GATT processing chains. Agricultural products are defined by GATT to include ten agricultural categories (fruit and vegetables; coffee, tea, cocoa, sugar, and so forth: grains; animals and products; oilseeds, fats and oils; cut flowers, plants, vegetable materials; beverages and spirits; dairy products; tobacco; other agricultural products) plus agricultural tropical products (tropical beverages; spices and plants; certain oilseeds and oils; tropical roots, rice and tobacco; tropical fruits and nuts).*

[3] *The reported percentage tariff reduction for these products is given in GATT (1993) Table 20. Pre-Uruguay Round tariffs were estimated using the World Bank - UNCTAD SMART Database. These statistics. plus the percentage reductions reported by GATT were used to derive the post - Uruguay Round rate.*

[4] *Computed using 1992 OECD country trade weights.*

low overall rates facing the middle-East include the extension of GSP treatment for many ME products and the EU-Israel and EU-Turkey Free Trade Agreement.[15]

Conversely, the relatively high tariffs that are found in the United States are the result of two factors: the exclusion of OPEC members from the US GSP scheme, and the fact that GSP preferences are not extended to textiles, clothing and footwear. Box 5 gives more detailed information on the tariffs facing Egypt's exports.

For the most part, the regional NTM trade coverage ratios that are shown in Table 12 are also low with one or two exceptions. More than 30 percent of Egypt's non-oil exports to the European Community (EC) and US encounter NTMs, but the product sectors affected differ in the two markets. In the EU, Egypt faces major import restrictions on foodstuffs while most of the US barriers are in the textile and clothing sector.

How did the Uruguay affect tariff barriers facing ME exports? The Round's accomplishments can be summarized as follows;

i) Manufactured goods: A 40 percent cut in industrial countries' tariffs on manufactures with an increase in bindings (legal maximum rates) from 94 to 98 percent of all imports. GATT data indicate tariffs will be lowered by approximately 2.4 percentage points to 4.0 percent. Lower than average cuts occur in sectors of major importance to developing countries such as textiles, clothing, footwear and transport equipment. Reductions will take place in five equal annual stages beginning with the entry into force of the World Trade Organization (January 1, 1995).

ii) Industrial tropical products: These are goods like jute, hemp, sisal, tropical wood and rubber. A 57 percent reduction in tariffs will result. Tariffs should decline from 4.2 to 1.9 percent.

iii) Natural Resource Based Products: Preliminary information suggests a 38 percent cut for these products. Larger than average reductions will occur for some mineral and metal products with lower than average reductions for fish. Tariffs on natural resource based manufactures should decline from 3.2 to 2.0 percent – a 40 percent reduction.

Table 13 provides more detailed estimates of the impact of the Uruguay Round on average OECD tariffs. One of the most disappointing results of the UR, in as far as most developing countries are concerned, were the far smaller than average reductions on leather manufactures, textiles and clothing (19 and 25 percent, respectively). In addition, while the Round did make some progress in reducing the extent of tariff escalation, this issue will likely remain a (post-Uruguay) point of contention between developing and developed countries.

Table 14: Estimated Effects of the Uruguay Round Tariff Cuts on Middle Eastern Countries' Exports

Exporting Country	1992 Exports to ($ million)			Projected UR Trade Effects (%)			Overall Export Change ($ million)
	EU	Japan	USA	EU	Japan	USA	
Bahrain	172.9	304.1	71.2	1.12	0.42	7.42	8.5
Cyprus	422.2	2.1	11.7	0.21	-1.74	4.54	1.4
Egypt	2,893.4	91.0	465.6	0.30	1.42	2.41	21.2
Iran	6,649.1	2,604.5	0.8	0.02	2.73	0.49	72.4
Israel	3,731.3	694.6	3,903.3	-0.14	-0.81	-0.16	-17.1
Jordan	88.2	24.1	18.6	-0.55	0.76	2.30	0.1
Lebanon	96.8	2.2	28.5	7.92	-0.11	-0.16	7.6
Libya	7,021.0	0.7	0.0	-0.13	-1.14	0.00	-9.1
Oman	165.7	1,962.4	207.3	0.88	3.04	0.93	63.0
Qatar	55.8	2,175.5	75.9	--	2.94	1.30	64.9
Saudi Arabia	11,150.4	10,181.1	11,285.7	-0.08	2.40	0.46	287.3
Syria	1,225.1	8.5	45.8	-0.20	0.12	0.33	-2.3
Turkey	4,208.4	202.2	1,183.4	-0.08	0.98	3.06	34.8
UAE	1,713.7	9,733.3	871.0	0.95	2.46	1.56	269.3
ALL MIDDLE EAST	39,594.0	27,986.3	18,168.8	0.02	2.42	0.64	802.2

Source: Author's calculations from World Bank-UNCTAD SMART data.

Empirical Evidence on the Round's Effects

In recognition of developing countries' need for technical assistance in the UR negotiations, UNCTAD and the World Bank initiated a joint project to help them evaluate various trade liberalization proposals. This project (named SMART – Software for Market Analysis and Restrictions on Trade) developed a desk-top system that allows a country to analyze the level, structure and restrictive effects of trade barriers on its exports.[16] SMART includes, with its other elements, a simulation model that projects the change in a country's exports following a change in foreign trade barriers (see Laird and Yeats, 1990). SMART projections are made at the tariff line level (US and EC tariff schedules identify over 8,000 tariff line products) and these estimates can be summed up to more aggregate groups. SMART accounts for trade creation (the substitution of foreign goods for domestic production) and trade diversion (the substitution of one foreign supplier for another) as a result of preference erosion (see Box 6 for information on how Egypt's preferences will be affected).

Before proceeding, it should be noted that there are UR effects that SMART does not account for. These include a (potentially important) stimulus to merchandise trade from the UR liberalization in services trade, and the stimulus resulting from strengthened rules on how trade is conducted. There is also ample evidence that a lowering of trade barriers in developing countries will increase their ability to compete in foreign export markets (see Nash and Thomas, 1990). Such factors are omitted because of problems in their quantification and not because of the assumption that they are unimportant. In addition, there are major problems in projecting the impact of the Round's elimination of NTMs – particularly in the agricultural, textile and clothing sectors where information on relative production costs in individual developing countries are required. Finally, it should be noted that the SMART projections are "short-term" estimates of trade changes and do not allow for efficiency gains associated with larger export volumes or the addition of new production capacity.

With the above qualifications, Table 14 summarizes SMART projections of the UR effects on regional country exports to the EC, Japan and the US markets.[17] These estimates are expressed as percentage changes from a 1992 trade base and in overall dollar terms (see the right-most column of the table). These data suggest the UR liberalization of these major OECD markets' trade barriers could increase all regional countries' exports by $800 million – an annual change of less than one percent. This is the estimated net effect of: (i) trade losses on products receiving preferences, and (ii) gains of products facing MFN duties that were lowered. However, Israel, Syria and Libya are projected to experience overall losses from the Round due to the erosion of their preferences.

Several specific points should be noted regarding these projections. First, they admittedly understate regional countries' trade gains since they do not account for the UR liberalization of barriers in countries like Australia, Canada, New Zealand and EFTA members. If the same import response occurs in these markets as that projected for the EC, Japan and United States, regional country gains could be approximately $100 million higher. Second, the projections do not fully incorporate the effects of the erosion of intra-OECD preferences (they do, however, account for reductions in EFTA's preferences in the EC). Some regional countries may achieve trade gains by displacing this exchange. Finally, the projections do not incorporate any estimates of the trade effects of the removal of MFA and other nontariff measures. For some regional countries, the impact of the NTM removal may be negative.

Elements of the Negotiations on Nontariff Barriers

The UR made important progress in liberalizing nonnative measures – especially in agriculture, textiles and clothing. Basically, what was achieved can be summarized as follows,

Agriculture. NTM restrictions are subject to "tariffication" with subsequent cuts by industrial countries of 36 percent over 6 years with a minimum reductions of 15 percent on all tariff lines. There are a few exceptions and, in these cases, 4 percent of domestic consumption in the 1986-88 period is a minimum access guarantee that must increase by 0.8 percent annually to 8 percent over the implementation period. Market access for agricultural products will involve the elimination of quantitative restrictions and other government interventions. Reductions of 36 percent were also negotiated in budgetary outlays on export subsidies and in quantities of subsidized exports.

Textiles and Clothing. The MFA will be phased out. Products accounting for not less than 16 percent of the total 1990 volume of imports covered by the MFA are to be integrated into GATT in 1994 upon entry into force of the World Trade Organization. After the third year of the phase-out period, at least an additional 17 percent of the total 1990 import volumes are to be integrated, followed by at least an additional 18 percent after the seventh year, and the remainder (49 percent) at the end of the ten-year period. Each phase-out must encompass products (chosen by the restricting country) from four groups – tops and yarns, fabrics, made-up textiles, and clothing.

Other Sectors. Elimination of "voluntary" export restraints (VERs). According to the World Bank-SMART Database, the US and EC each have VERs on over 400 tariff line products which cover such major sectors as metals, transport equipment, footwear and domestic utensils.

Table 12 documents the importance of industrial countries pre-Uruguay NTMs by showing the share of regional countries' exports that encounter these measures – both in total and for all non-oil products.[18] Overall, about 10 percent of all regional countries' nonfuel exports encountered NTMs with Egypt and Cyprus' coverage ratios the highest (32 and 16 percent, respectively) due to the relatively large share of temperate zone agricultural products, textiles and clothing in their exports.[19] (Box 8 provides more detailed information on specific Egyptian exports that encounter NTBs). Within manufactures, the coverage of textiles and clothing is particularly high – over 40 percent of ME clothing (SITC 84) exports face these measures, as do 38 percent of textile (SITC 65) products.

As a result of the UR NTM concessions, the profile of protection facing regional countries' exports has been altered substantially. Post-Uruguay Round NTM coverage ratios should fall from their current 10 percent level to between 1 to 2 percent.[20] The average decline for Egypt will be dramatic – the ratio will fall from 32 to approximately 2 percent. Essentially, this is due to the fact that all NTBs formerly applied to Egyptian and other regional countries' agricultural products, textiles, clothing and ferrous metals have been removed. As a result, Low and Yeats (1994) estimate the share of all developing countries exports facing NTMs fell from 18 percent before the Uruguay Round to about 3 percent after.[21]

Possible Effects of the Round's NTB Liberalization

The Uruguay Round's elimination of NTMs applied under the Multifiber Arrangement is clearly a positive development for developing countries as a whole, yet there may be negative implications for individual exporters. Under the MFA, and its predecessor the Short-Term-Textile Arrangement (STA), developing countries were allocated quotas for their textile and clothing exports to industrial countries. When the MFA quotas are phased out, textile and clothing trade will be subject to intense international competition and the displacement of many established suppliers could occur. Stated differently, some regional countries may be uncompetitive in this new international environment and could find their exports displaced by more efficient producers whose trade is now restrained by the MFA. As such, some ME countries may have to give a high priority to restructuring their industries, reducing costs, and improving quality to compete in a post-Uruguay Round world.

Summary and Conclusions

Overall, the exports of ME countries are anticipated to increase by approximately $800 to $900 million as a result of the Uruguay Round tariffs cuts.

This represents an annual expansion of less than one percent of regional exports. The projected overall gains are small due to the erosion of tariff preferences ME countries receive in OECD markets which offset the positive effects of reduced MFN tariffs on non-preference receiving products. Also, the major ME export product (petroleum) generally faces zero or very low tariffs so this item's trade could not be affected by the Uruguay Round reductions. Egypt's projected gains (about $20 million – which is less than one half of a percent of total exports) are largely concentrated in agricultural exports to the EU and manufactures exports to the US. Israel is projected to experience net trade losses from the Round due to the erosion of its FTA preferences in the EU and US.

The Uruguay Round made major progress in removing nontariff measures facing ME exporters – especially in agriculture, textiles and clothing. As a result, the average OECD NTM coverage ratio for ME exports will fall from its current 10 percent level to between 1 to 2 percent. The decline in the coverage ratio for Egypt is dramatic. Prior to the Round, 32 percent of Egypt's exports to the OECD faced NTMs – this share will go down to about 2 percent following the removal of the MFA and agricultural restrictions.

Although the liberalization of NTMs is clearly a positive development from the viewpoint of all developing countries, some may experience negative effects. With the removal of the MFA, international trade in textiles and clothing will be subject to increasing international competition. ME countries will need to adopt major cost cutting and efficiency increasing measures to remain viable exporters. Similarly, net food importing countries could be adversely affected by higher international food prices which are expected to result from the Uruguay Round Agreements. While there is a considerable uncertainty about the extent of price increases, there is a clear priority for net food importing countries to adopt reform measures aimed at stimulating domestic production. A key element in these reforms is the adoption of incentives to increase domestic food production.

This chapter also examined the prospects for increased intra-regional trade. The most important constraints to this exchange are the similarities in revealed comparative advantage and export profiles of many ME countries, as well as the high levels of tariff and nontariff measure protection that exist in some markets. The most favorable prospects for increased intra-regional trade appear to be between countries like Cyprus, Israel, Lebanon and Turkey, which are net energy importers, and the rest of the region.

Notes

1   In this study countries included in the definition of the Middle-East region include: Bahrain, Cyprus, Egypt, Iran, Iraq, Israel, Jordan, Lebanon, Libya, Oman, Qatar, Saudi Arabia, Syria, Turkey and the United Arab Emirates. Iraq is, however, excluded from much of the current analysis due to the United Nations embargo and its effects on this country's trade. There is, however, no general agreement as to which countries should be included or excluded in the region. See Fisher 1993 for a review and analysis of some of the alternative country definitions that have been employed.

2   Under its free trade area arrangements with the United States, the European Union, and European Free Trade Association (EFTA), Israel had virtually duty free access to these markets. The Uruguay Round's average 40 percent reduction in MFN tariffs will erode Israel's FTA preferences and may result in significant trade diversion. Yeats 1994 estimates that between 5 to 8 percent of Israel's textile and clothing exports to the United States may be displaced due to preference erosion.

3   About 60 percent of Oman's 1991 exports went to three regional markets, namely, Iran, Saudi Arabia and the UAE. One-fifth of Jordan's exports went to India, while China accounted for an additional 5 percent. Bahrain's official trade statistics did not specify the destination of roughly 40 percent of its total exports, but these shipments do not appear to have gone to OECD countries. Official trade data for Lebanon are not available and UNCTAD estimates (upon which Table 1 is based) do not specify individual markets for Lebanon's exports.

4   Based on 1990 trade flow information Cyprus, Jordan, Lebanon, Israel and Turkey were all net importers of petroleum products in SITC 3. Of these countries net imports of $1.2 billion Israel accounted for 28 percent of the total and Turkey for 21 percent.

5   In 1992, OECD countries imported $1.2 billion of fresh fruit and nuts from the region and close to $400 million of fresh vegetables. There may be additional opportunities for further processing of these goods (freezing, canning, drying, and so forth) that could increase their value added content and also have important job creating effects. Since food processing normally increases the usable life of a product further processing could also be an important factor reducing food spoilage. Other major crude material exports that may be suitable for further regional processing include unmanufactured tobacco ($432 million, undressed hides and skins ($112 million), raw cotton ($200 million), oilseeds ($60 million) and crude minerals such as natural asphalt, clays, borates and mica ($241 million).

6   These agricultural product exports have varied destinations. Turkey receives all of the region's barley exports and over half the shipments of unmilled wheat. Over 40 percent of the region's rice exports go to Switzerland while more than two-thirds of the wheat meal exports go to the European Union.

7   For example, Beissner and Hemmer 1981 note that "As clearly shown by many empirical studies the problem of absolute poverty in the developing countries is primarily a rural problem. Selective measures against absolute poverty must therefore focus on agricultural production. Not only must the production of food for domestic consumption be increased, but it should be examined how far an expansion of export-oriented agricultural production could contribute to improved living conditions in rural areas. There would, however, be no point in this if large economic regions like the European Community apply protectionist measures against the outside world."

8   For example, Lebanon did not report its exports to the region in 1990. This

exchange was estimated using reported imports from Lebanon by partners such as Egypt, Turkey, Cyprus, and so forth. Two problems should be noted with regard to this approach. First, imports are normally valued on a c.i.f. basis while exports are reported f.o.b.As such, the partner country data will overstate true exports by the margin of transport and insurance costs. Second, if some partner countries did not report data (like Lebanon-Iran in 1990) these bilateral flows would have to be excluded from these estimates of intra-regional trade. See the notes to Table 7 for details on how the regional trade data were estimated. These procedures did produce several interesting anomalies. For example, in 1990 Saudi Arabia reported no exports to the region yet regional countries reported about $1.4 billion in imports from Saudi Arabia.

9 The "trade intensity" index is defined as the share of one country's exports doing to a partner divided by the share of world exports going to the partner. That is,

(1) $TI_{ij} = [x_{ij}/X_{it}] \div [x_{wj}/X_{wt}]$

where x_{ij} and x_{wt} are the value of its exports and world exports to j, X_{it} is i's total exports and X_{wt} are total world exports. An index of more (less) than unity indicates a bilateral trade flow that is larger (smaller) than would be expected given the partner country's importance in world trade.

10 Import statistics are normally reported on a cost-insurance-freight (c.i.f.) basis while exports are typically reported in terms of free-on-board (f.o.b.) values. As such, partner country import statistics would tend to overestimate the value of (missing) export statistics. The IMF often employs an adjustment factor of 10 percent to express import data to the same basis as export statistics.

11 That is, if x_{ij} is the value of country i's exports of j, and X_{tj} is the country's total exports i's revealed comparative advantage index is:
$RCA_{ij} = (x_{ij}/X_{tj}) \div (X_{iw}/X_{tw})$ where the w subscripts refer to world totals.

12 Numerous studies show that OECD countries tariffs typically have a common structure Balassa 1968, Helleiner and Welwood 1978, Yeats 1987. Zero, or very low tariffs, are normally applied to raw material imports and these duties increase or "escalate" as the commodity experiences further processing.

13 The previous negotiations and their completion dates were: Geneva (1947), Annecy (1949), Torquay (1951), Geneva (1956), Geneva (1961), Kennedy (1967) and Tokyo Round (1979). Subject to confirmation by governments, the Uruguay Round Agreement will enter into force on July 1, 1995. Its market access offers will be phased in over periods as long as ten years. Certain additional issues, including the relationship between trade and the environment, labor standards, and competition policy, are under discussion and may be incorporated in a future work program for the World Trade Organization.

14 The following types of nontariff measures are included in the NTM trade coverage ratio: variable import levies and other special charges, all quotas and quantitative restrictions on imports, anti-dumping and countervailing duties, "voluntary" export restraints, minimum import price regulations, prohibitions, surcharges, tariff quotas, and all MFA restrictions.

15 One potential problem relating to the statistics in Table 12 is that ceilings are applied to some products receiving GSP treatment. Once these ceilings are exceeded additional imports are taxed at the MFN rate. Due to the lack of required information Table 12 assumes that all trade occurred within the pre-established GSP limits. If this is not the case Table 12 could understate the importance of applied tariffs.

16 SMART shows tariff line level information on trade barriers a country faces in about 40 major markets. The system also indicates: (i) unit values of competing

exports, (ii) the level and type of tariffs (MFN, GSP, Lome Convention, CBI, EC Regional Preferences) that are applied, and (iii) information on nontariff measures facing the product. SMART provides procedures for aggregating tariff line statistics to broad aggregates like; foodstuffs, agricultural raw materials, or manufactures. See Laird and Yeats 1991, Erzan and Yeats 1992, Safadi and Yeats 1993, or World Bank 1992 for illustrative applications.

17 These projections are based on an across-the-board reduction of MFN tariffs of approximately 40 percent except in the case of agriculture, textiles and clothing. In agriculture, estimates of NTMs nominal equivalents were drawn from Laird and Yeats 1991 and these measures were reduced by 36 percent. The simulations for textiles and clothing are based on a 20 percent reduction of nominal equivalents published in World Bank 1992 and Laird and Yeats 1991 over the 10 year phase out period specified in the draft agreement.

18 Coverage ratios show the percentage of trade in a product group that encounter NTMs. The measure has shortcomings (see Laird and Yeats, 1991). No trade, for example, may occur under restrictive NTMs – this would cause the index to take zero or low values. The index issensitive to the types of NTMs included in its computation. The coverage ratios in Table 6 were computed for the following measures: surcharges, variable levies, quantitative restrictions (including prohibitions, quotas, non-automatic licensing, "voluntary" export restrictions, and restraints under the MFA and similar textile arrangements and state monopolies), price control measures (including minimum, reference or basic import price systems, price surveillance and voluntary export price restraints, additional customs formalities and other entry control measures, and local content regulations.

19 Laird and Yeats 1991 surveyed published estimates of ad valorem equivalents of OECD countries' nontariff measures. Their findings indicate EC protection for grains is between 100 to 150 percent depending on the level of world prices while nominal rates of 200 to 350 percent occur for dairy products. Even higher ad valorem equivalents occur in Japan – between 200 to 350 percent for rice, beef and sugar. Japanese NTM protection for wheat and barley exceeds 400 percent.

20 These estimates hold regional countries' exports constant. The value of pre-UR NTM covered trade in the textile, clothing and agricultural sectors is determined by multiplying the coverage ratio times total trade in the group, and then subtracting the result from total NTM covered trade. These new NTM covered trade values are divided by actual total pre-UR trade values to estimate the post-UR ratios. The resulting coverage ratios are upward biased since they do not account for the increase in ME countries' exports that will result from the liberalization.

21 Given the Round's accomplishments regarding NTMs, what remains to be done if a further post-UR liberalization is attempted? Analysis of the Bank's NTM data shows that antidumping and countervailing duties (which may be far more widely used in a post-UR world), followed by QRs should be the most important remaining restrictions. These are mostly concentrated in chemicals (SITC 5) and miscellaneous manufactures (SITC 8). In short, the focus of post-Uruguay initiatives on NTMs would shift markedly in terms of the types of measures applied, the sectors affected, and the overall importance of these restrictions.

References

Balassa, Bela. 1968. "Tariff Protection in Industrial Nations and its Effects on the Exports of Processed Goods from Developing Countries." *The Canadian Journal of Economics*. Vol.1:583-594.

Baldwin, Robert, and Tracy Murray. 1977. "MFN Tariff Reduction and Developing Country Benefits Under the GSP." *The Economic Journal*. Vol. 87, March.

Baldwin, Robert, and Andrey Sapir. 1983. "India and the Tokyo Round." *World Development*. Vol.11.

Beissner, Karl-Heinz, and Hans-Rimbert Hemmer. 1981. "The Impact of the EC's Agricultural Policy on its Trade with Developing Countries." *Inter-Economics*. March/April.

Cable, Vincent. 1987. "Tropical Products," in J. Michael Finger and Andrzej Olechowski (eds.), The Uruguay Round: A Handbook on the Multilateral Trade Negotiations. Washington, DC: World Bank, November.

Cline, William et. al. 1978. Trade Negotiations in the Tokyo Round: A Quantitative Assessment. Washington, DC: The Brookings Institution.

Erzan, Refik, and Alexander Yeats. 1992. "Free Trade Agreements with the United States – What's in it for Latin America." World Bank Policy Research Paper Number 827. Washington, D.C.

Finger, J. Michael, and Andrzej Olechowski. 1987. *The Uruguay Round: A Handbook on the Multilateral Trade Negotiations*. Washington, DC: World Bank, November.

GATT 1993. *An Analysis of the Proposed Uruguay Round Agreement, With Particular Emphasis on Aspects of Interest to Developing Economies."* (MTN.TNC/W/122)(MTN.GNG/W/30) Geneva: GATT, 29, November.

Helleiner, G.K., and D. Welwood. 1978, *Raw Material Processing in Developing Countries and Reductions in the Canadian Tariff.* Ottawa: Economic Council of Canada.

Kirmani, N., et. al 1984. "Effects of Increased Market Access on Exports of Developing Countries." IMF Staff Papers, Vol.34, No.4, December.

Low, Patrick, and Alexander Yeats. 1994. "Nontariff Measures and Developing Countries: Has the Uruguay Round Leveled the Playing Field?". World Bank Policy Research Working Paper. Washington, D.C.

Laird, Sam, and Alexander Yeats. 1986. "The UNCTAD Trade Policy Simulation Model: A Note on Methodology, Data and Uses." UNCTAD Discussion Paper No. 16, Geneva.

___. 1990. "Trends in Nontariff Barriers of Developed Countries, 1966-1986." *Weltwirtschaftliches Archiv*, Band 126, Heft 2.

Laird, Samuel, and Alexander Yeats. 1991. *Quantitative Methods for Trade Barrier Analysis*. London: Macmillan Press.

Lydall, Harold. 1985. *Trade and Employment*. Geneva: ILO.

Nash, John, and Vinod Thomas. 1992. *Best Practices of Trade Policy Reform*. Cambridge: Cambridge University Press for the World Bank.

OECD. 1982. *Problems of Agricultural Trade*. Paris: OECD.

___. 1987a. *National Policies and Agricultural Trade: Country Study Japan*. Paris:

___. 1987b. *National Policies and Agricultural Trade: Study on the European Economic Community*. Paris: OECD.

Olechowski, Andrzej. 1987. "Nontariff Barriers to Trade" in J. Michael Finger and Andrzej Olechowski (eds.), *The Uruguay Round: A Handbook for the Multilateral Trade Negotiations*. Washington, DC: World Bank.

Pomfret, Richard. 1986. "The Effects of Trade Preferences for Developing Countries." *Southern Economic Journal*, Vol. 53.

Primo Braga, Carlos, Raed Safadi, and Alexander Yeats. 1994. "Regional Integration in the Western Hemisphere: Deja Vu All Over Again." *The World Economy,* Vol.17, July 1994.

Safadi, Raed, and Alexander Yeats. 1993. "Asian Trade Barriers Against Primary and Processed Commodities." World Bank Policy Research Paper No. 1174. Washington, D.C.

___. 1994. "The North American Free Trade Agreement: Its Effect on South Asia." *Journal of Asian Economics,* Summer.

Stern, Robert, et. al. 1976. *Price Elasticities in International Trade.* London: Macmillan Press.

UNCTAD. 1968. *The Kennedy Round: Estimated Effects on Tariff Barriers.* New York: United Nations.

___. 1982. *Assessment of the Results of the Multilateral Trade Negotiations.* (TD/B/778/Rev.1). New York: United Nations, 1982.

___. 1986. *Protectionism and Structural Adjustment.* New York: United Nations.

United Kingdom Political and Economic Planning Commission. 1962. *Atlantic Tariffs and Trade.* London: UKPEP.

USITC. 1989. *The Economic Effects of Significant U.S. Import Restraints, Phase I: Manufacturing.* Washington, DC: USITC Publication No. 2222, October.

Varangis, Panayotis, Carlos A. Primo Braga, and Kenji Takeuchi. 1993. "Tropical Timber Trade Policies: What Impact will Eco-Labeling Have?". World Bank Policy Research Working Paper No. 1156. Washington, D.C.

World Bank-UNCTAD. 1989. *A User's Manual for SMART.* Washington, DC.

World Bank. 1992. *Global Economic Prospects and the Developing Countries.* Washington, DC: World Bank, April.

Yeats, Alexander. 1981. "Agricultural Protectionism: An Analysis of its International Effects and Options for Institutional Reform." *Trade and Development: An UNCTAD Review,* Winter.

___. 1984. "On the Analysis of Tariff Escalation: Is There a Methodological Bias Against the Interest of Developing Countries?". *Journal of Development Economics.* Vol.15, Spring.

___. 1987. "The Escalation of Trade Barriers" in J. Michael Finger and Andrzej Olechowski (eds.), The Uruguay Round: A Handbook on the Multilateral Trade Negotiations. Washington, DC: World Bank, November.

___. 1994. "What Are OECD Trade Preferences Worth to Sub-Saharan Africa." World Bank Policy Research Working Paper. Washington, D.C

Appendix

Box A.1
The Geographic Destination of Egyptian Exports: 1965 to 1992

While Table 1 provides information on the current destination of Egypt's exports one would also want to know how the relative importance of different markets has changed. If an important shift occurred more attention should be given to changes in access conditions for markets that were gaining in relative importance and less to those which were declining.

Destination of Egyptian Exports

Year	World	All OECD	OECD Europe	North America	Japan	All Non-OECD	Eastern Europe	Middle East
Value of exports in terms of US $ millions								
1965-67	591,695	160,360	125,896	16,106	17,904	431,335	267,758	17,834
1970-72	792,066	162,302	123,127,4	9,062	29,990	629,793	448,612	36,713
1975-77	1,543,977	485,549	12,171	31,958	41,336	1,058,970	760,255	102,368
1980-82	3,132,778	1,821,143	1,538,343	180,159	102,559	1,311,634	343,701	502,836
1985-87	2,029,883	970,913	830,608	86,116	53,570	1,058,428	447,741	293,746
1990-92	3,108,179	1,634,028	1,297,845	269,469	65,399	1,474,150	340,888	611,774
Share of Total Egyptian Exports								
1965-67	100.0	27.1	21.2	2.7	3.0	72.9	45.2	3.0
1970-72	100.0	20.5	15.5	1.1	3.8	79.5	56.6	4.6
1975-77	100.0	31.4	26.7	2.1	2.7	68.5	49.2	6.6
1980-82	100.0	58.1	49.1	5.8	3.3	41.9	10.9	16.1
1985-87	100.0	47.8	40.9	4.2	2.7	52.2	22.1	14.5
1990-92	100.0	52.6	41.8	8.7	2.1	47.4	11.0	19.7

The above statistics show the share of Egypt's exports destined for OECD and other markets for select intervals over the periods 1965-67 to 1990-92. Two key trends are apparent. First, the growing relative importance of OECD markets is clear as the share of exports going to these destinations roughly doubled. Within the OECD, Europe was the dominant market, absorbing 42 percent of Egypt's exports. Second, the above statistics show a major decline in exports destined for Eastern Europe – a development that was accelerated by the break up of the former Soviet Union (in 1970-72 the FSU received 37 percent of Egypt's exports). Another noteworthy point concerns the rapid increase in Egypt's exports to other ME countries as this share increased more than six-fold between the periods 1965-67 and 1990-92.*

The importance of European markets for Egyptian trade prospects is clear. Thus, developments relating to the formation of the EU, further regional integration arrangements (particularly with Eastern Europe), or the impact of the Uruguay Round on European trade barriers should receive priority attention. Since North America receives less than 10 percent of Egypt's total exports, it is unlikely that NAFTA will have important direct implications for Egypt. However, the indirect effects could be important if countries which are displaced in North America attempt to shift these exports to Europe thereby increasing competitive pressures on Egypt.

---

* *In 1992, 40 percent of Egypt's exports to the region went to Israel and 30 percent went to Saudi Arabia. Crude petroleum accounted for about 95 percent of the shipments to Israel. About 40 percent of Egypt's exports to Saudi Arabia were live animals, fresh fruit, and fresh vegetables.*

Box A.2
Secular Changes in the Composition of
Egyptian Exports: 1965 to 1992

Historically, major changes have occurred in the commodity structure of Egypt's exports with a key factor being the increase in the importance of petroleum and petroleum-based products.* In addition, the volatility in international prices of energy goods has been a major factor causing the sizable year-to-year changes of petroleum and other groups' shares in total exports. For example, in 1980-82 mineral fuels accounted for about 65 percent of total exports, but by the early 1990s the share had fallen to about 44 percent. According to UNCTAD (1992, Table 2.7) crude petroleum prices fell by approximately 40 percent over the decade.

Product Group as a Percentage of Total Egyptian Exports

| | | | | | | of which: | | |
Year	Total Exports ($ million)	All Foods	Agricul- tural Material	Fuels	Ores & Non- Ferrous Metals	All Mfgs.	Textiles	Clothing
1965-67	591,695	16.7	54.5	5.4	1.6	21.6	16.1	0.4
1970-72	792,066	18.2	48.5	4.1	0.4	28.7	17.9	1.8
1975-77	1,543,977	18.6	32.1	20.0	1.5	27.7	15.3	3.4
1980-82	3,132,778	7.1	15.1	65.0	3.5	9.2	6.7	0.6
1985-87	2,029,883	8.0	13.0	51.2	6.0	21.8	16.7	1.3
1990-92	3,108,179	9.5	4.7	43.8	6.4	35.5	15.6	5.2

Note: 1992 Major Export Items in Each Group and Share of Group Total
  (i) Foods – Fresh Vegetables (SITC 054) - 28%; Rice (SITC 042) - 17%;
  (ii) Agricultural Materials – Cotton (SITC 263) - 56%; Crude Vegetable Material
      (SITC 292) - 30%
  (iii) Fuels – Crude Petroleum (SITC 331) - 87%
  (iv) Ores and Nonferrous Metals – Aluminum (SITC 684) - 90%
  (v) Manufactures – Textile Yarn (SITC 651) - 23%; Clothing (SITC 841) - 15%

The relative importance of agricultural raw materials in Egypt's exports has also changed – the share of these goods fell from about 55 percent in the mid-1960s to under 5 percent today. Cotton was the major product accounting for this decline as the value of cotton exports in 1992 ($53 million) was about six times lower than in 1965 ($337 million). Part of the decline is accounted for by further local processing of domestically produced cotton into yarns, textiles and clothing, although the international price competitiveness of Egyptian cotton has also declined.

Increased aluminum exports account for almost all of the change in the ores, minerals and nonferrous metals group. The share of manufactures in Egypt's exports increased by approximately 14 percentage points over the period with textile yarn, clothing, iron and steel products, and manufactured fertilizers accounting for much of the increase.

Although the share of food products in Egypt's total exports declined by about 7 percentage points (to 9.5 percent), several items within this sector (cereal preparations, fresh meat, fresh fish) recorded growth rates that were among the highest for any three-digit SITC product group (see Table 6). Since increased agricultural production and exports could help alleviate rural poverty, special attention should focus on the removal of foreign trade barriers facing these goods.

---

* Egypt has departed from established UN practices and does not include petroleum produced and exported by foreign firms in its official trade statistics. Exclusion of these shipments causes Egypt's annual exports to be under-reported by some $1 to $1.5 billion.

Box A.3
Egypt's Largest Three-Digit Global Exports: 1970-72, 1980-82 and 1990-92

As was the case with all regional countries as a group, major changes have occurred in the structure of Egyptian exports over the last two decades. The following statistics based on 1970-72, 1980- 82 and 1990-92 exports (three year averages were used to reduce the importance of any irregularities that might occur in a single year), show how the shares of major three-digit SITC export products have changed. Altogether, the 20 items listed below currently account for approximately 85 percent of Egypt's total exports and have made up as much as 95 percent in 1980-82. An important point to note is that these data understate the true importance of petroleum (by about $1 to $1.5 billion) due to Egypt's unusual practice of not reporting oil produced and exported by foreign firms in its official export statistics.

Description (SITC)	Value of Exports ($000)			Percent of Total Exports (%)		
	1970-72	1980-82	1990-92	1970-72	1980-82	1990-92
Crude Petroleum (331)	29,267	1,750,025	1,111,555	3.7	55.9	35.8
Textile Yarn and Thread (651)	88,106	159,023	317,069	11.1	5.1	10.2
Petroleum Products (332)	2,527	284,602	190,409	0.3	9.1	6.1
Aluminum (684)	227	90,397	185,127	--	2.9	6.0
Nonfur Clothing (841)	14,094	19,415	160,855	1.8	0.6	5.2
Cotton (263)	376,354	446,766	107,443	47.5	14.3	3.5
Cotton Fabrics (652)	40,881	36,334	88,505	5.2	1.2	2.8
Fresh Vegetables (054)	25,605	57,158	80,340	3.2	1.8	2.6
Fresh Fruit and Nuts Dry (051)	16,715	52,179	56,163	2.1	1.7	1.8
Natural Gas (341)	4	0	45,764	--	0.0	1.5
Furniture (821)	6,296	2,669	41,035	0.8	0.1	1.3
Rice (042)	61,887	29,811	38,806	7.8	1.0	1.2
Textile Products, nes (656)	6,208	7,658	36,682	0.8	0.2	1.2
Perfumes and Cosmetics (553)	4,247	4,591	28,414	0.5	0.1	0.9
Crude Vegetable Materials (292)	2,438	11,140	27,730	0.3	0.4	0.9
Floor Coverings (657)	5,044	6,192	27,647	0.6	0.2	0.9
Iron and Steel Shapes (673)	225	121	25,219	--	--	0.8
Chemicals, nes (599)	182	266	22,535	--	--	0.7
Manufactured Fertilizers (561)	1,786	838	21,546	0.2	--	0.7
Medicinal Products (541)	2,051	6,298	20,519	0.3	0.2	0.7
TOTAL OF ALL ABOVE ITEMS	**684,144**	**2,965,483**	**2,633,263**	**86.2**	**94.8**	**84.8**

Perhaps the two most striking statistics relate to crude petroleum (irrespective of the under-reporting problem) and cotton. Petroleum's share in total exports rose almost ten-fold between 1970-72 and 1990-92 and now accounts for almost 36 percent of all exports (41.9 percent if refined petroleum products are also included). It is worth noting that crude petroleum generally faces no, or very limited, OECD trade barriers so a large share of Egyptian exports would not be affected by either OECD integration efforts or the Uruguay Round.* However, the textile and clothing products that are among Egypt's major exports will certainly be affected by the multi-fiber arrangement (MFA) phase-out. Whether this is a positive or negative development will depend on Egypt's ability to compete on even terms with other developing countries.

---

* *With the exception of those products for which Egypt does not receive important GSP preferences and to which high MFN tariffs are applied. In North America, textiles, clothing and footwear products do not receive either GSP or Caribbean Basin Initiative preferences so the potential for a sizable NAFTA-induced displacement may exist. However, Safadi and Yeats (1994) and Primo Braga, Safadi and Yeats (1994) show that Mexico appears to have important supply constraints that should limit its capacity to displace third country exports to the United States.*

Box A.4
Egypt's Largest Three-Digit Regional Exports: 1970-72, 1980-82 and 1990-92

What is Egypt exporting to the region and how has the product composition of this exchange been changing? The following tabulations show that crude petroleum accounts for over 50 percent of Egypt's intra-regional exports – up from approximately 2 percent in the early 1970s (the share of petroleum may be even higher given Egypt's practice of not including foreign company exports in official trade data). Approximately 97 percent of the petroleum exports go to Israel, with small amounts destined for Turkey and the UAE. Foodstuffs play an important role in Egypt's intra-regional trade as these products comprise four of Egypt's eight largest three-digit exports. In 1992, 55 percent of Egypt's total intra-regional food exports went to Saudi Arabia, 12 percent to Libya and 15 percent to Syria and Lebanon combined.

Description (SITC)	Value of Exports ($000)			Percent of Total Exports (%)		
	1970-72	1980-82	1990-92	1970-72	1980-82	1990-92
Crude Petroleum (331)	705	395,830	268,777	1.9	78.7	53.5
Fresh Vegetables (054)	1,611	16,518	36,282	4.4	3.3	7.2
Rice (042)	7,778	5,048	24,864	21.2	1.0	4.9
Textile Yarn (651)	2,487	1,146	19,061	6.8	0.2	3.8
Fresh Fruit and Nuts (051)	774	16,051	14,581	2.1	3.2	2.9
Aluminum (684)	0	7,012	14,401	0.0	1.4	2.9
Live Animals (001)	1,550	21,155	14,259	4.2	4.0	2.8
Nonfur Clothing (841)	323	677	13,837	0.9	0.1	2.8
Medicinal Products (541)	721	4,443	11,140	2.0	0.9	2.2
Iron and Steel Shapes (673)	27	121	9,957	0.1	--	2.0
Cotton Fabrics (652)	3,373	4,443	9,643	9.2	0.9	1.9
Chemicals, nes (599)	5	70	6,877	--	--	1.4
Footwear (821)	10	256	6,208	--	0.1	1.2
Natural Gas (341)	4	0	5,970	--	0.0	1.2
Petroleum Products (332)	325	0	5,100	0.9	0.0	1.0
Furniture (821)	288	649	5,046	0.8	0.1	1.0
Cereal Preparations (048)	84	113	4,796	0.2	--	1.0
Base Metal Household Equip. (697)	67	142	4,583	0.2	--	0.9
Glassware (665)	11	1	4,576	--	--	0.9
Metal Manufactures (698)	151	121	4,520	0.4	--	0.9

Several of the products listed above (textile yarn, nonfur clothing, cotton fabrics and footwear) are normally manufactured by labor intensive production processes so their appearance is something of a surprise. The direction of this exchange conforms to what would be predicted by factor proportions theory as over 50 percent of the shipments of these products go to Saudi Arabia and Libya – both relatively high income and high wage cost countries.

In terms of total intra-regional exports Israel is currently the largest single destination receiving 41 percent of Egypt's exports, followed by Saudi Arabia (28 percent) and Syria (5 percent). These shares, however, are highly affected by oil exports. When petroleum is excluded, Saudi Arabia emerges as the largest destination receiving 48 percent of Egypt's exports followed by Libya with 14 percent. In contrast, Israel only receives under 3 percent of non-energy goods exported by Egypt.

In 1990, the exports of Egypt to Iraq were only $31 million. Thus, the Gulf war has not had a major impact on the structure of intra-regional exports. Four two-digit SITC products: plastics (SITC 58); iron and steel (SITC 67); metal manufactures (SITC 69); and plumbing equipment (SITC 81) accounted for over two-thirds of Egypt's exports to Iraq.

Box A.5
Average Applied Tariffs on Products Egypt Exports to OECD Markets

Do tariffs on Egyptian exports to the OECD discriminate in any important way against particular industries or sectors? Table 12 suggested that the overall level of import duties was low in the EU and Japan (in the one to two percent range) while US duties were higher since this country does not extend GSP treatment to textiles, clothing and footwear. Are there specific sectors where Egypt's exports encounter significantly higher import tariffs? The statistics provided below show average "applied" (in the sense that they are the average of the GSP or MFN duty actually levied) tariffs on Egypt's exports of broad product groups.

Product Group (SITC No.)	1992 OECD Imports from Egypt ($million)	Average Applied Tariff (%)		
		EU	Japan	USA
All Items (0 to 9)	3,898.3	0.6	2.0	4.6
All Foods and Feeds (0+1+22+4)	158.0	12.0	21.2	0.6
Food and Live Animals (0)	153.3	12.2	7.6	0.6
Beverages and Tobacco (1)	0.7	5.6	90.0	1.9
Animal and Vegetable Oils (4)	0.1	0.4	--	--
Agricultural Materials (2-22-27-28)	73.3	0.0	0.0	0.0
Ores & Nonferrous Metals (27+28+68)	180.8	0.0	0.0	0.0
Mineral Fuels (3)	2,429.1	0.0	3.2	0.5
Manufactures (5 to 8-68)	1,020.1	0.0	3.0	8.8
Chemicals (5)	81.3	0.0	0.0	0.0
Textiles (65)	304.3	0.0	4.9	8.3
Transport & Machinery (7)	252.1	0.0	0.0	0.0
Clothing (84)	241.9	0.0	11.0	17.4
Miscellaneous Manufactures (89)	25.1	0.0	0.0	0.0

Source: World Bank-UNCTAD SMART Data Base

The tariff averages show different patterns of protection exist in Japan and the EU as opposed to the United States. Exclusion of textiles and clothing from the United States GSP scheme accounts for the relatively high tariffs (8.8 and 17.4 percent) on these goods, but outside these two sectors import duties average under two percent. In contrast, in the EU and Japan the highest duties are applied to agricultural products (clothing in Japan is an exception) with tariffs of 90 percent facing Egypt's beverage and tobacco exports to Japan (mostly cured tobacco leaf).

Tariff "peaks" are also evident. The highest tariffs in the EU are 35 percent. The are levied on various pastry products exported from Egypt while several jam and fruit preserve products face tariffs between 27 to 30 percent. In the United States, the highest duties Egypt faces range between 33 and 35 percent on clothing products like sweaters and cotton undershirts.

Box A.6
The Impact of Preference Erosion on
Major Egyptian Exports

In 1989 Egypt exported 1,209 different tariff line level products to the EU (EU customs schedules distinguish between some 8,700 individual tariff line items). A zero MFN duty was applied to 120 of these products and the remainder (1,089) were affected by a positive tariff. However, the GSP accorded Egypt tariff preferences on 765 of these lines, i.e, on 70 percent of all lines with MFN tariffs and on 63 percent of all lines exported, which allowed exporters from Egypt to pay no duties or charges below the prevailing rate.* As a result of this preferential access, Egyptian exporters enjoyed a competitive edge over those in countries which faced the MFN tariff.

	Egypt's Exports: Number of Tariff Line Level Products			
Import Market	**Zero MFN Duty Lines**	**Lines With Nonzero MFN Duties**	**Lines Receiving GSP Treatment**	**Total Lines Exported**
European Union	120	1,089	765	1,209
Japan	20	74	48	94
United States	79	306	137	385

Source: World Bank-UNCTAD SMART Database

The above tabulations show the extent to which Egyptian products receive preferential market access in the EU, Japan and US. Egypt receives preferential access on 65 percent of (non-zero MFN) line items exported to Japan and on 45 percent of the shipments to the United States. The relatively low US figure is due to the exclusion of textiles and clothing from this country's GSP scheme.

The following statistics give another perspective on the GSP by showing the share (in terms of values) of total EU, Japan and US imports that are covered by these preferential tariffs. About 15 percent of EU's imports from Egypt receive GSP treatment while the corresponding US and Japanese shares are about 4 percent. Japan's largest imports from Egypt are raw cotton and crude petroleum – products which are imported under zero MFN duties.

	Share of Egypt's Exports Under Different Tariff Regimes			
Import Market	**Zero MFN Tariffs**	**Under Zero GSP Rates**	**Nonzero GSP Rates**	**Nonzero MFN Rates**
European Union	58.3	14.4	0.2	27.1
Japan	40.8	3.7	0.1	55.4
United States	12.0	3.9	0.0	84.1

Source: World Bank-UNCTAD SMART Database

The Uruguay Round made substantial reductions in OECD countries' MFN tariffs – about 40 percent on average (see Table 13). These cuts will reduce the margins of preference that Egypt's exports formerly received – the margins would be completely eliminated if the MFN rate were cut to zero. As a result of this reduction (or elimination) of preferences, some of Egypt's exports could be displaced by other countries that formerly faced MFN duties. How large this displacement will be depends on the ability of Egyptian exporters to offset these competitive losses. It should be noted, however, that Egypt would experience positive export gains on those items where it faced MFN tariffs that were cut in the Round. (See Box 7 for estimates of the size of these positive and negative effects).

---

* *There is a complication in that ceilings or quotas may be applied to products receiving GSP treatment in OECD markets. Once these quotas are exceeded, further imports are taxed at the prevailing MFN tariff rate.*

Box A.7
The Nature of Egypt's Uruguay Round Induced Export Changes

Table 14 suggested that the Uruguay Round tariff cuts should produce only minor gains for Egypt – probably about $20 million in increased exports to the EU, Japan and US combined. The possibility exists that this aggregate figure may conceal important differences in the effects on various product sectors. The statistics provided below examine this possibility by showing the projected gains and losses for major product groups exported to the EU and United States.

Product Group (SITC No.)	1992 Imports ($000)	Projected Trade Change Value ($ 000)	Percent Change (%)
EUROPEAN UNION			
All Items (0 to 9)	2,893,427.0	8,680.3	0.30
All Foods and Feeds (0+1+22+4)	111,294.4	8,224.7	7.39
Agricultural Materials (2-22-27-28)	26,549.4	2.7	0.01
Ores & Nonferrous Metals (27+28+68)	126,555.1	-189.8	-0.15
Mineral Fuels (3)	1,969.5	-1.6	-0.08
Manufactures (5 to 8-68)	649,156.4	644.3	0.10
Textiles (65)	168,934.9	-270.3	-0.16
Clothing (84)	83,064.3	-91.4	-0.11
UNITED STATES			
All Items (0 to 9)	465,598.3	11,220.9	2.41
All Foods and Feeds (0+1+22+4)	6,230.3	16.2	0.26
Agricultural Materials (2-22-27-28)	6,210.0	-7.5	-0.12
Ores & Nonferrous Metals (27+28+68)	312.7	-1.2	-0.37
Mineral Fuels (3)	242.4	0.8	0.34
Manufactures (5 to 8-68)	191,698.0	11,212.6	5.84
Textiles (65)	42,493.1	871.1	2.05
Clothing (84)	122,678.5	4,858.1	3.96

Source: World Bank-UNCTAD SMART Database.

In the European Union, the Uruguay Round tariff cuts on food products should lead to an increase in Egypt's exports by about $8 million which represents about 7 percent growth. Small net gains are also projected for the manufactures sector as a whole in spite of losses associated with the erosion of preferences on textiles and clothing.

In the United States, Egypt's projected trade gains are concentrated in the manufactures sector with over 50 percent of the increase accounted for by increased textile and clothing exports. Outside manufactures, very small positive or negative changes are projected. The decline for agricultural materials is almost entirely associated with the erosion of GSP preferences for several combed or carded wool products. Erosion of preferences for refined copper products accounts for the slight decline within the ores and nonferrous metals group.

Box A.8
Nontariff Measures Facing Egypt's Major Exports

Compared to the situation facing developing countries in total, Egypt's exports do not appear to be more affected by OECD nontariff measures. As shown below, 17.6 percent of all shipments to the US face NTMs, while the coverage ratio is about 4 points lower in the EU. No NTMs have been reported on Egypt's exports to Japan. Elsewhere, it was found that about 18 percent of all developing countries' exports to the OECD encounter nontariff measures (Low and Yeats, 1994).

Product Group*	1992 Imports from Egypt ($ million)			Egypt's NTM C overage Ratios (%)		
	EU	Japan	USA	EU	Japan	USA
All Items	2,893.4	91.0	465.6	13.2	0.0	17.6
All Foods and Feeds	114.6	0.4	6.2	19.6	0.0	0.0
Food and Live Animals	111.3	0.4	5.9	19.8	0.0	0.0
Beverages and Tobacco	0.2	--	0.3	47.4	0.0	0.0
Animal and Vegetable Oils	--	0.0	--	0.0	--	--
Agricultural Materials	26.5	21.9	6.2	0.0	0.0	0.3
Ores & Nonferrous Metals	126.6	2.0	0.3	0.0	0.0	0.0
Mineral Fuels	1,969.5	57.0	242.4	0.0	0.0	0.0
Manufactures	649.2	9.1	191.7	69.5	0.0	40.2
Chemicals	72.0	0.1	2.2	0.0	0.0	0.0
Textiles	168.9	2.5	42.5	98.6	0.0	87.0
Transport & Machinery	245.1	--	1.7	0.0	0.0	0.0
Clothing	83.1	0.1	122.7	95.5	0.0	34.3
Miscellaneous Manufactures	6.9	0.4	14.5	0.0	0.0	0.0

See Box 6 for the SITC numbers of the product groups.

Coverage ratios well above the average affect Egypt's textile and clothing exports to the EU and US, and foodstuffs exported to the EU. European MFA restrictions are applied to almost all of Egypt's textile and clothing exports with quotas on cotton yarns primarily responsible for the 98 percent coverage ratio for SITC 65.

Foodstuffs exported to the EU also have relatively high NTM coverage ratios due to the application of two or three different types of measures. For example, Egypt's exports of cane molasses (its largest food export with over $9 million traded) face variable import levies while globe artichokes and fresh oranges encounter reference import prices. Tariff quotas are applied to most EU bovine meat imports while quotas are applied to coffee and coffee-based food preparation.

The tariffication of agricultural NTBs (and reduction in associated levels of protection) could lead to increases in world prices of previously subsidized agricultural products, including cereals, meat, dairy products and sugar. Price increases should occur because of the increased international demand for agricultural products associated with a lowering of OECD trade barriers and the new Uruguay Round regulations regarding subsidies. These changes would benefit developing countries which are important exporters of these products. Some studies have concluded that prices of some previously subsidized products could rise by 4 to 10 percent in total when the full effects of the Round are felt.

A number of developing countries which are net food importers have expressed concern about possible higher food prices. Provided that these higher prices are passed on to farmers there will be an offsetting increase in domestic production. Nevertheless, if world food prices do rise, those countries that remain net importers of food will incur higher costs. Probably the best way to counter such a development is through the adoption of efficiency and cost cutting reforms to help stimulate domestic agricultural production.

The Uruguay Round and Trade in Financial Services in the Arab Countries*

Introduction

Rapid advances in information and telecommunication technology are expanding the boundaries of tradability in services – the fastest growing component of both trade and foreign direct investment. Until recently, it was common to view the services sector as a collection of mainly non-tradeable activities with low productivity growth potential. This conventional view of services is fast changing; the development of certain services activities is increasingly being regarded not as a consequence of common growth but as one of its preconditions. Trade in commercial services has grown faster than trade in merchandise over the past decade.[1] Commercial services encompass transport, travel, insurance and financial services among others. Services now account for close to one-quarter of world trade. The internationalization of services will likely lead to the next stage of economic globalization.[2] Liberalization of trade in services provides for important new opportunities and at the same time brings new challenges for developing countries and for the countries in the Middle East and North Africa (MENA) region as well.

This chapter discusses the prospects for trade liberalization in services, specifically in financial services, for developing countries in general and Arab countries in particular. It is worth noting at the outset that assessing the impact of liberalization of trade in financial services is a difficult task. Meaningful data on flows of financial services by category and by trading partners are not available. Cross-country comparisons regarding the costs of providing the service do not exist.[3] Apart from the OECD data set for 1984-85, which was published in 1990 in restricted distribution,[4] other publications such as those of the International Monetary Fund (IMF) do not provide adequate data for empirical analysis of trade in financial services. Moreover, the analytical literature does not sufficiently cover the special economic characteristics of financial services that take place over time, that is, banking; or those between agents, such as retailing and wholesale.[5] Accordingly, this chapter adopts a cautious approach in its assessment of the prospects of freeing trade in financial

* The authors wish to thank Sübidey Togan, Bernard Hoekman and the participants of the ERF Conference on Trade Liberalization in Istanbul, Turkey for helpful comments. The first author wishes also to thank John Whalley for useful discussions and Rania Sherif and Mohamed El-Baz for excellent research assistance. The usual disclaimers apply.

services in selected Arab countries.

The chapter is organized in seven sections. The following section discusses the achievements of the Uruguay Round in the area of trade in services. The next section highlights the characteristics of trade in services, including trade in banking services, regulation and protection of services, and the different kinds of barriers to trade in financial services. Then, the chapter discusses financial liberalization and the issue of appropriate sequencing, and then compares the commitments undertaken in the General Agreement on Trade in Services (GATS) and those that are found in regional agreements with respect to liberalization in the services sector. The next section highlights the distinctive characteristics of the structure of the banking system and its regulation in selected Arab countries. The final section offers some concluding remarks.

The Uruguay Round

The Uruguay Round (UR) was the eighth time in which contracting parties (now Member countries following the establishment of the World Trade Organization on 1 January 1995) negotiated on a multilateral basis the reduction of tariffs and non-tariff barriers (NTBs) to trade. The UR was the most comprehensive and hence complex round of multilateral trade negotiations (MTNs) ever undertaken. It was entrusted with a comprehensive agenda which aimed, among other things, to deal with shortcomings of the General Agreement on Tariffs and Trade (GATT) which were undermining the institution's systemic integrity. The UR was in addition unique from the viewpoint of developing countries. More than ever developing countries engaged actively as their interests in the UR's outcome heightened. At stake were issues that concerned: (i) the extension of trade liberalization in traditional areas as well as in areas not yet covered by the GATT; (ii) bringing trade that has moved outside the multilateral framework back into the GATT; (iii) bringing discipline to the trade-related aspects of intellectual property; (iv) enhancing the provisions concerning trade-related investment measures; (v) providing a framework of principles, rules and disciplines on trade in services; (vi) improving the rules and dispute settlement system of the GATT; and (vii) the creation of a World Trade Organisation, and doing so as a single undertaking.[6]

The inclusion of trade in services and trade-related investment measures (TRIMs) under the umbrella of the WTO has brought a vast new sphere of economic activity within the purview of the multilateral trading system. While services exports accounted for some 17 percent of world trade in 1980, the share had risen to over 22 percent in 1993. Annual average growth in services trade was approximately 8 percent from 1980 to 1993, compared to some 4 percent for merchandise trade. Moreover, it is important to note that the preferred choice for delivery of many services is through commercial presence of a supplier in the jurisdiction of consumers. And foreign direct investment (FDI) in services industries has been the most dynamic component of international FDI flows (Safadi, 1997).

Notwithstanding the fact that the General Agreement on Trade in Services (GATS) is the most comprehensive attempt to negotiate services liberalization based on reciprocity, the Agreement is a cautious one. It provides signatories with ample scope to condition their multilateral commitments. The GATS rests on the concept of the most-favored nation (MFN) treatment. MFN is a general obligation, though its application is subject to a negative list approach to the extent that countries may invoke exemptions to MFN for specific industries and for a limited time. Market access and national treatment are, however, specific obligations in the sense that they apply only to identified services activities listed by each country in its schedule of commitments at the level of each mode of supply and subject to the limitations made explicit in the offer;[7] in other words, a conditional positive list approach has been adopted in defining the coverage of the commitments.

If one examines the commitments of developing countries (LDCs) with respect to trade in services in the Uruguay Round, it seems clear that the majority of these countries did not use the GATS negotiations as a vehicle to promote further liberalization of their services industries. This is not a surprising finding to the extent that the GATS results entail mainly a standstill promise in terms of protectionist policies, that is, a commitment not to introduce new distortions in the services sector. Nonetheless, LDCs covered fewer services in their commitments than did industrial countries. Tourism and travel–related services were the only activities in which a substantial number of developing countries made commitments. By late 1994, seventy eight developing countries had offered commitments in services, indicating their support for multilateral discipline for services.[8]

Table 1 breaks down the number of commitments in services activities by region. North America was the region most committed to liberalization of services activities, followed by Western Europe. The MENA region stands out as the one which offered the lowest number of commitments compared to other regions (106). As a percentage of maximum possible services commitments, the only other region which offered less than the MENA region was Africa. Thus, it is evident that the countries in the MENA region remain the least convinced of the necessity to subject their service providers to the rigors of international competition.

Table 1. Commitments on Market Access for Services

Country Group[9]	Number of commitments in services	Services commitments as share of maximum possible (%)
High-income countries	2423	53.8
Developing countries	2159	17.2
North America	193	59.9
Latin America	738	15.3
Western Europe	2002	59.2
Central Europe	351	43.6
Africa	396	9.8
Middle East	106	16.5
Asia	796	26.0

Source: GATT 1994, reprinted in World Bank (1995).

Trade in Services

Two particular features of services activities that distinguish them from production and trade in goods should be noted at the outset. First, production and consumption of a service may occur simultaneously, since no possibility exists of storing certain services produced now for consumption later. In such cases, a transaction requires that the consumer and the supplier of the service must be in one location. For other services, arms-length supply is not possible since the service is not transportable. This implies that if a government grants market access rights to foreign suppliers in relation to non-storable or non-transportable services, it may have to accept either that foreign enterprises can establish a commercial presence in its territory, or that the service suppliers in question may enter its territory on a temporary basis. Traditional banking and insurance services can, in principle, be supplied at arms-length since loans could be secured by mail or phone and insurance policies are often so purchased (Bhagwati, 1987). The second distinguishing feature of services activities is that they tend to be subject to a greater degree of regulatory supervision than are physical goods. In part, this reflects concerns about consumer protection, or in case of financial services, prudential issues.

International trade is traditionally seen as an activity involving the movement of goods across borders. However, a quarter of world trade flows, representing some $600 billion annually, is now accounted for by services such as banking, insurance and telecommunications (Watkins, 1992). These exports have become increasingly significant to the OECD economies where the services sector now accounts on average for half of national income (70 percent in the United States). This is not a surprising result in view of the fact that services industries rely heavily on information technology which is a high capital, high skill industry. In addition, OECD countries have been exhibiting the highest total factor productivity (TFP) in the services sector. For example, TFP in transportation and communication in OECD countries rose 2.4 percent on an annual basis during the period 1979-93, three times faster than the 0.8 percent overall TFP growth rate during the same period (World Bank, 1995). In summary, the export advantage in many services as revealed by existing patterns of trade in services, seems to lie substantially with the OECD countries.

Services account for nearly 20 percent of total exports of goods and services from OECD countries to developing countries, but only 7 percent of total trade flows in the opposite direction. Because LDCs are net importers of services, they have not offered wholehearted support to the GATS. Developing countries fear that many of their own services industries are insufficiently developed to withstand foreign competition.

Trade in Banking Services

The most used estimates of trade in services, in general, are derived from the IMF's reports on Balance of Payment (BOP). The reports use trade in invisibles to refer to transactions that relate neither to goods nor to capital flows. Remaining services, which appear in one miscellaneous category, cover a wide range of financial and non-financial transactions such as insurance, commissions, advertising, and so forth. Clearly, separating financial services on a functional basis using the BOP reports is not possible.[10] A direct measure of the value of each financial service traded internationally is required. As suggested by Whalley (1995), this measure should include all fees and charges received by domestic banks from non-residents and has to adequately cover the value of financial intermediation. It is worth noting that the treatment of financial services within an economy requires the same suggested improvement which should be reflected in the national accounts.

The methodology developed by Whalley (1995) to estimate international trade in banking services in three developed countries can in principle be replicated to derive similar statistics for the Arab countries, Turkey and Iran. Because the BOP estimates do not distinguish between the different components of receipts and payments related to banking services, Whalley constructed estimates for international trade in banking provided by domestic and foreign intermediaries:

The method used involves applying estimates of the spread between deposit and lending rates both for US, UK, and Canadian banks and banks in their largest partner countries to corresponding data on assets and liabilities of both domestic banks with non-residents, and with non-resident banks with residents. These yield an estimate of the value of intermediation services provided by domestic banks to both depositors and borrowers abroad, and by non-resident banks to domestic depositors and borrowers. The combined financial intermediation charge is apportioned between the parties to calculate the internationally traded component. (Whalley, 1995, p. 29)

Whalley's results, which assume that the costs are borne equally by depositors and borrowers are summarized in Table 2 below. Unfortunately, most of the data required for this straightforward exercise are not available for any country in the MENA region.

Table 2: Estimates of International Trade in Financial Intermediation Services, US, UK, and Canada in 1984 (billions of US dollars)

	USA	UK	Canada
Estimate of exports of banking services	4.03	2.55	0.72
Estimate of imports of banking services	3.04	4.40	0.42

Source: Whalley (1995).

Regulation and Protection of Services

As has been stated earlier, regulation applies more pervasively to services than to goods' trade. Since fraud and sub-standard output may be difficult or impossible to detect and prevent before the damage is done, governments feel obliged to control supply ex ante rather than output on an ex post basis. Another consideration is that some services sectors, such as banking, have economy-wide effects, such that regulation erring on the side of caution is considered necessary to avoid the widespread damage that would be caused by specific sectoral failures. What this regulatory difference between services and goods implies is that, while local establishment by a foreign entity to provide a service will permit the fulfillment of local regulatory criteria, sale of such services from a base abroad will not. (Bhagwati, 1987).

Services industries are heavily protected by investment regulations. Such regulations are especially extensive in LDCs where governments regard the development of indigenous financial services industries as vital for both social and economic reasons. Hesitant LDCs regard some services activities, such as banking, as part of their infrastructure which they must control for political reasons. The structure of LDCs' banking sector illustrates some of the factors that underline state intervention. In the majority of LDCs, there are two sub-markets where the banking sector operates: a well diversified modern sector integrated with insurance and other operations, and a relatively underdeveloped rural sector. The latter, which serves the vast majority of agricultural producers, has limited access to capital and operates with lower returns because of income differentials between rural and urban sectors. Countries have several devices for protecting domestic suppliers of services from foreign competition. These include, inter alia, visa requirements, investment regulations and restrictions on the ability to repatriate earnings.

A feature common to many services activities is that they are used as intermediate inputs. For example, banking and insurance services translate to higher costs of providing the service. This not only impedes the development of efficient banking and insurance sectors and their ability to compete in the international market, but in addition, it hinders export opportunities of goods. The effects of protecting intermediate services are similar to those that result from raising the cost of intermediate inputs used in goods production. In some instances, such as in the present example of banking and insurance services, protective policies not only deny access to cheaper credit, but in addition, they deny exporters access to the entire vector of services that modern international banks can provide so as to facilitate international commerce. Therefore, the protection of intermediate services generates direct and indirect costs both of which have not been presumably properly assessed by LDCs (Bhagwati, 1987).

There is a wide variety of policy instruments that can be used to restrict access to markets. Five broad categories of policy instruments can be distinguished as impediments to trade in services:
i)   measures that are quantity-based (that is, those that explicitly restrict the volume or value of transactions);
ii) those that are price-based;
iii) those that require physical or commercial presence in a market;
iv) those relating to standards, certification requirements and industry-specific regulations, and
v)   measures relating to government procurement practices and subsidization.

Quantitative restrictions and standards are the most important access restrictions in the services context. Although import tariffs rarely impede trade in services, price controls are common. These involve either price-setting by government agencies and/or price monitoring and approval procedures. Examples of services activities that are subject to price controls in many countries include financial services.

Sapir (1985) argues that many modern services activities embody technology. The acquisition of these services is equivalent to technological transfer. Therefore, import of certain services leads to capital accumulation which will have a wholly beneficial effect on the development and future patterns of trade. The newly industrialized countries all have small positive patterns of trade, but they have been successful in accumulating human and physical capital.

Barriers to Trade in Financial Services

Barriers to trade in financial services have existed for many years, but in recent years they have experienced significant growth. Such barriers are measures that accord different treatment to competing domestic and foreign suppliers of the same financial service.[11] In the selected sample of countries in the Middle East, these barriers include one or more of the following:[12]

1. Discrimination against services supplied to the domestic consumers by foreign-based firms.
2. Limitations on the establishment of branches for foreign financial firms.
3. Various restrictions on the activities of foreign firms in the domestic markets, and so forth, restriction on the number of branches and their location and constraints on the transfer of profits.
4. Certain restrictions on the number of foreign staff and their movement in the host country.

These restrictions have existed for a long time and were introduced historically for different reasons. Exploring the underlying reasons will help us better understand the position of the sampled countries in respect of their hesitation to liberalize trade in services all the while providing some policy initiatives that would help to alleviate any possible negative effects of the removal of these barriers. These reasons can be grouped under six main categories:

1) OECD countries enjoy a comparative advantage over LDCs in the services sector. Recent regression estimates show that countries with relatively abundant human capital have a comparative advantage in insurance and other financial services.[13] One response may be to protect the financial service industry in LDCs. However, this response is based on a static understanding of comparative advantage. Accumulation of physical and human capital would help a developing country to gain a comparative advantage over time in certain financial services.

2) We argue that even if a developing country manages to accumulate physical and human capital, this would not be necessarily reflected in substantial gains in the international financial industry in which reputation has an

important role to play. Hence, efficient new entrants in the market of international financial services will not be able to compete with well-established firms, especially when customers are not adequately equipped to differentiate between the products supplied by the new and old firms through the study of their characteristics and attributes. So, if a developing country manages to improve its comparative advantage in financial services, a developed country would still be in a superior position owing to both its comparative and competitive advantages. This enforces the argument for protection or at least according a developing country a differential treatment in the competition game.

3) The previous two issues indicate that the infant industry argument may be a relevant one for the financial services industry in LDCs; they in addition help explain why the majority of LDCs were reluctant to offer more GATS commitments as they feared for the very survival of their domestic financial services industry. Their fear is justified by the fact that the internationally traded financial services are based on sophisticated technology and are capital-intensive, in both human and physical terms.[14]

4) The financial repression school views the sector as a source of cheap funding for the public sector and the state budget deficit in LDCs. This school believes that allowing foreign firms to enter the domestic market would jeopardize the stability of such funding and raise its costs.

5) The experience of LDCs with foreign banks, before and after independence, has not overall been very satisfactory. Foreign banks have been regarded as institutions that more often than not concentrate their activities in short term credits which are usually directed towards financing trade and a few services. They are also accused of cream skimming.[15]

6) In addition, LDCs had other reasons for erecting barriers to trade in financial services such as controlling key sectors of the economy as a way of ensuring their independence and national security; employment policy that favors the employment of nationals, and so forth.[16]

Financial Liberalization

Following the conclusion of the Uruguay Round and reaching a WTO deal on freer trade in financial services,[17] LDCs are now encouraged to liberalize their financial restrictions that discriminate between domestic and foreign providers. Technological innovations, especially in information technology, together with liberalization are contributing to rapid movement of capital across borders in pursuit of the best available returns, and that these flows are increasingly independent of trade in goods. According to Peter Drucker, "capital movements unconnected to trade – and indeed largely independent of it – greatly exceed trade finance." He cites two sets of figures to support this conclusion: first, the London Eurodollar market, where the world's financial institutions borrow from and lend to each other, turns over of world trade; second, foreign exchange transactions, in which one currency is traded against another, run to 35 trillion dollars a year – twelve times global trade in goods and services (Kakabadse, 1987).

No single event accounts for the outburst of capital flows, but the speed of change is such that the politics and economics of deregulation in capital markets have received less attention than they deserve. Deregulation in one financial market inevitably leads to some deregulation in another if the latter is to remain attractive to investors. Simultaneously, protectionist measures that discriminate against foreign suppliers are exacting heavy tolls on the domestic economy: this denies the economy access to new technologies and it limits the development of financial instruments. More efficient markets are being demanded by users as technology continues to decrease the economic distance among nations.

Although different countries may have different political reasons to move to deregulate their domestic markets, they all share the desire to stimulate competition and to attract more international financial business. Overall, the pronounced deregulatory drive reflects the intense competition between different financial centers and also the inability or unwillingness of governments and central banks to resist the changes that the accelerating pace of international capital flows is forcing upon them. As far as the banks are concerned, these changes are apparently quite timely because they coincide with the trend towards investment banking. Commercial banking (converting deposits into loans) is now less important than investment banking (the business of raising funds for customers by underwriting and dealing in securities). For many capital users, securities finance is cheaper and more flexible than loans. With tight government monetary policies limiting the expansion of banks in the foreseeable future, entry into securities has become for many banks the only option to grow. However, the commitment and costs of setting up competitive securities operations in the world's major markets are daunting.

Successful banks will need the widest possible geographical reach, an ability to deal in all the big financial markets, a strong dealing team in securities backed by top-class research and technology, and a wide range of institutional and corporate contacts. International banking is going through a fundamental process of change. Traditionally, it was the jealously guarded flagship of each sovereign state but now it is under pressure to become a single and highly competitive world market with a much wider choice to borrowers and investors. Corporate strategy, once a luxury the banks could do without, is now a condition of survival (Kakabadse, 1987, pp. 29-43).

Sequencing of Financial Liberalization

It has been argued that "the main objectives of external and internal financial liberalization are the integration of the domestic financial market with the international market in order to improve the role of the financial markets in the allocation of resources."[18] However, judging from the liberalization experience in Latin American countries, it is argued that if the domestic financial sector suffers from financial repression and noncompetitive structure, then the external financial liberalization should take place after internal financial liberalization.

Despite the fact that the literature on the issue of sequencing is still inconclusive,[19] there is nonetheless a wide agreement, based again on the Latin American experience, that the domestic financial sector should be liberalized after the reform of the domestic real sector. It is also widely accepted that controls on capital movements should be maintained until the domestic financial sector and the external trade sector are liberalized and until the stabilization program is implemented.[20]

Figure 1: Sequencing of Economic Liberalization

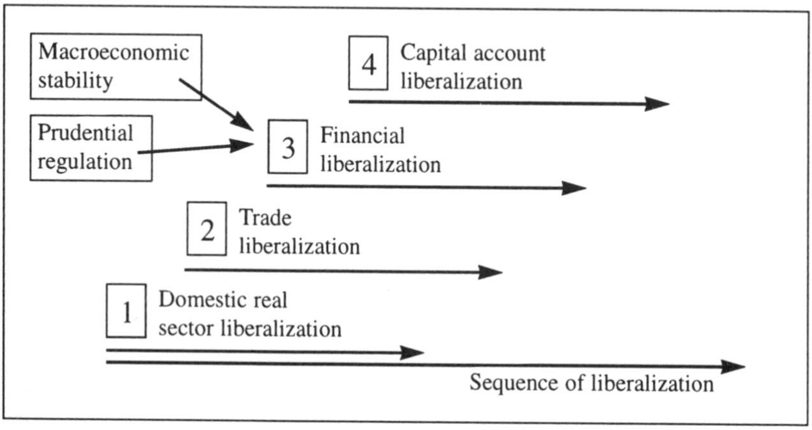

Source: Mohieldin (1994), p. 40.

The capital account should be the last in the liberalization sequence as shown in Figure 1. Several reasons have been put forward in support of this recommendation:

1. It is argued that capital markets adjust faster to changes in incentives than goods and labor markets and hence need a shorter period to respond to liberalization measures.[21]

2. If the liberalization of the domestic financial sector is undertaken before that of the trade sector, this would result in a higher allocating of credit to

the tradable sector owing to the existence of trade barriers.[22]

3. If capital controls are removed before the full liberalization of the domestic financial sector, then capital flight would be inevitable.[23]

4. Further to the previous point, capital flows into an economy that lacks an efficient and a liberalized financial system may be inefficiently allocated.[24]

5. If the capital account is liberalized before the external trade sector, then capital inflows into the economy may result in an exchange rate appreciation. This, in turn, would undermine the competitiveness of tradable goods and add more difficulties to trade liberalization attempts.[25]

6. If the inflow of capital precede fiscal discipline, this may lead to further complication of the budget deficit problem.[26]

It should be said that the sequencing of liberalization outlined above should not be considered immutable. The initial economic condition, political environment and credibility of government have important contributions to sequencing decisions as well as the extent of success or failure of financial opening.

Regional Integration Agreements[27]

Considerable interest has been generated in recent years by the dynamism driving regional integration agreements and the lessons this may provide for other countries contemplating such initiatives. The formation of the North American Free Trade Area (NAFTA), the Central European Free Trade Area (CEFTA) and the South American common market formed by Argentina, Brazil, Paraguay and Uruguay (MERCOSUR), the continuous widening and deepening of the European Community, major developments in the Asia-Pacific Economic Cooperation Forum (APEC), preparatory work on a Free Trade Area of the Americas (FTAA) and a New Trans-Atlantic Agenda, and the range of initiatives elsewhere all provide evidence that the fever of regional trading arrangements has taken hold. It is worth noting that back in 1990, regional trading arrangements affected approximately 40 percent of international trade flows on a global scale, up from 30 percent during the 1960s.

The expansion of regional trading arrangements has generated its own competitive momentum. In a world in which national barriers are becoming so many self-inflicted wounds – a sure way of being isolated from increasingly global investment and production decisions – all countries are facing irresistible pressures to keep pace with market liberalization. Countries enter into free trade relations only to find others joining the race for fear of losing out on investment, technology and market access. And the time has come for countries in the MENA region to revisit this option.

For those familiar with the history of regional initiatives in the MENA region, the above proposition may raise more doubts than excitement. However, it would be erroneous to judge the chances of success of any new arrangement (or the injection of new life into existing ones) by the failures of the past. The underlying premise is whether or not the current policy environment in the region is different from the one that characterized earlier experiments.

First, a cursory examination of the trade instruments still "in vogue" in the MENA countries reveals the presence of a multitude of trade-inhibiting measures, be they at the borders (of the tariff and non-tariff barriers kind) or increasingly within each countries' borders.[28] Such a picture emerges even where account has been taken of the trade preferences countries in the region accord each other through a multitude of minilateral and plurilateral agreements. True, many countries in the region have started to shift direction, though the pace of implementation and the strengths of reforms vary significantly across countries. However, and as of this day, much remains to be done in order to end up with trade and payments regimes that will further promote the openness of markets to regional competition, and eventually to global competition.

Second, intra-regional infrastructure including the institutional kind that should facilitate intra-regional trade remains either absent or at best non-responsive. For example, the Inter-Arab Investment Guarantee Corporation (IAIGC) – which was set up in 1974 and started activities in 1975, provides guarantees against non-commercial risks for Arab investors, including guarantees for trade credits, and loans to promote investments within Arab countries. In 1993, the value of guarantee contracts signed by IAIGC amounted to US$ 14.4 million for investment contracts and (a mere) US$ 47 million for export credit contracts. Another pan-Arab institution, the Arab Trade Financing Program (ATFP) was set up in 1989 with the objective of promoting inter-Arab trade through rediscounting of trade financing instruments from member countries covering pre-and post-shipment finance, loans and lines of credit, and guarantees accepted if issued by IAIGC. Between 1991 and 1993, ATFP approved 94 applications for lines of credit totaling US$ 263 million.

The third and last aspect to consider in this respect is whether or not the economies in the region have become more interdependent in trade, finance, or production over the last two or three decades. If the answer is yes, this would be a positive factor favoring further integration efforts. Growing interdependence might manifest itself in numerous ways, including increasing intra-industry trade, a rising share of intra-regional trade in total imports or exports, or by increased trade in components that will be assembled in the importing country. Whether the comparative advantage of MENA countries has evolved along complementary (or competing) lines would also be a consideration, as would persistent regional trade imbalances (a negative factor). Space limitations do not allow a comprehensive analysis of all these factors. Suffice it to say that in 1995, intra-regional trade in the region accounted for 7 percent of the total trade, and that share has remained more or less constant, at least during the last decade. However, this apparently low level of intra-regional trade should be put in perspective as the countries in the region absorb a total of 4 percent of global exports; in other words, MENA countries trade amongst themselves twice as much as they trade with the rest of the world.

Moreover, MENA countries continue to exhibit divergent interests as each one of them finds itself at a very different stage of economic development than the other. Development disparities amongst MENA countries remain much wider than among any other group of countries that have attempted to integrate their economies. In 1993, per capita incomes in the region ranged from a low US$ 660 in Egypt to a high of US$ 21,430 for the UAE, a difference of over 32 fold. In contrast, the largest difference in the European Union in the same year was between Greece and Denmark: the first recorded a per capita income of US$ 7,390 while the second achieved a high of US$ 26,730, a difference of only 3.6 fold. By the same token, the divergence in incomes under NAFTA between Mexico and the United states is only sevenfold.

While the above may lead one to question the merits of new regional initiatives in MENA, the analysis that follows will show that such pessimism may not after all be warranted.

First, it is no revelation to state that in the past, regional trading arrangements had set themselves an ambitious scope. What is less known is perhaps the fact that the emphasis was on using regional integration arrangements to advance the goals of import substitution industrialization. The anti-export bias inherent in such a development strategy, however, tended to choke off opportunities for specialization, and hence retarded economic development and the opportunities to expand the export base of countries in the region in line with their comparative advantage. Fortunately, more and more countries in the MENA region are in the process of abandoning such policies.

Second, it is worth noting that much of the excitement surrounding the new regional trading initiatives around the globe reflects expectations about North-South arrangements,[29] and countries in the MENA region are no exception as evidenced by the large number of countries that are negotiating FTAs with the EU. Although these agreements may implicitly increase trade barriers against non-members (and so forth, factories that outsource inputs in the regional market may be forced to redirect their purchases in order to qualify as local producers), the concerned countries in the MENA region have demonstrated their willingness to pay this premium for the "insurance effect" of an FTA with a large country. Moreover, the potential investment-diversion effects of such an agreement generate an additional incentive for countries that are interested in attracting large transnational corporations. The FTAs with the EU, which should be concluded by 2010, would provide for free circulation of manufactured products, progressive liberalization of trade in agricultural products, liberalization of the right of establishment for companies, provision of trans-border services, and free movement of capital. There would be largely identical rules of origin among the different parties, mutual recognition of standards, a high level of protection of intellectual property rights and provisions concerning rules of competition. What is important to note in this respect is the potential role of the EU in new initiatives in the MENA region. Specifically, to the extent that the MENA countries that have concluded an FTA with the EU extend (at the very least) the same preferences they have granted to the EU to other regional partners, this would go a long way in promoting both opportunities for intra-industry trade among MENA countries through the rationalization of economic activities, as well as external and internal investment flows to the region.

Third, while unilateral liberalization by each of the MENA countries, at whatever speed and sectoral composition, is to be preferred to preferential liberalization, from a political perspective it might be easier to pursue such liberalization as part of coordinated efforts in the MENA region. Coordinated liberalization within MENA, coupled with an FTA with an industrialized country, could be politically useful as it serves to lock-in the liberalization in each of the countries since reversal will compromise the FTA with the industrialized country.

Fourth, the emerging regional arrangements are distinctive, and in many instances have been labeled as "new" because they have included for the first time ever ambitious liberalization agendas that cover not only trade in goods, but also trade in services, foreign direct investment, intellectual property rights and many other "market access" issues broadly defined. While regional trade liberalization requires the removal of border barriers to promote intra-regional trade, it has been increasingly recognized that the development of regional production systems requires deeper forms of integration of national regulatory systems and policies. Many countries in the MENA region have embraced, mainly on a unilateral basis, a reform strategy that addresses most if not all of these sectors, and their commitment to stay the course appears unrelenting.

The fifth and last point that gives rise to optimism has to do with changed attitudes in the region. MENA countries have accumulated a wealth of information and knowledge, not only in respect of the reasons that have led their integration attempts to falter, but equally importantly, they have assimilated the lessons of experiences of other countries that have successfully integrated. Thus, MENA countries are more aware today than ever before of the need to focus their initiatives on a small, modest core of issues initially, and gradually moving to more ambitious goals as confidence builds up. MENA countries have in addition learned the value of cooperation amongst themselves, and the benefits of good citizenry, be that in their own backyard or increasingly on a global scale.

The above projects hope that new initiatives in the region have the potential of being more influential and successful than earlier attempts. In part, this simply reflects the potential role of the EU in these new initiatives. Still, structural changes and progress in unilateral liberalization reinforce such a conclusion. Nevertheless, a word of caution: like previous attempts at regional integration in the area, they can easily become instruments for trade diversion favoring special interests at the expense of society at large. From this perspective, they may end up having more in common with their forerunners than one would wish.

GATS and Regional Integration Agreements

Should countries in the MENA region decide to further their integration attempt, the experiences of other regions, for example, the EU, NAFTA, and the Australia-New Zealand Closer Economic Relations Agreement (CER) may offer some useful lessons. Six criteria for comparison between regional agreements and the GATS have been used (Hoekman and Sauvé, 1994):[30]

1. the modalities and instruments that are used to liberalize access to service markets,
2. sectoral coverage,
3. disciplines regarding government practices in areas such as subsidization and public procurement,
4. enforcement/dispute settlement procedures,
5. rules of origin, and
6. safeguard provisions.

Whether regional liberalization of services should be viewed as a complement or substitute to multilateral liberalization depends on whether regional agreements effectively lead to significant liberalization and if such arrangements go substantially beyond what is already feasible in the multilateral context. Given the outcome of the GATS, a review of regional trade agreements among OECD countries that cover the services sector suggests that regional and multilateral agreements display a fairly strong degree of complementarity. One important reason for this is the fact that regional agreements appear to have been useful laboratories in which to experiment with ever more sophisticated rules and disciplines covering services, investment and government procurement. There has been a substantial amount of cross-fertilization between the regional agreements and the GATS. The decision to launch the GATS negotiation was heavily influenced by the EU program and the NAFTA. The progress that was made in the multilateral discussions was in part driven by the existence of regional liberalization agreements (Hoekman and Sauvé, 1994).

An important effect of the regional liberalization of services markets is to enhance the competitiveness of firms – whether producers of goods or services – located within the region. The costs of intra-regional exchange are reduced as services providers are induced to specialize and differentiate their products. The main issue then from a policy perspective is what the economic impact of regional liberalization of service markets will be, which in turn depends importantly on the extent of such liberalization.

The consideration of services in the trade policy context has revealed that standard political economy arguments apply as much to services as to goods, and are helpful in understanding why a regional approach to liberalization of service markets has been pursued. There is a need for reciprocal liberalization in order to satisfy political constraints: export interests must balance those groups that oppose the liberalization of domestic markets.

As Hoekman and Sauvé (1994) argue "the non-storability and intangibility of services create incentives to go regional." Because services tend to be non-storable, services transactions often require that the supplier of the service and the consumers interact. Not only will a physical presence often be necessary, but such establishment will be subject to regulatory regimes insofar as governments attempt to offset the quality uncertainty that is associated with the intangible nature of many services. For liberalization to be effective, some harmonization of regulatory regimes and agreement to recognize the standards and regulations of partner countries may well be needed. To the extent that this is feasible, it will be more easily achieved in a bilateral or regional setting.

This raises an important question: does the regulatory environment in which the banking systems operate in the selected countries satisfy the requirements for the liberalization of trade in financial services under the GATS or even under regional arrangements? We summarize these requirements in the context of a liberalized banking system with a competitive structure and an adequate prudential regulation. We provide below a profile of the banking systems in the selected countries. It is worth noting that our efforts are limited by the dearth of information on some of the issues under consideration.

The Arab Banking Systems: Structure, Regulation and Performance

During the last two decades some Arab banks managed to adapt to the changes in the political climate, economic conditions and advances in technology. However, the Arab banking sector remains non-competitive owing to heavy intervention by both governments and influential political groups in the functioning of the Arab central banks and the operations of the banking units. If we use nominal interest rate spread as a proxy for competition in the banking sectors of the selected countries, we find that Arab banking markets do suffer from lack of competition and inefficiency in financial intermediation (Table 3).

Table 3. Nominal Interest Rate Spread in Arab Countries

	1981	1983	1985	1987	1989	1991	1993
Egypt	5.0	4.0	4.0	5.3	6.6	....	....
Bahrain	....	....	....	2.5	....	....	....
Kuwait	2.3	2.3	2.3	2.3	2.3	0.4	1.8
Jordan	....	....	....	....	....	6.75	5.75
Lebanon	....	4.52	4.05	15.36	22.32	21.25	12.97
Tunisia	4.1	4.0	4.28	3.86	....	....	....
Morocco	1.0	0.5	-0.2	0.5	0.5	0.5	....
UK	2.58	-1.34	0.54	1.07	2.49	1.48	2.16
Korea	1.2	2.0	0.0	0.0	1.3	0.0	0.0

Source: IMF, International Financial Statistics Yearbook (1994).

The problems that plague the banking sector in the Arab countries can be attributed to several factors such as:
1. The structure of the banking system in Arab countries which is typically dominated by a few inefficient state-owned banks.
2. Heavy financial repression in the form of government intervention in setting interest rates and allocation of credit, in addition to imposing high required reserves and liquidity ratios.
3. Lack of central bank independence.
4. The prevailing of unfavorable economic conditions such as high inflation rates and vulnerability to external shocks.

Table 4 shows the structure, regulation and performance of the banking systems in the Arab countries. It is clear from the entries in the different cells that the selected countries are not completely ready to face up to the challenges of competition in the international financial market. Financial opening means that Arab banks have to deal with critical issues such as mergers and acquisition, improving the quality of services provided, cost reduction, and so forth. Banks in the Arab countries will find themselves forced to diversify their revenue sources, improve their capital adequacy requirements up to the international standards,[31] and to solve the problems of non-performing loans and excess liquidity.[32] Effective liberalization requires harmonization of regulatory practices among trading partners. Thus, it is clear that to capture the opportunities offered by freeing trade in financial services, Arab countries will need to adapt their regulatory environments and develop supportive physical and human infrastructure.

Concluding Remarks

Although the integration of financial services into the world trading system has been considered one of the most important achievements of the Uruguay Round negotiations, this however made today's trading environment a vastly complicated one for several reasons: first, the financial services sector is the largest and the most sophisticated amongst the sectors on which negotiations are still taking place. Second, liberalizing trade in financial services through the reduction or elimination of barriers to trade is a major undertaking in as far as the majority of LDCs are concerned, and that includes the majority if not all of the Arab countries. Liberalization of financial services requires detailed negotiations of within-border laws and regulations.

Due to lack of data we cannot determine whether the GATS provides significant and substantive liberalization of trade in financial services. However, given the structure, regulation and recent performance of the banking sector in the Arab countries, we argue that they do not meet the prerequisites of successful financial liberalization, and major steps are required to improve their competitiveness. Internal reform of the domestic banking system and external financial liberalization are complementary processes and should be undertaken with the right sequencing, taking into account the initial economic and structural conditions of the financial sector and the economy as a whole.

We argue that allowing foreign banks to enter the domestic market is not enough to weaken the monopolistic structure or to improve the efficiency in financial intermediation as incumbent banks may squeeze out the new entrants or collude with them. The experience of Egypt after approximately two decades of opening its financial market to foreign banks is a case in point.

The progress in negotiations in trade in financial services has not been accompanied by a concomitant improvement regarding the regulatory framework. We argue that the establishment of an appropriate international regulatory framework for trade in banking services has become a necessary condition for a stable and sustainable growth of the international financial market.

Table 4: Structure, Regulation and Performance of the Banking Systems in Selected Arab Countries

Country	Structure	Regulation	Performance and Prospects
Egypt	The banking system consists of 101 institutions at the end of 1993. There are 44 commercial banks, including 4 state owned banks which dominate the banking system; 33 business and investment banks including 22 branches of foreign banks and 21 specialized banks; and 3 non-registered banks. Commercial banks account for 81 percent, 90 percent, 75 percent of total assets, deposits and loans respectively.	- In accordance with financial reform measures, that started with freeing interest rates in January 1991, a new law no. 37 of 1992 was promulgated. - This law raised the authorized and paid-up capital to $29 million and $14.5 million respectively. - The law also allowed foreigners to hold shares in banks and permitted foreign banks to deal in domestic currency. According to this law the Central Bank of Egypt (CBE) was granted further regulatory powers. The collapse of BCCI in 1991 made such increase of the powers of the CBF, justifiable. - A deposit insurance scheme was established according to the same law. - All banks were asked to adhere to the Basle standards on risk-weighted capital adequacy.	- The banking structure still suffers from the domination of public sector banks which will continue to be the major players in the banking sectors. - The problem of non-performing loans is still awaiting a solution. The banking system has an excess liquidity problem that reveals inefficiency in the intermediation process. - Foreign banks may find some profit opportunities from the privatization process and the development of the stock market.

Table 4: Continued (1)

Country	Structure	Regulation	Performance and Prospects
Lebanon	The banking system consists of 80 banks. 70 percent of total assets are held by the biggest 15 banks.	- Banque du Liban, which survived the Civil War, regulates the banking system. - The National Assembly may intervene in the central banking operations, for example, in 1991 it refused to pass a law that would have liquidated small banks that cannot meet the minimum capital suggested by Banque du Liban. - 10 percent of local currency deposits must be placed with the Central Bank, interest-free and a further 3 percent must be used for a compulsory purchase of law-rate-treasury bills.	- Before the start of Civil War in 1975 Beirut was the unrivaled banking center of the Middle East. Lebanon after the ending of hostilities in 1991 had the aspirations to regain its former position in the region and to compete with the business centers already established in Bahrain, Dubai and Cairo. - Many banks are under-capitalized because their equity was denominated in Lebanese Lira. However, banks had to meet a capital adequacy ratio of 6 percent in 1993 and 8 percent in 1995 in accordance with the Basle standard.

Table 4: Continued (2)

Country	Structure	Regulation	Performance and Prospects
Jordan	The Jordanian banking system consists of 8 commercial banks, 6 investment banks, 5 branches and 2 representative offices of foreign banks and an Islamic bank, in addition to specialized credit institutions for housing, agriculture and industry. Eight Jordanian banks had 31 branches in the West Bank and Gaza. Several banks have applied for opening and/or re-opening branches after the signing the Jordanian-Palestinian economic cooperation agreement.	- The Central Bank of Jordan (CBJ), regulates the banking system. The main aim of CBJ in the early 1990s was to curb the growth of liquidity using loans to deposits ceilings. - To attract foreign exchange, especially in from workers' remittances, foreign banks are now allowed to offer foreign currency investment portfolios for non-residents. - Interest rates have been liberalized. Foreign currency transfers are free from restrictions since February 1995.	- Four cases of bank failure had disturbed the financial sector in Jordan, in the late 1980s; Petra Bank was unable to provide the required reserves on its foreign currency deposits to the CBJ; the Jordan Gulf Bank suffered a serious liquidity problem; malpractice of the Mashreq Bank forced its closure; the Islamic Investment House was liquidated because of quality problems of its portfolio and divergence from the terms of its license. The four cases were met with firm decisions from the CBJ which restored confidence in the banking system. - Constrained by size of the economy, the Jordanian banking system will remain relatively small. The peace process may not necessarily widen the scope of the banking sector as it has two contradicting effects. Business opportunities may increase in accordance with cooperation agreements but Palestinian entrepreneurs who play a crucial role in the Jordanian financial system may choose to invest in Palestine rather than Jordan.

Table 4: Continued (3)

Country	Structure	Regulation	Performance and Prospects
Bahrain	The financial system in Bahrain is recognized at the international level as an offshore banking center. The offshore market was established as a result of oil euphoria. There are 18 commercial banks including 5 local ones. The two local banks account for 60 percent of local assets. There are also 22 investment banks of which there 6 locally incorporated institutions. The offshore market, which can be divided into locally incorporated and subsidiaries of banks as at the end of 1993. At the peak in 1984 there were 74 offshore banks.	- The Bahrain Monetary Agency (BMA), which replaced the old currency board in 1973, acts as a Central Bank and regulates the commercial, investment and offshore markets. The BMA, for historical reasons, is influenced by the Bank of England, and thus its deposit insurance scheme is modeled on that run by the latter.	- The Bahraini financial system, being based on offshore business, has been vulnerable to international financial changes; for example the National Bank of Bahrain has been negatively affected by the bond market crash of 1994. However, the performance of most of the local banks was sound as they issued healthy dividends. Despite the rise of Dubai as a competing center, it is apparent that Bahrain will continue to be a favored base for banks seeking syndicated lending and advisory business in the Gulf.

Table 4: Continued (4)

Country	Structure	Regulation	Performance and Prospects
The United Arab Emirates	There are 19 locally incorporated commercial banks and 28 branches of foreign banks. Despite the existence of 2 investment banks, in practice it is hard to discriminate between investment and commercial banking in the UAE. In terms of market share, five banks dominate the UAE banking scene.	- The Central Bank of the UAE, which is a federal body, regulates the banking system. - A few incidents have raised serious questions regarding the quality of regulation of the banking system in the UAE, for example, the closure of the BCCI and the failure of Niscorp. The case of the BCCI revealed that the banking system was subject to political influence that had overridden the regulatory framework. -The Central Banks must conform to Basle guidelines.	- It is hard to assess the performance of banks in the UAE as many banks do not operate according to the usual commercial criteria; some banks receive subsidies in a form of cheap deposits from their host Emirates and some of them are over-capitalized.

Table 4: Continued (5)

Country	Structure	Regulation	Performance and Prospects
Saudi Arabia	The Saudi banking system comprises 12 commercial banks, which are owned, wholly, or at least majority, by Saudi interests. There are also state development banks that extend subsidized loans, and so forth, to infrastructure and agriculture. Since 1988 the banking market has been closed to newcomers and no single license for operation was offered. Before 1976 foreign banks were allowed to operate in Saudi Arabia, but after that year they had to be put under majority local ownership through joint ventures.	- The Saudi Arabian Monetary Agency (SAMA), established in 1952, is the Central Bank. Although SAMA is granted considerable power over the banking units sometimes it can be paralyzed from performing its functions due to political pressure and civil groupings. For example one of the major commercial banks did not issue its financial annual accounts for two years, fearing that this would reveal the huge credit granted to influential persons without sufficient collateral. The bank became troubled with nonperforming loans beyond its provision and SAMA was not able force a solution to this problem.	- The banking system grew rapidly during the 1980s and early 1990s but started to shrink afterwards as a reflection of the general economic decline. However, with 15 percent return on average equity in 1993, the Saudi banks appear as the most profitable in the GCC.

Table 4: Continued (6)

Country	Structure	Regulation	Performance and Prospects
Kuwait	With assets of $26.3 billion the Kuwaiti banking system is the third largest in the GCC. In the late 1970s and during 1980s the banking system in Kuwait was comparable to that of Saudi Arabia, but after the Al-Manakh crash the economy was thrown into deep recession that had negative effects on the growth of the banking system. When some signs of recovery started to appear the banking system was hit by the Iraqi invasion. There are 6 commercial banks, 2 specialized banks and an Islamic bank. Foreign banks are not allowed to have branches or even representative offices. All commercial banks are wholly owned by Kuwaiti interests, that is, government or royal family. However, in order to attract foreign expertise, a law was passes in 1994, to allow foreign investors to hold up to 40 percent of local banks.	- All operating banks, except the Kuwait Finance House are regulated by the Central Bank of Kuwait (CBK). The CBK has been effective in applying a standard array of regulatory measures to monitor and control the banking system. Because of resistance of influential bank share holders, the CBK could not enforce the scheme of bank mergers that aimed to strengthen the banking system after the troubles of Al-Manakh financial crisis.	- The heyday of the banking system was before the financial crisis of 1982. Until the implementation of debt settlement scheme (DSS) all banks, except one, were technically insolvent and dependent on CBK subsidies. The DSS replaces bad loan portfolios with government bonds. By implementing the DSS, balance sheets of the banks were cleared out and the introduction of a disclosure standard improved the transparency of these banks. Nevertheless, the reduction of government bonds in bank portfolios is conditional on the government ability to recover the debts it took over from banks, which is doubtful.

Table 4: Continued (7)

Country	Structure	Regulation	Performance and Prospects
Tunisia	The banking system comprises 12 commercial banks, 8 development banks and 8 offshore banks and a merchant bank. There is not any significant problem facing the establishment of branches of foreign banks. The biggest bank in Tunisia is double the size of its nearest rivals in terms of assets.	- The Central Bank of Tunisia (CBT), which is granted some degree of independence, regulates the banking units. - The CBT is competent but there are complaints of its excessive intervention in the banking operations. Despite the adoption of some liberalization measures in 1992, there were more than 100 categories of credit subject to direct control of the CBT.	- The prospects of the Tunisian banking sector are limited by the size of its economy that despite intense efforts to develop remains a marginal one in the region. Hence, it is believed that the Tunisian banking market will continue to be a niche one in the Middle East. - It is argued that the country is 'overbanked' and considering the development of an offshore market in Morocco, the validity of a Tunisian offshore to serve the Mahreb region is questionable.

Table 4: Continued (8)

Country	Structure	Regulation	Performance and Prospects
Morocco	Since the early 1960s the banking system has been divided into three main parts: 2 state owned banks, other commercial banks owned jointly by local and foreign interests and 4 state-owned specialized banks.	- Bank Al-Maghreb, the Central Bank does not control exclusively the banking system or monetary policy. Regulation of credit institutions, control and discipling, which are normally undertaken by a central bank are divided in Morocco between three separate bodies, which raises the issue of coordination problems. A new law was passed in 1993 to standardize the legal framework and to support deregulation measures undertaken by the government. Although the law covers all credit institutions, the three main development banks are exempted. The Central Bank in 1991 lifted credit ceilings and allowed some freedom for banks to set interest rates. In 1993 banks were asked to adopt the Basle standards.	- The recent creation of an offshore center in Tangier and the privatization of government shares started to bring a significant change in the banking structure.

Source: Based on Cunningham, A. (1995), pp. 27-49; pp. 73-112; 121-135; and pp. 155-171.

Notes

1   See World Bank (1995), pp. 43-55.
2   Ibid.
3   Whalley (1995), pp. 2-3.
4   Moshirian (1994), p. 327.
5   Whalley, op. cit., p. 4.
6   See Safadi and Laird (1996) for a comprehensive analysis of the Uruguay Round Agreements and their impact on developing countries.
7   Article I of the GATS defines trade in services in terms of four modes of supply. The first mode involves the cross-border supply of a service from one jurisdiction to another. The second mode of supply requires the movement of consumers to the jurisdiction of suppliers. The third mode of supply is through commercial presence of supplier in the jurisdiction of consumers. The is the investment mode which caused so much difficulty in the early stages of the services negotiations. Many developing countries argued that commitments on services transactions under this mode of supply were tantamount to a surrogate obligation on FDI, and they expressed unwillingness to ties their investment regimes in this manner. Finally, the fourth mode of supply entails the movement of natural persons from one jurisdiction to another.
8   World Bank, op. cit., p. 55.
9   The regional classification in the table corresponds to that of the GATT Secretariat.
10 On this issue see Appendix (A) in Whalley (1995).
11 Schultz (1993), p. 215.
12 Ibid.
13 See Sapir and Winter (1994), p. 283.
14 Schultz (1993), p. 218.
15 See for example Germidis and Michalet (1984).
16 Schultz (1993), p. 216.
17 The deal was reached on June 29th 1995.
18 Blejer and Sagari (1988), p. 20.
19 Williamson (1993), p. 25.
20 Ibid., Greenaway and Morrissey, op. cit., p. 257, Gibson and Tsakalotos (1994), p. 591, Hanson (1994), p. 337.
21 Greenaway and Morrissey, op. cit., p. 258.
22 Ibid.
23 Edwards (1990), p. 2.
24 Williamson, op. cit., p. 26.
25 Greenaway and Morrissey, op. cit., p. 257-258.
26 Williamson, op. cit., p. 26.
27 This section draws from Safadi (1996).
28 Once, trade policy was about regulating commercial relations between national economies. Now it is being extended beyond countries' borders and into an ever increasing number of areas that have traditionally been considered to belong solely in the domestic policy domain: standards and regulations, investment policy, competition policy, labor policy and environment policy.
29 The potential of North-South agreements to expand Heckscher-Ohlin type of trade (for example, trade based on differences in relative factor endowments) is significant.
30 See Appendix (1) for further details.
31 Arab countries except Saudi Arabia have been classified as high risk countries considering their capital adequacy standards.
32 *Arab Banking and Finance* (1994). pp. 9-10.

References

Arab Banking and Finance. 1993-4. 10th edition, Tele-Gulf Directory Publications.

Bhagwati, Jagdish. 1987. "Services", in J. Michael Finger and Andrzej Olechowski (eds.), *The Uruguay Round: A Handbook on the Multilateral Trade Negotiations.* Washington, DC: World Bank.

Blejer, M., and S. Sagari 1988, "Sequencing the Liberalization of Financial Markets." *Finance and Development.* March.

Cooper, Richard. 1987, "Why Liberalization Meets Resistance?" in J. Michael Finger and Andrzej Olechowski (eds.), *The Uruguay Round: A Handbook on the Multilateral Trade Negotiations.* Washington, DC: World Bank.

Cunningham, A. 1995. *Banking in the Middle East. London*: FT Financial Publishing.

Edwards, S. 1990. "The Sequencing of Economic Reform: Analytical Issues and Lessons from Latin American Experience." *The World Economy.* Vol. 13, No. 1:1-14.

Finger, J. M., and A. Olechowski. 1987. (eds.), *The Uruguay Round: A Handbook on the Multilateral Trade Negotiations.* Washington DC: The World Bank.

Germidis, D., and C.A. Michalet. 1984. *International Banks and Financial Markets in Developing Countries.* Paris: OECD.

Gibson, H., and E. Tsakalotos. 1994. "The Scope and Limits of Financial Liberalization in Developing Countries: A Critical Survey." *The Journal of Development Studies.* Vol. 30. No. 3: 578-628.

Greenaway, D., and O. Morrisey. 1993. "Structural Adjustment and Liberalization in Developing Countries: What Lessons Have We Learned?". *KYKLOS*, Vol. 46: 241-61.

Hanson, J. 1994. "An Open Capital Account: A Brief Survey of the Issues and Results" in G. Caprio, I. Atiyas and J. Hanson (eds.), *Financial Reform: Theory and Experience.* Cambridge: Cambridge University Press.

Hoekman, Bernard, and Pierre Sauvé. 1994. "Liberalizing Trade in Services." World Bank Discussion Papers. Washington DC: The World Bank.

International Monetary Fund. 1994. *International Financial Statistics Yearbook.* Washington: IMF

Kakabadse, Mario. 1987. "International Trade in Services: Prospects for Liberalization in the 1990s." The Atlantic Institute For International Affairs Papers, No. 64, USA: Croom Helm.

Mohieldin, M. 1994. "On the Sequencing of Financial Liberalization." Mimeo, Dept. of Economics, University of Warwick.

Moshirian, F. 1994. "Trade in Financial Services." *The World Economy*, May, Vol. 17, No. 3: 347-362.

Safadi, R. 1995. "Global Challenges and Opportunities Facing MENA Countries at the Dawn of the Twenty First Century." Paper presented at the conference organized by the World Bank and ERF on Liberalization of Trade and Foreign Investment, Istanbul, Turkey, 16-18 September.

___. 1996. "Is MENA Likely to Go Regional: Promoting the Regional Option." A background paper prepared for ERF. Cairo, Egypt.

Safadi, R., and S. Laird 1996. "The Uruguay Round and Developing Countries". *Journal of World Development*, Vol. 24, No. 7, July.

Safadi, R. 1997. "Trade, Investment and Finance in a Globalizing World Economy." in *Globalization and Linkages to 2020: Challenges and Opportunities for OECD Countries.* Processed. Paris: OECD.

Sapir, A. 1985. "North-South Issues in Trade in Services." *The World Economy*, Vol. 8, March: 27-42.

Sapir, A. and C. Winter 1994. "Services Trade" in D. Greenaway and L. Winters (eds.), *Surveys in International Trade*. Oxford: Blackwell.

Schultz, S. 1993. "Barriers in Services Trade: The State of Negotiations and Prospects." *Intereconomics*. September.

Shafik, Nemat. 1994. "Economic Cooperation in The Middle East: Prospects and Challenges." Mimeo, Cairo University.

Watkins, Kevin. 1992. *Fixing the Rules: North-South Issues in International Trade and the Uruguay Round*. UK: Russell Press Ltd.

Whalley, John. (ed.), 1989. "The Final Report from the Ford Foundation Project on Developing Countries and the Global Trading System." *The Uruguay Round and Beyond*. London: Macmillan Press Ltd.

Whalley, John. 1989. *Developing Countries and the Global Trading System*. London: Macmillan Press Ltd.

___. 1995. "Services in the Uruguay Round and Beyond." UNCTAD Project on the Implications of the Uruguay Round on Developing Countries. Geneva.

Williamson, J. 1993."A Cost-Benefit Analysis of Capital Account Liberalization" in H. Reisen and B. Fischer (eds.), *Financial Opening: Policy Issues and Experiences in Developing Countries*. Paris:OECD.

Wolf, Martin. 1987. "Why Trade Liberalization is a Good Idea" in J. Michael Finger and Andrzej Olechowski (eds.), *The Uruguay Round: A Handbook on the Multilateral Trade Negotiations*. Washington, DC: World Bank

World Bank. 1995. *Global Economic Prospects and the Developing Countries*. Washington, DC: The World Bank.

Appendix 1: A Brief Comparison between the GATS, the EU, NAFTA and NAFTA

AGREEMENT CRITERIA	EC-92	NAFTA	CER	GATS
1) Modalities and instruments of liberalization.	Four freedoms: goods, services, capital, labor. Non-discrimination: all modes of supply liberalized. Mutual recognition of diplomas and certification of professional service providers. Harmonization of prudential and safety regulations. Implicit right of non-establishment. No exemption to general nondiscrimination requirements. Common labor market. Accession negotiations.	National treatment, 'reverse'-MFN, freedom of mode of supply, including right of non-establishment (no local presence). No grandfathering. Allows for exemptions to national treatment, MFN and local presence. No disciplines on non-discriminatory QRs., but all such measures to be listed. Ratcheting provision for unilateral liberalization. Abolition of residency requirements for professions. Generic blueprint for use by service providers seeking recognition agreements. Work programs on standards harmonization (land transport and telecoms). Accession clause.	National treatment and market access. Freedom of mode of supply, but right of establishment remains subject to national investment laws. Right of non-establishment. No residency requirements for professionals. Common labor market. MFN for excluded sectors. Encouragement of recognition agreements for licensing and certification requirements. Accession clause.	All modes of supply covered in principle. Transparency, MFN, and dispute settlement as basic general right of non-establishment. Encouragement of recognition agreements. No general disciplines on non-discriminatory QRs., but these prohibited under the market access article unless explicitly reserved.

Appendix 1: Continued (1)

AGREEMENT CRITERIA	EC-92	NAFTA	CER	GATS
2) Sectoral coverage	All services covered. Sector-specific directives and regulations. Common EC policy for transport.	Negative list approach to coverage. Universal coverage, except for air services subject to bilateral air agreements. Annexes on: reservations of existing non-conforming investment and cross-border services measures at federal and state/provincial levels; 'unbound' reservations in sensitive sectors; activities reserved for the state; exceptions to MFN; and existing non-discriminatory QRs. Separate chapters on telecommunications (access to and use of public networks and services); financial services; temporary entry of business people. Timetables for the liberalization of land transport and specially air services.	Negative list approach to coverage. Annexes for exceptions to national treatment and market access obligations. No indefinite exclusions. A number of reserved services were removed from reservation lists in 1992 review of the Agreement.	Positive list of scheduled sectors. Most air transport services excluded via an annex (indefinite). Other annexes deal with telecommunication (access to and use of public networks and services); financial services (complemented by an understanding of commitments on financial services); movement of natural persons.
3) Disciplines on related government policies	State aid subject to restrictions and monitoring. Government procurement of services, including construction, covered.	Government procurement of services and construction covered. Positive list for entity coverage; negative list approach for services coverage. No disciplines on subsidies for services.	Export subsidies for services prohibited. Government procurement of services and other subsidies exempted from national treatment obligation.	No disciplines for Government. procurement or subsidies. MFN obligation for subsidies. Subsidy disciplines to be negotiated in future. Services and construction procedures. under discussion in context of GATT code on Government. procedures.

Appendix 1: Continued (2)

AGREEMENT CRITERIA	EC-92	NAFTA	CER	GATS
4) Enforcement and dispute settlement	EC law has direct effect: supersedes national law. Enforcement by private parties and the EC Commission. Supranational court of justice. No service specific procedures.	Generic procedures apply to all covered areas under the Agreement. Binding dispute settlement available to determine whether relation in response to non-implementation of a panel finding is 'manifestly excessive'. Regime for investor-state arbitration for enforcement of obligations under the investment chapter. Retaliation between goods and services allowed, with the exception of financial services.	Informal and non-binding procedures. Only consultation required.	General procedures under the WTO. Consultation followed by panel. Strict time limits imposed for the various stages of the dispute settlement process. Non-implementation of panel findings may result in authorization of retaliatory measures.
5) Rules of origin	Incorporation in an EC Member Sates and headquarters or principal place of business in the EC.	National or incorporation for investment; substantial business activity within any NAFTA country for cross-border trade in services.	Nationality or residency for natural persons; incorporation for legal persons.	Nationality or residency for natural persons; incorporation under law of a Member State and substantive business operations in a Member; or control - ownership by nationals of a Member. Ownership requires more than 50 percent of assets; control requires the power to direct the actions of the enterprise.

Appendix 1: Continued (3)

AGREEMENT CRITERIA	EC-92	NAFTA	CER	GATS
6) Safeguards	Only one service specific provision relating to the common transport policy. General balance of payments and public health and safety provisions.	No service-specific safeguards, other than periodic review of bus and truck liberalization with scope for modification of phase-in schedule. Emergency protection for goods only. General balance of payments and public health and safety provisions.	Currently no safeguard measures for goods or services. A GATT-type Article XIX safeguard provision applied during the transitional period, which has now expired.	Provides for services-specific measures to safeguard the balance of payments and to protect service industries injured by import competition. However, specific rules on the latter to be negotiated. Also provides for modification of commitments, subject to compensation of affected Members.

Source: Hoekman and Sauvé (1994), Table (4), pp. 45-48.

Part II
Country Studies

Tiger or Turtle?
Exploring Alternative Futures for Egypt to 2020[*]

Introduction

In the 1980s and early 1990s, the Egyptian economy suffered from slow growth in both GDP and productivity, declining real wages, growing unemployment, and falling household incomes. This discouraging performance was combined with chronic macroeconomic imbalances that were manifested in large budget deficits and high inflation rates. The simultaneous occurrence of a foreign exchange crisis and high levels of food imports in the late 1980s suggested that the country's food security was at risk. Over the last few years, the situation has improved in important respects, primarily as a result of a program for macroeconomic stabilization: the current account is in surplus, inflation has declined, and the budget deficit has been brought under control. However, economy-wide growth is still low and incomes are stagnant; Egypt has yet to emerge as a Middle East tiger. As Egypt approaches the turn of the millennium, the key challenges facing economic policymakers include raising real incomes and reducing unemployment given manageable internal and external macro imbalances.

Egypt's success in meeting these challenges will clearly depend on a wide range of factors. This chapter focuses on three critical areas: productivity growth, investment and foreign trade, and agricultural water scarcity. In order to simulate the effects of alternative scenarios over the period 1990 to 2020, a dynamic computable general equilibrium (CGE) model of the Egyptian economy was developed. The different scenarios were defined drawing on Egyptian and South Korean data, the latter were used as proxy for successful East Asian economies that provide some indication of potential achievement. The next section presents the model structure and the data base, followed by a definition of the alternative scenarios and an analyzation of the results. The chapter then concludes with a brief discussion of the main findings.

The CGE Model: Structure and Data Sources

Our dynamic CGE model of Egypt, called AGRO-CGE, starts from the static Egyptian Land-Water (ELW) model of Robinson and Gehlhar (1995). These

* *The authors would like to thank Monica Scatasta for research assistance, and Natasha Mukherjee, Farha Ghannam and Marcelle Thomas for editorial comments.*

models are in the tradition of trade-focused CGE models of developing countries described in Dervis, de Melo, and Robinson (1982). Both the ELW and AGRO-CGE models draw on earlier models of Egypt, including Löfgren (1995a; 1995b).[1] Among the distinguishing features of the ELW model is an activity-analysis representation of agricultural resource (water and land), technology, and supply-demand constraints. Compared to earlier CGE models of Egypt, the representation of the agricultural sector in the ELW model is relatively detailed.[2]

The AGRO-CGE model extends the ELW model in a number of ways: (1) the data base is now updated from 1986/87 to 1989/90 and disaggregated to match the detailed treatment of the agricultural sector; (2) the treatment of the agricultural sector has been disaggregated to capture seasonality in land use and links between crop and livestock activities; and (3) the model is now dynamic (using a multi-period recursive formulation). Conceptually, the model can be divided into two modules: a static, within-period, module, the core one-period CGE model, and a dynamic, between-period, module where parameters and exogenous variables of the core CGE model are updated over time. Appendix 1 presents a simplified version of the equations of the static module, with a focus on the activity-analysis features of the model. The discussion here uses no equations.

The Static Module

Table 1 shows the disaggregation of factors, institutions, and activities in the model. The treatment of institutions is quite aggregate. Among the factors, labor and capital are used by all sectors, while water, summer-land, and winter-land are used only by agricultural crop activities. Given the long-run nature of the analysis, it is assumed that all factors are sectorally mobile. For capital, the model solves endogenously for the intersectoral allocation that equates the rental rate across sectors and fully employs the aggregate capital stock. In the labor market, however, we allow for unemployment. The labor supply function is assumed to be infinitely elastic at the 1990 real wage until aggregate employment reaches 95 percent of the labor force (a 5 percent unemployment rate), at which point the supply curve becomes vertical. For water and the two land types, a similar dual regime is specified. If there is excess supply, the price is zero. When the resource is scarce, a flexible price adjusts to clear the market.[3] Like capital rent, the water price is uniform across all sectors. However, for land and labor, the price (the rent or the wage) is differentiated across the demanding sectors on the basis of fixed ratios (calculated from base-year data). This is a reflection of real-world phenomena that are not modeled explicitly. Proportional variations in each of these differentiated sectoral prices clear the markets when the relevant demand-supply balances are binding.

The model includes 22 activities and 22 commodities, with 13 agricultural sectors in both. This relatively fine disaggregation of agricultural commodities and activities is unique to CGE models of Egypt. The crop activities are differentiated according to period of land occupation into winter crops, summer crops, and perennial crops. With a few important exceptions, there is a one-to-one mapping between activities and commodities. The exceptions are the two berseem (clover) activities, which produce the same commodity (berseem), and a crop fodder commodity which is also the second output (byproduct) of five crop activities: maize, rice, wheat, other summer crops, and other winter crops. Among the commodities, all except berseem, (raw) cotton, crop fodder, and government labor services have both exports and imports.

Table 1: Disaggregation of Factors, Institutions, and Activities

Set	Elements
Institutions	1. Households 2. Enterprises 3. Government 4. Rest of the world
Factors of production	1. Capital 2. Labor 3. Water 4. Summer-land 5. Winter-land
Activities (22 sectors)	
Crop Agriculture (12)	**Winter crops** Short Berseem, Long Berseem, Wheat, Winter Vegetables, Other Winter Crops **Summer crops** Cotton, Maize, Rice, Summer Vegetables, Other Summer Crops **Perennial crops** Fruit. Sugarcane
Other activities (10)	Livestock, Oil (Crude Oil and Natural Gas), Food Processing, Cotton Ginning, Textiles, Other Industry, Electricity, Construction, Government Labor Services, Other Services

The production technologies are summarized in Figure 1. Producers are assumed to maximize profits given their technology, specified by a nested CES (Constant Elasticity of Supply) value-added function, and fixed (Leontief) intermediate input coefficients. The arguments of the value-added functions are labor, capital and, for the crop sectors, a land/water aggregate. The latter is made up of land and water in fixed proportions. Thus, for crops, substitutability is possible between land, capital and the land/water aggregate on the level of the value-added functions; there is no substitutability between land and water. Two major agronomic area constraints are captured: the area of short berseem is constrained to equal the cotton area, and the cotton area is limited to one third of the land not covered by perennial crops. For the oil activity (crude oil and natural gas), it would be erroneous to assume that output levels and factor use can vary in response to profitability considerations in a manner which parallels other sectors. Instead, the quantities of output and factor use for the oil activity are fixed at the 1990 level. In the absence of a more detailed treatment of this activity, its behavioral rules and sustainable productive capacity (most importantly determined by the levels of petroleum and gas reserves), such an assumption is an appropriate simplification of a more complex reality. Finally, the output of the activity for government labor services is in effect fixed; the government, the sole demander, demands a fixed quantity of the non-traded commodity produced by this activity.

Figure 1: Sectoral Production Technology

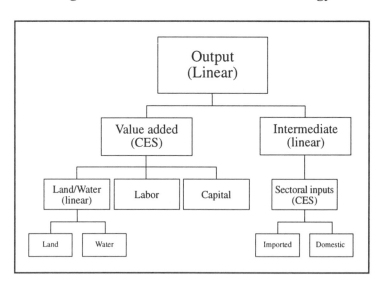

There is one exception to the assumption of fixed intermediate input coefficients: the intermediate (feed) input coefficients of the livestock activity are flexible in the context of livestock producer minimization of feed costs subject to a limited degree of substitutability between different feeds (given by a CES function) and a fixed aggregate feed requirement per unit of the livestock activity. The livestock sector is treated differently given the crucial importance of links between crop and livestock activities in Egypt's agriculture, as crop activities supply the livestock activity with the bulk of its intermediate feed inputs.

Domestic factor incomes are split among the domestic institutions (government, enterprises, and households) in fixed shares. The fact that, if water is scarce, its income (like land incomes) accrues to the household. This is compatible with the assumption that proprietary rights to water have been assigned to the current users.[4] In addition to factor incomes, government revenue consists of transfers from the rest of the world (fixed in foreign currency) and taxes, direct taxes from households and enterprises, indirect taxes from domestic activities, and import tariffs. All taxes are ad valorem. Transfers from the government and aggregate government consumption are fixed shares of nominal GDP. After having paid for a fixed quantity of labor, the government consumes remaining commodities in fixed value shares. Enterprise income (from factors and government transfers) is distributed to households after subtracting taxes, savings, and transfers to the rest of the world (fixed in foreign currency). In addition to factor income and payments from enterprises, households receive transfers (labor remittances) from the rest of the world (fixed in foreign currency). Total household income is used to pay taxes, save (according to an exogenous saving propensity), and consume. Sectoral consumption demand is determined by a linear expenditure system, expressed in per-capita form.

The rest of the world supplies imports and demands exports. Import prices are exogenous in foreign currency (an infinite price-elasticity of supply). Exports are demanded according to constant-elasticity demand curves, the price-elasticities of which are high but less than infinite. The treatment of oil exports deviates from this pattern: Egypt, being a small supplier of this highly homogeneous commodity, is facing an infinitely elastic demand at the exogenous world price. The Armington assumption is used to model the choice between imports and domestic output, which are assumed to be imperfect substitutes. More specifically, to the extent that a commodity is imported, all domestic demands, household and government consumption, investment demand, and intermediate demands, are for the same composite commodity, with the mix between imports and domestic output determined by the assumption that domestic demanders minimize cost subject to imperfect substitutability, captured by a CES aggregation function. Similarly, the allocation of domestic output between exports and domestic sales is determined on the assumption that domestic producers maximize profits subject to imperfect transformability between these two alternatives, expressed by a constant-elasticity-of-transformation (CET) function. These assumptions, imperfect substitutability and transformability, grant the domestic price system a certain degree of independence from international prices and dampen export and import responses to changes in the producer environment. Domestic prices of domestic outputs and composite commodities are all flexible, performing the task of clearing relevant markets in a competitive setting where both suppliers and demanders are price-takers.

The macro system constraints (or macro closures) determine the manner in which the accounts for the government, the rest of the world, and savings-investment are brought into balance. Government savings are fixed; the government adjusts the direct tax rates of enterprises and households proportionally to generate the desired savings level. Foreign savings are also fixed (but in foreign currency), leaving the task of generating balance for the rest-of-the-world account (that is, equality between Egypt's foreign currency earnings and outlays) to a flexible real exchange rate. On the spending side of the savings-investment balance, aggregate investment is a fixed share of real GDP. On the savings side, the enterprise savings rate is assumed to be flexible, varying to generate a level of total savings needed to finance aggregate investment.[5]

The primary data sources for the disaggregated model SAM (a 56x56 matrix) are: CAPMAS' SAM and input-output tables for 1989/90 (CAPMAS 1995; 1994); USAID and Ministry of Agriculture data on agricultural crops (USAID 1992); and FAO (Food and Agriculture Organization) data on agricultural trade. Compared to the CAPMAS' SAM, the disaggregated model SAM is rearranged and has a more aggregate representation of non-agricultural sectors (9 sectors instead of 14), but provides a considerably more detailed view of agriculture (13 sectors instead of 2). A macro version of the model SAM, identical to the disaggregated SAM except for the aggregated depiction of activities and commodities, is shown in Table 2. A variety of sources were used for estimates of elasticities for the Armington, CET, CES (production), LES (household consumption), and export-demand functions (the values used are given in Table A2.1 in the Appendix). Sectoral wage and land rent differentials were derived from CAPMAS (1993) and USAID (1992). On the basis of SAM data, and independent estimates of the capital stock (£Ebn113.3) and depreciation (£Ebn4.48), rates of depreciation

(4.0 percent) and net profitability (36.5 percent) were calculated (World Bank 1994, Annex B, Table 42; CAPMAS 1995, p. 75). Sectoral capital stocks were derived on the assumption of equal sectoral depreciation and gross profit rates.

The Dynamic Module

The within-period, static model is solved for 1990 (the base year), 1993, 1995, and every five years thereafter until 2020. Between the static-model solutions, selected parameters are updated in the dynamic (between-period) module, either using lagged endogenous variables (from solutions in previous periods) or exogenously (on the basis of trends). Parameters for the capital stock and consumer demand equations are changed endogenously. The capital stock is updated given previous investment and depreciation, extrapolating for the inter-period years. Simulated per-capita incomes and budget shares enter the functions for updating the parameters of the LES consumer demand functions.[6] The parameters for population, labor force, and total factor productivity by activity are updated exogenously.

Approach to Model Solution

CGE models are typically formulated and solved as systems of simultaneous equations exclusively made up of strict equalities. To permit the inclusion of inequality constraints for resources generating the desired dual-price regime, the ELW model was solved as an optimization problem, maximizing an objective function, subject to a set of constraints, made up of a mixture of strict equalities and inequalities. The AGRO-CGE model deals with this phenomenon in a different manner: it is formulated as a mixed complementarity problem (MCP), consisting of a set of simultaneous equations (once again a mix of strict equalities and inequalities), but without an objective function. The inequalities, which are linked to bounded (price) variables, apply to labor, land and water. The GAMS modeling software is used both to generate the disaggregated SAM and to implement the model. The model is solved with PATH and MILES, two solvers for mixed complementarity problems.[7]

Simulations

The model is used to simulate the Egyptian economy for the period 1990-2020. The simulations are divided into three categories exploring, respectively, the effects on economic performance of alternative scenarios for productivity growth and investment rates, foreign trade and agricultural water supplies.

The basic assumptions for the dynamic (30-year) simulations are presented

Table 2: Macro SAM for Egypt, 1989/90 (billion 1989/90 £E)

	Act.	Comm.	Factors			Institutions				Savings	Taxes/Subsidies/Tariff			
	1.	2.	3a.	3b.	3c.	4a.	4b.	4c.	4d.	5	6a.	6b.	6c.	6d.
1. Activity		106.6							14.5					
2. Commodity	52.8					54.2		4.9		24.7				
3. Factors														
3a. Labor	17.9							7.2	8.3					
3b. Capital	39.8													
3e. Land	8.0													
4. Institutions														
4a. Households			33.5	19.8	8.0		4.6	-1.2	1.0					
4b. Enterprises				19.8				1.4						
4c. Government				0.0					2.0					
4b. Rest of World		27.2					2.5							
5. Savings						10.4	11.3	-0.9	3.9					
6. Taxes/Subs/Tariffs														
6a. Ind.Taxes	4.3													
6b. Subsidies	-1.9													
6c. Dir. Taxes						1.1	3.1							
6d. Tariffs		2.9												
7. Total	121.0	136.6	33.5	39.8	8.0	65.7	21.4	11.5	29.7	24.7	4.3	-1.9	4.2	2.9

Note: Only column totals are shown; for each account, the row total is identical to the column total.

in Table 3. The values for transfers from the rest of the world and the current-account deficit for 1993 and onward reflect a judgement about what is considered reasonable and sustainable in light of recent improvements in Egypt's current account balance.[8] They imply that Egypt's trade deficit remains unchanged in absolute real terms but, as the economy grows, will decline relative to the overall size of the economy. The annual growth rate for export demand is at the level of Egypt's export growth for the period 1983-1994 (World Bank 1995, pp. 256-257). Future changes in the supply of two key agricultural resources, land and water, are difficult to predict. With regard to land, reclamation of less fertile lands and the transfer of older, more fertile lands to non-agricultural uses represent two opposing forces. For water, opposing forces are also at work: increased efficiency and improved exploitation may raise the supply while growing demands from upstream Nile countries and non-agricultural sectors domestically may force the agricultural sector to manage with less.[9] Here, it is assumed that water availability declines gradually between 1990 and 2020, reaching a supply in 2020 that is 20 percent less than in 1990.[10] For agricultural land, there is no supply change: in "efficiency" units, land reclamation is assumed to equal loss of lands to non-agricultural uses.

Scenarios for Productivity Growth and Investment

The specific assumptions underlying the three scenarios that are simulated are presented in Table 4. On the pessimistic side, the "Turtle" extrapolates the relatively dilatory economic performance of the 1980s and early 1990s, a period characterized by unfavorable external conditions and stagnant domestic policies. The more optimistic "Tiger" scenario postulates a decisive break from the past, incorporating investment rates and productivity growth, but not export growth, typical of successful East Asian economies. The third scenario, labeled the "Urban Tiger", explores the consequences of low agricultural productivity growth in a setting with high aggregate investment rates and rapid productivity growth for the rest of the economy.

Table 5 shows selected results for these three scenarios, compared with data for 1990 when relevant.[11] The message of the Turtle scenario is strong: extrapolation on the basis of the investment and productivity performance of the 1980s produces a very discouraging outcome. Per-capita GDP and household consumption decline and an unsustainable level of unemployment emerges in the labor market. In face of a growing budget share for foodstuffs, the food trade deficit increases.

Table 3: General Assumptions for Simulations 1990-2020

Item	1990 value	1993-2020 projection
Population size (mn.)	56.3	+1.65% per year
Labor force (mn.)	15.5	+2.62% per year
Labor force participation (%)	27.5	gradual increase to 37.2% in 2020
Export-demand	---	+6% per year
Transfers from RoW to household (1990 £Ebn)	9.3	12.5
Transfers from RoW to government (1990 £Ebn)	2.0	2.7
Current-Account Deficit (1990 £Ebn)	3.9	0.0
Current Government Savings (1990 £Ebn)	-0.9	0.0
Agricultural land (mn. feddans)	6.1	no change
Agricultural water supply (bn m^3)	32.9	gradual decline to 80% of base supply in 2020

Sources: World Bank (1994b, p. 210) and United Nations projections.
Note: In 2020, the size of the population and the labor force are 92.0 and 33.6 million, respectively. Water quantities are measured in terms of consumptive use (after deducting losses in the distribution system). For1990, it is assumed that water supply very marginally exceeded recorded water use, 32.9 bn m^3 (World Bank 1993a, p. 24).

Table 4: Assumptions for Alternative Productivity and Investment Scenarios

Item	Turtle	Tiger	Urban Tiger
Investment share of GDP (%)	20.2	25.0	25.0
Factor Productivity Growth (%/year)	0.32	2.5	Agriculture: 0.32 Oth. sectors: 2.50
Incremental Capital-Output Ratio	4.8	4.0	4.0

Sources: World Bank (1993c, pp. 42 and 56; 1993b, p. 45; 1994a, Annex B, Table 42); authors' calculations.
Note: For 1990 the investment share implicit in CAPMAS' SAM, 21.6 percent, is used. A slightly lower value is used for later periods in the Turtle scenario in light of an observed decline in the GDP investment share in the early 1990s.

In reality, one would expect that the dramatic increase in unemployment for the Turtle scenario would be tempered by a decline in real wages. To test the sensitivity of these results to the current assumption of a downwardly rigid real wage, the Turtle scenario was repeated with a flexible market-clearing wage at the 1990 unemployment rate throughout the period 1990-2020. The general trend was similar. The main difference is that the increase in unemployment was replaced by a decline in real wages, by 3.2 percent per year, signaling a dramatically different impact on income distribution. With a steady unemployment rate and declining wages, output growth was stronger, GDP at factor cost grew by 1.5 percent per year, and the small fall in household consumption was replaced by a minor increase (the index for household per capita income ended up at 104.7 in 2020, from a base of 100 in 1990). Nevertheless, the overall results are quite insensitive to the assumption about the labor market.

The outcome for the Tiger scenario dramatically illustrates the impact of achieving higher levels of investment and productivity growth over a 30-year period. GDP per capita grows at more than 3 percent a year, per-capita real household consumption is almost doubled, and the unemployment rate now declines slightly. The trade deficit, which is fixed in foreign currency, represents 16 percent of GDP in 1990 but, as GDP grows rapidly, it falls to 6 percent in 2020. Disaggregating the trade deficit, by the year 2020 there is an increase in the food deficit and a shift to a surplus in non-food items, a highly plausible tendency for a land- and water-constrained economy. While the real exchange rate appreciates for the slow-growth Turtle scenario, it now depreciates. This reflects the fact that, with relatively rapid growth in output and demand (including import demand), depreciation is needed to encourage exports and discourage imports up to the point of generating the fixed aggregate trade deficit.

The GDP share of agriculture declines strongly for the Tiger scenario and, to a lesser extent, also for the Turtle scenario, as growth in agriculture is much lower than growth in the rest of the economy. This trend, typical of growing economies, reflects the inverse relationship between growing income and the share spent on food, as well as the constraining impact on agriculture in Egypt of fixed or declining levels of scarce, sector-specific resources. Another structural change shown in Table 5 that is particularly strong for the Tiger scenario revolves around Egypt's economic relationship with the outside world: in the context of a liberal trading environment and a declining trade deficit (as share of GDP), the shares of export and import in GDP, which were substantial already in 1990, expand dramatically.

Table 5: Results for Alternative Productivity and Investment Scenarios

	Value: 1990	2020 Value or 1990-2020 Growth Rate:		
		Turtle	Tiger	Urban Tiger
GDP per capita at market prices (% growth/year)	---	-0.6	3.1	2.4
Household per capita consumption(index 1990 = 100)	100.0	98.9	194.0	157.8
Unemployment (%)	20.0	55.7	18.5	31.1
Imports (% of Nominal GDP)	34.7	35.8	55.0	57.5
Exports (% of Nominal GDP)	18.5	26.3	49.0	50.6
Trade deficit (% of Nominal GDP)				
Total	16.3	9.6	6.0	6.9
Food & agriculture	10.2	13.6	11.8	17.2
Other	6.1	-4.1	-5.7	-10.2
Exchange rate (£E/$: index 1990 = 100)	100.0	86.1	127.9	113.3
Wheat self-sufficiency rate (%)	44.6	24.5	40.8	11.3
Food self-sufficiency rate (%)	79.3	73.5	76.0	71.2
GDP at factor cost (% growth/year)				
Total	---	1.1	5.1	4.5
Agriculture	---	0.4	3.3	1.5
Non-Agriculture	---	1.3	5.6	5.2
Share of agriculture in real GDP at factor cost (%)	29.1	23.7	17.4	12.0

Note: Units are indicated in the first column. "1990" column refers to base year values; a dash (---) indicates "not applicable" (for rows indicating % growth/year 1990-2020).

The third scenario, the "Urban Tiger", was formulated to gauge the importance of the agricultural sector in the (Tiger) context of rapid growth and a diminishing agricultural share in GDP. It differs from the basic Tiger scenario in that, for the agricultural sectors, the optimistic assumption of annual total factor productivity growth at a rate of 2.5 percent is replaced by the Turtle rate of 0.32 percent (Table 4). Compared to the Tiger scenario, performance deteriorates (Table 5), aggregate growth is significantly lower, agricultural growth falls by more than 50 percent, and unemployment in 2020 is much higher than in 1990. In the food and agricultural area, Egypt is becoming more heavily reliant on the outside world; in particular, there is a dramatic fall in the rate of wheat self-sufficiency which probably would be considered unacceptable to Egyptian policymakers. The overall implication is that the performance of the agricultural sector will remain crucial also in the next century, even if non-agricultural growth is fairly rapid. Hence, it is important to nurture supporting activities (such as agricultural research and extension services) while preserving existing agricultural resources from environmental degradation and other sources of productivity losses.

Sensitivity Analysis: Foreign Trade

The above scenarios assumed that import tariff rates remained at the levels of 1990 whereas export demand grows at an annual rate of 6 percent.[12] We will here assess the effects of tariff cuts and more successful penetration of export markets in the context of the Tiger scenario. For tariff cuts, the first scenario assumes the removal of all agricultural tariffs, and the second the removal of tariffs across all sectors. In both cases, the relevant tariff rates are set at zero starting from 1993. For export demand, we test the impact of doubling the annual growth rate to 12 percent, close to South Korea's record for the period 1973-1993 (World Bank 1995, pp. 396-397).

Table 6 shows the results for these three scenarios compared to the basic Tiger scenario and 1990 data. For both tariff cuts scenarios, the aggregate impact is positive but very minor: the indicators for per-capita GDP growth, household consumption, and unemployment all show some small improvement. The positive effects are slightly stronger for the scenario with full tariff removal. In reality, tariff cuts may boost productivity growth by increasing the exposure of domestic producers to international competition; however, such potential effects are not captured in the current model. Given the closure rule for the government account, the tariff cuts lead to a shortfall in government revenue that is compensated by an increase in direct tax rates. Compared to the basic Tiger scenario, the direct tax rates are 8 percent higher for the agricultural tariff cut and 72 percent higher for the economy-wide tariff cut.[13] For both scenarios, there is some additional depreciation, strengthening the competitiveness of tradables sufficiently to generate the same trade deficit as with tariff protection, but in a less distortionary fashion.

For the third scenario, with more rapid growth in export demand, the repercussions are quite strong. By 2020, the economy has reached "full" employment, an unemployment rate of 5 percent,[14] as opposed to 19 percent for the basic Tiger scenario, an achievement that marginally boosts aggregate growth. To validate the initial trade deficit (fixed in foreign currency), the exchange rate appreciates strongly compared to the other Tiger scenarios; this has a strong positive impact on real household consumption. Thus, this scenario demonstrates that strong export performance can have a decisive impact on real household welfare and on the economy's ability to absorb marginal labor.

Table 6: Results for Alternative Foreign Trade Scenarios

		2020 value or 1990-2020 growth rate		
	Value: 1990	Tiger	Agricultural Tariffs Removed	All Tariffs Removed	Rapid Export demand Growth
GDP per capita at market prices (% growth/Year)	--	3.1	3.1	3.1	3.5
Household per capita consumption (Index 1990=1000)	100.0	194.0	194.4	194.6	288.8
Unemployment (%)	20.0	18.5	17.7	15.5	5.0
Imports (% of Nominal GDP)	34.7	55.0	56.2	59.3	36.9
Exports (% of Nominal GDP)	18.5	49.0	50.1	53.0	34.1
Trade deficit (% of Nominal GDP)					
Total	16.3	6.0	6.1	6.4	2.8
Food & agriculture	10.2	11.8	12.2	12.7	10.3
Other	6.1	-5.7	-6.1	-6.3	-7.6
Exchange rate (£E/$; inddex 1990=100)	100.0	127.9	131.0	135.3	83.0
Wheat self-sufficiency rate (%)	44.6	40.8	38.5	39.7	10.8
Food self-sufficiency rate (%)	79.3	76.0	75.8	76.5	78.3
GDP at factor cost (% growth/year)					
Total	--	5.1	5.1	5.1	5.4
Agriculture	--	3.3	3.3	3.3	3.7
Non-Agriculture	--	5.6	5.6	5.7	5.8
Share of agriculture in real GDP at factor cost (%)	29.1	17.4	17.3	17.1	18.3

Note: See Table 5 for explanations.

In the Egyptian environment, water is not priced and the right to use water is associated with land ownership. In our model, the simulated value of the land/water aggregate arises from its marginal productivity in production and incorporates both the value of the raw land and the water right associated with land ownership. It is assumed that both land and water are allocated efficiently across the different crops. The model simulations can be use to allocate the total value of the land/water aggregate between raw land and water, a value which is unobservable in Egypt since there are not separate and liberalized markets for raw land and water.

Figure 2 shows the water share of the total value of the land/water aggregate for three of the above scenarios: Turtle, Tiger, and Urban Tiger. The results indicate that over time, as water becomes relatively scarce, its value to farmers will exceed that of raw land. The differences in the water shares across the scenarios and over time reflects the extent to which agricultural commodity demands are directed toward water-intensive crops, in its turn a reflection of economic interactions, both domestically and with the outside world. The fact that, water-intensive crops (for example rice) tend to have relatively low income-elasticities of demand lowers the value share for water, other things being equal.

Figure 2: Share of Total Value of Land/Water Aggregate Allocable to Water

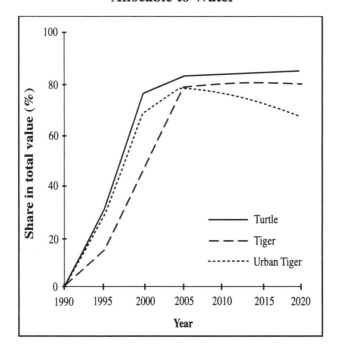

Sensitivity Analysis: Water Supply and Productivity Growth

In the long run, there is considerable uncertainty about Egypt's future agricultural water supplies. In the basic Tiger scenario, the assumption of a simultaneous 2.5 percent productivity growth in output per unit of both land and water may be excessively optimistic. While the Green Revolution has led to increases in land yields of this magnitude, they have often been associated with an increase in water use per land unit.

Table 7: Results for Tiger Scenarios with Different Cuts in Water Supply

	Value: 1990	2020value or 1990-2020 growth rate:			
		Tiger-0	Tiger-20	Tiger-40	Tiger-60
Water supply cut (%)	---	0.0	20.0	40.0	60.0
GDP per capita at market prices (%growth/year)	---	3.19	3.10	2.93	2.61
Household per capita consumption (index 1990=100)	100.0	199.6	194.0	182.5	164.3
Unemployment (%)	20.0	15.0	18.5	24.0	34.4
Imports (%of Nominal GDP)	34.7	54.5	55.0	59.8	63.5
Exports (%of Nominal GDP)	18.5	48.5	49.0	53.4	56.4
Trade deficit (% of Nominal GDP)					
Total	16.3	6.0	6.0	6.5	7.1
Food & agriculture	10.2	10.4	11.8	15.8	19.5
Other	6.1	-4.4	-5.7	-9.4	-12.4
Exchange rate (£E/$: index 1990=100)	100.0	132.3	127.9	128.2	124.3
Wheat self-sufficiency rate (%)	44.6	32.7	40.8	47.8	32.6
Food self-sufficiency rate (%)	79.3	77.0	76.0	69.6	65.8
GDP at factor cost (% growth/year)					
Total	---	5.16	5.09	4.99	4.75
Agriculture	---	3.52	3.33	2.91	2.01
Non-Agriculture	---	5.65	5.61	5.56	5.43
Share of agriculture in real) GDP at factor cost (%)	29.1	18.0	17.4	15.8	13.0

Note: See Table 5 for explanations.

To explore the sensitivity of the results to different assumptions about water use, we ran a series of variations on the Tiger scenario. We reduced agricultural water supplies in steps of 10 percent, with declines ranging from 0 to 60 percent and taking place gradually between 1990 and 2020. (The basic Tiger scenario specified a 20 percent decline.) These experiments can be seen as simulating the impact of smaller water supplies or, alternatively, they can be interpreted as exploring the impact of lower productivity growth for water relative to other factors, including land. For example, a 50 percent decrease in the water supply (or in water productivity) in 30 years corresponds to an annual productivity decline of 2.28 percent. The same outcome could be achieved by reducing water productivity growth from 2.5 percent to 0.22 percent per year; that is, to a growth rate below the Turtle level.[15]

The results of these sensitivity simulations are summarized in Table 7 and Figures 3 and 4. Cuts up to 20 percent do not impose severe constraints on the economy. It is apparently not too difficult to marginally change the crop mix to make better use of water, especially given that the water constraint was not binding in the base year. For larger cuts, the effects are more severe. Never-the-less, the changes in most economy-wide indicators, GDP growth, house-hold consumption, and trade, are manageable even for a 60 percent cut in water availability (or, from a different perspective, an annual decline in water supplies by 0.5 percent with no change in water productivity). The major exception is unemployment: in 2020, it encompasses 34 percent of the labor force (as opposed to 19 percent for the basic Tiger), illustrating the high sensitivity of labor absorption to marginal changes in growth.

Figure 3: Factor Unemployment Rates with Reduced Water Supplies, Tiger Scenario

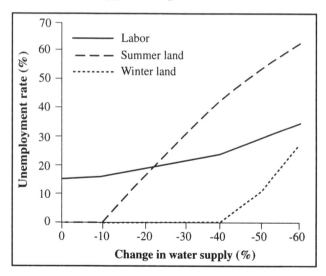

Within the agricultural sector, the changes are more drastic. Compared to the basic Tiger, agricultural growth shrinks considerably, reaching merely 2 percent per year, when a 60 percent water cut is imposed. In response to water cuts, agricultural capital and labor intensities increase along with increased relative agricultural prices.[16] In 1990, the real share in agricultural value-added of the land/water aggregate was 38 percent. By 2020, this share ranges from 26 percent for no water cut to 21 percent for a 60 percent cut. As shown in Figure 3, a growing share of summer land is left uncultivated and, starting between 40 percent and 50 percent cuts, winter land also is taken out of production. Accordingly, as shown in Figure 4, the water share in aggregate water and land incomes climbs from zero to 100 percent. As land returns decline, it would become easier to convert agricultural land to non-agricultural uses. Reduced water supplies bring about significant changes in the cropping pattern; in this environment, cotton, fruit and vegetables are relatively competitive whereas other crops, including rice, virtually disappear. Given their lower water requirements, winter crops, including wheat, are favored since they make more productive use of the remaining scarce water. (See Table A2.4 for details.)

Figure 4: Share of Land/Water Income with Reduced Water Supplies, Tiger Scenario

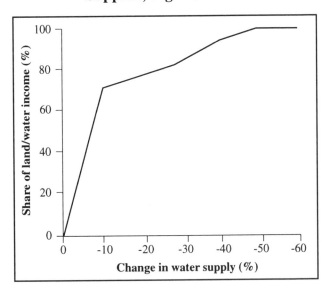

Conclusions

In 1960, Egypt's per capita income was 60 percent above South Korea's. Thirty years later, it reached merely 11 percent of the South Korean level (Mason 1984, p. 8; World Bank 1992, p. 219). The exceptional South Korean performance and the relatively lackluster Egyptian growth reflect differences

over the long run in investment levels, choice of development strategy, policy management, and other considerations. This chapter considers alternative
future scenarios for Egypt from 1990 to 2020, also a period of 30 years, using
a dynamic CGE model with a detailed treatment of the agricultural sector. In
terms of method, the model, expressed as a mixed-complementarity problem,
formulates agricultural resource constraints in a fashion that is innovative in
the context of CGE models, permitting not only full utilization with flexible
prices but also excess supplies with a zero price. In all scenarios, we assume
that Egypt's economy will be market-oriented and competitive; that there will
be mechanisms in place for achieving an efficient allocation of water in agriculture; and that growth will occur in an environment of general macroeconomic balance. As indicated by its title, this chapter should be seen as
exploratory: the model needs to be more closely adapted to Egypt's economic structure; better data is needed; and the empirical foundations for the alternative scenarios may be strengthened.[17]

We consider two broad scenarios: the "Turtle," which extrapolates on the
basis of the productivity growth and investment levels characteristic of
Egypt's recent past; and the "Tiger," which combines key aspects of successful East Asian economic performance (using Korean data as a proxy) with
Egyptian resource constraints and production structure. The results for the
Turtle scenario are grim. Per-capita income remains roughly the same in 2020
as 30 years earlier. As the country's labor force grows dramatically, the labor
market moves toward a crisis, with some unsustainable combination of
increasing unemployment and falling real wages. On the other hand, the
"Tiger" scenarios, which assume that Egypt achieves rates of investment and
productivity growth typical of South Korea and other high-performance East
Asian economies, are more encouraging. When combined with rapid growth
in export demand, per-capita household income almost triples, while full
employment is also achieved.

Sensitivity analysis of the results for the Tiger scenario suggests that
export-demand growth and balanced rapid productivity growth (not excluding
agriculture) are of crucial importance. While having a positive effect, the
removal of distorting import tariffs is alone of minor importance. Increasing
water scarcity (due to water cuts or lower water productivity growth) have a
strong negative impact on agricultural performance and labor absorption without, however, significantly reducing growth in aggregate output and income.
The unemployment rate is the aggregate indicator that is most sensitive to
changes in economic performance, assuming downward rigidity of real wages.

The broader policy implications from this analysis are clear: Egypt should
attach top priority to measures that promise to raise balanced long-run

productivity growth (covering both agriculture and other sectors); encourage high investment rates; and seek foreign trade agreements that give access to export markets while lowering import tariffs in return. The gains from increased exports far outweigh the costs of structural adjustments required from opening domestic markets. In searching for a successful Egyptian development strategy, it is potentially fruitful to learn from South Korea and other successful East Asian economies.[18]

Notes

1   For surveys of earlier CGE models of Egypt, see El-Laithy (1994) and Löfgren (1994b).
2   Dethier (1985) is an early agriculture-focused CGE model of Egypt. Hazell et al. (1995) use a detailed, partial-equilibrium, programming model of the Egyptian agricultural sector, extended in Löfgren (1995b) for analysis of water policy. Löfgren (1995a) is a CGE model adapted to the structure of Egypt's economy. The representation of agriculture in the AGRO-CGE model is in the tradition of Hazell et al., although less detailed.
3   Compared to labor, the difference is that, for these agriculture-specific resources, the supply curve is horizontal at a price of zero whenever demand is less than the fixed quantity supplied
4   For a survey of issues related to water markets in LDCs, see Rosegrant and Binswanger (1994).
5   Savings from the other sources, government, households, and the rest of the world, are not free to equilibrate aggregate savings-investment. Government and rest-of-the-world savings are exogenous while household savings are a fixed share of income.
6   More specifically, simulated values for per-capita consumption, commodity prices, and real per-capita income enter the relationships from which the LES parameters are derived. The Frisch parameter is adjusted on the basis of changes in simulated per-capita income, drawing on a function estimated by Lluch, Powell and Williams (1977, p. 248): $F=-36X^{-0.36}$ where F = Frisch parameter, X = per-capita income.
7   For GAMS, see Brooke et al. (1988). Rutherford (1995) provides more information on PATH and MILES.
8   The current account was in deficit between 1974 and 1990, when it moved into surplus. Since 1992, the surpluses have declined gradually from a high of $2.8bn. (EIU 1995, pp. 3 and 9). We simply assume a zero deficit throughout the period 1993-2020.
9   For a discussion of the different factors involved, see Abu-Zeid (1993) and World Bank (1993a, pp. 23-29). The basic scenarios of this chapter have been formulated in the spirit of Richards (1995): Egypt's agriculture is or is about to become supply-constrained for water as total supply is unlikely to increase significantly at the same time as non-agricultural water demands are likely to grow.
10 The impact of declines in water supplies are indistinguishable from the impact of lower rates of productivity growth for water. The sensitivity of the results to alternative cuts in agricultural water supply (or productivity) is analyzed later.
11 Tables A2.1-3 in Appendix 2 present cropping patterns and resource prices for the different scenarios.

12 For import tariffs, aggregate figures in CAPMAS' SAM implied higher rates for individual commodities than suggested by available disaggregated information (American Embassy 1992, p. 41). Drawing on this information, this inconsistency was overcome by assuming a uniform low tariff for staple crops (primarily grains, set at 8 percent), and a uniform high tariff for other crops (primarily vegetables and fruits, calibrated to 77 percent). The results presented in the chapter do not seem to be sensitive to the specific levels of these two uniform rates.

13 For example, in 2020 for the Tiger scenario, household and enterprise direct tax rates are, respectively, 1.8 percent and 15.5 percent. For the scenario with an economy-wide tariff cut, the corresponding rates are 3.1 percent and 26.7 percent.

14 However, the improvement in the average real wage is quite small, indicating that the labor-market bottleneck constrains aggregate growth only to a minor extent.

15 The corresponding annual rates of decline are 0.35 percent for a 10 percent cut, 0.74 percent for a 20 percent cut, 1.18 percent for a 30 percent cut, 1.69 percent for a 40 percent cut, and 3.01 percent for a 60 percent cut.

16 The ease with which this takes place is determined by the elasticity of substitution between factors in the agricultural value-added functions, here a value of 0.4 is used. The fact that substitutability between water and land is zero may lead to a negative bias for these scenarios.

17 In terms of the model structure, it may be desirable to strengthen the hydrological aspects, and explore means of making the mix between water and land price-responsive (while still permitting a dual market regime for both water and land). It would be of interest to incorporate stylized facts reflecting the impact of economic openness on productivity growth along the lines in Lewis et al. (1995).

18 For recent research assessing the relevance of East Asian industrial policy to Egypt, see Said et al. (1995).

19 See Rutherford (1995) for a description of MCP algorithms, their application to CGE mod-els, and their implementation in the GAMS language.

20 For other choices of numeraire, relative solution prices will equal relative shadow prices.

References

Abu-Zeid, M. 1993. "Egypt's Water Resource Management and Policies." in M. A. Faris and M. H. Khan (eds.), *Sustainable Agriculture in Egypt*. Boulder, Colorado: Lynne Rienner.

American Embassy. 1992. *Agricultural Situation Annual Report*. Cairo, March.

Brooke, A., D. Kendrick, and A. Meeraus. 1988. GAMS: A User's Guide. Redwood, California: The Scientific Press.

CAPMAS. 1993. StatisticalYearbook. Cairo, June.

___. 1994. *National Accounts for Egypt: Input-output Tables for 1989/90*. Cairo, June

1995. *National Accounts for Egypt: A Social Accounting Matrix for 1989/90*. Cairo, January

Central Bank of Egypt. 1994. *Annual Report, 1993/94*. Cairo. (In Arabic.)

Dervis, K., J. de Melo, and S. Robinson. 1982. *General Equilibrium Models for Development Policy*. New York: Cambridge University Press.

Dethier, Jean-Jacques. 1985. "The Political Economy of Food Prices in Egypt." Ph.D. Dissertation, Department of Agricultural and Resource Economics, University of California at Berkeley.

Economist Intelligence Unit. *Country Report: Egypt*. Various issues.

El-Laithy. H. 1994. "Review of Macroeconomic Policies and Economic Modeling."
    Paper prepared for the IFPRI Project on Food Security and Structural Adjustment
    in Egypt. January. (Processed)

Lewis, J. D., S. Robinson, and Z. Wang. 1995. *Beyond the Uruguay Round: The
    Implications of an Asian Free Trade Area.* January. (Processed)

Lluch, C., A. A. Powell, and R. A. Williams. 1977. *Patterns in Household Demand and
    Saving.* World Bank Research Publication. New York: Oxford University Press.

Löfgren, H. 1994a. "A Brief Survey of Elasticities for CGE Models." Paper presented
    to the Ford Foundation. December.

___. 1994b. "Egypt's Experience from CGE Modeling: A Critical Review." ERF
    Working Paper WP 9411, Cairo: Economic Research Forum for the Arab
    Countries, Iran and Turkey.

___.1995a. "Macro and Micro Effects of Subsidy Cuts: A Short-run CGE Analysis for
    Egypt." *Middle East Business and Economic Review.* Vol. 7, No. 2: 18-39.

___. 1995b. "Water Policy in Egypt: An Analysis with IFPRI's Agricultural Sector
    Model." Trade and Macroeconomics Division Discussion Paper No. 7.
    Washington, DC: IFPRI.

Mason, E. S. 1984. "The Chenery Analysis and Some Other Considerations" in
    Syrquin, M., L. Taylor, and L. E. Westphal (eds.), *Economic Structure and
    Performance: Essays in Honor of Hollis B. Chenery.* New York: Academic Press.

Richards, Alan. 1995. "The Economic Value of Water: Concepts, Measurements and
    Options for Implementation." Ministry of Public Works and Water Resources,
    Cairo. June. (Processed)

Robinson, S., and C. Gehlhar. 1995. "Land, Water, and Agriculture in Egypt: The
    Economy-wide Impact of Policy Reform." TMD Discussion Paper No. 1.
    Washington, DC: IFPRI.

Rosegrant, M. W., and H. P. Binswanger. 1994. "Markets in Tradable Water Rights:
    Potential for Efficiency Gains in Developing Country Water Resource Allocation."
    World Development, Vol. 22, No. 11:1613-1625, November .

Rutherford, T. 1995. "Extensions of GAMS for Complementarity Problems Arising in
    Applied Economic Analysis." *Journal of Economic Dynamics and Control.* Vol.
    19, No. 8:1299-1324.

Said, M., H.J. Chang, and K. Sakr. 1995. "Industrial Policy and the Role of the State
    in Egypt: Relevance of the East Asian Experience." ERF Working Paper WP 9514.
    Cairo: Economic Research Forum for the Arab Countries, Iran and Turkey.

USAID. 1992. *Agricultural Data Base.* Cairo. January.

World Bank. 1992. *World Development Report 1992.* New York: Oxford University
    Press.

___. 1993a. *Arab Republic of Egypt: An Agricultural Strategy for the 1990s.* A World
    Bank Country Study. Washington, D.C.

___. 1993b. *Arab Republic of Egypt: Public Sector Investment Review,* Vol. I, Main
    Report.

___. 1993c. *The East Asian Miracle: Economic Growth and Public Policy.* A World
    Bank Policy Research Report. New York: Oxford University Press.

___. 1994a. *Private Sector Development in Egypt: The Status and the Challenges.*
    World Bank Resident Mission, Cairo.

___. 1994b. *World Development Report 1994.* New York: Oxford University Press.

___. 1995. *World Tables 1995.* Baltimore: Johns Hopkins University Press.

Appendix 1: The Egyptian AGRO-CGE Model

The Egyptian model is an economy-wide, computable general equilibrium (CGE) model that disaggregates the agricultural sector and provides special treatment of land and water. The AGRO-CGE model combines an activity-analysis representation of agricultural resource (land and water) technology with a neoclassical representation elsewhere. Inequality constraints impose upper limits on the use of agricultural resources. While the activity-analysis specification of agricultural technology in this version is simple, the model is capable of replicating or being linked to more elaborate agricultural sector models.

Table A1.1 provides a listing of the equations of a simplified version of the AGRO-CGE model. The simplified model in Table A.1.1 focuses on production technology and ignores international trade, income distribution, and macro aggregates such as savings, investment, the balance of trade, and the government deficit. Equations 1 to 5 give the production structure, following the nesting in Figure 1. Equations 6 to 13 define cost prices and the various first-order conditions for profit maximization. Equations 14 and 15 map factor income to product demand, while equations 16 to 20 provide market-clearing conditions. Finally, equations 21 to 26 bring together a number of revenue-expenditure identities arising from the homogeneity of the various underlying functions. These identities are implied by the other equations and are hence not independent equations. The simple model has $(13+i + i+j + 5)$ endogenous variables and, assuming all constraints are binding, $(13+i + i+j + 6)$ equations. The model, however, satisfies Walras' Law and therefore has only $(13+i + i+j + 5)$ independent equations.

Except for the land/water aggregate (LND), the model has a standard neoclassical specification. The CES functions for real value added yield well-behaved first-order conditions for profit maximization (equations $10 + 12$), conditions which will generally yield a solution with all factor prices strictly positive. The land/water aggregate, however, is a linear function of water and land (H2O and FED), with separate supply constraints (equations 17 and 18). The full model has two land types, corresponding to summer and winter cropping. Given that there are multiple agricultural sectors with quite different water and land coefficients, it is certainly possible to have both constraints binding. If either the water or land constraint is especially binding, however, it is also possible that the constraint on the other will not be binding. For example, the water constraint might be so binding that it is impossible to find a crop mix that utilizes all the land; the land constraint equation would then be satisfied as a strict inequality. If the land or water constraint is not binding (equations 17 and 18), the corresponding market price of land or water (W^{fed} and W^{H2O} in equation 9) should be zero in equilibrium. The solution prices in the

CGE model display the same kind of complementary slackness as the shadow price system in an agricultural sector mathematical programming model.

A neoclassical CGE simulation model will generally have a unique solution that satisfies all the non-linear first-order conditions with all prices strictly positive and all constraints satisfied as equalities. No maximand is needed, since the model includes explicit supply and demand equations for all goods and factors. In the LW-CGE model, the first-order conditions for the land and water constraints are summarized in the linear cost functions in equation 9. There is a problem, however, in that there is an infinite number of solutions that satisfy the cost function (equation 9) and the two inequality constraints (equations 17 and 18). Without an explicit maximand, there is nothing in the cost equations that prevents the model economy from operating within the production possibility frontier for agriculture. In the usual CGE simulation model, this possibility is eliminated by expressing the resource constraints as strict equalities.

Given the inequalities for the land and water constraints, there are two approaches that can be used to solve the model. First, the model can be seen as a nonlinear mixed complementarity problem (MCP) in which the land and water prices, W^{FED} and W^{H2O}, are "complementary" to the land and water supply-demand inequalities. Complementarity simply means that the product of the non-negative price times the corresponding excess-supply inequality must equal zero, as noted earlier. Imposing the two complementary slackness conditions explicitly guarantees that the model operates on the production possibility frontier while also satisfying the market equilibrium pricing equations. Recently developed MCP solvers work well on this particular model.[19] This is the approach we have used in this chapter.

The second approach to solving the AGRO-CGE model is to introduce an explicit maximand and treat the model as a nonlinear programming problem. Since the CGE model is designed to simulate the operation of a market economy, it is important to specify a maximand that generates a solution that can be seen as simulating a market outcome. However, we explicitly specify in equation 9 that the price of the land/water aggregate must equal the cost of the water and land used, a condition that is true in a competitive equilibrium in which there are no excess profits. In general, any solution that is on the production possibility frontier and satisfies equation 9 with non-negative prices can be seen as a market outcome. Factor wages would equal marginal revenue products for land and water in all agricultural sectors, a condition which characterizes a profit-maximizing market equilibrium.

Given that the AGRO-CGE model has a single consumer, the obvious choice of maximand is consumer welfare. In a competitive economy with no distortions, maximizing consumer welfare will generate a profit-maximizing and utility-maximizing market equilibrium, and is equivalent to maximizing the sum of consumers' and producers' surplus in the economy. In addition, the various supply-demand balance constraints will then have shadow prices that measure the welfare gains from relaxing the constraints. If there are distortions in the market price system, for example from sectoral tariffs, taxes, and subsidies, the model will generate a market solution and any differences between the simulated market prices and the shadow prices, given the maximand, measure the welfare costs associated with the distortions.

In this model, we have chosen as numeraire (Equation 13) the cost of living index associated with the utility function that underlies the expenditure functions (Equation 15). In this case, the variable Y, which measures aggregate income and expenditure, is a direct measure of utility. Given the numeraire, it corresponds to expenditure in the indirect utility function. Changes in Y are a direct measure of "equivalent variation," which is a standard measure of welfare change. In addition, for this choice of maximand, if there are no distortions in the model economy, the shadow prices associated with the supply-demand balance equations should exactly equal the endogenous market-clearing prices at the simulated market equilibrium.[20]

While the AGRO-CGE model solves for market rental rates for land and water (FED and H2O) at the bottom of the production nest, it is not necessary to interpret these rates as occurring in an actual market. In fact, Egypt does not charge for water use, so there is currently no market for water. However, we do assume that, at the next level, the solution rental rate for the land/water aggregate does reflect a market valuation. In effect, we are assuming that, when a farmer uses land to grow a particular crop, he is entitled to the needed water, and the market return to his land reflects that entitlement.

The model separately prices land and water and so decomposes the rental value of the land/water aggregate into components reflecting pure land rent and the value of the water entitlement. The model solution generates information about the counter-factual "what if" question: If Egypt were to institute a market for water, what would be the market-clearing price?

Table A1.1: Equations of a Simplified AGRO-CGE Model

Production

1	X_i	$= LIN_i (V_i, INT_i)$	Linear production function.
2	V_i	$= CES_i (K_i, L_i, LND_i)$	CES value added function.
3	X_{ij}	$= LIN_{ij} (INT_i)$	Intermediate inputs.
4	FED_i	$= LIN_i (LND_i)$	Land input.
5	$H2O_i$	$= LIN_i (LND_i)$	Water input.

Prices and Factor Demand

6	$(1 - t_i^x) \cdot P_i^x$	$= LIN_i (P_i^V, P_i^{INT})$	Output cost price.
7	P_i^{INT}	$= LIN_i (P_{ji}; j)$	Intermediate input cost price.
8	P_i^V	$= CES_i (W^K, W^L, W_i^{LND})$	Value added cost price.
9	W_i^{LND}	$= LIN_i (W^{FED}, W^{H2O})$	Land/water cost price.
10	W_i^{LND}	$= \dfrac{\partial V_i}{\partial LND_i} P_i^V$	Demand for land/water.
11	W^K	$= \dfrac{\partial V_i}{\partial K_i} P_i^V$	Demand for capital.
12	W^L	$= \dfrac{\partial V_i}{\partial L_i} P_i^V$	Demand for labor.
13	$\overline{p}$	$= \pi_i (P_i^x)^{\beta_i}$	Numeraire cost of living index.

Income and Final Demand

14	Y	$= \sum_i (P_i^V \cdot V_i + t_i^x \cdot P_i^x \cdot X_i)$	Aggregate income.
15	$P_i^x \cdot C_i$	$= \beta_i \cdot Y$	Consumption demand.

Supply-Demand Balances

16	X_i	$= C_i + \sum_j X_{ij}$	Prouct supply-demand.
17	$\overline{FED}$	$\geq \sum_i FED_i$	Land supply-demand.
18	$\overline{H2O}$	$\geq \sum_i H2O_i$	Water supply-demand.
19	$\overline{L}$	$= \sum_i L_i$	Labor supply-demand.
20	$\overline{K}$	$= \sum_i K_i$	Capital supply-demand.

Identities

21	$(1 - t_i^x) \cdot P_i^x \cdot X_i = P_i^V \cdot V_i + P_i^{INT} \cdot INT_i$		Sales/income.
22	$P_i^V \cdot V_i \quad = W^K \cdot K_i + W^L \cdot L_i + W_i^{LND} \cdot LND_i$		Value-added/ factor payments.
23	$P_i^{INT} \cdot INT_i \quad = \sum_j P_{ji}^x \cdot X_{ji}$		Intermediate input expenditure.
24	$W_i^{LND} \cdot LND_i = W^{FED} \cdot FED_i + W^{H2O} \cdot H2O_i$		Land/ water payments.
25	$\sum_i P_i^x \cdot C_i \quad = Y$		Income / expenditure.
26	$Y = W^K \cdot \overline{K} + W^L \cdot \overline{L} + \sum_i W_i^{LND} \cdot LND_i +$		Income / factor payments.

Variables and Parameters

Variables

X_i	Output
V_i	Real value added
INT_i	Aggregate intermediate input use
K_i	Capital input
L_i	Labor input
LND_i	Aggregate land/water input
X_{ji}	Intermediate input from sector j to sector i
FED_i	Land subfactor input into land / water aggregate
$H2O_i$	Water subfactor input into land / water aggregate
P_i^X	Output market price
P_i^V	Value added price
P_i^{INT}	Aggregate intemediate input price
W^K	Rental rate of capital
W^L	Wage of labor
W_i^{LND}	Rental rate of sectoral land / water aggregate
W^{FED}	Rental rate of land subfactor
W^{H2O}	Price of water subfactor
Y	Aggregate income
C_i	Consumption demand

Parameters

t_i^X	Indirect tax rate (or subsidy, if negative)
J_i	Consumption expenditure shares
$\overline{FED}$	Aggregate supply of land subfactor
$\overline{H2O}$	Aggregate supply of water subfactor
$\overline{L}$	Aggregate supply of labor
$\overline{K}$	Aggregate supply of capital

Notation

LIN	Linear function
CES	Constant elasticity of substitution function

Appendix 2: Supplementary Tables

Table A2.1: Elasticity Values Used in Model

Sector	LES	Armington	CET	CES	Export demand
Berseem	--	--	--	0.80	--
Cotton	0.58	0.60	--	0.40	--
Fruit	1.26	0.30	0.80	0.40	-7.5
Maize	0.29	8.00	0.50	0.40	-7.5
Other summer crops	0.29	0.30	1.50	0.40	-7.5
Other winter crops	0.29	0.30	1.50	0.40	-7.5
Rice	0.29	6.00	0.50	0.40	-7.5
Sugar Cane	--	2.00	--	0.40	--
Summer vegetables	1.26	0.30	0.80	0.40	-7.5
Winter vegetables	1.26	0.30	0.80	0.40	-7.5
Wheat	0.29	8.00	--	0.40	--
Livestock	1.26	0.30	1.50	0.40	-7.5
Oil	1.26	2.00	2.00	--	--
Food Processing	0.87	0.33	2.00	0.60	-7.5
Cotton Ginning	0.29	0.33	2.00	0.60	-7.5
Textiles	1.07	0.33	2.00	0.60	-7.5
Other Industry	1.07	0.33	2.00	0.60	-7.5
Electricity	1.26	0.33	1.50	0.40	-2.5
Construction	1.29	0.33	2.00	0.60	-2.5
Services	1.26	0.33	2.00	0.60	-2.5

Note: For a brief survey of elasticities of CGE models. Löfgren (1994a).
Abbreviations:
LES = Household income elasticity of demand in LES demand functions;
Armington = Elasticity of substitution between imports and domestic goods in CES aggregation function;
CET = Elasticity of transformation between exports and domestic sales in CET function;
CES = Elasticity of factor substitution in CES value-added functions.

Table A2.2: Cropping Patterns and Resource Prices for Alternative Productivity and Investment Scenarios

	Value 1990	Value for the year 2020:		
		Turtle	Tiger	Urban Tiger
Summer Land		---- Percent composition ----		
Cotton	16.5	22.7	27.8	26.2
Fruit	12.6	16.0	13.5	18.0
Maize	39.3	16.0	23.2	13.5
Other Crops	2.7	3.9	2.8	4.6
Rice	17.2	10.2	7.6	7.9
Sugar Cane	4.4	3.3	3.0	3.4
Vegetables	7.3	7.4	7.1	10.7
Excess Supply	0.0	20.5	15.1	15.7
Total Supply	100.0	100.0	100.0	100.0
Winter Land				
Long Berseem	25.0	26.8	24.2	29.6
Short Berseem	16.5	22.7	27.8	26.2
Fruit	12.6	16.0	13.5	18.0
Other Crops	7.6	9.4	6.3	10.3
Sugar Cane	4.4	3.3	3.0	3.4
Vegetables	3.1	3.0	2.8	3.9
Wheat	30.8	18.9	22.4	8.6
Excess Supply	0.0	0.0	0.0	0.0
Total Supply	100.0	100.0	100.0	100.0
Resource rents/prices		---- 1989/90 £E -----		
Summer land (£E/feddan)	701	0	0	0
Winter land (£E/feddan)	628	343	1624	1671
Water (£E/'000m^3)	0	359	1287	712

Table A2.3: Cropping Patterns and Resource Prices for Tiger Scenarios with Alternative Foreign Trade Assumptions

		Value for the year 2020:			
	Value 1990	Tiger	Agricultural tariffs removed	All tariffs removed	Rapid Export Growth
Summer Land		----- Percent composition -----			
Cotton	16.5	27.8	27.9	27.9	25.7
Fruit	12.6	13.5	13.5	13.3	19.6
Maize	39.3	23.2	22.8	23.0	14.4
Other Crops	2.7	2.8	2.8	2.7	3.6
Rice	17.2	7.6	7.6	7.7	7.0
Sugar Cane	4.4	3.0	3.0	2.9	3.3
Vegetables	7.3	7.1	7.3	7.3	12.3
Excess Supply	0.0	15.1	15.2	15.2	14.1
Total Supply	100.0	100.0	100.0	100.0	100.0
Winter Land					
Long Berseem	25.0	24.2	25.3	24.7	34.2
Short Berseem	16.5	27.8	27.9	27.9	25.7
Fruit	12.6	13.5	13.5	13.3	19.6
Other Crops	7.6	6.3	6.2	6.2	7.2
Sugar Cane	4.4	3.0	3.0	2.9	3.3
Vegetables	3.1	2.8	3.0	2.9	3.3
Wheat	30.8	22.4	21.2	22.0	6.0
Excess Supply	0.0	0.0	0.0	0.0	0.0
Total Supply	100.0	100.0	100.0	100.0	100.0
Resource rents/prices		----- 1989/90£E -----			
Summer land (£E/feddan)	701	0	0	0	0
Winter land (£E/feddan)	628	1624	1588	1563	3354
Water (£E/'000m^3)	0	1287	1206	1242	882

Table A2.4: Cropping Patterns and Resource Prices for Tiger Scenarios with Alternative Water Cuts

	Value 1990	Value for the year 2020:			
		Tiger-0	Tiger-20	Tiger-40	Tiger-60
Summer Land	----- Percent composition -----				
Cotton	16.5	27.1	27.8	28.1	18.5
Fruit	12.6	13.9	13.5	13.2	10.9
Maize	39.3	29.3	23.2	3.7	0.3
Other Crops	2.7	2.3	2.8	2.3	1.9
Rice	17.2	14.1	7.6	2.2	0.3
Sugar Cane	4.4	4.9	3.0	2.4	1.6
Vegetables	7.3	8.4	7.1	5.7	4.4
Excess Supply	0.0	0.0	15.1	42.4	61.9
Total Supply	100.0	100.0	100.0	100.0	100.0
Winter Land					
Long Berseem	25.0	25.4	24.2	21.3	18.8
Short Berseem	16.5	27.1	27.8	28.1	18.5
Fruit	12.6	13.9	13.5	13.2	10.9
Other Crops	7.6	6.3	6.3	6.2	5.6
Sugar Cane	4.4	4.9	3.0	2.4	1.6
Vegetables	3.1	3.5	2.8	2.4	1.9
Wheat	30.8	18.9	22.4	26.3	15.3
Excess Supply	0.0	0.0	0.0	0.0	27.4
Total Supply	100.0	100.0	100.0	100.0	100.0
Resource rents/prices	----- 1989/90 £E -----				
Summer land (£E/feddan)	701	4056	0	0	0
Winter land (£E feddan)	628	3602	1624	418	0
Water (£E/000m^3)	0	0	1287	2071	3090

Export Policies and Export Performance:
The Case of Turkey[*]

Introduction

A remarkable transformation in prevailing views about the role of trade in economic development has occurred throughout the developing world during the last two decades. This sweeping change is not just a result of a drive to avoid the bottlenecks arising from foreign exchange shortages, but also and perhaps more importantly, to achieve higher and more sustainable growth. Thus, discussions on trade and trade policies have become often debated issues in the recent literature on diverse topics as stabilization and growth. Export promotion schemes, exchange rate policies and domestic demand policies have become central issues in the analysis of export policies.

Turkey's experience provides a good case study. Over the last three decades the Turkish economy has experienced many changes in its foreign trade policies, export performance and growth. Turkey was one of the first countries that had gone through a foreign debt crisis at the end of the 1970s. The debt crisis promoted the adoption of an adjustment program whose central feature included the change of orientation of the economy, from inward to outward. More recently, Turkey has experienced a post-liberalization crisis in early 1994, which pre-dated the Mexican crisis of a similar nature at end-1994.

The primary purpose of this chapter is to make a comparative evaluation of export policies pursued in Turkey during the period from the late 1970s to the mid-1990s. In this context, the effects of exchange rate policies, different export promotion schemes and domestic demand policies are discussed and analyzed. The different policy regimes that were adopted are scrutinized with the help of an export supply function. The main objective is to analyze empirically to what extent are these policies different in terms of their long and short-run effects.

The next section takes stock of the theoretical arguments and empirical findings on the relationship between export expansion and growth, and tackles the issue of whether free trade or policy intervention is the optimum policy stance for export growth and welfare maximization.

* *My thanks to Hanaa Kheir-El-Din and to Fatih Özatay for their comments on the first draft of this chapter. The usual disclaimer applies.*

The chapter then provides a summary evaluation of the policies and macroeconomic developments in Turkey from the early 1970s to the mid-1990s with a view of assessing export policies within the context of the overall Turkish macroeconomic environment. It next evaluates different export policies on the basis of an export supply equation estimated with quarterly data from the fourth quarter of 1977 to the second quarter of 1995. Estimation results indicate that in the short term real exchange rate, excess demand, fixed capital investment and export subsidies contribute significantly to the explanation of export supply with economically meaningful parameters. In the long term estimation, however, export subsidies turn out to have a negative effect on long term export supply while the parameters of the remaining variables have the same meaningful signs as in the short term estimation. The short and long term estimation results imply that export subsidies make a positive effect in the initial growth of exports when the subsidies exceed a certain threshold value, but they do not contribute and/or their contribution turns negative in the long term. The chapter then concludes.

Exports, Growth and Export Promotion

The Relationship Between Exports and Growth

The relationship between export expansion and sustainable and faster growth is based on several arguments. First, it can be shown that plants of minimum efficient size can be established and production technologies with indivisibilities can be introduced. A second argument is that export expansion allows for the exploitation of scale economies in general since the world market is very much larger than the domestic market.

A third argument states that since the export industries face keen competition from the rest of the world, they have to use up to date technologies and employ highly skilled workers, the latter perhaps being partly trained by the producers/exporters themselves. Dynamic spill-over effects and the diffusion of technology across other sectors are other arguments that support the positive relationship between export growth and economic growth. "In many cases and particularly in small countries, exports may constitute the only reasonably efficient means of shifting the sectoral composition of output away from traditional primary activities and thus deriving dynamic benefits from industrialization" (Helleiner, 1990, p.888).

The above-listed factors combine to induce faster total factor productivity (TFP) growth in the export industries. This in turn would lead to a reallocation of resources from the relatively inefficient non-traded sectors to the more efficient export sectors. Higher growth of export demand, at least potentially, as compared to domestic demand, and higher overall TFP growth would result in a higher overall rate of economic growth.

There are, however, some qualifications to the above results. First, exports refer more specifically to manufacturing exports. "An important distinction between a success story such as South Korea and a failure such as Honduras is that the former has grown through exporting manufactured goods to the developed countries, whereas the latter has remained backward while exporting primary goods such as bananas and coffee" (Eswaran and Kotwal, 1993, p. 163).

Second, some manufacturing activities are known to contribute more to growth than others, in terms of generating scale economies, learning effects, technology adoption, and even income distribution. Thus, while the exports of some industries might bring about higher overall growth rates, exports of some others might not produce significant growth rates.

Third, the Solow-type neoclassical growth model does not provide a framework that can be used to show export growth contributing to overall economic growth. In this model, only the level of output can be raised by exports since the long run growth rate is determined by the exogenously given technological change. The recent endogenous growth models provide mechanisms through which higher export growth leads to the acceleration of economic growth, as explained by Romer (1990), Rivera-Batiz and Romer (1991a and 1991b), Grossman and Helpman (1991) and others. However, these models address the more general issue of the relationship between growth on the one hand and trade and openness on the other.

It is important to note that empirical studies on the relationship between export growth and economic growth have not resolved the issue. Indeed, they have added more fuel to the debate. In the early studies of Michaely (1977) and Balassa (1978), simple rank correlations were used to show that there was a significant positive relationship between export growth and growth in gross domestic product (GDP). The work by Feder (1983) was based on two neoclassical production functions, one for the non-export sector and the other for the export sector. Feder reiterated the findings of Michaely and Balassa and found that the marginal productivities of both labor and capital were higher in the export sector than in the non-export sector.

Gray and Singer (1988) and Kohli and Singh (1989) found that although export growth has a significant effect on GDP growth when world demand is strong, the effect becomes insignificant when world demand is low. Thus, export growth may not at all times cause GDP growth. Jung and Marshall (1985), after testing for Granger causality, conclude that although in some countries exports cause growth, evidence in support of this type of causality is not as strong as was previously thought. Hutchinson and Singh (1987) found that in only less than one-third of the sample countries investigated, Granger-type export growth causes GDP growth.

Levine and Renelt (1992) examined the sensitivity of several variables that enter the "endogenous growth" equations. Of their results, two are important. First, they have shown that all the results that specify the share of exports in GDP can be reproduced, almost identically when either the share of total trade or imports are used. Thus, studies that use export variables should not be interpreted as studying the relationship between growth and exports per se, but rather as investigating the relationship between growth and trade defined more broadly. And second, a large variety of trade policy measures are not robustly correlated with growth when the estimated equation includes the investment share (Levine and Renelt, 1992).

Greenaway and Sapsford (1994) noted that while those studies that use cross-section data tend to find significant positive relationships between exports and growth, those that employ time series data are inconclusive. Based on the time series estimation of a modified production function for nineteen countries which implemented trade liberalization policies, Greenaway and Sapsford found little support for the effect of exports on growth, and no support for the effect of trade liberalization on exports.

Sengupta (1994) found a substantial externality effect associated with the export sector on the rest of the economy in Korea. The Korean externality effect is indeed the highest within a group of six countries. Sengupta and Espana (1994) tested whether there is a long-run equilibrium relationship between export growth and overall growth in Korea. They explained that such a relationship exists in Korea since the two series are cointegrated. They also found a considerable scale effect in manufacturing production stimulated by exports.

Whatever the arguments in the theoretical and empirical studies, the success of such countries as South Korea and Taiwan provides concrete examples in favor of a positive relationship between rapid export expansion and higher economic growth. For the large majority of the developing countries, export-led growth has therefore become a dominant strategy in the process of development. The debt crisis of the early 1980s and the conditionalities of the multilateral organizations such as the World Bank and the International Monetary Fund that followed have also encouraged the pursuit of such strategy.

Free Trade and Export Promotion Policies

The pursuit of export-led export strategy requires the adoption of certain policies. There is a general agreement that a stable macroeconomic environment with minimum uncertainty and a realistic and stable real exchange rate are necessary conditions for long term export growth. However, beyond this point and on the most appropriate trade strategy, considerable controversy arises.

One can distinguish two schools of thoughts. One school believes that sustainable export expansion is best achieved through the adoption of a free trade strategy, which involves de-control, liberalization and no policy intervention in the foreign trade markets and, indeed, in all the markets. Their reasoning is based on the premise that perfect competition ensures efficient allocation of resources and eliminates factors that deter export expansion. Liberalization of imports, for instance, is considered as a process that eliminates the anti-export bias that is inherently present in import quotas and tariffs.

The other school calls for the adoption of interventionist policies in promoting exports. This school has received a new shot in the arm with the advent of the "new" trade theory and "strategic" trade policy. Its arguments rest on the following two basic observations: (1) perfect competition does not exist in the international markets, and (2) the export industries are dominated by increasing returns to scale - rather than constant returns to scale, externalities and learning by doing.

Brander and Spencer (1985) showed that in a duopolistic situation with Cournot behavior and no retaliation by rivals, export subsidies lead to a higher welfare level when compared with a policy of no intervention. Krugman (1986) and Helpman and Krugman (1989), among others, have also shown that given the above characteristics of the export markets, specific export subsidies may induce higher market shares and raise the growth rate and the welfare level of the exporting country.

In spite of the optimality of policy interventions in theory under certain circumstances, there are cautionary statements about the adoption of strategic trade policy in the real economy. For example, Baldwin (1992), Krugman (1993) and McCulloch (1993) all have argued that (i) the appropriate strategic policy is highly sensitive to details of market structure that governments may not get right, (ii) the pay-off of such a policy may not be large, and (iii) as a result of political economy considerations on the part of the governments, tools of policy interventions such as export promotion schemes might become instruments in the allocation of rents to the politically favored or strong groups.

Krugman (1993) therefore favors what he calls "the broad argument" for free trade "to which many economists implicitly subscribe, is essentially political: free trade is a pretty good if not perfect policy, while an effort to deviate from it in a sophisticated way will probably end up doing more harm than good (Krugman, 1993, p. 364)." McCulloch (1993, p. 371) concludes with a similar sentiment: "The theoretical suboptimality of free trade is the product of science; the belief in the practical suboptimality of most intervention reflects an appreciation of what lies beyond the narrow limits of that science."

The strategic trade policy approach has nevertheless shown that there need not be a one-to-one relationship between outward-orientation and free trade. Actually, as pointed out by Helleiner (1990), the case of Korea has already made it clear that outward orientation may be accompanied by substantial interventions in the export markets. There is by now a wide agreement that for export growth in developing countries, in addition to the stability of the macroeconomic environment and the real exchange rate, government support may be required for some time, especially at the time of entry into the world export markets. In this sense, as illustrated by the example of Korea, export promotion may take the form of import controls, regulated capital markets and targeted/selective direct subsidies.

Export promotion schemes have of course been in effect long before the strategic trade policy arguments were promulgated, and they have been evaluated in some studies. In an assessment of these schemes for eight Latin American Countries, Nogués (1990) found that only in Brazil export subsidies were effective in increasing and diversifying exports. The performance of Argentina was the worst, since, among other factors, the real exchange rate showed large fluctuations and overvaluations. Nogués reviews other studies and mentioned, in addition to Brazil, Korea and Turkey among the successful export subsidizers. He cited Caballero and Corbo (1988), who used data from seven developing countries to emphasize that export response is not only a function of current export incentives, but also a function of the stability of these incentives.

On the other hand, Rodrik (1993) criticized the appeals to political economy arguments for non-intervention. Instead, he emphasized the role of other elements such as "state capability", "state autonomy" and "policy coherence" in helping to understand the effectiveness of economic policies in general and export subsidies in particular. In terms of the implementation of the latter, Rodrik examined two successful countries, Korea and Brazil, two failures, Kenya and Bolivia, and two intermediate cases, Turkey and India. The evidence from the case studies led Rodrik to conclude that "policies work best when autonomy and coherence are both present; they fail when neither is" (Rodrik, 1993, p. 8).

Referring to the available econometric evidence from Korea, Rodrik (1993, p. 12) stated that exports were highly sensitive to subsidies: Jung and Lee (1986) estimated that a 1 percent increase in export subsidies eventually led to more than a 2 percent increase in export supply. They found that the elasticity of export supply with respect to the real exchange rate was smaller than this value. Rodrik noted however that without certain institutional innovations, such as the practice of setting and monitoring export targets, export incentives would not have been as effective. In the case of Brazil, the other successful subsidizer, Rodrik considers the BEFIEX program as a crucial one among the various promotion schemes, in that it entailed long term export commitments on the part of the exporters.

Rodrik has categorized Turkey as an intermediate case in terms of the effectiveness and success of export promotion policies. This was based on the premise that (i) the Turkish state is not considered to be an autonomous one, since it is open to the influences of the organized private interests, but (ii) export promotion policies were coherent and the leadership declared their commitment to export growth, at least until the mid-1980s. Uygur (1993) explains the factors that created uncertainty in export policies after this date. Again in line with the categorization of Rodrik, the export supply of Turkey was found to be significantly responsive by Uygur to export promotion schemes particularly in the early 1980s, but not after the mid-1980s.

The Macroeconomic Environment and Export Policies since the 1970s[1]

The Macroeconomic Environment Since the 1970s

For two decades, from the early 1960s to the end of the 1970s, Turkey followed an import substitution industrialization and development strategy. This strategy, formulated and implemented through five-year plans and annual programs, was justified on the grounds that the two-gap model was relevant for Turkey. Insufficiency of domestic savings and foreign exchange earnings were considered to be the two factors that limited investments and consequently the rate of growth of output. A significant rise in foreign exchange earnings was thought to be difficult due to fixed exchange rates and, more importantly, due to the low income elasticity of Turkey's exports. Import substitution was therefore considered to be the easiest way to escape from the foreign exchange constraint.

Foreign exchange shortages started to occur in the late 1960s, mainly because the inward-looking industrialization strategy had resulted in a sustained increase in the demand for imported capital goods and imported raw materials. In August 1970, a stabilization package was put into effect which included a devaluation and improvement in export promotion measures. In response, there was a considerable rise in export earnings and workers remittances. Together with a large rise in exports until 1974, the sectoral composition of exports also changed.

By the mid-1970s, the inward-looking industrialization process had reached its most difficult phase and, simultaneously, the economy was experiencing a variety of internal and external shocks. The oil shock of 1973-74 raised Turkey's import bill dramatically. On the other hand, the upward trend in remittances was reversed from 1975 onwards and exports stagnated. These developments called for an assessment and reshaping of the policies but that was not done in a vigorous manner. Devaluations were made but they did not stop the real appreciation of the Turkish Lira. In the mean time, inflation shifted from single to double digit rates.

Crisis in the Late 1970s and the 1980 Adjustment Program

In 1977, trade and current account deficits reached an all time high. External debt increased sharply together with a jump in the share of short term debt. Foreign exchange shortages were translated into higher black market activity. In 1979, GDP growth was negative for the first time in decades. Inflation accelerated and, from an average rate of about 20 percent in the mid-1970s, it reached 71 percent in 1979. At the end of the 1970s, Turkey was in a full fledged economic and social crisis.

January 1980 witnessed the beginning of the reversal of the earlier policies and, from then on, a series of changes and measures were introduced under a stabilization and liberalization program. The program was supported by multilateral organizations including the International Monetary Fund (IMF), the OECD and the World Bank and also by bilateral creditors, especially the major OECD countries.

The first objective of the program was to reduce the rate of inflation while not causing a major slowdown in the growth of output. The second aim was to promote exports through continuous adjustments of the exchange rate and export incentives, and subsequently, to liberalize imports. The third objective was financial liberalization, which, it was hoped, would increase private savings and investments. The fourth, longer term, aim was to liberalize foreign capital movements and to take measures towards making the Turkish Lira convertible. A final major aim of the program was to reduce the role of the public sector in the economy by both reducing the size of the central government and by privatizing public enterprises.

The 1980 adjustment program included the simultaneous implementation of stabilization and liberalization policies. As far as the sequencing of liberalization was concerned, the program addressed first the product market, then foreign trade and domestic financial markets, and finally, foreign capital transactions. As regards the speed of the liberalization policies, gradualism was their characteristic.

The stabilization program first sought to correct the misalignment in prices and to eliminate the disequilibria in certain markets. To this effect, multiple exchange rates were eliminated and, with a large devaluation reaching 100 percent, a uniform rate was established. Government-controlled prices were likewise increased sharply. The result was a three digit wholesale price index inflation at 107.2 percent in 1980. In addition to the price adjustments, domestic demand was reduced and import bottlenecks arising from the balance of payments crisis were eliminated with support from the multilateral organizations including the IMF, the OECD and the World Bank.

In May 1981 the Central Bank was authorized to make daily adjustments in the exchange rate. The commercial banks were allowed to fix their own rates within a narrow band around the official rate. With continuous adjustments, the lira depreciated in real terms and the real effective exchange rate (REER) increased considerably until 1986-87 as can be seen in Table 1.[2] The margin between the official and market exchange rates was eliminated in mid-1980s. Changes in the direction of domestic financial liberalization started in July 1980 when the ceilings on the deposit and credit interest rates were abolished. In December 1983, residents were allowed to open foreign exchange deposits with the commercial banks.

Outward orientation in the early 1980s was pursued more in terms of export promotion. Import liberalization was more gradual and cautious for fear of balance of payments problems. The major change in this direction started in December 1983 by the removal of quantitative restrictions on a large proportion of import items and by reductions in tariff rates. The overall tariff plus surcharge rates were lowered again in 1989 and 1990. These changes, accompanied by a substantial decline in the real exchange rate, resulted in a jump in imports and a large trade deficit of over US$ 10 billion in 1990.

Together with the liberalization of the current account, changes were made in the direction of capital account liberalization in 1984, when some restrictions on foreign exchange transactions were relaxed. However, major changes in this area had to wait until August 1989 before being introduced. Since then, Turkish nationals have been permitted to purchase foreign securities abroad and foreigners can buy Turkish securities; Turkish Banks can extend foreign currency credits to foreign trade companies; Turkish nationals are no longer required to obtain government permission to borrow abroad; and foreigners can open Turkish lira accounts convertible into foreign exchange.

These changes made it easier for Turkish corporations to borrow abroad

Table 1: Selected Economic Indicators

	1981-3	1984	1985	1986	1987	1988	1989	1990	1991	1992	1993	1994	1995
Inflation Rate	31.4	50.3	43.2	29.6	32.0	70.5	63.9	52.3	55.4	62.1	58.4	120.7	88.5
Exchange Rate													
US $, % Change	45.7	62.1	40.9	30.5	26.7	67.3	47.4	23.4	57.9	65.2	59.5	170.4	54.0
Effective, % Change	37.8	55.9	41.1	46.4	37.6	67.7	44.0	32.1	55.5	70.5	54.7	173.5	62.9
REER, 1990=100	107.7	124.8	122.2	130.3	129.8	128.7	118.1	100.0	94.9	96.1	90.1	121.1	104.9
Real Wage 1990=100	79.8	67.1	64.0	61.9	66.4	62.5	79.9	100.0	134.4	136.3	139.6	106.3	90.9
Investment/GNP	19.8	19.5	20.2	22.9	24.7	26.2	22.5	22.6	23.5	22.8	25.3	24.3	23.4
Private	11.1	11.2	10.8	12.4	14.7	17.3	15.0	15.7	16.1	15.5	18.4	19.0	19.6
Public	8.7	8.3	9.4	10.5	10.0	8.9	7.5	7.0	7.4	7.3	6.9	5.3	3.8
Savings/GNP	19.9	19.8	21.6	24.1	23.9	27.2	22.1	22.0	21.2	20.9	21.8	23.0	n.a
Private	13.2	13.7	13.9	16.0	17.3	20.4	17.4	18.6	20.6	21.9	24.5	24.8	n.a
Public	6.7	6.1	7.7	8.1	6.6	6.8	4.7	3.4	0.6	-0.9	-2.8	-1.8	n.a
Foreign Deficit/GNP	-2.2	-2.3	-1.4	-1.3	-1.8	1.1	-0.2	-3.1	-2.1	-2.0	-5.0	1.5	-3.5
Exports/GDP	12.5	16.1	16.3	13.8	15.6	19.2	16.7	13.3	13.7	14.3	13.5	21.3	20.3
Imports/GDP	15.4	19.2	18.5	15.8	17.8	18.0	18.4	17.6	16.4	17.3	19.1	20.3	25.0

Notes and Sources: 1.) Figures for the 1981-3 period are the simple arithmetic averages for these three years.
2.) Inflation: Rates are computed from the wholesale price index (with 1987= 100) of the State Institute of Statistics (SIS).
3.) Exchange Rates: Percentage changes are obtained from annual average exchange rates. The effective exchange rate is defined as the basket comprised of Dollars and D. Marks, with weighs 0.5 for each. In defining the REER, consumers price index for Turkey and wholesale price indices for the USA and Germany are used. Date are from the Central Bank of Turkey, Monthly and Quarterly Bulletins and IMF, International Financial Statistics.
4.) Real Wage: Hourly manufacturing wage rate (including side payments) deflated by the consumer price index. Data are from the SIS.
5.) Investment, Savings, Foreign Deficit, Exports and Imports: Investment refers to gross fixed investment, foreign deficit is defined as the sum net exports (X - M) and net factor income from abroad (GNP - GDP). Data are from the SIS, Monthly Bulletin of Statistics and State Planning Organization, Main Economic Indicators.

and for foreign capital to exploit arbitrage opportunities arising from interest rate differentials. The real appreciation of the Turkish Lira from 1989 onwards was partly a consequence of the speculative capital inflows. In an environment of high and rising public sector deficits, these were not appropriate and desired developments; but the policy makers thought differently. The real appreciation of the Lira was considered as an opportunity in the fight against inflation.

Although the fight against inflation was given top priority in the 1980s, and although it fell to an average of 36.2 percent in terms of wholesale prices during the 1981-86 period with the help of restrictive monetary and fiscal policies, the overall inflation record of this decade was rather poor and deteriorated from 1987 onwards, as can be observed in Table 1. The importance of 1987 is that it was an election year when expansionary monetary and fiscal policies were implemented owing to electoral considerations. Higher inflation rates were recorded despite a considerable decline in the real exchange rate from 1989 onwards. The view that the basic cause of this outcome was the growing deficits of the public sector has generally been accepted.

After experiencing a negative growth rate in 1980, GDP growth averaged 5.2 percent during the 1981-1986 period. However, this growth was not investment-led. Utilization of the existing capacity at higher rates accounted for a considerable proportion. Yet, the sustainability of outward-orientation and liberalization processes critically depended on investment growth. The adjustment program relied on the assumption that financial liberalization would stimulate private savings and that larger funds would be available for fixed investments. Neither aspect materialized to the extent desired.[3] The growth rate was pushed up to a peak of 9.5 percent by expansionary policies in 1987. Between 1988 and 1991 the growth rate fluctuated widely and averaged a relatively low 3.2 percent.

Export growth until 1987 was one of the best achievements of the 1980 adjustment program. Supported by exchange rate policies and export promotion schemes, exports more than tripled, and the share of manufacturing increased from about 36 percent to about 79 percent between 1980 and 1987. Export growth slowed considerably after 1987-88, in response to policies that raised domestic demand and lowered the real exchange rate, which also coincided with the poor performance of other macroeconomic variables.

The years 1989 and 1990 were crucial ones in many respects. First, following restrictive policies in 1988, policies turned expansionary once again in 1989 to gain electoral support. Second, as mentioned above, the Turkish Lira appreciated in real terms in 1989 and 1990, reaching a total of about 30 percent in these two years. Third, with more freedom in trade union bargaining power and more concern about income inequality, real (consumption) wages in the manufacturing industry increased sharply in 1989 and 1990. These changes, which can be seen in Table 1, resulted in an upswing in demand and, combined with the growing public sector deficits, high inflation continued into the 1990s.

The 1994 Crisis and the Adjustment Program Once Again

As was pointed out above, economic policies became expansionist at the close of the 1980s. Political economy considerations were important in the shaping of such policies. The party in power, which implemented the January 1980 adjustment program, was loosing its electoral support. To regain popularity, the stabilization aspects of the 1980 program were left aside. Warnings were made at times that given the degree of openness of the economy, expansionist policies would have severe current account repercussions. However, there was a belief that the liberalized markets would solve the problem and that the public and trade deficits were sustainable.[4]

Expansionist policies did not produce the desired results, and the ruling party lost the general election at the end of 1991. A coalition government was formed which continued populist policies. During 1992 and 1993, public sector deficits continued to increase and Turkey was in a high interest rate-repressed exchange rate trap. The experience of several countries showed that this trap was not sustainable and stability was at stake. It can be seen in Table 1 that the share of exports in GDP declined to the levels of the early 1980s. There was also a long-term effect. Resources were driven away from the tradable sectors to the non-tradable ones.

Given the limits in domestic borrowing and the drive to create downward pressure on interest rates, the government turned to foreign borrowing to finance both the public and current account deficits. However, starting in Autumn 1993, foreign creditors warned that they would not finance Turkey's deficits at the same pace and scale, as they looked unsustainable. It was evident that a crisis was brewing but the government declared that corrective measures will be taken after the municipal elections to be held in March 1994. However, the crisis did not wait until after the elections.

From November 1993 onwards, there was a rush to buy foreign exchange. Then came the reduction in the credit rating of Turkey by the international rating institutions. To calm the panic and keep the exchange rate within certain limits, the Central Bank intervened in the foreign exchange market by selling its foreign reserves, and raised the official dollar exchange rate by 13.6 percent in one day in mid-January 1994. That did not stop the demand for foreign exchange, and the Central Bank continued selling its reserves. From

November 1993 to end-March 1994 the sale of foreign exchange reserves amounted to almost $ 7 billion, leaving the reserves at about $ 3.3 billion. Concomitantly, the demand for treasury bills was dwindling at the going interest rates indicating lack of trust in the government.

Finally, some measures were drafted and a stabilization program was announced on April 5, 1994. Nevertheless, and despite the signing of a stand-by agreement with the IMF, turbulence in the financial markets continued. The government was unable to borrow in the domestic market. Borrowing resumed at end-May 1994 when the three-month bills could be issued at an annual compound interest rate of 406 percent. This implied phenomenal real rates, at well over 100 percent.

The crisis reached the real sector with some delay and created major losses. In 1994, the decline in manufacturing output was nearly 8 percent. Wholesale price inflation reached an all time record of 120.7 percent. Following the prediction of the Dornbusch model, there was overshooting in the exchange rate which increased by over 170 percent, as can be observed in Table 1. One year later in mid-1995, stability was established; inflation was down to two digit figures, though still in the range of 70-80 percent, and growth resumed.

An important element in the stabilization program of April 1994, as was the case in the earlier 1980 program, was the reduction of domestic demand. Coupled with the higher real exchange rate, lower demand was expected to lead to higher exports, offsetting part of the negative growth effect. Hence, the importance of exports was realized, but at the time of another crisis. A further and more important dimension was the inability of the government to borrow from abroad between 1994 and until mid-1995. Thus, foreign exchange earnings in general and export activities in particular became crucial variables and export policies found a central place once again in another stabilization program.

Export Policies Since the 1970s

The above account identifies important aspects that are particular to the Turkish export policies since the 1970s. These policies have not been part of a longer term plan, or a policy framework that sought to achieve higher growth by export expansion as was the case for example in Korea, Taiwan and Brazil. Export policies in Turkey aim and serve rather short term needs for foreign exchange.

Exchange Rate and Domestic Demand Policies

Export policies, including export promotion schemes, were in full use even in the heyday of import substitution strategy in Turkey. The central feature of the

1970 adjustment program, which was implemented in a fixed exchange rate regime, was a devaluation. This devaluation was accompanied by improvements in export promotion measures. The tax rebate system, which dates back to 1963, was made simpler, and two funds were established to support the export credit scheme and the availability of foreign exchange was increased for manufacturing exporters. These measures were necessary in order to overcome the balance of payments difficulties and to meet the foreign exchange needs of the import substitution growth strategy.

The adjustment program of 1980 sought and declared outward-orientation and export-based growth strategy right from the very beginning. In line with this objective, and given the need for foreign exchange, the program inhibited domestic demand and used the exchange rate exclusively to promote exports during the 1980-84 period. Between 1985 and 1988, the exchange rate was almost neutral regarding export promotion, as can be seen in Table 1. But there was confusion in export promotion schemes. While some schemes were improved in 1985 and 1986, it was announced in the meantime that the subsidy element in some other schemes would be phased out. Uncertainty surrounded export policies in the second half of the 1980s.

After 1988, not only expansionary policies were pursued, but the Turkish Lira appreciated considerably in real terms, when the exchange rate was used as an anchor against inflation. Expansionary policies and real appreciation of the Lira lasted until the 1994 crisis when domestic demand was cut substantially, public and foreign deficits were reduced and the Lira depreciated in real terms. As in the earlier cases, exports responded strongly to these changes.

It should be noted, however, that the real appreciation of the Lira in 1994 was due to the jump, or overshooting of the exchange rate, in the first half of the year. Otherwise, from the mid-1994 onwards, the exchange rate began to be used as a nominal anchor in the fight against inflation. It was agreed with the IMF that the exchange rate basket, formed of one dollar and one and a half of Deutsch Marks, was to be raised by a certain rate each month. Initially, this policy was perceived to be a temporary one that would last until the end of 1994. Yet, the nominal anchor policy continued in 1995 and the real exchange rate declined considerably. This resulted in a sharp rise in imports and a slowdown in the growth of exports.

Export Promotion Schemes

All export incentives in Turkey are linked to the issuance of an export incentive certificate,[5] which grants automatic entitlement to the full range of incentives. The incentive schemes were too fragmented even for the exporters, but they have been made more compact and reduced to manageable numbers in the recent years. Important incentive schemes include the following:

The Tax Rebate Scheme. This scheme, which was introduced as early as in 1963 and was abolished at the beginning of 1989, allowed exporters to be refunded for the indirect taxes paid during the process of production. The rebate rates were largely determined according to the rate of indirect taxes paid in stages of production, but there were also other considerations such as the value-added content of the product. The rates differed across commodity groups and were altered each year. The maximum rate was 15 percent in January 1980 and was raised to 20 percent in May 1981.

In addition to the basic rebate rates, there were additional rebates for large exporters which varied between 6 percent and 10 percent until April 1984. The additional rates were used to channel exports through the foreign trade companies. The rebate rates were almost halved in late 1984, when it was also announced that the system would be eliminated at the end of 1988, mainly because it was abused by the so-called fictitious exports[6] and had a large burden on the budget.

Table 2 contains data on exports eligible for rebates and on ex-post tax rebate payments as a proportion of the value of exports. Column (2) of the table indicates that during 1980-88 over two thirds of the manufacturing exports were eligible for tax rebates. Column (3) shows that in the same period about 90 percent of the exports eligible for tax rebates originated from the same sector. The industries that benefited most from the rebates were iron and steel, transportation equipment and machinery. Rebates as a proportion of exports reached a peak in 1984 and they declined thereafter. Note that, even though the tax rebate system was abolished at the beginning of 1989, payments to exporters continued after that date in smaller amounts, due to accruals from the previous periods.

Payment of Cash Premiums. At the time when the tax rebate rates were reduced in 1984, plans were made to compensate at least for part of the reduction. In December 1984 an extra-budgetary fund, Resource Utilization and Support Fund (RUSF), was established to provide low cost funds for exports and investments. However, RUSF was used to make cash premium payments to exports at rates ranging between 2 percent and 4 percent of the value of exports. The RUSF scheme was short-lived. After the premium rates were lowered in March 1986, the scheme was abolished at the end of that year. Premium payments from RUSF are given in Table 3.

Another extra-budgetary fund that was utilized for the payment of cash premiums to exports was Support and Price Stability Fund (SPSF), which was established in January 1980. Premium payments from the SPSF to iron and steel exporters started in 1984. But general export promotion with the SPSF scheme started in December 1986. The government decided to end this scheme effective from 1993. Due to accruals, however, payments continued after this date. Unlike the RUSF system, the SPSF system was selective and the payments were made on the basis of a comparison between domestic costs and foreign prices. The sectoral distribution of the SPSF premiums is very much similar to the sectoral distribution of the tax rebates and around 90 percent of the SPSF premiums went to manufacturing. Premium payments to exports from the SPSF are given in Table 3.

There are two other fund related cash premium schemes. The first is a

Table 2: Exports Eligible for Rebates and Rebates as a Proportion of Exports

| Year | Exports Eligible for Rebates | | | Rebates/Manufactures | |
	Total (1)	Manufactures (2)	(1)/(2) (3)	Total (4)	Manufactures (5)
1979	32.5	82.9	87.8	4.4	11.0
1980	24.8	61.2	88.7	2.2	5.6
1981	32.8	63.9	94.8	4.7	9.1
1982	44.0	71.6	97.0	9.2	15.1
1983	51.4	76.4	94.9	11.4	17.4
1984	60.7	80.8	96.0	12.6	17.0
1985	54.6	70.3	96.9	6.9	8.7
1986	55.1	66.5	86.2	5.6	6.6
1987	58.6	65.7	88.7	5.0	5.7
1988	47.0	51.6	84.2	4.0	5.2
1989	21.0	19.5	72.7	1.6	2.0
1990	1.0	1.1	86.8	0.1	0.1
1991	0.0	0.0	--	0.0	0.0
1992	0.0	0.0	--	0.0	0.0
1993	0.0	0.0	--	0.0	0.0
1994	0.0	0.0	--	0.0	0.0

Sources: Milanovic (1986), Çelebi (1991), and Uygur (1991).

transportation subsidy scheme applied to exports transported on ships. The source of payment for the transportation subsidy is again the SPSF. This subsidy is higher when transport is made with ships sailing under the Turkish flag. The SPSF payments in Table 3 cover transportation subsidies as well. The second is an energy subsidy scheme that was established to offset part of the higher electricity price in Turkey. This scheme started in 1992 and the payments, which are negligibly small, are made from the Encouragement Fund (EF). The energy subsidy payments from the EF are also presented in Table 3.

It is evident from Tables 2 and 3 that the direct subsidy schemes have been used in a decreasing manner. One reason for this is that particularly since 1990, premium payments from the SPSF have become strained due to budgetary constraints. Another and perhaps more important reason is the prohibition of direct premium payments in the General Agreement on Tariffs and Trade's Subsidies Code, of which Turkey is a signatory. Export promotion in recent years has been implemented increasingly through indirect measures such as tax exemptions and subsidized export credits.

Export Credits. Subsidized export credits were instituted in 1968 and since

Table 3: Direct Payments from Funds as Proportion of Exports (%)

Year	SPSF Premium (1)	RUSF Premium (2)	EF Premium (3)	Total Premium 1+2+3	Manufactured Premium (5)
1979	0.0	0.0	0.0	0.0	0.0
1980	0.0	0.0	0.0	0.0	0.0
1981	0.0	0.0	0.0	0.0	0.0
1982	0.0	0.0	0.0	0.0	0.0
1983	0.0	0.0	0.0	0.0	0.0
1984	0.2	0.0	0.0	0.2	0.3
1985	0.2	1.1	0.0	1.3	1.5
1986	0.2	2.9	0.0	3.1	4.1
1987	1.7	0.9	0.0	2.6	3.0
1988	2.0	0.1	0.0	2.1	2.4
1989	3.0	0.0	0.0	3.0	3.5
1990	3.7	0.0	0.0	3.7	4.3
1991	3.3	0.0	0.0	3.3	3.9
1992	2.7	0.0	0.0	2.7	3.0
1993	2.4	0.0	0.2	2.6	2.8
1994	2.0	0.0	0.1	2.0	2.2

Notes: 1) SPSF premium includes transportation subsidies. 2) In the computation of the manufacturing premiums given in column (5), the share of manufacturing in total is assumed to be equal to this industry's share in tax rebates, which ranged between 85 percent in 1979 and 95 percent during 1988-90. For 1991-94, the average of which is 92 percent during 1980-88. As explained elswhere, the share manufacturing in export credits is also around 90 percent.
Sources: Until 1990, Central Bank and Uygur (1991). After 1991, column (1),
Undersecretariat of Foreign Trade; column (3), Arslan (1994).

then have been supplied in different forms and from three different sources, namely the Central Bank, the commercial banks and the Export-Import Bank (Eximbank). Until the end of 1980, the Central Bank supplied more than 50 percent of export credits through the commercial banks. Between 1980 and 1983, Central Bank credits increased but commercial bank credits expanded much faster. During 1984, subsidy rates were lowered considerably, the maturities of the credits were shortened and credits of the Central Bank fell to a fraction of what they were in the earlier years. Commercial banks were not able to make up for the decline and total export credits decreased in 1984 and 1985, even in nominal terms.

The subsidized export credit scheme was terminated in January 1985, but was reintroduced after almost two years in November 1986 when it became apparent that there was a fall in exports of that year. Export credits in the second half of the 1980s differed from those in the early years of the 1980s in two respects. Firstly, they overwhelmingly became short-term credits after 1986, with maturities ranging from one month to six months. Secondly, there were no direct subsidy payments after 1986, whereas significant subsidies were paid to credit receivers in the early 1980s.

After its establishment in August 1987, the Eximbank began to extend part of the preferential credits to exporters. On its part, the Central Bank channeled most of its export rediscount funds to Eximbank from 1988 onwards. Eximbank extended only pre-shipment export credits until 1990. These are Turkish Lira denominated credits disbursed through the intermediation of the commercial banks and still constitute the bulk of Eximbank credits. In 1993, for instance, the share of these credits out of total flow was 79.9 percent. During the 1994 crisis, Eximbank credits denominated in foreign exchange increased substantially and reached almost 45 percent of the bank's credit flow. The share of Eximbank in total export credits has not been significant. It increased during the 1994 crisis, but even then it was about 7.2 percent. Thus, in the recent years exporters have depended on commercial bank credits to a large extent.

The subsidy value of export credits can be taken as the difference between the effective rate of interest charged on non-preferential short term commercial credits and the lower rate of effective interest on export credits. In Turkey, the difference between these two rates has stemmed from three factors. First, the base rate for the export credits had at times been lower than that for the general short term credits. Second, while short term non-preferential credits have required the payment of certain taxes and surcharges, such as the transactions tax and contributions to funds and stamp duties, export credits have been exempt from these. Third, export credits received additional subsidies between 1980 and 1983.

From the beginning of 1980 and until the termination of export credits at the beginning of 1985, the difference between the base rates for short term credits and export credits varied between 10 and 15 percentage points. When tax exemptions and subsidy payments were accounted for, the difference between the resulting effective interest rates reached as high as 27.1 percentage points in 1981[7] but declined in the subsequent periods, as can be seen in column (3) of Table 4. During 1985 and 1986, the only subsidy elements were the exemptions from taxes and surcharges. Starting in 1988, the rate of subsidy increased somewhat primarily because of the lower cost Eximbank credits.

Table 4 provides a clear and informative picture of governments' views in respect of foreign exchange earnings and export policies. In the late 1970s and the early 1980s, there was a balance of payments crisis and exports were promoted by both larger credits and higher subsidies on these credits. In the mid-1980s, foreign exchange shortages were not felt as before and exporters were faced with lower incentives. Some months before and during the 1994 crisis, foreign exchange became crucial due to supply falling short of demand. Consequently, the volume of subsidized export credits expanded substantially and there was a significant rise in subsidy rates.

Foreign Exchange Allocations and Duty Free Imports. Foreign exchange allocations to exporters for imports at the official exchange rate have been in practice since 1968. Until the end of 1983, allocations could not exceed 60 percent of the free-on-board (FOB) value of pledged exports. In December 1983, this rate was reduced to 40 percent but raised again to 50 percent in 1985 and to 80 percent in 1986. The latter rate was still effective at the end of 1995. The allocation scheme was valuable especially when there were foreign exchange shortages and when the market exchange rate carried a premium over the official exchange rate. This premium, which constituted a subsidy to exporters, stopped being significant after 1983, as the official exchange rate approached the market rate.

The duty free importation of raw materials and intermediate goods used by exporters started in 1980 and has operated on the same basis as the foreign exchange allocations. Once the latter has been granted, the exporters obtain the right for duty free importation up to the amount allocated. The subsidy element of this scheme is equivalent to the tariffs and surcharges not paid by the exporters who qualify. Subsidies, as a proportion of exports, that resulted from foreign exchange allocations and duty-free imports are provided in columns (3) and (4) of Table 5. These subsidies are computed as follows: First, the effective tariff plus surcharge rate that the exporter is exempt from is calculated for each period. Second, exchange rate premiums are obtained

Table 4: Export Credits, Interest Differentials and the Subsidy Element of Export Credits

| | Export Credits, Year-End, BTL | | Effective Interest Rate Differential (%) | Subsidy Element of Export Credits | |
| | Central Bank | Commercial Banks | | Total (%) | Manufactures (%) |
Year	(1)	(2)	(3)	(4)	(5)
1979	24	16	13.1	5.2	11.2
1980	48	43	21.3	6.0	12.4
1981	113	94	26.7	7.1	10.8
1982	101	379	20.8	7.3	9.7
1983	182	547	18.5	7.1	8.9
1984	34	561	15.8	3.7	4.3
1985	7	718	7.1	1.4	1.6
1986	4	1,691	7.6	3.1	3.9
1987	55	2,142	6.9	2.2	2.5
1988	343	3,050	11.2	3.1	3.7
1989	590	5,727	15.5	5.7	6.6
1990	229	9,628	10.4	4.6	5.3
1991	0	20,068	11.9	6.4	7.6
1992	0	39,459	12.3	7.7	8.5
1993	0	75,741	12.2	8.7	9.7
1994	0	1,670,141	24.2	12.5	13.4

Notes: 1) Commercial Bank's credits include credits of Eximbank. 2) The effective interest rate differential in column (3) is the difference between the effective rates on general non-preferential credits and export credits. While the former includes tax and surcharge payments.
the latter are exempt from these costs, provided the exporter has an incentive certificate. 3) In the computation of the subsidy elements in columns (4) and (5). first the stocks of export credits were converted to flows by multiplying the former with the following turnover ratios: 0.8 for 1979-83, 1.2 for 1984. 1.3 for 1985, 1.4 for 1986, 1.5 for 1987, 1.6 for 1988, 1.7 for 1989, 1.8 for 1990-91, 1.9 for 1992-93 and 2 for 1994. These values reflect the shortened maturities of export credits, and indeed of all credits, in Turkey. Credit flows so obtained were then multiplied by interest differentials in column (3). 4) On the basis of available information, the share of manufacturing in total export credits were taken as follows: 75 percent in 1979-81,80 percent in 1982-83, 85 percent in 1984-85, 90 percent in 1986-90 and 92 percent in 1991-94. 5) Only those exporters with an incentive certificate are entitled to subsidized credits. On the other hand, exports with incentive certificates constitute, on average, about 85 percent of total. Thus, 85 percent of export credits are taken as subsidized credits.
Sources: Central Bank and Undersecretariat of Foreign Trade.

by comparing the official and market exchange rates. It should be noted that the market rate exceeded the official rate considerably before 1980 by a margin that reached 50 percent. The official and market rates converged in the early 1980s and the difference between the two became negligible after 1983. In the early days of the 1994 crisis, particularly during the first quarter of that year, the two rates diverged again, raising the premium on the exchange rate. The subsidy value of duty-free imports and exchange rate premia are

determined by the amount of foreign exchange allocation given in columns
(1) and (2) of Table 5.

Table 5: Subsidy from Foreign Exchange
Allocations and Duty Free Imports

Year	Foreign Exchange Allocations (M US$)		Rate of Subsidy (%)	
	Total (1)	Manufactures (2)	Total (3)	Manufactures (4)
1979	135	122	6.6	7.1
1980	172	170	1.9	5.3
1981	395	338	2.8	4.9
1982	542	530	2.8	4.5
1983	873	859	4.1	6.3
1984	1,256	786	3.2	2.7
1985	1,819	1,452	4.7	5.0
1986	2,614	1,670	8.5	7.6
1987	2,586	1,880	7.0	6.4
1988	3,058	2,205	6.8	6.4
1989	3,409	3,064	5.7	6.1
1990	3,244	3,182	6.0	6.8
1991	3,486	3,207	6.9	7.9
1992	3,848	3,540	7.1	7.7
1993	4,562	4,197	8.1	8.8
1994	6,171	5,677	7.3	7.8

*Notes: 1) Data for the share of manufacturing in foreign exchange allocations were not avail-
able after 1990. This share is assumed to be 90 percent during 1991-94.*
*Sources: Columns (1) and (2); 1980-84, Milanovic (1986), 1985-89, Çelebi (1991, pp. 80-81),
1990-94, Undersecretary of Foreign Trade. Effective tax rate used in the computation of
columns (3) and (4) is taken from the SIS. Market exchange rates used in the computation of
the last two columns are from Uygur (1991) and Central Bank.*

Allocations for duty free imports increased considerably after 1984 and,
consequently, there was a similar increase in the subsidy rate of the two
schemes. In certain years, such as 1984 and 1988, subsidy rates declined significantly mainly because of the elimination of the foreign exchange premium on the market exchange rate and lower tariff rates that accompanied
import liberalization efforts. The latter also affected the distribution of allocations among industries.

Partial Exemption from Corporate Taxes. This scheme was introduced in
1980 and the rules were made simpler and more uniform in 1981. According
to the scheme, industrial firms that export over $ 0.25 million are allowed to
deduct up to 20 percent of their export revenues from taxable earnings. If
exports are made through a trading company, one-fourth of the tax allowance

is forwarded to that company. Manufacturing and total corporate taxes not paid due to this promotion scheme are shown in Table 6.

Table 6: Corporate Tax Allowance;
Total and Manufacturing

	In Billion TL		As Percent of Exports	
Year	Manufactures (1)	Total (2)	Manufactures (3)	Total (4)
1980	n.a	n.a	n.a	n.a
1981	n.a	n.a	n.a	n.a
1982	n.a	n.a	n.a	n.a
1983	n.a	n.a	n.a	n.a
1984	37	47	2.0	1.8
1985	63	77	2.0	1.9
1986	92	130	2.6	2.6
1987	303	358	4.3	4.1
1988	715	785	5.5	4.7
1989	1,138	1,258	5.9	5.1
1990	1,307	1,452	5.0	4.3
1991	1,535	1,705	3.5	3.0
1992	1,621	1,801	1.9	1.8
1993	2,134	2,371	1.5	1.4
1994	5,249	5,832	1.1	1.0

Sources: 1980-89, Çelebi (1991, p.79); 1990-93, Arslan (1994). 1994 is an estimate.

Apart from the above-mentioned allowances, exporters are also exempt from the payment of value-added tax (VAT) and extra-budgetary fund contributions in transactions such as insurance. No attempt is made for the quantification of the subsidy component of these exemptions since they are considered marginal.

The subsidy components of the export promotion schemes in the manufacturing industry are brought together in Table 7. The table also includes the percentage change in REER to facilitate comparison. The table shows that:

(1) export promotion efforts in terms of both subsidies and real exchange rate changes were substantial in the early years of the 1980s. They reached a peak of about 35 percent of the value of exports in 1983. The REER, on the other hand, showed jumps in 1980 and 1982. A similar pattern is observed in the more recent crisis in 1994. However, export subsidies could not be raised in this year as much as before due to (a) GATT provisions, (b) the scheduled

customs union with the European Union, and (c) constraints imposed by large budget deficits.

(2) There was a rather sharp downturn in export promotion in general in 1984-85, after which the exchange rate policy was either neutral or played a negative role.

(3) The sum of all the subsidies seems to have stabilized at just over 20 percent in the late 1980s and early 1990s.

(4) The findings of other studies such as Çelebi (1991) and Togan (1993), which cover the period between 1980 and 1990, are in general agreement with the data presented in Table 7 and the findings of this study.

Table 7: Percentage Change in REER and Subsidies in Manufacturing

Year	REER Change (1)	Direct Payments (2)	Export Credits (3)	Duty Allowances (4)	Tax Allowances (5)	Total (2+3+4+5) (6)
1979	-5.3	11.0	11.2	7.1	0.0	29.2
1980	24.1	5.6	12.4	5.3	2.0*	25.3
1981	7.1	9.1	10.8	4.9	2.0*	26.8
1982	12.4	15.1	9.7	4.5	2.0*	31.3
1983	5.8	17.4	8.9	6.3	2.0*	34.6
1984	7.6	17.3	4.3	2.7	2.0	26.3
1985	-2.1	10.2	1.6	5.0	2.0	18.8
1986	6.6	10.7	3.9	7.6	2.6	24.8
1987	-0.4	8.7	2.5	6.4	4.3	21.9
1988	-0.8	7.6	3.7	6.4	5.5	23.2
1989	-18.2	5.5	6.6	6.1	5.9	24.1
1990	-15.3	4.4	5.3	6.8	5.0	21.5
1991	-5.1	3.9	7.6	7.9	3.5	22.9
1992	1.3	3.0	8.5	7.7	1.9	21.1
1993	-6.2	2.8	9.7	8.8	1.5	22.8
1994	34.4	2.2	13.4	7.8	1.1	24.5

Notes: (*) These are assumed values.
Sources: Tables 1 through 6.

Export Performance and a Comparative Evaluation of Export Policies

Export Performance in the 1980s and the 1990s

During the 1980-87 period, both the growth and the change in the composition of exports were impressive: exports more than tripled, and the share of manufacturing in total exports increased from about 36 percent to over 75 percent, as can be observed in Table 8. However, the performance of exports in the 1988-93 period can be described as one of stagnation or marginal growth.

On the supply side, the strong performance of exports until 1987 was achieved through the utilization of excess production capacity in manufacturing which was created largely in the 1970s. Excess capacity was large particularly in the early 1980s due to reduced domestic demand.

There has been a considerable rise in the exports of relatively new products, such as basic metals, iron and steel, and chemicals. Yet, in spite of the incentives for diversification, textiles, food and iron and steel, which are among the most labor-intensive industries, have kept their large share of about 70 percent in total exports. This reflected the comparative advantage of Turkey in labor-intensive industries, and the fact that diversification has not been achieved to the extent desired.

It is explained in Uygur (1991 and 1993) that export growth in the late 1980s and early 1990s was constrained by the fact that in addition to expansion of domestic demand, fixed capital investment growth in that period was not high. Diversification was also limited by the same factor. For the same reason, total factor productivity growth was not as high as anticipated. The large increase in particularly manufacturing exports in 1994 resulted from both a reduction in domestic demand and a considerable rise in the real exchange rate.

Manufacturing exports in dollar terms increased by about 18 times between 1980 and 1995, but a large proportion of this rise was recorded during the 1981-85 period. The rise in the quantity of manufacturing exports was even more pronounced during this period as can be seen in column (8) of Table 8. These high growth rates were comparable with the rates achieved in countries such as Korea, Taiwan, Malaysia and Thailand. However, while these countries attained sustained growth in manufacturing exports, growth of Turkish manufacturing exports could not be sustained for the reasons explained above.

A Comparative Evaluation of Export Policies: Econometric Estimation Results

All export policies, but particularly export promotion schemes carry direct and indirect costs. The direct cost of a scheme would be equivalent to the subsidy value, which in turn is an income transfer from generally public funds to exporters. Indirect costs are more difficult to assess. An important one is the increase in public sector spending or foregone revenue which may make the public deficit more difficult to control, with attendant inflationary effects.

Table 8: Exports by Sectors

Year	Million $				Percent Distribution			Real
	AGRX (1)	MINX (2)	MANX (3)	TOTX (4)	AGRX (5)	MINX (6)	MANX (7)	MANX (8)
1977	1,309	127	664	2,100	62.1	6.2	31.8	78.9
1980	1,672	191	1,047	2,910	57.5	6.6	35.9	100.0
1981	2,219	193	2,290	4,703	47.2	4.1	48.7	234.6
1982	2,141	175	3,429	5,746	37.3	3.1	59.7	377.2
1983	1,881	189	3,658	5,728	32.8	3.3	63.9	425.1
1984	1,749	240	5,145	7,134	24.5	3.4	72.1	642.4
1985	1,719	244	5,995	7,958	21.6	3.1	75.3	762.3
1986	1,886	247	5,324	7,457	25.3	3.3	71.4	742.7
1987	1,853	272	8,065	10,190	18.2	2.7	79.2	982.4
1988	2,341	377	8,944	11,662	20.1	3.2	76.7	1,042.8
1989	2,126	413	9,086	11,625	18.3	3.5	78.2	1,010.1
1990	2,388	329	10,242	12,959	18.4	2.6	79.0	1,034.9
1991	2,732	286	10,575	13,593	20.1	2.1	77.2	1,073.2
1992	2,259	264	12,191	14,714	15.4	1.8	82.8	1,266.0
1993	2,381	238	12,726	15,334	15.5	1.6	82.9	1,328.7
1994	2,470	272	15,364	18,106	13.6	1.5	84.9	1,772.8
1995	2,314	406	18,916	21,636	10.7	1.9	87.4	1,820.3

Notes: 1) Data for 1977-79 are annual averages of these three years. 2) AGRX: Agricultural exports; MINX: Mining exports; MANX: Manufacturing exports; TOTX: Total exports; Real MANX: Index of real manufacturing exports with 1980 = 100.
Sources: State Institute of Statistics. Summary of Monthly Foreign Trade.

In what follows, the relative effects and effectiveness of export policies in general and promotion schemes in particular are estimated with the use of manufacturing export supply equations. The estimated equations are based on the export supply function of a representative exporter that aims to maximize profits. The derivation of such functions can be seen in, for example, Aspe and Giavazzi (1982) and Funke and Holly (1993). The export supply function of an exporter is specified as:

$$X = X(I, D, P^x/P^d, S), \qquad (1)$$
$$\text{where } X_I, X_{P^x/P^d}, X_S > 0 \text{ and } X_D < 0.$$

where X is export supply, I is gross fixed investment, D is domestic excess demand, P^x is the price of goods exported, P^d is the price of goods sold in the domestic market and S is export subsidy. $X_I, \ldots X_D$ denote partial derivatives.

It should be noted that adoption of a single supply equation, rather than of both demand and supply simultaneously, requires the assumption that export demand is infinitely elastic. This is true only in the case where it is possible to sell any quantity at the existing price. The infinite elasticity assumption can be meaningful if the exporting economy is small in that it does not have a sizable share in the international export markets. Considering that the Turkish exports do not constitute a significant proportion of world exports, at least at the level of aggregation taken here, estimation of a single export supply equation can thus be justified.

Equation (1) describes ex-ante supply and it implies instantaneous adjustment since the time factor is not explicitly accounted for. Yet, there may be time lags in the adjustment process due to (i) adjustment costs, (ii) the sluggishness of export prices which in turn may reflect menu costs, (iii) information lags, and (iv) transportation lags. Thus, a dynamic specification of equation (1) may be necessary, incorporating lags of the dependent and the explanatory variables.

Another form of dynamism, in terms of differences of the variables involved, may be required due to the time series properties of the variables in equation (1). It has long been established that the variables in an econometric equation should be stationary in the sense that their means should not drift and their variances and covariances should not change with time. Yet, most macroeconomic variables are non-stationary. These non-stationary variables can be made stationary by taking their differences.

However, when the variables under consideration are differenced, the relationships that are sought are short-run relationships and the long-run ones are lost. To recover this lost information and reflect it in the short run relationship, a long-run relationship is also specified and estimated. Such an equilibrium relationship exists if the variables under consideration are "co-integrated". Obviously, there may be deviations from the co-integration or long-run relationship in the short-run, which can be represented by the residuals in this latter relationship. These residuals are called "the error-correction terms" and they are included in the short run equations if long-run co-integrating relationships exist. Thus, equation (1) may, in the end, contain another explanatory variable, namely an error-correction term, which comes about as a result of the econometric approach followed in the estimation of the export equation.

Variants of equation (1) are estimated by using ex-post quarterly manufacturing data which cover the period from 1977-IV to 1995-II. Estimation of this equation is not straightforward as it involves several steps. Among these steps, there are the long term and short term estimations of the export supply equation. This estimation methodology allows us to answer the following questions: (i) What are the time series properties of the variables in equation (1)? (ii) Are there long-run co-integrating relationships between the variables of equation (1)? (iii) What is the short-run dynamic specification of equation (1)? (iv) What are the policy implications of the short-run and long-run specifications?.

Time Series Properties of the Variables of Export Supply Equation

Given the upward trend in manufacturing exports and the convenience in interpreting the coefficients, the variables of equation (1) are expressed in logarithms. The dependent variable of this equation is:

LRMANX = Log(Real manufacturing exports).

Consistent data for manufacturing investment are not yet available particularly for the 1990s. Thus, non-residential investment is used in estimations:

LRNHI = Log(Real non-residential investment).

Non-residential investment includes investment in manufacturing, energy, transportation, communications, agriculture and so on. Available information shows that manufacturing investment closely follows non-residential investment. On the other hand, one can argue that non-residential investment is a more appropriate variable in explaining aggregate manufacturing exports any way, since these exports require a coordinated activity of not only manufacturing but also communications, transportation and energy, among others.

Excess demand in the manufacturing industry is defined as follows:

LEXDDT = Log (Manufacturing capacity utilization / Percentage of manufacturing firms which report insufficient domestic demand).

Capacity utilization per se is not taken as an indicator of excess demand since it can be affected by supply factors. Data that relate to the proportion of firms which report insufficient domestic demand are obtained from the quarterly manufacturing surveys of the State Institute of Statistics.

Figure 1: Logarithms of Manufacturing Exports (LRMANX), Non-residential Investment (LRNHI) and Excess Demand (LEXDDT)

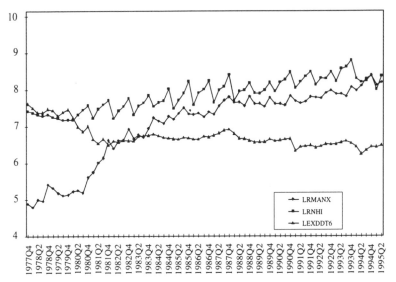

Note: To facilitate comparison with a similar scale, 6 is added to LEXDDT.

Figure 1 shows that there is both seasonality and trend in all three of the LRMANX, LRNHI and LEXDDT variables. To see whether LRMANX, LRNHI and LEXDDT are stationary, the unit root test of Hylleberg et.al. (1990) is used. With this test, which is shortly referred to as the HEGY test, one can check for both seasonal unit root and non-seasonal unit root and for this reason it may be preferred to the usual Dickey-Fuller (DF) or the Augmented Dickey-Fuller (ADF) tests. The HEGY test requires the estimation of equations which contain four different transformations of the LRMANX, LRNHI and LEXDDT variables. Estimation results of the HEGY equations and the definitions of the transformed variables are given below in Table 9.

Assume that the four transformed variables are labeled X1(-1), X2(-1), X3(-2) and X3(-1). In the HEGY procedure, the test for non-seasonal unit root is carried out on the coefficient of the X1(-1) variable. For no unit root, this coefficient should pass the HEGY test, that is it should be less than zero. To test for seasonal unit root, in addition to the individual tests on the coefficients of X2(-1), X3(-2) and X3(-1), a joint F-test on the coefficients of the last two variables is required. If the coefficient of X2(-1) does not pass the test, there is biannual seasonal unit root. If the coefficients of both X3(-2) and X3(-1) do not pass the test, which will also imply failure of the joint F-test, then there is annual seasonal unit root. If only one of these coefficients fail the individual test but they pass the joint F-test, then one can reject, though with some doubt, the presence of annual seasonal unit root. For a variable not to have a unit root at all, seasonal and non-seasonal, so that it is stationary, it should pass all the individual tests

Consider first the dependent variable LRMANX. The t-ratio for the coefficient of X1LRMX(-1) given in Table 9 does not pass the HEGY test since it is lower in absolute terms than the critical values provided by HEGY for no trend and no dummy, which are approximately -3.55 for 1 percent and -2.92 for 5 percent. Thus, there is non-seasonal unit root in the LRMANX data. To see if there is seasonal unit root in the same data, first the individual t-tests are done. The absolute t-ratio for the coefficient of X2LRMX(-1) barely exceeds the 5 percent critical value of HEGY, but is considerably lower than the 1 percent critical value of -2.65. One can therefore suspect the presence of biannual seasonal unit root.

While the coefficient of X3LRMX(-2) passes the HEGY test, the coefficient of X3LRMX(-1) does not, at both 1 percent and 5 percent. To make a decision on annual seasonal unit root, the joint significance of the coefficients of X3LRMX(-2) and X3LRMX(-1) is tested with the following F-statistic:

$$F_{n-k}^r = \frac{(RSS_{(R)} - RSS_{(U)}) / r}{RSS_{(U)} / n - k}$$

where $RSS_{(R)}$ is the residual sum of squares from the restricted equation which excludes X3LRMX(-2) and X3LRMX(-1) and $RSS_{(U)}$ is the residual sum of squares from the unrestricted equation given in Table 9, r is the number of restrictions, 2, and n - k is degrees of freedom. The F-statistic computed is 8.80 and exceeds the critical value given by Hylleberg et.al. Thus, one can say that LRMANX does not contain annual seasonal unit root. Note however that the coefficient of X3LRMX(-1) did not pass the test.

The results for LRNHI are similar to those for LRMANX. The t-ratio for the coefficient of X1LRNHI(-1) does not pass the HEGY test since it is lower in absolute terms than the critical values provided by HEGY for constant, trend and dummy, which are approximately -4.25 for 1 percent and -3.60 for 5 percent. There is therefore non-seasonal unit root in the LRNHI data. The absolute t-ratio for the coefficient of X2LRNHI(-1) is lower than the 1 percent and 5 percent critical values of HEGY, -3.72 and -3.02, implying the presence of biannual seasonal unit root.

While the coefficient of X3LRNHI(-2) does not pass the HEGY test, the coefficient of X3LRNHI(-1) barely passes this test at 5 percent; the t-ratio of the latter's coefficient is almost equal to the critical value given by HEGY. This is reflected in the computed F-statistic which is very close to the critical value given by HEGY at 1 percent. Thus, in addition to biannual seasonal unit root, there may be annual seasonal unit root in the LRNHI data.

The excess demand variable LEXDDT does not have a non-seasonal unit root at 5 percent, but it does have at 1 percent. This variable does not have a biannual seasonal unit root since the absolute t-ratio of the coefficient of X2LEXD(-1) exceeds the critical HEGY values for constant and dummy, which are -3.69 at 1 percent and -3.00 at 5 percent. Although the F-statistic for the joint test of the coefficients of X3LEXD(-2) and X3LEXD(-1) indicates no annual seasonal unit root, the coefficient of the latter variable does not pass the individual test. Thus, annual seasonal unit root cannot be completely ruled out.

The test results indicate that LRMANX, LRNHI and LEXDDT are not stationary. More specifically, (i) there is non-seasonal unit root in all three of them, (ii) there is biannual seasonal unit root in the LRMANX and LRNHI data, and (iii) one can not rule out the presence of annual seasonal unit root in all three of the variables under consideration. This information should be taken into account in the co-integration tests and in differencing the variables when making short-term dynamic estimations of equation (1).

The other two variables of equation (1), relative manufacturing export price and manufacturing export subsidy are also expressed in logarithms and denoted by LRMAXP and LTOTSU, respectively.

LRMAXP = Log(Manufacturing Export Price / Domestic Manufacturing Wholesale Price)

LTOTSU = Log(Manufacturing Export Subsidies / Value of Manufacturing Exports)

As can be observed in Figure 2, there is no apparent seasonality in LRMAXP and LTOTSU. Hence, the ADF test, rather than the HEGY test, is used to test for the stationarity of these two variables.

Estimation results of the equations that are used to carry out the ADF tests are given in Table 10. According to these results, the t-ratios obtained exceed, in absolute terms, the critical values of the ADF test at both 1 percent and 5 percent. (The critical values are approximately -2.60 for no constant and no trend and -3.55 for constant and no trend at 1 percent.) Thus, LRMAXP and LTOTSU do not contain unit roots and are stationary.

Table 9: Unit Root Tests for LRMANX, LRNHI and LEXDDT

Dependent variable: X4LRMX
Current sample: 1978:3 to 1995:2
Durbin's h alternative = -.350819 [.726]
Breusch/Godfrey LM2 = 1.21780 [.544]
Breusch/Godfrey LM4 = 6.51015 [.164]

Number of observations: 68
Breusch/Godfrey LM1 = .178354 [.673]
Breusch/Godfrey LM3 = 4.73028 [.193]
Augmented Dickey - Fuller = -8.05802 [.000]

Regressor	Coefficient	Standard Error	T-Ratio [Prob]
CONST	.353209	.140081	2.52146 [.014]
X1LRMX(-1)	-.010365	.004809	-2.15529 [.035]
X2LRMX(-1)	-.170823	.085645	-1.99455 [.051]
X3LRMX(-2)	-.445455	.129196	-3.44791 [.001]
X3LRMX(-1)	-.262709	.131244	-2.00167 [.050]
X4LRMX(-1)	.366597	.152999	2.39607 [.020]
X4LRMX(-2)	-.141186	.114456	-1.23353 [.222]

X1LRMX = LRMANX + LRMANX(-1) + LRMANX(-2) + LRMANX (-3)
X2LRMX = -(LRMANX - LRMANX(-1) + LRMANX(-2) - LRMANX(-3))
X3LRMX = -(LRMANX - LRMANX(-2))
X4LRMX= LRMANX - LRMANX(-4)
LRMANX: Logarithm of real manufacturing exports.

Dependent variable: X4LRNHI
Current sample: 1979:4 to 1995:2
Durbin's h alternative = -.159214 [.873]
Breusch/Godfrey LM2 = 2.26561 [.322]
Breusch/Godfrey LM4 = 2.75780 [.599]

Number of observations: 63
Breusch/Godfrey LM1 = 1.13702 [.286]
Breusch/Godfrey LM3 = 2.31347 [.510]
Augmented Dickey-Fuller= -8.48633 [.000]

Regressor	Coefficient	Standard Error	T-Ratio	[Prob]
CONST	4.64232	1.48428	3.12766	[.003]
TIME	.013312	.0043822	3.03766	[.004]
DUM2	.314839	.090979	3.46055	[.001]
DUM3	.357386	.082559	4.32885	[.000]
DUM4	.340578	.081094	4.19980	[.000]
X1LRNHI(-1)	-.172732	.052580	-3.28515	[.002]
X2LRNHI(-1)	-.200339	.088158	-2.27249	[.027]
X3LRNHI(-2)	-.376712	.108436	-3.47405	[.001]
X3LRNHI(-1)	-.314577	.112737	-2.79037	[.007]
X4LRNHI(-1)	.284470	.139572	2.03817	[.047]

X1 LRNHI = LRNHI + LRNHI(-1) + LRNHI(-2) + LRNHI(-3)
X2LRNHI = -(LRNHI - LRNHI(-1) + LRNHI(-2) - LRNHI(-3))
X3LRNHI = -(LRNHI - LRNHI(-2))
X4LRNHI = LRNHI - LRNHI(-4)
LRRNHI: Logarithm of real non-residential investement

Dependent Variable: X4LEXD
Current sample: 1979:2 to 1995:2
Durbin's h alternative = -.620164 [.535]
Breusch/Godfrey LM2 = .808034 [.668]
Breusch/Godfrey LM4 = 4.51161 [.341]

Number of observations: 65
Breusch/Godfrey LM1 = .417309 [.518]
Breusch/Godfrey LM3 = 3.97292 [.264]
Augmented Dickey-Fuller= -8.08259[.000]

Regressor	Coefficient	Standard Error	T-Ratio	[Prob]
CONST	.076283	.034198	2.23065	[.030]
DUM4	.055085	.029627	1.85928	[.068]
X1LEXD(-1)	-.040022	.011595	-3.45169	[.001]
X2LEXD(-1)	-.492314	.123339	-3.99514	[.000]
X3LEXD(-2)	-.562006	.110219	-5.09900	[.000]
X3LEXD(-1)	-.038078	.132512	-.287354	[.775]
X4LEXD(-1)	.290388	.138159	2.10185	[.040]
X4LEXD(-3)	-.171636	.085990	-1.99599	[.051]

X1LEXD = LEXDDT + LEXDDT(-1) + LEXDDT(-2) + LEXDDT(-3)
X2LEXD = -(LEXDDT - LEXDDT(-l) + LEXDDT(-2) - LEXDDT(-3))
X3LEXD = -(LEXDDT - LEXDDT(-2))
X4LEXD = LEXDDT - LEXDDT(-4)
LEXDDT: Logarithm of excess demand in manufacturing.

Note: Estimations were carried out with TSP386.

The Long-run Relationship Among the Variables of Export Supply Equation

Given the time series properties of the variables in the export supply equation, the short-run dynamic version of equation (1) can be estimated. However, in this estimation, which will require differencing of the variables with unit roots so that these variables can be made stationary, only the short-term relationship between LRMANX and the explanatory variables can be established. Information regarding the nature of the long-term relationship between LRMANX and the explanatory variables will be lost. Yet, one can seek for a long-term, cointegration relationship among the variables of equation (1). Two methods are available in this respect. One is that of Engle and Granger (1987) and the other is that of Johansen (1988).[8] The Johansen procedure, which is basically a Vecor Auto Regression (VAR) methodology, is more appropriate here since it is better suited for multivariate analysis.

Figure 2: Logarithms of Relative Manufacturing Export Price (LRMAXP) and Total Manufacturing Export Subsidies (LTOTSU)

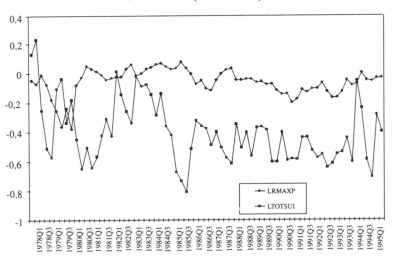

Note: To facilitate comparison with a similar scale, 1 is added to LTOTSU.

In the search for a cointegration relationship, the following procedure is followed:

1) In the application of the Johansen procedure, variables with unit root (LRMANX, LRNHI and LEXDDT) as well as variables without unit roots, LRMAXP and LTOTSU, are included in the VAR system. This may not seem

conventional, since in the Johansen procedure cointegration is generally sought among the variables with a unit root. LRMAXP and LTOTSU are included since their exclusion from the VAR system would imply that prices do not play a role in the determination of long-run export supply. Economically, this is not plausible. Johansen stated:

> Thus the question of stationarity of individual series can be formulated in a natural way in terms of parameters in the multivariate system, and is a hypothesis that is conveniently checked inside the model rather than a question that has to be determined before the analysis starts. Thus one can include in the cointegration analysis the variables that are considered economically meaningful as long as they are I(1) or I(0). By including a stationary variable in the vector Xt we add an extra cointegrating vector, that is, an extra dimension to the cointegrating space. It is this possibility to have unit vectors as cointegrating vectors that forces us to have a definition of I(1) that allows both I(1) and I(0) components. (Johansen, 1995, p. 74).

Table 10: Unit Root Tests for LARMAXP and LTOTSU

Dependent variable: D1LRMXP
Current sample: 1978:1 to 1995:2 — Number of observations: 70
Durbin's h alternative = -.0962 [.923] — Breusch/Godfrey LM1 = -2.26349 [1.00]
Breusch/Godfrey LM2 = -2.12043 [1.00] — Breusch/Godfrey LM3 = -1.42984 [1.00]
Breusch/Godfrey LM4 = 1.36472 [.850] — Augmented Dickey-Fuller = -8.5163 [.000]

Regressor	Coefficient	Standard Error	T-Ratio [Prob]
LRMAXP(-I)	-.17665	.061919	-2.85291 [.006]
D1LRMXP(-2)	.265042	.112639	2.35301 [.022]

Dependent variable: D1LTOTS
Current sample: 1978:1 to 1995:2 — Number of observations: 70
Durbin-Watson statistic =2.00215 — Breusch/Godfrey LM1 = .676121 [.411]
Breusch/Godfrey LM2 = .238411 [.888] — Breusch/Godfrey LM3 = 1.74659 [.627]
Breusch/Godfrey LM4 = 2.74478 [.601] — Augmented Dickey-Fuller = -8.783[.000]

Regressor	Coefficient	Standard Error	T-Ratio [Prob]
CONST	-.641492	.134484	-4.77003 [.000]
LTOTSU(-1)	-.450432	.094476	-4.76771 [.000]

Note: Estimations were carried out with TSP386.

Just as pointed out by Johansen, when the two price variables, LRMAXP and LTOTSU, are excluded from the VAR system, one is faced with the outcome that either it is not possible to obtain cointegration vector(s) with a plausible number of lags in the VAR system or, even when such vectors are obtained, the parameters are not economically meaningful.

2) Seasonal unit roots in the LRMANX, LRNHI and LEXDDT variables were eliminated by summing each of these three series for four quarters. This is done to avoid seasonal interference in the long-term relationship.

3) A dummy variable, DU841, is added to represent an announcement effect. It was declared at the end of 1983 and the beginning of 1984 that subsidies on exports would be lowered considerably during 1984. Thus, exporters rushed to take advantage of the subsidies before they were reduced. It is generally accepted that part of this rush represented fictitious exports. See for example Celasun and Rodrik (1989).

4) If and when a meaningful cointegration relationship was found, it was checked whether the error correction term from this relationship had a significant coefficient with the expected (negative) sign in the short-term equation. Only when this condition was met, the cointegration relationship was kept for further analysis.

The results of the Johansen cointegration procedure with 7 lags in the VAR system are given in Table 11. (Similar results were obtained with 6 and 8 lags.) The table indicates that on the basis of the LR (Likelihood Ratio) tests based on both the maximal eigenvalue and the trace of the stochastic matrix, 4 cointegration vectors can be found between the variables of the export supply equation. Any one of these vectors can be chosen on the basis of the meaningfulness of the parameters.

On the basis of the signs of the parameters, vectors 1, 2 and 3 should be ruled out. In vector 1, the signs of the elasticities of relative export price (FLRMAP) and excess demand (FLEXD) are incorrect. In vector 3, the signs of the elasticities of relative export price and investment (FLRNHI) are not acceptable. In vector 2, not only the sign of the elasticity of excess demand is incorrect (positive), but also the magnitudes of the elasticities of all the variables are too high to be acceptable. There remains only vector 4, where the elasticities of investment, relative export price and excess demand have correct signs and acceptable magnitudes. In vector 4, however, the sign of the elasticity of export subsidy (LTOTSU) is negative, implying that in the long run export subsidies lead to a decline in export supply.

This is an interesting result and on the basis of the cointegration analysis we cannot reject the statement that subsidies may reduce manufacturing export supply in the long run. The magnitudes of the other elasticities imply that in the long run relative export price has the largest effect on export supply. The elasticity of domestic excess demand is just over unity and a decline in excess demand leads to slightly more than a proportional increase in exports. Investment has an elasticity close to unity implying that a sustainable rise in export supply requires a proportional increase in investment.

These results, particularly the negative effect of export subsidies on export supply require further elaboration. To be able to do such an elaboration, we first need to find out the short term influence of the above mentioned explanatory variables on export supply. This can be done by short term dynamic estimation of the export supply equation. Following this estimation, additional tests and explanations can be made on the medium term effects of different export policies, particularly of subsidies.

Table 11: Estimation of Long-Term Manufacturing Exports; Johansen Maximum Likelihood Procedure (Trended Case, Trend in DGP)

Sixty observations from 1980Q3 to 1995Q2. Maximum lag in VAR= 7, chosen r=4.
List of variables included in the cointegrating vector: FLRMX, FLRNHI, FLEXD,
FLRMAP, FLTOSU. List of additional I(0) variables included in the VAR: DU841.
List of eigenvalues in descending order: .69663 .49335 .42946 .21371 .043586

i) Cointegration LR Test Based on Maximal Eigenvalue of the Stochastic Matrix:

Null	Alternative	Statistic	95% Critical V.	90% Critical V.
r= 0	r=1	71.5674	33.4610	30.9000
r<=1	r=2	40.7966	27.0670	24.7340
r<=2	r=3	33.6699	20.9670	18.5980
r<=3	r=4	14.4254	14.0690	12.0710
r<=4	r=5	2.6739	3.7620	2.6870

ii) Cointegration LR Test Based on Trace of the Stochastic Matrix

Null	Alternative	Statistic	95% Critical V.	90% Critical V.
r=0	r>=1	163.1331	68.5240	64.8430
r<=1	r>=2	91.5658	47.2100	43.9490
r<=2	r>=3	50.7692	29.6800	26.7850
r<=3	r>=4	17.0993	15.4100	13.3250
r<=4	r=5	2.6739	3.7620	2.6870

iii) Estimated Cointegrated Vectors in Johansen Estimation (Normalized in Brackets)

	Vector 1	Vector 2	Vector 3	Vector 4
FLRMX	.19780	.052927	-.039372	-.25442
	(-1.0000)	(-1.0000)	(-1.0000)	(-1.0000)
FLRNHI	-.52304	-.59566	-.30261	.24729
	(2.6443)	(11.2543)	(-7.6858)	(.97198)
FLEXD	-.46353	-.67535	-.55676	-.27449
	(2.3435)	(12.7600)	(-14.1409)	(-1.0789)
FLRMAP	.39236	-.70055	-.16521	1.3502
	(-1.9836)	(13.2359)	(-4.1960)	(5.3070)
FLTOSU	-.43723	-.23193	-.78818	-.26710
	(2.2105)	(4.3821)	(-20.0184)	(-1.0498)

iv) Estimated Adjustment Coefficients of Vector 4 (Normalized in Brackets)

FLRMX	FLRNHI	FLEXD	FLRMAP	FLTOSU
.19810	.13831	.092763	-.014573	-.076050
(.050402)	(.035188)	(.023601)	(-.0037076)	(-.019349)

Notes: As explained in the text, LRMX, FLRNHI and FLEXD are the four quarter sums (at t, t-1, t-2 and t-3) of LRMANX, LRNHI and LEXDDT, respectively. The summation is done to eliminate seasonality in these variables. In order not to effect the parameter values with this procedure, LRMAXP and LTOTSU were multiplied by four. Thus, FLRMAP = 4*LRMAXP and FLTOSU =4*LTOTSU.

Short-run Dynamic Estimation of the Export Supply Equation

In the short term dynamic estimation of the export supply equation, the following procedure is followed:

(i) An error-correction term was added to the export supply equation. This term is basically the residual of the cointegration vector 4 of Table 11 and is defined as follows:

ERCOEX = FLRMX - .97198*FLRNHI + 1.0789*FLEXD
         - 5.3070*FLRMAP + 1.0498*FLTOSU

(ii) In order to eliminate both the non-seasonal and seasonal unit roots in the dependent variable LRMANX and the explanatory variables LRNHI and LEXDDT, these were differenced by four quarters.

(iii) The other two explanatory variables, LRMAXP and LTOTSU, did not have unit roots. They therefore did not require differencing. Nevertheless, estimations were carried out after these variables were differenced one quarter so that comparative evaluations on their estimated parameters can be made. Since the dependent variable is differenced, it would not be easy to evaluate the parameters of undifferenced LRMAXP and LTOTSU.

(iv) Several diagnostic tests, a total of 14 of them, were used in choosing the final short-term equation. (v) In line with the "from general to specific" modeling approach, several lagged as well as the current values of the explanatory variables were initially included in the equation but the insignificant lags were eliminated.

(v) Alternative lags, ranging from one to four, were tried in choosing the most appropriate number of lags for the error correction term ERCOEX. Estimations with one lag, ERCOEX(-1), yielded meaningful and econometrically acceptable results.

Estimation results and the diagnostic tests of the short term error correction investment equation are given in Table 12. The table contains three different estimations of the same equation; the difference arises from alternative treatments of the lagged variables. In the first estimation, the lags of the lagged dependent variable, D4LRMAX(-1), and the relative export price variable, D1LRMXP, are not constrained. In the second estimation, the lags of these variables are constrained to lie on a polynomial. This polynomial distributed lag (PDL) or Almon lag estimation was done to avoid multicollinearity between the different lags of D4LRMAX(-1) and D1LRMXP.

Table 12: Short-Term Estimation of the Manufacturing Export Supply Equation

1. Dependent Variable: D4LRMAX

Current sample: 1979:2 to 1995:2   Number of observations: 65

R-squared = .848537   Adjusted R-squared = .813584

Durbin-Watson statistic = 2.09410   Durbin's h alternative = -.582803 [.560]

Breusch/Godfrey LM1 = .381024 [.537]   Breusch/Godfrey LM2 = 1.14407 [.564]

Breusch/Godfrey LM3 = 3.05104 [.384]   Breusch/Godfrey LM4 = 8.82237 [.066]

Aug Dickey-Fuller =-8.20191 ** [.000]   ARCH test = 1.15710 [.282]

Chow test = 1.33960 [.233]   LR het. test (w/Chow)= 11.3653 [.000]

F-statistic = 24.2765 ** [.000]   Jarque-Bera normality test = .747485 [.688]

Akaike Information Crit. = -1.38380   Log of likelihood function = 57.9735

Regressor	Coefficient	Standard Error	T-Ratio[Prob]
C	-.079628	.032933	-2.41787 [.019]
D4LRMAX(-1)	.571057	.115410	4.94808 [.000]
D4LRMAX(-2)	.104237	.115584	.90183 [.371]
D4LRMAX(-3)	.154049	.106351	1.44850 [.153]
D4LRMAX(-4)	-.516421	.110672	-4.66624 [.000]
D4LRMAX(-5)	.214877	.097855	2.19588 [.033]
D4LRNHI(-3)	.262207	.096835	2.70778 [.009]
D1LRMXP	.901651	.264286	3.41165[.001]
D1LRMXP(-1)	.218518	.287092	.76114 [.450]
D4LEDDTC(-2)	-.159813	.094080	-1.69869 [.095]
D1LTOTS(-1)	.162481	.086266	1.88350 [.065]
ERCOEX(-1)	-.031650	.010180	-3.10893 [.003]
DU841	.494003	.115815	4.26543 [.000]

II. Dependent variable: D4LRMAX

Current sample: 1979:2 to 1995:2   Number of observation: 65

R-squared = .847557   Adjusted R-squared= .812378

Durbin-Watson statistic = 2.08949   Breusch/Godfrey LM1= .360236 [.548]

Breusch/Godfrey LM2= 1.23029 [.541]   Breusch/Godfrey LM3= 3.36623 [.339]

Breusch/Godfrey LM4= 7.78228 [.100]   Aug Dickey-Fuller =-8.18439 ** [.000]

ARCH test = 1.29267 [.256]   Chow test = 1.02810 [.446]

LR het. test (w/Chow) = 6.22667 [.013]   Jarque-Bera normality test = .749710 [.687]

F-statistic =24.0926 ** [.000]   Akaike Information Crit. =-1.37735

Log of likelihood function = 57.7639

Regressor	Coefficient	Standard Error	T-Ratio[Prob]
C	-.065601	.033496	-1.95848 [.056]
D4LRMAX(-1)	.582412	.115216	5.05494 [.000]
D4LRMAX(-2)	.121386	.115079	1.05481 [.296]
D4LRMAX(-3)	.153362	.107530	1.42622 [.160]
D4LRMAX(-4)	-.512157	.110849	-4.62030 [.000]
D4LRMAX(-5)	.208480	.098452	2.11758 [.039]
D4LRNHI(-3)	.281455	.097097	2.89871 [.005]

Table 12: Continued

DILRMXP	.807575	.264930	3.04826 [.004]
DILRMXP(-1)	.483612	.170353	2.83888 [.006]
DILRMXP(-2)	.159650	.295642	.54001 [.591]
D4LEDDT(-2)	-.174716	.093695	-1.86473 [.068]
DILTOTS(-1)	.171792	.086029	2.00000 [.050]
ERCOEX(-1)	-.026173	.010363	-2.52566 [.015]
DU841	.501594	.115790	4.33192 [.000]

(*) Note: Coefficients of D4LRMAX(-1) and D1LRMXP were estimated with a PDL.

	Sum of Lag Coefficients	Standard Error	t-statistics
D4LRMAX(-I)	0.5535	0.0961	5.759
DILRMXP	1.451	0.5111	2.839

III. Dependent variable: D4LRMAX

Current sample: 1979:2 to 1995:2
R-squared = .845957
Durbin-Watson statistic = 2.05679
Breusch/Godfrey LM2 = .563317 [.755]
Breusch/Godfrey LM4 = 4.63127 [.327]
ARCH test= .983201 [.321]
LR het. test (w/Chow) = 11.5541 [.000]
F-statistic = 44.7181 ** [.000]
Akaike Information Crit. = -1.52076

Number of observations: 65
Adjusted R-squared = .827040
Breusch/Godfrey LM1 = .075434 [.784]
Breusch/Godfrey LM3 = 2.35243 [.503]
Aug Dickey-Fuller = -8.03970 ** [.000]
Chow test= 1.75179 [.110]
White het. test = 33.6607 [.214]
Jarque-Bera normality test = 1.59854 [.450]
Log of Likelihood function = 57.4246

Regressor	Coefficient	Standard Error	T-Ratio [Prob]
C	-.061158	.027096	-2.25713 [.028]
D4LRMXA(-1)	.590419	.061023	9.67537 [.000]
D4LRNHI(-3)	.290129	.089919	3.22657 [.002]
DILMXPA	1.33656	.374926	3.56486 [.001]
D4LEDDT(-2)	-.194931	.084606	-2.30397 [.025]
DILTOTS(-1)	.166041	.076216	2.17855 [.034]
ERCOEX(-1) -	-.024578	.007561	-3.25048 [.002]
DU841	.502940	.110618	4.54664 [.000]

Notes:
D4LRMAX = LRMANX - LRMANX(-4)
LRMANX: Logarithm of real manufacturing exports.
*D4LRMXA(-1) = D4LRMAX(-1)+0-2*D4LRMAX(-2)+0.25*D4LRMAX(-3)-*
*D4LRMAX(-4)+0.5*D4LRMAX(-5).*
D4LRNHI = LRNHI - LRNHI(-4)
LRNHI: Logarithm of real non-residential investment.
D4LEDDT= LEXDDT-LEXDDT(-4)
LEXDDT: Logarithm of excess demand in manufacturing.
DILRMXP = LRMAXP-LRMAXP(-I)
*DILMXPA = O.6O*DILRMXP+0.25*DILRMXP(-1)+0.15*DILRMXP(-2);*
LRMAXP: Logarithm of relative manufacturing export price.
DILTOTS = LTOTSU-LTOTSU(-1)
LTOTSU: Logarithm of the value of manufacturing export subsidies as a proportion of the
value manufacturing exports.
DU841: Dummy variable that takes the value of 1 in 1984:1 and 0 at other times. In the third
estimation, instead of the lags of D4LRMAX(-1) and DILRMXP, their weighted sums, labeled
D4LRMXA(-1) and DILMXPA are used. These weighted sums are defined in Table 12.

The results show that (i) all the parameter estimates have correct signs and (ii) the magnitudes of the estimates are smaller than those of the long term parameters given in Table 11. It can be stated on the basis of the diagnostic tests that there are no econometric problems in the estimations. We can only suspect the presence of heteroskedasticity. According to the LR (Likelihood Ratio, Chow) test, this problem is present. But according to the LM (Lagrange Multiplier, White) test heteroskedasticity is rejected.

The short term price change effect on export supply in the current quarter, given by the parameter estimate of D1LRMXP, is close to unity but declines sharply after the second quarter. Note, however, that since the dependent variable is differenced by four quarters while the price variable is differenced by one quarter, the parameter estimate of D1LRMXP reflects the effect of quarterly price changes on annual export changes. The three quarter effect of price change on annual export change is 1.45 in estimation II and 1.34 in estimation III. These results are supportive of the large long term price elasticity of exports obtained from the cointegration estimation given in Table 11.

It is worth noting that although the long term investment and excess demand elasticities of exports are almost equal, the short term effect of investment on exports is higher than that of excess demand. As already mentioned in the context of cointegration estimation, the dummy variable DU841 represents the effect of an announcement made at the end of 1983 that export subsidies would be lowered considerably during 1984. This resulted in a rush of the exporters at the beginning of 1984 to take advantage of the subsidies before they were reduced.

Of particular interest in these estimations is the short term effect of export subsidies on exports, given the negative long term effect of the former on the latter. The parameter of the export subsidy variable is positive in all three estimations.[9] The same parameter is also significant in the last two estimations where the problem of multicollinearity is reduced. These results imply that in the short run and with one quarter lag, exports respond to higher subsidies positively and significantly.

One important conclusion that comes out from the long run and short run estimation results is the following. The cointegration relationship shows that export subsidies have a negative effect on export supply in the long term. On the other hand, dynamic estimations show that export subsidies have a positive effect on export supply in the short term. Can these seemingly conflicting results be reconciled and explained? These results are explained below on the basis of economic reasoning. But before that, the export supply equation is estimated by rolling regressions to see whether the parameter estimate of export subsidies change in time. If, for instance, this parameter declines in time, then it can be stated that the effect of export subsidies diminishes in time.

In rolling regressions, repeated estimations are carried out with a certain window size (number of observations). The window is shifted one step ahead at each estimation while keeping its size unchanged. In this way, a sequence of parameter estimates and their standard errors are obtained. Here, the third equation in Table 12 is estimated with rolling regressions; window size is taken to be 46 and the initial estimation started at 1990-1993. Due to space considerations, only the graph of the parameter estimates of export subsidies is provided in Figure 3.[10]

Figure 3: Coefficient Estimates of Export Subsidy Variable D1LTOTS(-1) in Rolling Estimations of Export Supply Equation III (Window Size:46)

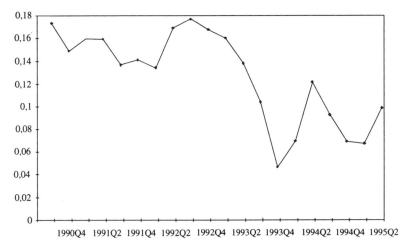

The figure indicates that the coefficient of D1LTOTS(-1) has a negative trend and there is a sharp decline starting in 1993I. Considering that the window size is 46, it is evident that this sharp decline is observed when the observations that reflect the 1981-83 jump in export subsidies are left out. Note that there is some rise in the coefficient after 1994I when there was another large increase in export subsidies.

The rolling regression results are not comparable with cointegration estimations. However, it can be reiterated that export subsidies, as promotion schemes, raise export supply if and when they exceed a certain threshold and this effect diminishes in time.

The economic explanation of the above results can be made in terms of the arguments of the "irreversibility" or "sunk cost" approach. This approach is used in the explanation of investment behavior and can easily be extended to the explanation of export behavior. As explained by Pindyck (1991) and Dixit and Pindyck (1994), an investment expenditure is considered to be a sunk cost, and therefore irreversible, basically because it is industry specific and cannot be used productively by others in a different industry. An irreversible investment project has an opportunity cost that must be included as part of the cost of investment. This opportunity cost can be high and is highly sensitive to uncertainty over the future value of the project. Thus, changing economic conditions that affect the perceived risk of the future cash flows can have a large negative effect on investment expenditure. This latter effect may be larger than for instance the effect of a change in interest rates.

Export activity requires not only investment but also, for instance, marketing by which considerable sunk costs can be incurred. Dixit (1989) explains that such sunk costs combined with exchange rate uncertainty create sizable opportunity costs of entering and exiting international markets. Uncertainties over future product prices, input costs, exchange rates, future regulations and tax policies affect export activity in a manner similar to that of investment activity. Thus, "if uncertainty over the economic environment is high, tax and related incentives may have to be very large to have any significant impact on investment" and exports. Pindyck (1991, p. 1141).

The implication of the irreversibility argument for the above econometric results is clear. In Turkey, uncertainty has all along surrounded export subsidies themselves. First, governments considered export subsidies as part of emergency measures or stabilization programs to raise foreign exchange earnings especially at times when the supply of foreign exchange was not sufficient. In other words, subsidies were not considered as part of a longer term plan that aimed at sustainable export growth.

Second, as subsidies reached high levels during 1980-83, it became evident as early as in 1984 that these high levels were unsustainable. Large and rising budget deficits put a limit both on direct premium payments and foregone tax revenues. There were times in the late 1980s and the early 1990s that the realization of the subsidies had to be postponed due to large public sector deficits. There were also the GATT provisions that prohibited direct payments at the end of the 1980s. The scheduled customs union with the European Union, by which the subsidy regulations of the latter would become effective, was an additional factor in the perceived unsustainability of export subsidies.

Uncertainty also characterized government policies in general and domestic (excess) demand and real exchange rate policies in particular. Thus, export subsidies had a positive effect on exports in the short term by way of higher utilization of the existing capacity. But this effect was temporary and could not last long. A long lasting positive effect could not be observed because of the negative effect of uncertainty and risk on long term decisions that, for instance, relate to the expansion of productive capacity.

In terms of the effects and effectiveness of export policies, econometric results imply the following. The most effective policy seems to be the real exchange rate policy. The effect of this variable is clearly dominant in both the short term and the long term. Then comes the domestic (excess) demand policy. Export subsidies can be used in expanding export supply in the short term but their effect is reversed in the long term. An export policy which heavily depends on export subsidies will fail in the long run. Thus, if a choice has to be made between the exchange rate and subsidy policies, the former should be preferred as against the latter.

Conclusions

Expansion and diversification of exports are generally considered necessary for developing countries to achieve higher and sustainable growth. It is therefore important to make a comparative evaluation of different export policies such as exchange rate policies, domestic demand policies and export promotion schemes. Recently, there has been a concern over the implementation of export promotion measures with the conclusion of the Uruguay Round and the establishment of the World Trade Organization. Since, the "Agreement on Subsidies and Countervailing Measures" (SCM) has tightened the disciplines on subsidies, which may constrain export promotion schemes.

In the Turkish context, reduction of domestic demand, increases in the real exchange rate and improved and newly-introduced export promotion schemes were among the important elements of export policy. These measures were implemented with varying degrees of intensity from the mid-1970s to mid-1990s. Export policy worked well until the mid-1980s, with impressive performances in terms of both the growth and composition of exports. But these could not be sustained.

The sustainability of the growth and diversification of exports required a rise in fixed investment for two reasons. First, the strong performance of exports until mid-1980s was achieved, on the supply side, by the existence of excess production capacity created largely in the 1970s and not fully utilized due to reduced domestic demand. Repressed domestic demand could not be maintained for long. And second, gains in competitiveness in the export markets was achieved by lower real wages and higher real exchange rates. There was not much room left in terms of these variables and technical progress was called for. A related requirement for sustainable export growth and diversification was a stable and well managed macroeconomic environment. Since without such an environment it would be difficult to make long term plans to compete in the international markets.

During the period 1980 to mid-1990s, there was a fall in public sector investment. Although the rise in private fixed investment more than compensated for this decline, it was not as much as was anticipated and a considerable proportion of this rise went to housing. Thus, it was inevitable that export growth and diversification would be constrained from the investment and technology sides. Exports, and for that matter investments, were also constrained by the deterioration of the macroeconomic environment. In the second half of the 1980s and the early 1990s, persistent and large public sector deficits, chronic inflation, attempts to reduce inflation by real appreciation of the Turkish Lira, expansionary fiscal and monetary policies, considerable rises in real wages, electioneering and political economy considerations contributed to an uncertain macroeconomic environment. Under these circumstances, export policies themselves became uncertain.

Dynamic error correction estimations of an export supply equation, carried out with a Turkish data set that covers the period from end-1977 to mid-1995, show that in the short run real exchange rate is the most significant variable with the largest effect. Fixed investment, domestic demand and export subsidies, in descending order, also have significant effects. Hence, in terms of the short term effects and effectiveness of different export policies, at the top there is real exchange policy, then come domestic demand and export promotion policies. The cointegration estimation of the same export supply equation reveals that in terms of supply elasticities, the relative export price variable makes the largest effect implying that real exchange rate is the most effective policy in the long term as well. Domestic demand policy comes second in terms of long term effectiveness. On the other hand, export subsidies have a negative effect on export supply in the long term.

This may look like a controversial result. However, this is not the case in Turkey because of the uncertainties that surround the policies and the macroeconomic environment. On theoretical grounds, this result can be explained with reference to the irreversibility approach in investment. Export decisions, as is the case with investment decisions, take into account the opportunity cost arising from sunk costs which affect the cash flow from exports. This opportunity cost can be large and is highly sensitive to perceived uncertainty and risk. In turn, economic conditions that affect the perceived uncertainty and risk can have a large negative effect on both investments and exports.

Uncertainties over future demand, product prices, input costs, exchange rates, regulations, and tax and subsidy policies affect export activity in a manner similar to that of investment activity. Short run and long run estimations carried out in this study with a Turkish data set have shown the following. (i) If uncertainty over the economic environment is high, tax and subsidy incentives may have to be very large to have any significant impact on exports. (ii) When uncertainty and risk become pervasive in an economy, the effect of tax and subsidy incentives may turn out to be negative in the long run.

The policy implications of this study are clear. Real exchange rates, investment and domestic demand are the long run determinants of exports. Uncertainty and risk have important effects on export and investment decisions. Thus, a major cost of political and economic instability may be its depressing effect on exports and investments. If the goal of macroeconomic policy is to stimulate exports and investments, stability and credibility are crucial determinants, even more important than tax incentives and subsidies. More importantly, and in the absence of stability and credibility, uncertainty and risk are exacerbated with the result that incentives and subsidies discourage exports in the long run rather than encourage them.

Notes

1   This section is largely based on Uygur 1991, 1993b and 1994.
2   The exchange rate is expressed as the Turkish Lira equivalent of one unit of foreign currency. Following Edwards 1989a, the real effective exchange rate is defined in terms of the wholesale price indices for trade partners and consumer price index for Turkey. The precise definitions of the effective exchange rate and the real effective exchange rate are given at the bottom of Table 1.
3   Financial liberalization, savings and investment are discussed at length in Uygur 1993b.
4   Similar views were expressed later in 1993 when the deficits were even higher. See Yenal 1993 and Uygur 1994 on this point.
5   These certificates were issued by the State Planning Organization until 1992. Since then they have been issued by the Undersecretariat of Foreign Trade. The latter was part of the Undersecretariat of Treasury and Foreign Trade until 1995. The two were separated at the beginning of that year.
6   See, for example, Milanovic 1986, p. 12 and Celasun and Rodrik 1989, Chap. 7 on fictitious exports.
7   Yaöcy 1984, p.32 and Milanovic 1986, p.29 estimated this same differential to be 28.1 percent and 29.9 percent respectively.
8   The Johansen VAR methodology is also explained in detail in Johansen and Juselius 1990 and Johansen 1995.
9   It should be mentioned that the contemporaneous correlation between the manufacturing exports and export subsidies is negative. This is expected, since as explained at some length, subsidies were generally raised at times when exports declined or stagnated.
10 Rolling regressions were carried out with MFIT386.

References

Arslan, İsmail 1994. "Incentive Programs in Turkey." Mimeo. The World Bank Resident Mission, Ankara.

Aspe, Pedro, and Francesco Giavazzi. 1982 "The Short Run Behaviour of Prices and Output in the Exportable Sector." *Journal of International Economics.* Vol.12 No.1:83-93.

Balassa, Bela. 1978. "Exports and Economic Growth: Further Evidence." *Journal of Development Economics*, Vol.5, No.2:181-189.

Baldwin, Robert E. 1992. "Are Economists' Traditional Trade Policy Views Still Valid?". *Journal of Economic Literature.* Vol. XXX, No.2:804-829.

Brander, James A., and Barbara J. Spencer. 1985 "Export Subsidies and International Market Share and Rivalry." *Journal of International Economics.* Vol.18, No.1-2: 83-100.

Caballero, Ricardo, and Vittorio Corbo. 1988 "Export Pessimism: Empirical Evidence of the Role of Uncertainty and Imperfect Competition." Mimeo. Washington DC:The World Bank.

Celasun, Merih, and Dani Rodrik. 1989. "Debt, Adjustment and Growth: Turkey" in Jeffrey D. Sachs and Susan M. Collins (eds.), *Developing Country Debt and Economic Performance, Country Studies Vol. 3.* Chicago: NBER and The University of Chicago Press.

Çelebi, Ism. 1991. "Export-Led Growth Model in Turkey After 1980 and an Evaluation of Export Incentives in the Context of Industrialization." Ph.D. Dissertation. Dokuz Eylül Universitesi, Izmir. (In Turkish.)

Chow, P. C. 1987. "Causality Between Export Growth and Industrial Development." *Journal of Development Economics*, Vol.26, No.1:55-63.

Dixit, Avinash K. 1989. "Hysteresis, Import Penetration and Exchange Rate Pass-Through." *Quarterly Journal of Economics*, Vol.104, No.2: 205-228.

Dixit, Avinash K., and Robert S. Pindyck. 1994. *Investment Under Uncertainty.* Princeton: Princeton University Press.

Edwards, Sebastian. 1989. *Exchange Rate Misalignment in Developing Countries. Baltimore:* The Johns Hopkins University Press.

Eswaran, Mukesh, and Ashok Kotwal. 1993. "Export Led Development: Primary Versus Industrial Exports." *Journal of Development Economics,*Vol. 41, No.2: 163-172.

Feder, Gershon. 1983. "On Exports and Economic Growth." *Journal of Development Economics*, Vol.12, No.1-2: 59-73.

Funke, Michael, and Sean Holly. 1993. "The Determinants of West German Exports of Manufactures: An Integrated Demand and Supply Approach." *Weltwirtschaftliches Archiv*, Vol.129, No.3: 488-512.

Gray, Patricia, and Hans W. Singer. 1988. "Trade Policy and Growth of Developing Countries: Some New Data." *World Development*, Vol.16, No.3: 395-403.

Greenaway, David, and David Sapsford. 1994. "What Does Liberalization Do for Exports and Growth?". *Weltwirtschaftliches Archiv*, Vol.130, No.1: 152-173.

Grossman, Gene M., and Elhanan Helpman. 1991. *Innovation and Growth in the Global Economy.* Cambridge, M. A: MIT Press.

Helleiner, Gerald K. 1990. "Trade Strategy in Medium-Term Adjustment." *World Development*, Vol.18, No.6: 879-897.

Helpman, Elhanan and Paul Krugman. 1989. *Trade Policy and Market Structure.* Cambridge, M. A.: MIT Press.

Hutchinson, Michael and Nirvikar Singh. 1987. "Exports and Growth in Developing

Economies: Identifying Externality Effects." Working paper University of California, Santa Cruz.

Johansen, Soren. 1988. "Statistical Analysis of Cointegration Vectors." *Journal of Economic Dynamics and Control*, Vol.12, No.2: 231-254.

___. 1995. *Likelihood-Based Inference in Cointegrated Vector Autoregressive Models.* Oxford: Oxford University Press.

Johansen, Soren, and Katarina Juselius. 1990. "Maximum Likelihood Estimation and Inference on Integration: With Applications to the Demand for Money." *Oxford Bulletin of Economics and Statistics*, Vol. 52, No. 1:169-200.

Jung, Woo S., and Peyton J. Marshall. 1985. "Exports, Growth and Causality in Developing Countries." *Journal of Development Economics*, Vol.18, No. 1: 1-12.

Kohli, Indergit and Nirvikar Singh. 1989. "Exports and Growth: Critical Minimum Effort and Diminishing Returns." Journal of Development Economics, Vol. 30, No. 2: 391-400.

Krugman, Paul. 1986. "New Thinking About Trade Policy" in Paul Krugman (ed.), *Strategic Trade Policy and the New International Economics*. Cambridge, MA: MIT Press.

___. 1993. "The Narrow and Broad Arguments for Free Trade." *American Economic Review, Papers and Proceedings*, Vol.83, No.2: 362-366.

Levine, Ross, and David Renelt. 1992. "A Sensitivity Analysis of Cross-Country Regressions." *American Economic Review*, Vol. 82, No. 4: 942-963.

McCulloch, Rachel. 1993. "The Optimality of Free Trade: Science or Religion." *American Economic Review, Papers and Proceedings*, Vol. 83, No. 2: 367-371.

Michaely, Michael. 1977. "Exports and Growth: An Empirical Investigation." *Journal of Development Economics*, Vol. 4, No. 1: 49-53.

Milanovic, Branko. 1986. "Export Incentives and Turkish Manufactured Exports 1980-84." World Bank Staff Working Papers No. 768. Washington, DC: The World Bank.

Nogués, Julio. 1990. "The Experience of Latin America With Export Subsidies." *Welwirtschaftliches Archiv*,Vol. 126, No.1: 97-114.

Pindyck, Robert S. 1991. "Irreversibility, Uncertainty and Investment." *Journal of Economic Literature*, Vol. 29, No.3: 1110-1148, September.

Rivera-Batiz, Louis, and Paul M. Romer. 1991a. "Economic Integration and Endogenous Growth." *Quarterly Journal of Economics*, Vol.106, No.3: 531-556.

___. 1991b. "International Trade With Endogenous Technical Change." *European Economic Review*,Vol. 35, No.4: 971-1001.

Rodrik, Dani. 1993. "Taking Trade Policy Seriously: Export Subsidization as a Case Study in Policy Effectiveness." NBER Working Paper No. 4567. Cambridge, MA: NBER.

Romer, Paul M. 1990. "Endogenous Technological Change." *Journal of Political Economy*, Vol. 98, No.5: s71-s102.

Sengupta, Jati. 1994. "Rapid Growth in NICs in Asia: Tests of New Growth Theory for Korea." *Kyklos*,Vol. 44, No.4: 561-579.

Sengupta, Jati, and Juan R.Espana. 1994. "Exports and Economic Growth in Asian NICs: An Econometric Analysis for Korea." *Applied Economics*, Vol.26, No.1: 41-51.

Togan, Sübidey. 1993. *The Foreign Trade Regime and Liberalization of Foreign Trade in Turkey during the 1980s*. Ankara: Turkish Eximbank. (In Turkish.)

Uygur, Ercan. 1991. "Policy, Trade and Growth in Turkey: 1970-1990." Mimeo. Faculty of Political Science, Ankara University, Ankara.

___. 1993a. "Trade Policies and Economic Performance in Turkey in the 1980s" in

Manuel Agosin and Diane Tussie (eds.), *Trade and Growth: New Dilemmas in Trade Policy*. London:Macmillan Press.

___. 1993b. *Financial Liberalization and Economic Performance in Turkey*. Ankara: The Central Bank of Turkey.

___. 1994. "Economic Crisis in Turkey: Formation, Present and Future." *Yktisat, Ypletme, Finans*, Vol.9, No.100: 42-54. (In Turkish.)

Yenal, Oktay. 1993. "Thoughts on a Stabilization Programme for the Turkish Economy." Mimeo. Ankara. (In Turkish.)

Yagci, Fahrettin. 1984. "Protection and Incentives in Turkish Manufacturing: An Evaluation of Policies and their Impact in 1981." World Bank Staff Working Papers 660. Washington DC: The World Bank.

Trade Liberalization and Foreign Investment in Jordan

Introduction

The severe economic crisis that Jordan had experienced in 1988 prompted the implementation of two macroeconomic adjustment programs in cooperation with the International Monetary Fund (IMF) and the World Bank. A central feature of both programs was the launching of a trade reform package which was designed to open up the economy to international trade and subject it to the rigor of international competition. This objective gained additional momentum in the early 1990s following Jordan's 1993 request to join then the GATT (General Agreement on Tariffs and Trade) which on 1 January 1995 became the World Trade Organization (WTO). Tariffs and non-tariff barriers were reduced gradually and significant steps were undertaken in the quest to dismantle the import substitution policies which have historically characterized the underlying economic orientation of the economy. The trade reform package was also accompanied by the adoption of other economic reforms in various areas that sought to promote the industrial sector and to provide for a higher and more sustainable growth path.

This chapter provides a comprehensive analysis of Jordan's attempts to reform its trade regime, and the policy choices the country will be facing in light of developments in the Middle East peace process as well as in the country's negotiations for WTO membership.

Recent Economic Developments

Historically, Jordan has consistently pursued a relatively liberal economic policy, including in the areas of trade and investment. However, the increasing availability of foreign reserves in the 1970s and early 1980s, particularly from workers remittances and Arab assistance, prompted the Government to assume a more assertive role in economic activities. The Government's regulatory intervention was elaborated in all the spheres and sectors of the economy including exports, imports, counter trade, free zones, investment, and employment. The Government was also active in establishing, directly and indirectly, new public enterprises and companies that were totally or partially government-owned.

In addition, the Government's efforts at improving public utilities, services and infrastructural facilities, together with defense expenditures and subsidizing basic goods have resulted in large deficits. In the mid-1980s, the region witnessed an economic slowdown due to the sharp drop in oil prices and revenues. Consequently, official Arab assistance and workers remittances started to decline. The Jordanian economy experienced in 1988 and 1989 an acute economic crisis with rapidly growing imbalances in the Government budget and the balance of payments, and the rising debt and debt-service burden. With dwindling foreign reserves and inability to service external debt, the Jordanian Dinar was devalued in 1988 and again in 1989.

The economic crisis was manifested in the sharp decline in real GDP by 1.9 percent and 13.5 percent, respectively in 1988 and 1989, which marked the worst recession in the recent history of Jordan. At the same time, the Government budget experienced an overall deficit (after official grants) of 9.0 percent and 5.8 percent of GDP in 1988 and 1989, respectively. Money and quasi-money expanded due to an increase in domestic assets (in 1988) which resulted mainly from a rise in Government domestic borrowing. The severe imbalance was also reflected in the balance of payments. The trade deficit in 1988 accounted for 28.3 percent of GDP and external public debt rose from 169.4 percent of GDP in 1988 to 228.8 percent in 1989. The overall deficit amounted to Jordanian Dinars (JD) 120.3 million in 1988 (Table 1). Moreover, official reserves sharply declined in 1988 and Jordan was forced to depreciate its currency in 1988, 1989 and in 1990.

The severe economic crisis led the country to adopt a medium-term economic adjustment program for the period 1989-1993. The program aimed at correcting structural imbalances in the economy in both the balance of payments and Government's budget while maintaining a reasonable growth rate. The main elements of the macro-economic package of the program included tight monetary policy, the reduction of the budget deficit by generating more domestic revenues and constraining expenditures, export promotion, trade liberalization, encouragement of private investment, reliance on market forces and privatization. The objectives of the program appeared to be reachable in the first year. However, the implementation of the program was interrupted in 1990 in the wake of the Gulf War – which prompted the abrupt return of about 300,000 Jordanians from Kuwait and the Gulf states, and the cessation of Arab assistance to Jordan.

The relatively stable economic and political environment in the region in 1991 enabled the economy to achieve a moderate growth rate of 1.8 percent in real GDP which was attributed to the improved performance in the construction, trade and financial services sectors. However, the country had still to overcome a severe indebtedness problem and a rising unemployment rate which reached 18.8 percent in 1991. In 1992, Jordan adopted an amended

Table 1: Main Economic Indicators in Jordan 1988-1994

(Million JD)

Indicators	1988	1989	1990	1991	1992	1993	1994
GNP	2175.9	2180.7	2428.8	1634.0	3306.8	3733.4	4117.1
GDP	2264.4	2372.1	2668.3	2855.1	3493.0	3882.5	4266.2
Annual Changes in Percent							
Real GDP	-1.9	-13.5 1.0	1.8	16.1	5.8	5.7	3.9
GDP Deflator	3.1	21.0	11.4	5.2	5.4	5.1	3.6
Cost of Living Index	6.6	25.6	16.2	8.2	4.0	3.3	
Government Budget							
Total Revenue	721.3	855.5	938.2	1112.0	1358.7	1406.3	1492.3
Revenue	544.4	565.4	744.0	828.8	1168.9	1191.5	1270.0
Foreign Grants	155.4	261.7	164.3	225.2	137.4	163.3	167.3
Total Expenditures	925.9	992.6	1032.6	1099.6	1177.7	1336.6	1437.1
Overall Deficit	-204.6	-137.1	-94.4	12.4	181.0	69.7	55.2
In Percent of GDP at Current Prices							
Total Revenue	31.9	36.1	35.2	38.9	38.9	36.2	35.0
Revenue	24.0	23.8	27.9	29.0	33.5	30.7	29.8
Foreign Grants	6.9	11.0	6.2	7.9	3.9	4.2	3.9
Total Expenditures	40.9	41.8	38.7	38.5	33.7	34.4	33.7
Overall Deficit	-9.0	-5.8	-3.5	0.4	5.2	1.8	1.3
Monetary Aggregates							
Money and Quasi Money	2646.7	2971.1	3122.6	3717.5	4193.0	4481.8	4841.5
Foreign Assets	363.6	682.7	955.8	1694.9	1729.2	1689.6	1904.3
Domestic Assets	2279.9	2288.4	2166.8	2022.6	2464.8	2792.2	2937.5
Total Deposits	2346.0	2625.4	2642.6	4022.1	4749.0	4939.4	5391.5
Exchange Rate	2.692	1.753	1.507	1.469	1.471	1.443	1.433

Table 1: Continued

(Million JD)

Indicators	1985	1989	1990	1991	1992	1993	1994
Annual Changes in Percent							
Money and Quasi Money	11.4	12.4	5.1	19.1	7.4	6.9	8.0
Foreign Assets	-15.3	87.7	40.1	77.3	2.0	-2.2	12.7
Domestic Assets	17.2	3.7	-5.3	-6.7	21.8	13.3	5.2
Total Deposits	9.5	11.9	0.6	52.2	18.1	4.0	9.1
Real Effective Exchange Rate	-12.7	-15.6	-11.2	2.2	-2.3	--	--
Balance of Payments							
Exports	381.5	637.6	706.1	770.7	829.3	864.7	995.2
Imports	1022.5	1230.0	1725.8	1710.5	2214.0	2453.6	2362.6
Trade Balance	-641.0	-592.4	-1019.7	-939.8	-1384.0	-1588.9	-1367.4
Workers Remittances	335.7	358.5	331.8	306.3	573.1	720.7	784.3
Current Account	-105.5	-104.9	-272.8	-288.1	-568.7	-435.3	-231.9
Overall Balance	-120.3	-317.8	-317.8	108.1	-409.9	-557.3	-250.2
Official Reserves	218.5	330.1	370.8	949.1	1001.1	1689.6	1904.2
External Public Debt	3836.9	5409.4	6052.5	5516.8	5203.1	4803.9	4612.7
In Percent of GDP							
Trade Balance	-28.3	-25.0	-38.2	-32.9	-39.6	-40.9	-32.1
Current Account	-4.7	-4.4	-10.2	-10.1	-16.3	-11.2	-5.4
External Public Debt	169.4	228.8	226.8	193.2	149.0	123.7	108.1

Sources: Central Bank of Jordan, Monthly Statistical Bulletin. Feb. 1995. (Amman, Jordan);
Central Banks of Jordan, Annual Reports for 1992 and 1993 (Amman, Jordan).

economic adjustment program for the period 1992-1998 and formulated a policy-oriented development plan for the period 1993-1997. The macroeconomic policies which Jordan adopted in accordance with this adjustment program led to positive developments in the main economic indicators. The Government pursued a strict fiscal policy emphasizing the generation of local revenues and the constraining of public expenditures. Real GDP rebounded by 16.1 percent in 1992 as a result of buoyant activities in the construction, manufacturing, transport and communications, and agricultural sectors.

Since 1992 the Jordanian economy has been achieving significant improvements in its economic performance. Real GDP grew by 5.8 percent and 5.7 percent in 1993 and 1994, respectively. This was mainly attributed to the manufacturing, mining, transport and communications sectors. It is worth noting that the level of GDP growth which was achieved in 1994 had exceeded the target set in the five-year plan at 5.6 percent.[1] The strict fiscal policy which led to an overall surplus in 1991-1994, was supported by a tight monetary policy and prudent exchange rate management. Thus, external public debt declined due to reduction and rescheduling (from 228.8 percent of GDP in 1989 to 108.1 percent in 1994). Official reserves accelerated and the exchange rate of the JD stabilized. In addition, the foreign trade performance improved and for the first time in several years, the trade deficit in 1994 shrank.

Merchandise Trade

The Jordanian economy has been suffering from a chronic, and increasing trade deficit. This reflected Jordan's relatively narrow export base and its heavy reliance on imported consumer goods and energy products. The economy's structural characteristics and its level of development, along with the country's political and economic relations with the outside world have, to a large extent, determined the sources of imports and destination of exports. Merchandise trade deficits have been financed by remittances of Jordanians working abroad, official grants from neighboring Arab-oil exporting countries, external borrowing and a considerable drawdown of foreign exchange reserves.

Jordan's external merchandise trade has been expanding rapidly: excluding the year 1991, the average annual growth rate of imports and exports was about 19.4 percent during the period 1988-1994 (Table 2). While there was a substantial decline in foreign trade due to the Gulf crisis in 1991 and its aftermath, this sector recorded a remarkable recovery in 1992 as trade grew by 23.3 percent. This achievement was mainly a result of the notable performance of various economic sectors and population growth caused by the

Jordanian returnees from the Gulf States. Imports and exports accounted respectively, for 93.5 percent and 6.5 percent of the total expansion in foreign trade in 1992. However, external trade grew by 10.4 percent and 3.6 percent in 1993 and 1994 respectively, due to the slowdown in the growth of imports in 1993 and their notable decline in 1994 for reasons which will be discussed later.

Nonetheless, the trade deficits continued to increase as the fall in exports was larger than that of imports. Thus, the trade deficit, following its decline in 1991 by 7.8 percent, increased sharply by 47.3 percent and 14.7 percent in 1992 and 1993 respectively; and then it dropped by 13.9 percent to JD 1367.4 million in 1994 (Table 3).

Merchandise trade plays a vital role in the Jordanian economy. This is reflected in the ratio of external trade to GDP which rose from 59.5 percent in 1988 to 87.5 percent in 1990. However, due to the Gulf crisis it dropped to 80.8 percent in 1991; and stabilized at 81.0 percent during the period 1992-1993 before declining to 74.0 percent in 1994 owing to the considerable decrease in imports. At the same time, per capita share in external trade has been on the increase (Table 2). These indicators show the significant openness of the Jordanian economy.

Exports

Excluding the year 1991, the level of Jordan's exports has been rising. In 1994, they increased to JD 793.9 million from JD 691.3 million in 1993, a growth rate of 14.8 percent (Table 3). This was mainly due to the rise in demand for Jordanian consumer goods in the neighboring Arab countries and to public and private efforts to promote domestic exports in line with the objectives of the structural adjustment program.

Raw materials have always accounted for the bulk of Jordan's domestic exports, despite their decline in 1992 and 1993 by 6.5 percent and 13.4 percent, respectively. Their relative importance fell from 65.0 percent of total exports in 1991 to 57.4 percent and 45.5 percent in 1992 and 1993, respectively. This was mainly a result of the decrease in the exports of phosphates, potash and fertilizers owing to the weakening of demand and prices in the international market and emerging shipment difficulties from the Aqaba port.[2]

The above notwithstanding, the performance of raw material exports improved substantially in 1994 as they grew by 39.1 percent; and their relative importance rose to 55.1 percent. This was mainly due to the increase in the export of phosphates, potash and fertilizers by 2.6 percent, 7.7 percent and 60.4 percent, respectively,[3] as demand in the international market and prices picked up in 1994.

Table 2: Main Indicators of Jordan's External Trade 1988-1994

(Million JD)

Indicators	1988	1989	1990	1991	1992	1993	1994
Growth Rate (in percent)							
External Trade	15.7	30.9	32.5	-1.2	23.3	10.4	3.6
Domestic Exports	30.5	64.4	14.6	-2.2	5.9	9.1	14.8
Imports	11.7	20.3	40.3	-0.9	29.4	10.8	-3.7
Re-exports	-15.3	82.5	-9.4	83.5	13.6	-11.3	16.1
Percent of GDP							
External Trade	59.5	74.3	87.5	80.8	81.0	74.0	--
Domestic Exports	14.3	22.5	22.9	20.9	17.8	18.6	--
Imports	45.2	51.8	64.5	59.9	63.2	55.4	--
Re-exports	2.5	4.3	3.5	6.0	4.5	4.7	--
Per Capita Share (JD)							
External Trade	448.9	567.1	677.1	593.9	708.4	757.4	769.8
Exports	108.2	171.7	177.3	154.0	157.7	166.5	193.6
Imports	340.7	395.4	499.8	439.9	550.7	590.7	576.2
Re-exports	18.9	33.3	27.2	44.3	48.6	41.8	49.1

Sources: Central Bank of Jordan, Monthly Statistical Bulletin, Feb. 1995, (Amman, Jordan); Central Bank of Jordan, Annual Reports for 1992 and 1993, (Amman, Jordan).

With the exception of 1994, exports of consumer goods have been on the rise since 1988 in both relative and absolute terms even during the Gulf Crisis. This has been attributed to the growth and some diversification of manufacturing output along with the increasing demand in the Arab neighboring countries for Jordanian products. These exports grew from JD 200.5 million in 1991 to JD 356.7 million in 1993 before declining to JD 329.1 million in 1994, reflecting a rise in their relative importance to 51.2 percent in 1993 and a drop to 41.5 percent in 1994 (Table 3). The main contributors to the growth in 1991-1993 were pharmaceutical products, detergents and soap, plastic products, cloths, diary products and eggs, and fodder. The decline in the overall exports by 7.7 percent in 1994 was attributed mainly to the drop in the exports of food and live animals, cloths and plastic products by 34.8 percent, 2.2 percent and 25.3 percent respectively.[4]

Exports of capital goods have had a relatively small share in total exports. However, after a decline of 42 percent in 1991 they continuously increased to record a growth of 36 percent in 1994 (Table 3). Machinery and transport equipment have constituted the bulk of these exports. It has to be stated, however, that despite the efforts to diversify industrial production, there is still a high degree of commodity concentration in exports.

The prevailing economic conditions and political stability in the Arab region have play an important part in influencing the destination of Jordan's exports. Nevertheless, Arab countries have remained the main markets for Jordanian products. Due to the Gulf crisis, the share of Arab countries in total exports declined from 42 percent in 1988 to 28.8 percent in 1991, followed by a gradual recovery to reach 42.5 percent in 1994 (Table 4). Iraq is the main export market for Jordanian products, although its share in the total exports of Jordan dropped from 19.9 percent in 1988 to 7.7 percent in 1992 before increasing to 13.3 percent in 1994. At the same time, the share of Saudi Arabia fell sharply from 9.6 percent in 1988 to 1.8 percent in 1991, followed by a remarkable recovery to reach 10.4 percent per annum during the period 1992-1994.

Imports

Jordan's structural characteristics, level of development and narrow production base have resulted in its heavy dependence on commodity imports, leading to relatively high ratios of imports to both exports and GDP (Table 2). With the exception of 1991, imports in Jordan have been on the increase since the mid-1980s. After a decline of 0.9 percent in 1991, they achieved a remarkable growth of 29.4 percent in 1992 and 10.8 percent in 1993 before decreasing again by 3.7 percent in 1994 (Table 2). The high growth of imports in

Table 3: Jordan's External Trade by Economic Function 1988-1994

(Million JD)

	1988 Value	1988 %	1989	1990	1991	1992	1993	1994 Value	1994 %
Domestic Exports	**324.8**	**100.0**	**534.1**	**612.3**	**598.6**	**633.8**	**691.3**	**793.9**	**100.0**
Consumer Goods	79.9	24.6	123.3	173.5	200.5	255.6	356.7	329.1	41.5
Raw Materials	239.3	73.7	388.2	422.8	388.8	363.5	314.6	437.6	55.1
Capital Goods	5.6	1.7	13.6	-16.0	9.3	14.7	20.0	27.2	3.4
Re-exports	**56.7**	-	**103.5**	**93.8**	**172.1**	**195.5**	**173.4**	**201.3**	-
Imports	**1,022.5**	**100.0**	**1,230.0**	**1,725.8**	**1,710.5**	**2,214.0**	**2,453.6**	**2,362.6**	**100.0**
Consumer Goods	371.6	36.3	414.3	650.7	728.5	900.5	938.2	785.1	33.2
Raw Materials	393.7	38.5	523.8	730.1	680.2	789.9	882.6	1,141.7	48.3
Capital Goods	219.5	21.5	262.1	319.5	291.0	509.8	606.5	423.7	18.0
Miscellaneous	37.7	3.7	29.8	16.5	10.8	13.8	26.3	12.1	0.5
Trade Balance	**-641.0**	-	**592.4**	**-1,019.7**	**-939.8**	**-1,384.7**	**-1,588.9**	**-1,367.4**	

Sources: - *Department of Statistics, Statistical Year Book 1992, (Amman, Jordan), pp. 476-477.*
- *Central Bank of Jordan, Twenty Ninth Annual Report, 1992 (Amman, Jordan), p. 153.*
- *Central Bank of Jordan, Monthly Statistical Bulletin, Feb. 1995 (Amman, Jordan).*

1992 can be attributed to the general economic recovery following the sudden return of Jordanian expatriates and their investments. By contrast, the sharp drop in imports in 1994 was a result of the dwindling domestic demand for certain industrial products along with the rise in the prices of many commodities in the international market.

Consumer goods have accounted for about 36 percent of total imports per annum over the period 1988-1994. With the exception of 1994, they have been on the rise since 1988. Their sharp decline by 16.3 percent in 1994 was a result of the aforementioned factors. Foodstuff and manufactured consumer goods have constituted the bulk of these imports, reflecting the country's resource endowments.

The share of intermediate inputs and raw materials in the total annual import bill of Jordan has been about 41 percent. After a drop of 6.8 percent in 1991, they gradually grew to achieve a remarkable growth of 29.3 percent in 1994. Energy products, iron and steel, paper and cardboard, textile yarn and fabrics have accounted for the highest portion of these imports.

Imports of capital goods made up about 21 percent of the total annual import bill of Jordan during the period 1988-1994. The sharp increase in investment in the manufacturing sector reflecting a notable economic recovery generated a sizable rise in these imports which grew by 75 percent and 19 percent in 1992 and 1993, respectively (Table 3). However, they decreased by 30 percent in 1994 as a result of the sharp decline of 70 percent in imports of machinery and transport equipment which constitute the bulk of this category.

The European Community provides about 30 percent of Jordan's total imports, while Arab countries' share has been about 20 percent. The United States has accounted for the highest portion of Jordan's imports in comparison with other non-Arab countries (Table 5). Among Arab countries, Iraq has had the highest share of Jordan's imports. Arab countries have been the source of energy products and some consumer goods, whereas Western European countries, Japan and the United States have been the main source of capital and intermediate imports. Other countries such as Turkey, India, Taiwan, China and South Korea have mainly provided manufactured consumer goods to the Jordanian market.

Trade Reforms

Jordan initiated a gradual trade liberalization program in late 1988 and early 1989 to mitigate the balance of payments crisis of 1988. Although the exchange rate system became initially more restrictive in 1989 in an attempt to overcome the intensified balance of payments pressures, it was gradually liberalized with the improvement in the balance of payments. Trade reform

Table 4: Destination of Jordan's Domestic Exports 1988-1994

(Million JD)

	1988		1989	1990	1991	1992	1993	1994	
	Value	%						Value	%
Arab Common Market Countries	75.9	23.4	145.2	146.9	81.8	74.0	108.4	147.1	18.5
Iraq	64.6	19.9	123.9	118.5	55.8	48.8	77.5	105.3	13.3
Other Arab Countries	60.3	18.6	96.1	112.0	90.5	148.4	177.6	189.9	24.0
Saudi Arabia	31.3	9.6	47.7	46.8	11.0	70.1	80.1	72.3	9.1
Eastern Europe Countries	23.8	7.3	42.7	24.4	27.8	15.7	32.9	13.7	1.7
E.E.C.	25.4	7.8	25.0	22.1	18.5	19.1	27.9	40.4	5.1
India	55.4	17.1	94.9	129.1	109.6	96.4	65.9	88.1	11.1
Japan	6.6	2.0	18.2	13.0	10.6	12.1	9.8	12.6	1.6
Indonesia	11.0	3.4	27.3	30.4	24.2	29.0	37.6	28.0	3.5
Turkey	8.8	2.7	11.55	15.1	13.1	15.3	12.6	10.3	1.3
South Korea	6.7	2.1	9.8	7.6	10.0	12.1	7.5	14.4	1.8
Taiwan	7.3	2.2	11.3	13.6	10.7	10.4	10.0	9.9	1.2
Other	43.6	13.4	51.1	98.1	201.8	201.3	201.7	239.5	30.2
Total	**324.8**	**100.0**	**534.1**	**612.3**	**598.6**	**633.8**	**691.3**	**793.9**	**100.0**

Source: *Central Bank of Jordan, Twenty Ninth Annual Report, 1992 (Amman, Jordan), p. 156.*
        Central Bank of Jordan, Monthly Statistical Bulletin, Feb. 1995 (Amman, Jordan),p. 66.

Table 5: Sources of Jordan's Imports 1988 - 1994

(Million JD)

	1988 Value	1988 %	1989	1990	1991	1992	1993	1994 Value	1994 %
Arab Common Market Countries	139.6	13.7	250.6	306.4	239.6	363.3	388.9	385.1	16.3
Iraq	117.3	11.5	212.7	273.2	170.9	295.4	307.0	291.3	12.3
Other Arab Countries	122.1	11.9	86.9	132.0	99.1	98.7	109.9	138.0	5.8
E.E.C.	303.3	29.6	365.7	494.1	512.2	650.1	753.8	794.7	33.6
Germany	69.9	6.8	80.8	101.2	133.2	189.7	202.8	184.4	7.8
United Kingdom	64.8	6.3	74.0	89.4	77.6	108.4	127.9	120.8	5.1
France	39.6	3.9	72.6	97.9	73.6	78.1	98.5	111.8	4.7
Eastern Europe Countries	62.2	6.1	55.8	85.3	85.6	129.7	151.9	137.9	5.8
Other European Countries	46.7	4.6	58.2	59.8	59.2	75.0	81.7	68.6	2.9
U.S.A.	128.9	12.6	170.8	299.5	178.2	246.2	311.4	232.9	9.9
Japan	54.1	5.3	45.7	54.3	61.1	132.2	123.4	93.6	4.0
Turkey	29.0	2.8	28.1	46.1	57.1	97.4	58.4	62.7	2.7
Taiwan	20.5	2.0	23.1	30.2	40.1	52.7	43.7	39.1	1.7
China	17.5	1.7	21.9	25.0	29.1	52.1	50.6	62.4	2.6
South Korea	12.8	1.3	15.3	17.6	24.8	46.7	61.3	58.3	2.5
India	2.8	0.3	8.7	22.1	53.5	31.2	43.5	38.9	1.6
Other	83.3	8.1	99.7	153.4	2,270.9	238.7	274.9	250.4	10.6
Total	**1,022.5**	**100.0**	**1,230.0**	**1,725.8**	**1,710.5**	**2,214.0**	**2,453.9**	**2,362.6**	**100.0**

Source: *Central Bank of Jordan, Twenty Ninth Annual Report, 1992 (Amman, Jordan), p. 156.*
Central Bank of Jordan, Monthly Statistical Bulletin Feb. 1995 (Amman, Jordan), p. 67.

gained momentum in 1990 and 1992 when tariff and non-tariff barriers were reduced substantially with the aim of rationalizing the tariff structure, reducing tariff protection and gradually eliminating non-tariff barriers. This reform was accompanied by reforming investment regulations to attract more foreign investments, improving export incentives and initiating institutional reforms in various areas to promote the industrial sector and to support the shift towards the export-oriented strategy. Nevertheless, despite the progress that has been achieved in these fields, the country has not been very successful in offsetting the anti-export bias created by the trade regime and exchange system to establish an incentive regime conducive to outward-oriented growth.[5]

Import Policies

Jordan's import regime was substantially restrictive and characterized by high tariff and non-tariff barriers in the 1980s. This was a reflection of the import substitution strategy and high protection which led to considerable anti-export bias. Since late 1988, there has been a notable change in the direction of trade liberalization through the gradual reduction of tariffs and non-tariff import restrictions.

Tariffs

Tariff duties in Jordan have had three objectives: to protect import substituting industries, to raise government revenues, and to influence domestic savings and consumption patterns. The main aim of the tariff reform program that was initiated in late 1988 was to structure a more uniform tariff regime while at the same time ensuring revenue neutrality. Thus, the rates of the lowest tariffs were to be increased and those of the highest reduced; this was also supposed to serve the purpose of diluting the discrimination implied by a more differentiated tariff structure. Tariffs on certain consumer and intermediate goods have in fact been reduced and increased on luxury imports on several occasions since 1990. Although this reform has resulted in a more uniform tariff regime, it still implies significant distortions as the overall tariff level and the degree of tariff differential offered to various products and industries have not been reduced as much as planned. In addition, over half of total imports still enjoy some form of exemptions.[6]

Table (6) shows that the manufacturing sector is affected by an average tariff rate of 17.9 percent which was higher than that for the agricultural and mining sectors in 1993. The tariff rate on consumer goods (24.9 percent) was almost triple that on intermediate goods and slightly higher than that on capital goods. The highest tariff rate was for beverages (103.9 percent), while the lowest rate was for petroleum and coal products. Import surcharges ranged between 20.2 percent for wearing apparel and leather products, and 11.3 percent for printing and publishing items.

The combination of the new tariffs and surcharges have reshaped the nominal tariff protection structure. Nominal tariff protection is lower for mining (22.2 percent) and agriculture (23.7 percent) than it is for manufacturing (34.3 percent). It is also lower for intermediate goods (23.4 percent) and capital goods (37.9 percent) than it is for consumer goods (42.7 percent). As can be seen in Table 6, nominal tariff protection varies widely among manufacturing industries. The lowest rate is for petroleum and coal products (16.7 percent) and the highest is for beverages (123.6 percent). This reflects the fact that there is considerable variation in the levels of nominal protection for different industries and commodities. However, it has been reported that nominal tariff protection has declined on manufactured goods to about 21 percent in 1994 due to the reduction of tariff duties on consumer goods.[7]

Table 7 presents data on the effective rate of protection (ERP), which takes into account import duties on both the inputs and the output. All ERPs are positive for all sectors and industries. Effective protection for agriculture (5.1 percent) and for mining (8.5 percent) are very low relative to the significantly higher rate of 40.9 percent for manufacturing. The highest ERP rates are enjoyed by beverages (185.0 percent), tobacco (117.2 percent), wooden furniture (97.0 percent), wearing apparel (78.0 percent), plastic products (76.8 percent) leather products (64.0 percent), and rubber products (57.5 percent) industries. By contrast, the lowest rates are for petroleum and coal products (0 percent), and printing and publishing (9.1 percent) industries. What is important to note in this respect is the fact that the higher the effective protection, the higher the anti-export bias as output is encouraged to be directed toward the protected domestic market rather than for exports. In addition, protection gears investments towards industries with higher protection, i.e. towards consumer goods industries, rather than intermediate goods industries.

Moreover, it should be mentioned that manufactured exports are expected to benefit from a new World Bank-supported trade and financial sector adjustment project due for completion in July 1995. This project aims to simplify the customs regime, reduce the number of tariffs and produce sound customs laws. The new system is expected to cut costs and reduce the delays being experienced in the importation of raw materials and intermediate goods, which, in turn, would enhance the competitiveness of exports.[8]

Non-Tariff Measures

Prior to 1988, there were several quantitative restrictions affecting imports into Jordan. Since late 1988 and in the process of reforming the trade regime,

Table 6: Unweighted Average of Tariffs, Surcharges and Nominal Tariff Protection in Jordan, 1993

Industry	Tariff	Surcharges	Nominal Protection
AGRICULTURE	**10.5**	**13.2**	**23.7**
MINING	**9.3**	**12.9**	**22.2**
MANUFACTURING	**17.9**	**16.4**	**34.3**
Processed Food	16.3	15.7	32.0
Beverages	103.9	19.7	123.6
Tobacco	49.3	18.6	67.9
Textiles	14.7	15.8	30.5
Wearing Apparel	28.8	19.7	48.5
Leather Products	22.1	20.2	42.3
Footwear	30.0	20.2	50.2
Wood &Cork Products	15.7	17.1	32.8
Wooden Furniture	30.0	20.2	50.2
Paper Products	13.4	17.9	31.1
Printing & Publishing	8.7	11.3	20.0
Industrial Chemicals	7.4	14.0	21.4
Other Chemical Products	15.2	16.8	32.0
Petroleum Refineries	11.9	17.8	29.7
Petroleum & Coal Products	4.1	12.6	16.7
Rubber Products	12.0	17.0	29.0
Plastic Products	23.3	17.3	40.6
Non-Metallic Products	24.6	18.8	43.4
Non-Electric Products	10.4	14.6	25.0
Electric Appliances	31.4	18.5	49.9
Scientific Equipment	14.2	18.4	32.6
Transport Equipment	57.7	17.1	74.8
Fabricated Metal Products	19.9	18.4	38.3
Basic Metal Industries	6.7	15.9	22.6
Other Manufactured Goods	17.1	17.9	35.0
OVERALL ECONOMY	**16.8**	**16.1**	**32.9**
CONSUMER GOODS	**24.9**	**17.8**	**42.7**
INTERMEDIATE GOODS	**8.4**	**15.0**	**23.4**
CAPITAL GOODS	**21.3**	**16.1**	**37.9**

Source: The World Bank: Jordan-Consolidating Economic Adjustment and Establishing the Base for Sustainable Growth, (Washington D.C., December 30, 1993), p.52.

Table 7: Average Nominal Tariff Protection and Effective Rate of Protection by Sector and Sub-Sector in Jordan, 1993

Industry	Average Nominal Tariff Protection	Effective Rate of Protection
AGRICULTURE	**23.7**	**5.1**
MINING	**22.2**	**8.5**
MANUFACTURING	**34.3**	**40.9**
FOOD BEVERAGES, TOBACCO	**41.1**	**22.5**
Food Manufacturing	32.0	19.4
Beverages	123.6	185.0
Tobacco	67.9	117.2
TEXTILES & LEATHER	**36.3**	**48.6**
Textiles	30.5	32.6
Wearing Apparel	48.5	78.0
Leather Products	42.3	64.0
WOOD & CORK PRODUCTS	**33.6**	**51.4**
Wood & Cork Products	32.8	49.0
Wooden Furniture & Fixtures	50.2	97.0
PAPER & PRINTING MATERIAL	**28.3**	**19.8**
Paper Products	31.3	22.3
Printing & Publishing	20.0	9.1
CHEMICALS, PETROLEUM, COAL	24.9	24.8
Industrial Chemicals	21.4	13.8
Other Chemical Products	31.9	26.3
Petroleum Refineries	29.4	39.7
Petroleum & Coal Products	16.7	-
Rubber Products	29.0	57.5
Plastic Products	40.7	76.8
NON-METALLIC PRODUCTS	**43.4**	**48.5**
METAL PRODUCTS & MACHINERY	**40.3**	**99.4**
Non-Electric Machinery	25.0	14.7
Electric Appliances	49.9	-
Scientific Equipment	32.6	76.6
Transport Equipment	74.8	-
Fabricated Metal Products	38.4	57.0
BASIC METAL INDUSTRIES	**22.6**	**18.0**
OTHER MANUFACTURED GOODS	**35.0**	**55.6**
OVERALL ECONOMY	**33.0**	**30.3**
CONSUMER GOODS	**42.7**	-
INTERMEDIATE GOODS	**23.3**	-
CAPITAL GOODS	**37.9**	-

Source: The World Bank: Jordan-Consolidating Economic Adjustment & Establishing the Base for Sustainable Growth, (Washington D.C., December 30, 1993), p.54.

many non-tariff barriers have been phased-out. Three types of non-tariff measures remain in existence:

(a) *Import Bans*: There is an outright prohibition on the importation of five commodities: tomato paste, fresh milk, certain dairy products, mineral water and table salt. The Ministry of Industry and Trade (MIT) will not issue an import license for these commodities. In addition, the import of some 11 luxury goods is banned at times for balance of payments purposes.[9]

(b) *Licensing Requirements*: These affect the importation of five major categories, namely, fruits and vegetables, certain chemicals, pharmaceutical products, many foodstuffs and telecommunication equipment. Actually, all fresh fruits and vegetables cannot be imported without permission from the ministry of Agriculture prior to MIT issuing an import license. There are some 220 chemicals that cannot be imported without permission from the Ministry of Interior. The importation of all pharmaceutical products requires prior approval from the Ministry of Health. There are some 6 foodstuffs that require permission from the Ministry of Supply before an import license can be issued by MIT. These include white cheese, barley, animal feeds, meat, fish, butter, fresh juice, beans, cows and sheep. All telecommunication equipment e.g., telephones, facsimile machines, telexes, and so forth, are subject to licensing requirements from the Ministry of Telecommunications before they can be imported.[10]

(c) *Government Monopoly*: The Government has a monopoly on the importation of nine necessary commodities: sugar, wheat, rice, flour, dried milk, cigarettes, frozen chicken, lentils and olive oil. Importers of these items act as agents for the Ministry of Supply which sets their price and distributes them in the country. Sugar, wheat, rice and powdered milk are sold by the Government at subsidized prices in order to assist the poor.

Import Procedures

Import procedures in Jordan are considered relatively complex and restrictive despite the efforts that have been undertaken to simplify them since 1989. Importers go through the following customs procedures:

(a) *An import license* must be obtained from MIT for imports that exceed JD 2000. However, as mentioned earlier, the importation of many products require import permits from the concerned authorities prior to MIT issuing an import license.

(b) *A bank guarantee* is required. The Central Bank of Jordan demands cash requirements against import documents. In addition, a foreign exchange permit should be acquired from the Central Bank after the import license has been obtained.

(c) *Approval* from various departments is required. It has been reported that import documents typically require about 50 signatures.[11] Although many of these signatures were introduced as a result of the Gulf Crisis, they are still required even though the political and economic conditions have improved in the region.

(d) *Inspection* of imported products is carried out by various departments before they can be cleared. This involves the Ministries of Industry and Trade, Agriculture and Health along with the Customs Department.

Export Promotion Policies

Jordan has adopted an export promotion scheme since 1989 with the aim of reducing the anti-export bias inherent in its import regime, increasing manufactured exports, diversifying economic activity, and attracting more foreign investment. The following existing export incentives have been introduced and/or improved recently:[12]

(a) *Duty Drawback System*: This provides rebate of import duties and taxes paid on inputs used in exports. However, the system is a complex one and has several shortcomings, for example, the exclusion of spare-parts.

(b) *Temporary Admission or Duty Exemption*: Even though this system has some shortcomings, it works better than the duty drawback system.

(c) *Export Credit Guarantee Corporation*: The Government has recently established this corporation to improve credit and guarantee procedures for exporters.

(d) *Industrial Estates and Exports Processing Zones*: Jordan has two industrial zones and two free zones which have been operative for some time with the goal of promoting industrialization and the export of manufactured goods.

(e) *Jordan Export Development and Commercial Centers Corporation (JEDCO)*: This corporation provides a wide range of services directly to exporters and indirectly through the country's various private sector organizations with the aim of export promotion. These include product promotion, market information and research, technical assistance for product design and development, and process improvement and export development advisory services. It also encourages exporters to participate in national, regional and international trade fairs. JEDCO is responsible for the management of most of the trade protocols and counter trade agreements on behalf of MIT.

(f) *Export Procedures*: Although there have been efforts to simplify export procedures, they are still considered complex and time consuming. Despite the fact that exports are not subject to export taxes and there are no explicit restrictions on exports, exporters must obtain a certificate of origin from either the Chamber of Commerce or the Chamber of Industry prior to acquiring an export license from MIT. The Customs Department might require that the exporter must obtain an approval from the Ministry of Foreign Affairs and the Amman embassy of the foreign country to which the products are being exported. If products are being exported to a protocol country, exporters are asked to arrange for barter trade through JEDCO. After acquiring all of these documents, exporters must go to the Customs Department to obtain several approvals. It is reported that export documents often require more than 20 signatures.[13]

Foreign Exchange Regime

The foreign exchange system was liberalized substantially after the balance of payments crisis in late 1988. It has moved from a fixed exchange to a dual exchange rate system: an official rate and a free market rate. The reform included the elimination of several capital control policies and eased foreign exchange restrictions. Since late 1988, the JD has depreciated substantially in response to balance of payments pressures. Although there are still some restrictions on invisibles and capital payments, it has been reported that they do not hinder foreign investments or the repatriation of foreign capital. The following are the main characteristics and foreign exchange arrangements of the present foreign exchange and capital control system:[14]

1. The JD is pegged to the SDR. In December 1994, the official buying and selling rates quoted by the Central Bank of Jordan were JD 0.697 and JD 0.699, respectively, per one US dollar. The spread between the official rate which is determined by the Central Bank of Jordan and the free market rate which is largely set by the banking system has been minimal.

2. After its gradual increase overtime, the amount of foreign exchange that could be taken out of the country or transferred abroad by any one resident and non-resident annually reached the equivalent of JD 35,000. A fee of 0.10 percent is levied on exchange permits for invisible payments, except those of government departments and other certain institutions.

3. Jordanian nationals residing in Jordan may open foreign currency accounts with licensed banks in Jordan provided that each individual's holdings do not exceed the equivalent of JD 500,000.

4. Licensed banks and financial companies are authorized to open accounts in foreign currencies for nonresidents without any condition; withdrawals and transfers from these accounts are permitted freely.

5. Licensed banks and financial companies may extend credit facilities to

residents and nonresidents against their foreign currency deposits up to JD 100,000 without prior approval of the Central Bank.

6. Premium Development Bonds denominated in JD may be purchased with convertible currencies by nonresidents; proceeds from redemption at maturity, including interest are transferable to any convertible currency.

7. At the end of 1992 about 30 foreign exchange houses were allowed to resume operations. Presently, there are 25 foreign exchange houses in operation.

8. Importers are required to obtain a foreign exchange permit from the Central Bank, which is granted automatically when an import license has been obtained. A fee of 0.10 percent is levied on exchange permits approved by the Central Bank for sales of foreign exchange for the purpose of paying for imports, except imports of government departments and certain other approved institutions.

9. Importers into the free zones and transit trade are responsible to provide foreign currencies to finance such transactions. Their banks are authorized to set the percentage of advance import deposit.

10. Imports of gold in any form are permitted without the prior approval of the Central Bank, while importation of gold for the purpose of craftsmanship and re-exports is subject to the prior approval of the Central Bank.

11. Proceeds from merchandise exports of Jordanian origin must be repatriated through authorized banks; proceeds from merchandise re-exports must be repatriated within one month of shipment. Exporters are allowed to keep 10 percent of the proceeds in deposits at local commercial banks or financial institutions and to use them to pay for imports of inputs.

12. Foreign exchange receipts from invisibles must be repatriated through an authorized bank.

13. Exports of gold in any form other than gold that has been increased in value due to craftsmanship require the prior approval of the Central Bank

14. Inward transfers of capital are not restricted, but outward transfers require approval and are not normally permitted, except that the Central Bank may approve applications made by banks, insurance companies, industrial or trading firms, and contractors for permission to transfer funds abroad for specified investment or operating purposes.

15. The transfer of funds for the purpose of investing in Arab countries by individual investors is permitted only if mutual treatment or bilateral agreement exists between Jordan and the concerned Arab country, and it is the investor's responsibility to provide foreign currency to finance such investments.

16. Income resulting from non-resident investments in Jordan may be transferred abroad.

17. Under the encouragement of Investment Law of 1987, profits, dividends and interest from approved foreign investments may be remitted, subject to the approval of the Ministry of Industry and Trade in accordance with the guidelines of the Central Bank. After two years, repatriation of the capital is permitted with the approval of the Ministry of Industry and Trade and the Central Bank. The Investment Committee of the Prime Minister's office may approve more liberal provisions, and exchange permits are granted accordingly.

18. In accordance with the Foreign Companies Registration Law No. 46 (1975) foreign companies are permitted to establish branches in Jordan for the purpose of conducting business outside the country; such branches may also be granted non-resident status for exchange control purposes.

Foreign Investment Regime

As part of its strategic drive towards expanding the export sector, Jordan has exerted considerable efforts to attract foreign investment. The Encouragement of Investment Law of 1987 offers various tax and import duty incentives. However, Jordan has not yet been successful in attracting foreign investments. This may be due in general to the relatively unfavorable climate for foreign investment which includes deficiencies, ambiguities and weaknesses in investment laws, and red tape. Available information shows that foreign-registered investment in the country ranged between JD 2.2 million and JD 9.2 million annually during 1988-1993 in comparison with a range between JD 36 million and JD 233.3 million of domestic capital (Table 8). That is, the share of foreign investment in total registered investment fluctuated widely between 1.5 percent and 10.6 percent per annum. Not only was the registered level of foreign investment low, but the average size of projects also was small, ranging between JD 19,300 and JD 55,000 per project. There is no available information on the amount of this committed investment which actually took place.

Table 9 shows that during the period 1986-89, foreign-registered capital accounted for 7.3 percent and 4.5 percent of total registered capital for investment in the industrial, and trade and services sectors, respectively. These ratios increased substantially in 1990 to 16.2 percent and 7.5 percent, respectively, despite the relatively low level of foreign investment. In the first eight months of 1991, however, the shares of foreign capital in these two sectors were almost equal. It appears that foreign investment has been concentrated more in the industrial sector in comparison with other sectors.

Although the above mentioned investment law of 1987 offered attractive investment incentives, it still has principle deficiencies including an arbitrary differentiation between "approved economical projects" and "economic projects", inadequate monitoring of tax holidays granted, along with increasing evidence that tax holidays are an ineffective means of investment promotion, limited customs duty exemptions which provide limited relief for spare parts imports, and it does not include the imports of raw material and contains several highly anti-competitive provisions favoring local procurement.[15] Therefore, the reform of this law is urgently needed. It is worth noting that the government has exerted serious efforts since 1992 to replace the 1987 investment law by a new one to tackle these shortcomings. But these efforts have not yet produced the aspired results due to various domestic economic, social and political reasons.

Table 8: Number and Value of Foreign Registered Investments in Jordan 1988-1993

(Million JD)

	1988	1989	1990	1991	1992	1993
Number of Projects	1974	1840	2393	4145	4556	4409
Domestic Capital	35.9	41.0	41.3	89.6	160.2	233.3
Foreign Capital	3.4	2.2	4.9	4.4	2.4	9.2
Total Capital	39.3	43.2	46.2	94.0	162.6	242.5
Average Capital Per Project (JD)	**19,908**	**23,478**	**19,306**	**22,688**	**35,694**	**55,001**

Sources: - Ministry of Industry and Trade,unpublished information (Amman, Jordan).
*   - The World Bank: Jordan - Foreign Direct Investment Climate (Washington D.C.*
*   1992). Annex C.*

In addition, foreign investment in Jordan is subject to two other laws: the Companies Law of 1989 and the Law Governing Arab and Foreign Investment (No. 22 of 1992). Under the Companies Law, foreign investors are more restricted in their choice of business than either Jordanian or other investors of Arab origin. Foreign enterprises must form a Jordanian company if they intend to undertake operations in Jordan. Registration of a branch of a foreign corporation is generally permitted only in as far as specific projects of limited duration are concerned. The establishment of a full subsidiary of a foreign company is not allowed. The Government provides attractive incentives for foreign companies to establish regional or representative offices in Jordan, and undertake activities outside the country. These offices are considered non-resident and cannot conduct business activities within the country.

Although the Law Governing Arab and Foreign Investment (No. 22 of 1992) does not include specific incentives for foreign investors, it outlines general investment guarantees and other protection for foreign investors and

Table 9: Sectoral Distribution of Foreign Registered Investments in Jordan in 1986 - 1989, 1990 and 1991

(Million JD)

Sector	Total Registered Capital			Foreign Capital			Domestic Capital			% share of Foreign Capital in Total Registered Capital		
	1986-89	1990	1991¹	1986-89	1990	1991¹	1986-89	1990	1991¹	1986-89	1990	1991¹
Industry	46.4	16.7	15.1	3.4	2.7	0.8	43.1	14.0	14.4	7.3	16.2	5.3
Trade and Services	111.7	29.5	27.8	5.0	2.2	1.5	106.6	27.3	26.2	4.5	7.5	5.4
Total	**158.1**	**46.2**	**42.9**	**8.4**	**4.9**	**2.3**	**149.7**	**41.3**	**40.6**	**5.3**	**10.6**	**5.4**

¹ *For the first eight months*
Source: Ministry of Industry and Trade, unpublished information (Amman, Jordan).

specific sectors in which foreign participation is limited. While this law is an improvement over the previous law of 1987, it still contains a number of areas of ambiguity and weaknesses both of which greatly reduce its effectiveness. Principal deficiencies include the following:[16]

(a) Unequal treatment between Arab and non-Arab foreign investors.

(b) All non-Arab foreign investors are required to seek the approval of the Cabinet approval prior to registering a business in Jordan.

(c) Non-Arab investment in shares of public shareholding companies listed on the Amman Financial market must obtain approval from the Prime Minister's office.

(d) Ambiguity about the definition of sectors where foreign participation is permitted in full, and sectors where it is limited to a maximum of 49 percent of the equity.

(e) Lack of sufficient guarantees to protect non-Jordanian investment.

(f) Lack of internationally-recognized third party investment disputes resolution mechanisms.

Regional Trade Arrangements: The Triangle

The Declaration of Principles (DOP) between the PLO and Israel on September 13, 1993 and their subsequent agreement on the Protocol on Economic Relations on April 29, 1994 have defined the economic and trade relationships between Israel and the Palestinian Authority (PA) for the five year transitional period starting May 13, 1994. Jordan on the other hand has concluded a peace agreement with Israel on October 26, 1994, and the two parties are still negotiating the terms of an economic agreement. Jordan has also concluded an Economic Agreement with the PA on January 1994, and the two parties have agreed on a Protocol Trade Agreement on May 4, 1995 to direct their trade relations during the Interim Period.

The basis for future trade relations between Palestine and Israel, and between Jordan and Palestine have already been laid out by the aforementioned agreements. However, Jordan still has not concluded a trade agreement with Israel, and the three parties have not yet started negotiations for a trilateral trade agreement among them to regulate and facilitate their intra-trade relations.

The economic protocol between the PLO and Israel establishes a combination of a free trade area and a customs union between the two entities: there are goods that can be traded freely between them and goods that can be imported by the Palestinians using Israeli tariff rates and/or Palestinian tariffs. Although this protocol includes some policies that allow independent action by the Palestinians, it has other elements which reflect a continuity of Israeli policies in the West Bank and Gaza Strip. While Palestinians are allowed to import from Jordan, Egypt and other Arab and Islamic countries goods listed in the protocol, the Palestinian markets will remain open to Israeli products and Israeli tariffs and import policies will be applied to most of Palestinian imports.[17] However, Palestinian products, apart from tomatoes, potatoes, eggs, poultry, cucumbers and melons, will have free access to the Israeli market. Palestinians can levy tariffs on some imported goods, for instance, cars.

On the whole, and despite some shortcomings, the protocol may be considered advantageous to the Palestinians as it enhances their trade independence. Although Palestinian products are being exposed to Israeli competition, Palestinians should take advantage of the Israeli market through exports provided that Israel does not create administrative barriers to Palestinian exports. In addition, Palestinians should pay particular attention to diversifying both their production base and export markets to promote intra and extra-regional exports.

Although Jordan and Palestine aspire for establishing free trade between them, the May 1995 Protocol Trade Agreement regulates their trade relations during the transitional period by identifying two lists of goods that can be traded freely or partially exempted from tariffs. These lists include 61 Palestinian products and 100 Jordanian ones.[18] This is in addition to the goods that can be traded subject to tariff duties by both parties. It is important to note that the flow of trade between Jordan and Palestine is subject to the Israeli approval as Israel still retains control over the bridges that connect Jordan and Palestine.

The status of the trade negotiations between Jordan and Israel is as follows:

(a) Recognizing the fact that the Israeli economy is far more advanced than that of Jordan, Israel has already agreed to the principle of granting Jordan a preferential treatment in their future trade relations. But it desires to conclude a preferential trade agreement with Jordan with a stated goal of free trade within 12 years.[19] However, Jordan cannot make a free trade commitment with Israel for economic and socio-political reasons; in addition, Jordan has not signed a free trade agreement with any country. Accordingly, Jordan is willing to conclude a preferential trade agreement with Israel first and assess its impact on the Jordanian economy after three years.[20]

(b) The two countries have already agreed on the lists of goods that can be freely traded or partially exempted from tariffs.

Due to the close trade interrelationships among Jordan, Palestine and Israel as a result of the geo-politics and socio-economic relations among them, there is a need to layout their future trade relations, at least during the Interim Period. The following are the major issues that should be considered by the three entities to facilitate future trade cooperation among them through a trilateral trade agreement:

1. Freer trade should be the ultimate objective for their future trade relations as the establishment of a free zone or customs union among them is not economically feasible in the near future. This is due to the need to protect domestic production both in Jordan and Palestine against the Israeli competition, and for social and political factors in the region.

2. To regulate trade flows among them, tariffs, rather than quantitative restrictions should be used.

3. They should agree on the lists of goods, and their tariffs and legal status, that can flow between Jordan and Israel through the West Bank.

4. If Jordan is going to levy different tariffs on goods imported from Palestine and Israel, there should be an agreement on the status of Palestinian goods of high Israeli import content when exported to Jordan.

General Issues related to WTO Accession and Implications for Jordan

As was indicated earlier, Jordan applied in December 1993 for membership in the GATT, and following the establishment of the WTO, Jordan is now in the process of negotiating its WTO terms of accession.

a) WTO Accession Negotiations

The scope and coverage of the WTO is much broader than the GATT 1947. In the area of goods, in addition to the GATT 1994, the WTO includes 6 understandings on the interpretation of certain provisions of the GATT 1994, and 12 agreements dealing with matters such as agriculture, sanitary and phytosanitary (SPS) measures, textiles and clothing, trade-related investment measures, customs valuation, import licensing procedures, safeguards, and so forth. The WTO Agreement also includes a General Agreement on Trade in Services and an Agreement on Trade-related Aspects of Intellectual Property Rights.

Pursuant to Article XII of the WTO Agreement, any state or separate customs territory possessing full autonomy in the conduct of its external commercial relations and of the other matters provided for in the WTO may accede to the WTO Agreement on terms to be agreed with the WTO. Decisions on accession shall be taken by Ministerial Conference or by the General Council. The agreement on the terms of accession must be approved by a two-thirds majority of the members of the WTO. In pursuance of the decision of the General Council of 15 November 1995, accession decisions are adopted by consensus unless a member requests a ballot.

As a first step in accession, the countries applying for accession must submit a memorandum on the Foreign Trade Regime which covers goods, services, intellectual property, investment measures and so forth. Members of the WTO will ask questions in writing and the applicant will respond also in writing. The countries which had applied for accession to GATT 1947 are expected to update their Memorandum or to submit supplementary notes. The additional information should be submitted at the beginning of the activities of the Working Party. Members will also ask questions in writing in connection with the supplementary information.

The negotiations for accession to the WTO take place simultaneously in two parallel tracks. Firstly, the fact finding phase consists of the multilateral examination of the foreign trade regime of the acceding country. This multilateral phase is followed by the negotiations of specific commitments in the sectors where full compliance with WTO obligations is not possible from the time of accession. Secondly, the negotiations of bilateral market access concessions on goods and services. The Working Party will prepare a draft report reflecting the commitments and concessions that have been agreed between WTO members and the acceding country in the context of the Working Party. The bilateral market access agreements are consolidated by the WTO Secretariat into the schedule of the acceding country. The schedules of concessions on goods and services are annexed to the protocol of accession.

b) Consequences of Accession to the WTO

Accession to the WTO Agreement entitles the goods and services of members to the most favored nation treatment and the national principle treatment. The WTO serves as a multilateral forum to implement the Multilateral Trade Agreements annexed to the WTO Agreement and to carry out further trade negotiations. The WTO monitors the trade policies of the members through periodic reviews carried out in the Trade Policy Review Body. The WTO Agreement includes an Understanding on Rules and Procedures Governing the Settlement of Disputes concerning the trade matters covered by the WTO Agreement which sets up a Dispute Settlement Body as the jurisdictional mechanism to resolve impartially and expeditiously the trade disputes among members. In accordance with the single undertaking principle embodied in the WTO Agreement, all WTO members must comply with the provisions of the Multilateral Trade Agreements. Nevertheless, the WTO Agreement accords developing counties and countries with economies in transition reasonable transitional periods to implement certain obligations. Exceptions to those measures are not applied arbitrarily or discriminatorily or as a disguised restriction on international trade. Members may take the measures necessary to protect public morals, human, animal or plant life or health, the conservation of exhaustible natural resources, and so forth. In addition, the WTO Agreement gives members flexibility in the implementation of certain obligations if they face balance of payment difficulties or other emergency situations as foreseen in the respective Multilateral Trade Agreements. In exceptional circumstances, a member may request the WTO to waive certain obligations temporarily. Waivers are subject to precise conditions. If not adopted by consensus, the adoption of the decision concerning a waiver is subject to a high threshold of approval.

Finally, the WTO permits that, at the time of accession, both the acceding country and the current members invoke the non-application clause thus excluding WTO relations entirely. This is a one time right which must be exercised at the time of accession. Prior notice of the intention to invoke this provision must be given to the Ministerial Conference or the General Council prior to the approval of the agreement on the terms of accession.

c) Interagency Coordination

The experience of other countries negotiating accession is that interagency coordination is essential to prepare the documentation, respond to the questionnaires, and participate in the Working Party meetings and in the market access negotiations. Participation should include the Ministries of Commerce, Industry, Economy, Agriculture, Finance, Planning, Foreign Affairs, Central Bank, and so forth, represented preferably at the level of deputy minister or vice minister. The leader of the delegation that carries out the accession negotiations in Geneva should be a senior official empowered to carry out negotiations.

d) Standstill

Countries applying for accession to the WTO have observer status in the WTO. These countries do not have legal obligations in terms of the WTO and are free to change their customs duty rates and other foreign trade policy measures. Nevertheless, WTO members have repeatedly stated that countries negotiating for accession to the WTO should not introduce any measures inconsistent with the WTO Agreement. Therefore, since the time of accession the acceding country should refrain from introducing new measures inconsistent with the WTO.

e) Transparency and Notifications

The documentation submitted to the Working Party should be comprehensive and up to date. The acceding country is not expected to pronounce itself in consistency of measures with the WTO Agreement. In order to maximize transparency, acceding countries are expected to respond to the questionnaires on import licensing procedures, customs valuation, technical barriers to trade and state trading according to a pre-set outline. In addition, acceding countries have been invited to submit in draft form to the Working Party on Accession notifications which WTO members have undertaken to submit with regard to matters such as agriculture, SPS, subsidies, anti-dumping, safeguards, rules of origin, and so forth. The Working Party will review these draft notifications multilaterally. If these draft notifications are not submitted prior to the conclusion of the work, the report of the Working Party is likely to establish a precise time frame for their submission.

f) Transitional Periods

A number of WTO Agreements establish transitional periods for members to implement certain obligations. WTO members take the position that these transitional periods are applicable to the original members of the WTO exclusively. In their view, the countries negotiating for accession are not entitled to these transitional periods as a matter of right. WTO members have stated that countries negotiating for accession should implement all the obligations in full from the time of accession. Nevertheless, in certain cases transitional periods to comply with WTO obligations in full have been accepted concerning the taxation regime, the elimination of reference price mechanism, and so forth.

Since Jordan considers itself a developing country, it may be allowed more time than that accorded to developed nations to implement certain WTO provisions. Once again, it must be stated that the new WTO accession procedures do not grant automatic relief to any acceding member: all the terms of accession are in principle subject to negotiations. Put differently, only those developing countries that are already WTO Members have an automatic right to existing special and differential treatment; developing countries seeking membership in the WTO will have to negotiate each and every aspect of their terms of accession. For example, Jordan may or may not be allowed to maintain even on a temporary basis import restrictions for balance of payments purposes, or to delay the effect of tariff concessions to establish a new industry or to expand an existing one.[21] Jordan is in fact negotiating such derogations.

Jordan's membership in the WTO will strengthen the country's position in international trade through the following:[22]

1. Jordan would benefit from non-discriminatory trade as it will be granted the status of most-favored nation, which ensures that no trading partner would be able to discriminate against Jordanian products by imposing higher trade barriers than are applied to products originating from other WTO member countries.

2. WTO membership will provide Jordan with access to the WTO dispute settlement mechanism.

3. WTO membership would help Jordan in promoting trade liberalization policies that will support the growth of internationally-competitive domestic industries.

4. Jordan would benefit from the "market friendly" WTO rules as these rules promote the non-discriminatory use of tariffs, constrain the use of quantitative restrictions, and restrict the use of trade measures that are implemented for balance of payments purposes. Jordan's exports would be positively affected by WTO membership as follows:[23]

1. Jordan would benefit from the reductions in member trading partners' import barriers. Therefore, Jordan's exports would be able to compete more effectively in the domestic markets of these partners, and would have access to non-traditional markets.

2. When trade distortions are reduced world-wide by WTO agreements, Jordan would benefit from the increased demand for goods and services in its trading partners' markets.

3. When trade barriers are reduced in compliance with WTO principles, foreign competition in Jordan's domestic market would allow a more efficient allocation of resources.

Policy Recommendations

Jordan should intensify its efforts to achieve the ultimate objective of shifting from import substitution to an export-oriented development strategy in both trade and investment by enhancing domestic producers' competitiveness through market forces. Therefore, it has to implement its current trade liberalization program faster. This is concurrent with the objective of attaining freer trade with its close neighbors, namely Palestine and Israel. In addition, further liberalization coincides with the requirements of the WTO, which Jordan is keen to join.

The aforementioned goals can be achieved by the adoption of various interconnected fiscal, monetary and commercial policies, and public sector reforms. The following are the major trade and investment policy reforms that should be given the highest priority:

1. To reduce further all tariffs on consumer, intermediate and capital goods in order to reduce effective protection and to achieve a freer trade system.

2. To remove all non-tariff barriers and convert them to tariff-based duties.

3. To remove all surcharges in order to have a unified tariff structure.

4. To eliminate all tariff exemptions granted to both individual goods and institutions.

5. To grant more export incentives in order to reduce further the anti-export bias that has resulted from the import substitution strategy.

6. To overcome the shortcomings of the Duty Drawback and Temporary Admission schemes.

7. To simplify further export and import procedures.

8. To remove import licensing requirements.

9. To expedite the process of amending the current Encouragement of Investment Law.

10. To reform all foreign investment related legislations.

Notes

1   Ministry of Planning: *Economic and Social Plan 1993-1997.* (Amman, Jordan.)
2   Central Bank of Jordan: *Twenty Ninth Annual Report 1992* . (Amman, Jordan), p.69. *Jordan: Recent Economic Developments* (IMF, Washington DC, June 22, 1993), p.40.
3   Central Bank of Jordan: *Monthly Statistical Bulletin,* Feb. 1995, (Amman, Jordan), p.62.
4   Ibid, p.62
5   Jordan, *Consolidating Economic Adjustment and Establishing the Base for Sustainable Growth.* (The World Bank, Washington DC, December 30, 1993), pp.59 and 64.
6   Ibid, pp. 48-50.
7   *MEED:* 21 April 1995, p. 10.
8   *MEED*: 21 April 1995, p. 10.
9   IMF, op.cit., p. 93.
10 The World Bank, op.cit., p. 45.
11 Ibid, p.60.
12 Ibid, pp. 59-63
13 Ibid, p. 60.
14 Central Bank of Jordan: "Exchange Arrangements and Exchange Restrictions" unpublished report, (Amman, Jordan, December 31, 1993) and IMF, op. cit., pp. 52-53 and 95-97.
15 FIAS/World Bank: *Jordan-Foreign Direct Investment Climate* (World Bank, Washington, DC, November, 1992).
16 Ibid pp. 8-9.
17 The Protocol on Economic Relations between Palestine and Israel is presented in the Near East Economic Progress Report no. 2, September 1994, Institute for Social and Economic Policy in the Middle East, Kennedy School, Harvard University.
18 *Al-Aswaq* newspaper: May 6, 1995 (Amman, Jordan).

19 *Financial Times*: June 21, 1995 (London, UK) p. 7.
20 Ibid.
21 G. Boye and M. Lord: "The Economic Impact of GATT/WTO Membership on Jordan - An Assessment" draft report. (USAID, December, 1994), p. v.
22 Ibid. p. v, and Central Bank of Jordan: "Jordan's Membership in GATT and its Impact on the Jordanian Economy", unpublished report, (Central Bank of Jordan, Amman, January 1994) pp. 17-21.
23 G. Boye and M. Lord, op. cit., p. vi. and Central Bank of Jordan; op. cit., pp. 17-21.

Part III
The EU-Mediterranean Partnership

Catching Up with Eastern Europe?
The European Union's Mediterranean Free
Trade Initiative

Introduction

Since the early 1980s, a remarkable shift towards opening up to international trade has taken hold in many countries. To a large extent this reflected a recognition that trade interventions are often not only inefficient, but also ineffective and counterproductive. Governments around the globe are increasingly seeking to create an enabling environment allowing private individuals and firms to exploit the nation's resources more efficiently. Such an environment includes the provision of public goods such as a stable, business-friendly legal framework that allows contracts to be enforced rapidly and at least cost; a regulatory regime that fosters and maintains competition on product and factor markets; and the provision of basic education and health services. While trade liberalization is a powerful instrument for increasing competition, formal trade policies such as the level and dispersion of the tariff represent but one aspect of the trade regime. As important are trade institutions: the framework in which policies are determined and the administrative mechanisms through which they are implemented and enforced. Traders should operate under as little uncertainty as possible regarding the rules that apply, the taxes that must be paid, or the time taken up by customs clearance.

The critical policy challenge facing many of the countries in the MENA region is to follow the rest of the world in liberalizing, privatizing and deregulating markets. The role of the public sector in many MENA countries is still pervasive. In some parts of the region it accounts for more than one-half of gross domestic product (GDP), and employs over 60 percent of skilled workers (World Bank, 1995a). Trade barriers remain high. Average taxes on trade are around 15 percent, more than twice the average in Eastern Europe (Appendix Table 1). Para-tariffs of many kinds are prevalent, reducing the transparency of the trade regime.

A basic tenet of economic reform efforts undertaken in the last decade in many countries of the region has been that reforms be gradual. Given that gradual trade reform has often not been accompanied by actions to significantly reduce the role of the state in the economy, reform efforts have had a limited impact in terms of effectively increasing competition in product markets (Hoekman, 1995a). The slower the pace of economic reform and the less comprehensive its scope, the larger the gap between MENA's economic performance and that of the rest of the world is likely to become. The implicit rationale for gradualism in the region appears to be a perception that a "big bang" approach is not feasible politically.[1] What is needed is an institutional framework that enhances the credibility of a gradual reform strategy and thus ensures the needed supply response. The World Trade Organization (WTO) and the European Union's (EU) offer to establish a Euro-Mediterranean Economic Area are particularly relevant in this regard.

The need for reform is clear: economic performance has been lagging, and the incentive regime is steadily falling behind that of comparator countries (World Bank, 1995a). The aim of this chapter is to discuss the potential role of a Euro-Mediterranean Agreement (EMA) in helping MENA governments implement structural economic reforms.

The chapter is organized as follows: the next section discusses the arguments for and against preferential liberalization in the MENA region, comparing the potential costs and benefits of a multilateral (WTO) approach as opposed to a regional integration strategy. The chapter then describes the recent trade performance of Central and Eastern European countries (CEECs) to illustrate the possible impact of opening up the economy to trade in the context of a free trade agreement (FTA) with the EU. It then turns to the recently negotiated EMA between Tunisia and the EU, and analyses the extent to which this agreement will help MENA countries catch up with the CEECs. The analysis highlights the need to pursue significant supporting and complementary actions. Key issues in this connection are the regulatory regimes applying to inward foreign direct investment (FDI) and the services sector, the magnitude of tariffs applied to the rest of the world (trade diversion), the extent of privatization, and the imposition of hard budget constraints on state-owned enterprises. Most of these aspects are not subject to disciplines under the EMA. The chapter then concludes.

Why Go Regional?

Governments seeking to liberalize their trade and investment regimes can choose among a variety of approaches. These include unilateral action, multilateral liberalization based on reciprocity, and preferential (regional) liberalization. For a small country – one that cannot influence its terms of trade for most commodities – economic theory has established that a unilateral approach to freeing trade is welfare superior to the other options. In the context of multilateral negotiations, if other countries reciprocate, this will increase the welfare gains from unilateral liberalization efforts. However, given the small country assumption – which applies to the countries in the region – there are few if any gains to be expected from making liberalization conditional upon reciprocity by trading partners. Preferential liberalization through the negotiation of an FTA will also be an inferior strategy since the world market is always larger than a regional one. By not discriminating across potential trading partners, domestic firms and consumers will be allowed to buy goods and services from least cost suppliers, wherever they are located. By discriminating in favor of specific countries, the possibility of trade diversion arises from the substitution of inefficient regional suppliers at the expense of efficient suppliers in third countries on account of the tariff preference. This may be offset by trade creation which comes from a shift away from high-cost domestically produced goods to lower-cost imports from regional partner countries. The point, however, is that through unilateral liberalization losses from trade diversion do not occur, and the net gains are therefore greater.

The case against regional (preferential) trade agreements is particularly strong in the context of small countries that already have duty free access to a large partner country market while simultaneously maintaining tariffs on imports originating from this partner country. This is the case for the MENA countries which were granted duty-free access to EU markets for industrial (non-agricultural) goods under Cooperation Agreements negotiated in the 1970s. In such cases, as argued by Panagariya (1995), MENA countries that enter into an FTA with the EU will lose the tariff revenue presently collected on imports of EU origin. The EU accounts for 48 percent of total imports by all MENA countries, a share that will increase after the implementation of free trade with Europe. The revenue loss is therefore substantial. The static benefits arising from improved resource allocation are unlikely to offset this loss (Panagariya, 1995). Of course, dynamic benefits (induced growth effects driven by increased factor accumulation) may well ensure that longer term returns are positive. Again, the important consideration is that these benefits can in principle also be obtained through unilateral liberalization and without the losses associated with trade diversion.

Although these are powerful logical arguments in favor of nondiscriminatory liberalization, many countries nonetheless pursue preferential trade agreements. What explains this? More importantly, what are the necessary conditions for regional integration to be welfare enhancing for the countries involved?[2] Possible economic explanations or motivations for regional integration are manifold. Five will be mentioned here. But before doing so, it is worth noting that the decision to go regional may be driven by foreign policy and political considerations. Possible economic losses (inefficiencies) may thus be accepted as the price for attaining non-economic objectives. This aspect of regional integration is undoubtedly important in practice. However, from an economic perspective, what matters is that policy-makers (and voters) have enough information to allow them to judge whether non-economic benefits compensate for potential economic losses.

Credibility and dynamic gains: In some cases a regional integration agreement (RIA) may offer a stronger mechanism for locking in (anchoring) economic reforms than the WTO. In part this may be because the RIA addresses policy areas that are not covered by the WTO at all, or where WTO disciplines are weak. For example, investment or factor market policies are not addressed by the WTO. WTO disciplines pertaining to the services sector are also relatively weak.[3] Thus, unilateral reforms in these areas may be anchored through an RIA in ways that are not available in the WTO. Even in the area of trade policies, the traditional domain of the General Agreement on Tariffs and Trade (GATT)/WTO, disciplines may be weaker than under an RIA. Credibility under the WTO arises in large part from the binding of tariffs. The most that can be done in this connection is to bind tariffs at applied rates. This is something many developing countries have not done, in part because of the mercantilistic bias of the GATT/WTO negotiating process (governments wanted to keep "negotiating chips"), and in part because many did not desire to be bound by GATT rules. Although there is mounting pressure on governments to reduce the difference between bound and applied rates, there is no obligation to bind at applied rates. Binding at applied rates has been a voluntary step for developing countries' governments. In the RIA of the kind envisaged by the EU, binding is not voluntary, but required. An RIA may therefore help overcome internal political resistance to binding.[4] It may also lead to greater credibility if monitoring and enforcement mechanisms are stronger.

The greater credibility that may be associated with an RIA can lead to important dynamic growth effects insofar as more investment is fostered, greater adjustment efforts are made, and so forth. These effects are of course the important dimension. Unfortunately, quantifying them is very difficult. Nonetheless, the cross-border merger and acquisition activities that were associated with the EU's Single Market program in the late 1980s are indicative of the type of market responses that may emerge following the initiation of a credible regional liberalization strategy.

Harmonization: An important element of an RIA may consist of harmonizing regulatory regimes and administrative requirements relating to product standards, testing and certification procedures, mutual recognition agreements, common documents for customs clearance (for example, the EU's Single Administrative Document), coordination and cooperation on linking computer systems of Customs, and so forth. These are areas where the WTO is restricted to general principles (for example, national treatment and most favored nation (MFN)). While such cooperative efforts can be pursued uni-laterally, formal agreements may be necessary to induce the administrative bodies involved to cooperate. The associated reduction in trade and transactions costs will benefit all traders and consumers. Insofar as reductions in transactions costs are applied in a nondiscriminatory manner, trade diversion type issues do not arise.

Security of market access: One benefit of an RIA may be that it prevents partner countries from imposing contingent protection, such as antidumping actions. To the extent that a substantial share of total trade is with partner countries, this arrangement could be of great value. In the multilateral context, such an agreement does not look feasible in the near future. Harmonization of administrative requirements and procedures may also help to improve the security of market access. An important area in this connection relates to product standards and their enforcement.

Transfers: Another potential benefit of an RIA is that it may involve trans-fers from richer members to poorer ones. Such transfers may be financial, or take the form of technical assistance. To the extent that such transfers are con-ditional upon membership of the RIA (that is., they are additional), they will help offset the possible losses associated with the implicit transfer of tariff revenue and the costs associated with trade diversion. Additionality is impor-tant, and much may depend on how this is measured. For example, MENA countries already receive significant financial assistance from the EU, both through bilateral official aid, and through the Financial Protocols that are negotiated every 4 years under the auspices of the Cooperation Agreements. It can be argued that what matters in this connection is the comparison between the present discounted value of the expected transfers under the existing arrangements (Cooperation Agreements) and those that are anticipat-ed under the new regime (the EMA). Given the generally declining trend in official aid, and the emergence of the CEECs as new "claimants," taking past transfers as the basis for an "additionality" test is probably unrealistic.

Facilitation of general liberalization: A final, and very important potential rationale for regional integration along EMA lines relates to the opportunity to build on this preferential liberalization by liberalizing the economy more generally, that is., on a most-favored-nation (MFN) basis. The potential for trade diversion associated with an EMA will be curtailed if trade barriers against non-partner countries are also reduced. Adjustment costs associated with liberalization on an MFN basis are not likely to be much higher than those emerging from regional liberalization with the EU. The offer of finan-cial and other assistance from the EU can then be used to facilitate the transi-tion path to MFN reductions in trade barriers. Stated otherwise, the EMA may allow a government to enhance the political feasibility of MFN liberalization.

These are some of the economic arguments favoring a regional strategy. The extent to which they are sufficient to ensure a net welfare gain for any one MENA country in particular is an empirical matter. The scope of the trade agreement that is negotiated, the magnitude of the additional financial and other types of transfers, and the intentions of the governments involved are all factors that influence the outcome. In summary, the necessary conditions for the EMA to be welfare- improving are: (i) the transfer of tariff revenue/trade diversion costs is offset; (ii) the EMA goes significantly beyond the current WTO disciplines – especially in areas such as investment and services; and (iii) that significant progress be made in the area of trade facilitation – customs procedures, documentary requirements, product testing and certification. The case in favor of going regional will also be strengthened to the extent that the security of market access is enhanced. The next Section discusses the extent to which these necessary conditions appear to have been met. In general, most RIAs have not satisfied them. Indeed, the history of preferential trade agreements generally shows that they have not gone much beyond the GATT (Hoekman and Leidy, 1993).

The potential losses associated with an EMA will be reduced the more competitive are EU suppliers, and the lower are the tariffs imposed on imports of EU goods by MENA countries. As has been stated earlier, these losses may be further curtailed if efforts are made to reduce trade barriers confronting non-partner countries. Indeed, the importance of this cannot be over-emphasized. The strongest case that can be made in favor of regional integration along EMA lines is if it is used as part of a deliberate strategy to liberalize the economy more generally, that is, on an MFN basis. Very much depends in this connection on the willingness of the government to state clearly that general, MFN liberalization of the trade regime is indeed its objective. If this is not done, incentives may easily be created for the formation of coalitions between EU and domestic firms that oppose further opening of the market to (more efficient) third country suppliers. As noted by Bhagwati (1993), they may argue that the regional market is "our" market, that outsiders trade "unfairly" because they are subject to a more lenient regulatory environment, and so forth.

The Europe Agreements and Recent Trade Performance of the Central and Eastern European Countries (CEECs)[5]

This section briefly describes recent developments in MENA and CEECs trade with the EU, and explores the impact of measures to open the economy to international trade. While the comparison is somewhat "unfair" given the greater levels of industrialization and human capital that exist in Eastern Europe relative to the MENA region, the parallels between the two regions are close enough that a comparison is informative. Many countries in both regions started reforms in the late 1980s; the level of state intervention in both regions was high; and both are in geographical proximity to the European Union. Moreover, although CMEA-based trade dominated in the CEEC context, it was also significant for a number of Mediterranean countries (for example, Egypt)[6]. Clearly the similarities should not be exaggerated. But the CEEC experience is informative because it provides data on the possible impact of an EMA.

Figure 1: Per Capita Exports 1989-94

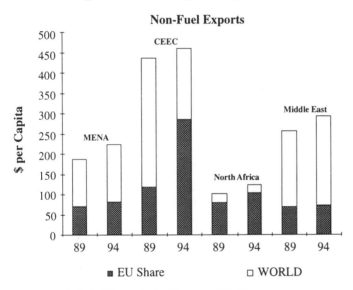

1. North Africa = Algeria, Morocco and Tunisia.
2. Middle East = Egypt, Israel, Jordan, Kuwait, Lebanon, Syria and UAE.
3. MENA = North Africa and Middle East.
4. CEEC = Bulgaria, Czech Republic, Hungary, Poland,
   Romania and Slovak Republic.

Per capita exports for the MENA region as a whole are around US $225. They rose slightly between 1989 and 1994, with the share of exports going to the EU declining to 36.6 percent (Figure 1). MENA exports to the EU originate largely from the North African countries, which export most of their manufactured goods to Europe. For the Middle Eastern countries, the EU is much less important. Although aggregate exports of the CEECs to the world initially declined after 1989 – reflecting a large drop in output and exports as enterprises adjusted to price liberalization and the demise of centralized trade – by 1993 per capita exports exceeded 1989 levels again. Whereas only some 29 percent of CEEC exports went to the EU in 1989, the proportion had risen to over 60 percent in 1994. The average annual growth rate of CEECs' exports to the EU (20.4 percent) is two and a half times that of MENA countries (Table 1).

Table 1: Non-Oil Exports to the EU, 1989 and 1994 (ECU million)

Country	Value			Market Share in EU	
	1989	1994	Growth	1989	1994
MENA	9,940	14,485	7.8	2.68	2.68
Jordan	86	152	12.1	0.02	0.03
Lebanon	100	87	-2.8	0.03	0.02
Syria	90	234	21.0	0.02	0.04
Israel	3,014	4,043	6.1	0.81	0.75
Egypt	790	1,107	6.9	0.21	0.20
Morocco	2,612	3,652	7.0	0.70	0.67
Tunisia	1,596	2,784	14.8	0.43	0.51
Algeria	219	328	8.4	0.06	0.06
Saudi Arabia	890	1,234	6.7	0.24	0.22
Kuwait	131	169	5.2	0.04	0.03
UAE	414	695	10.9	0.11	0.12
CEEC	10,336	26,115	20.4	2.79	4.83

Source: EUROSTAT, COMEXT database.

Intra-industry trade has been expanding very rapidly between the CEECs and the EU (Figure 2). Intra-industry trade is important because it is a major mechanism through which transfers of technology can occur. The Europe Agreements with the CEECs have created incentives for EU suppliers/retailers to engage in so-called outward processing trade (OPT). This consists of shipping components or assemblies to a CEEC where further processing occurs. The processed good is then exported back to the EU supplier/retailer. Such processing trade benefits from liberal access to the EU, and has been used intensively for sectors such as garments, electrical machinery and furniture. As part of the subcontracting that is involved, EU counterparts will often provide designs, monitor quality, take care of marketing, and so forth. This is a good way for firms in partner countries to reduce the costs and risks associated with development of export markets, while at the same time obtaining know-how from suppliers. While OPT is frequently restricted, at least in the initial stages, to labor intensive, low value-added activities, these can create significant employment.

Figure 2: Intra-Industry Trade with the EU

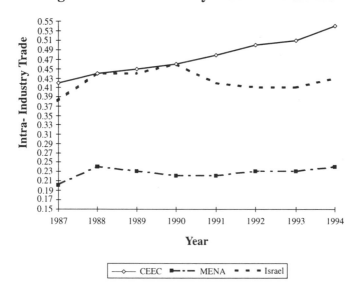

In the period following the implementation of the agreements with the CEECs, OPT exports accounted for about 18 percent of total CEEC exports to the EU in 1993, up from 10 percent in 1989. For Romania, processing activities generated 30 percent of exports to the EU in 1993. In contrast, exports to the EU of processed goods represented only 1.7 percent of total MENA exports in 1993, a share that has remained constant since 1989 (Table 2). Most of the processing occurs in leather/footwear, clothing, electrical machinery, precision instruments and furniture. OPT accounts for a substantial share (about one quarter) of the growth in exports from the CEECs to the EU (Hoekman, 1995a). In contrast, it plays a very minor role in MENA countries, the two exceptions being Morocco and Tunisia.[7]

The data reveal clearly that the CEECs are moving rapidly to exploit the advantage of their geographic proximity to the EU, which in conjunction with their relatively low wages and significant stocks of human capital make them formidable competitors for the MENA region. The geographic advantage that the MENA region used to enjoy – because Eastern Europe was effectively closed to open exchange with the West – has now disappeared. MENA firms must now compete head-to-head with companies located in the CEECs. This is indeed a challenge, not least because relative labor costs in the CEECs and MENA are not that different. Per capita incomes in the CEECs – one proxy for such costs – are close to MENA levels (World Bank, 1995a). Although factor endowments differ in important respects, it is also worth noting that some of the CEECs are producing and exporting similar products to the EU. Correlation coefficients between revealed comparative advantage indices of MENA and CEEC countries are sometimes significant.[8] Table 3 reports those cases where such correlation coefficients are above 0.1. In general, however, the data suggest that competition between firms located in different CEECs is more intense than that between the two regions.

Table 2: Exports After Outward Processing
(Share in Total Exports to EU)

	CEEC		MENA	
	1989	1993	1989	1993
Total	10.4	17.9	1.6	1.7
Leather	38.9	34.5	8.0	8.5
Garments	60.8	74.5	15.6	11.1
Machinery	8.1	14.4	5.4	2.6
Transport	12.3	4.7	4.5	2.3
Instruments	6.4	11.9	6.5	2.5
Furniture	26.5	13.9	1.2	1.5

Source: EUROSTAT, COMEXT database.

The extent to which the export performance of the CEECs is due to the Europe Agreements is very difficult to determine. It can be argued that to a large extent much of this would have been realized if the CEECs that were GATT contracting parties had simply locked in their trade liberalization through the WTO. Indeed, the GATT played a significant role in anchoring CEEC trade policy reforms, as most of the CEECs had low, bound tariffs. Once centralized trade was abolished, GATT commitments ensured a substantial amount of discipline. However, the Europe Agreements go far beyond the WTO, basically extending much of the EU's Single Market rules to the CEECs. They have provided an important political signal that the CEECs could aspire to membership of the EU – something that was acknowledged explicitly by the EU in June 1993 during the Copenhagen summit. The Agreements have thus greatly reduced uncertainty for investors regarding the future policy environment. Nonetheless, there are differences in opinion regarding the extent to which the Agreements were instrumental in preventing the re-imposition of protection. Sapir (1995) argues that at least in the case of Hungary, the Agreement helped the government resist pressures for protection;[9] Csaba (1995) argues that the Europe Agreements are too narrow in scope to create the institutional infrastructure needed to maintain a free trade stance. In his view it is the credible prospect of EU membership that is the key dimension in the CEEC context, as it is only this that will fundamentally constrain the use of various non-tariff barriers.

Table 3: Correlation Coefficients Between Revealed Comparative Advantage Indices, 1994

	Bulgaria	Czech Republic	Hungary	Poland	Romania
Bulgaria	1.00	--	--	--	--
Czech Rep.	0.19	1.00	--	--	--
Hungary	0.37	0.23	1.00	--	--
Poland	0.48	0.47	0.60	1.00	--
Romania	0.33	0.49	0.48	0.60	1.00
Jordan	0.23	0.14	0.05	0.22	0.08
Lebanon	0.23	0.03	0.17	0.08	0.06
Syria	0.01	0.01	0.13	-0.01	0.01
Tunisia	0.17	0.01	0.01	0.07	0.22
UAE	0.11	0.04	0.26	0.26	0.20
ALL MENA	0.13	0.02	0.05	0.05	0.06

Source: Authors' own calulations

EU membership is not on the agenda of Mediterranean countries. As far as MENA is concerned, the CEEC experience under the Europe Agreements that is perhaps of greatest relevance is the importance of OPT in driving export performance. While an EMA may enhance the incentives to use OPT, it should be recognized that MENA countries already have access to this customs regime. The lack of OPT in the MENA region suggests the existence of administrative or regulatory barriers in MENA countries themselves. These may be offset to some extent under an EMA through harmonization of procedures and technical assistance (economic cooperation). Action in this area is a priority to generate an export supply response.

The Euro-Mediterranean Agreement With Tunisia

Currently, economic relations between Mediterranean countries and the EU are governed by Cooperation Agreements dating from the 1970s. These agreements are not limited in their duration, and they provide duty-free access to

EU markets for industrial goods, and preferential access for agricultural commodities. The agreements are not reciprocal in that partner countries may continue to apply MFN tariffs to goods of EU origin. They are complemented by Financial Protocols, which establish the amount of financial resources the EU will provide each partner country over a five year period. The key changes that will be implied by an EMA is a move to reciprocal free trade in industrial goods, and the replacement of Financial Protocols with EMA-specific financial cooperation (see below).

The basic objectives of the Euro-Med proposal are to: achieve reciprocal free trade between the EU and Mediterranean countries in most manufactured goods; grant preferential and reciprocal access for agricultural products; establish conditions for gradual liberalization of trade in services and capital; and to encourage the economic integration of Mediterranean countries. The goals and constraints imposed by Mediterranean countries are perhaps best stated in the EU Commission's request for negotiating authority:

> in order to be able to enter progressively into free trade with the Union and to take on board a wide range of trade-related Community regulations (customs, standards, competition, intellectual property protection, liberalization of services, free capital movements, and so forth.) ... Mediterranean countries ... insist on four fundamental aspects ...: the need for long transitional mechanisms and secure safeguards; the need to obtain improved access for their agricultural exports; the need for increased financial flows ... [and] the possibility to count on the Community's help to accelerate the modernization of their social and economic systems.[10]

The first Euro-Med Agreement (EMA), negotiated with Tunisia, was initialed in April 1995 and signed in July of the same year. (Hamdouch, 1995). As it is very similar in structure to the other agreements that were concluded subsequently (Morocco) or are still being negotiated at the time of writing (Egypt, Jordan, Lebanon) what follows restricts attention to the Tunisian EMA. The agreement is unlimited in duration and is to be implemented over a twelve year period. Its operation is overseen by an Association Council (meeting at Ministerial level at least once a year) and an Association Committee (meeting at the level of officials, responsible for implementation of the Agreement). The EMA has six major elements: (1) political dialogue; (2) free movement of goods; (3) right of establishment and supply of services; (4) payments, capital, competition and other economic provisions (for example, safeguards); (5) economic, social and cultural cooperation; and (6) financial cooperation. The structure of the EMA is similar to those of the Europe Agreements with the CEECs. The major difference is that no commitment has been made by the EU that the longer term goal is accession by partner countries. Many of the provisions of the EMA are conditional upon the date it enters into force (for example, timing of tariff reductions). This in turn depends on how long it will take the 15 EU Member States and the Tunisian parliament to ratify the agreement.

Free movement of goods: As noted above, Tunisia already benefits from duty-free access to EU markets for manufactured goods under the 1976 Cooperation Agreement, and additional Protocols (1982, 1988) negotiated after the enlargement of the EU in 1981 and 1986. This implies that liberalization will mostly occur on the Tunisian side. As discussed below, the area where Tunisia potentially stands to gain significantly in terms of greater export opportunities – agriculture – was largely removed from the table. Quotas are to be abolished upon the entry into force of the agreement – except as allowed by GATT rules. In contrast to the CEEC Agreements, no special treatment was given to Tunisia as regards more rapid elimination of textile quotas than agreed under the GATT. However, Tunisia is reportedly only subject to two quotas, neither of which is close to being fully utilized (World Bank, 1994). Tunisia committed itself to gradually reducing tariffs on industrial products of EU origin to zero. Five groups of products – at the seven-digit Community Common Nomenclature (CCN) level – have been defined in this connection. Four of these groups have been defined explicitly in Annexes. Tariffs for the fifth group, the residual (that is., manufactured product that are not mentioned in any one of the Annexes) will be abolished upon the entry into force of the agreement. There are 470 six-digit tariff lines in this group, all of which are either intermediate inputs or machinery (capital goods), accounting for 10 percent of 1994 imports from the EU (Table 4).[11] Annex 3 to the Agreement contains a list of products for which tariffs and surcharges will be eliminated over a five-year period in steps of 15 percent, starting from the entry into force of the treaty. Products on this list, together with the group of goods to be liberalized immediately (that is, those not mentioned in an Annex) account for some 35 percent of 1994 imports by Tunisia. Annex 4 comprises a list of products that will be liberalized over the full 12 year transition period, in steps of 8 percent per year. Products listed in Annex 5 will be subject to tariff reductions four years after the entry into force of the agreement, with reductions spread out linearly over the remaining eight years of the transition period (that is., annual cuts of 11-12 percent). A final list of manufactured products contained in Annex 6 is exempted from tariff reductions. This list contains 37 six-digit tariff lines, comprising bread, pasta, and carpets.

Import weighted average tariffs applying to the groups of goods to be liberalized range from 21 to 34 percent (Table 4). Goods to be liberalized immediately have the lowest average tariffs, while those to be liberalized last have the highest average rates. Liberalization of intermediate inputs and capital goods is front-loaded, whereas liberalization of consumer goods has been back-loaded. Some 90 percent of the goods in Annexes 3 and 4 are intermediates or machinery; as compared to only 4 percent for Annex 5. It appears that some 75 percent of 1994 Tunisian exports to the EU involve goods contained in Annex 5. These products accounted for over 40 percent of domestic production in 1992. Annex 4 covers another 20 percent of domestic output. Much of the liberalization commitments affecting the domestic industry is therefore gradual and back-loaded. Although this might be supported with the argument that such a strategy will assist the domestic industries concerned to prepare for greater competition from imports in the future (in part by raising effective protection through the more rapid reduction in tariffs on inputs and capital goods), there is no guarantee this will occur. Much will depend on the perceived credibility of the government's commitment to the EU, and on the use of provisions allowing for safeguard protection to be imposed. To the extent that the increase in effective protection of domestic industries during the first part of the implementation period leads to inefficient investment or non-adjustment, pressures may emerge in the future to resist market opening or impose safeguard actions. Moreover, the transition path chosen implies that there may be static welfare losses quite apart from the revenue transfer problem identified by Panagariya (1995), because the effective rate of protection will increase during the first stage of the transition.[12]

The approach taken by Tunisia with respect to tariff elimination is similar to that of the CEECs, albeit much more gradual. Poland committed itself to do away with tariffs on about 30 percent of its imports from the EU in 1992, and to abolish the remainder over a seven year transition period, with duty reductions taking place during the last four years. Hungary agreed to liberalize 12-13 percent of its imports over a three year period in annual steps of one-third, another 20 percent between 1995 and 1997, again in steps of one-third and the rest (two-thirds) between 1995 and 2001, in steps of one-sixth per year. The Czech and Slovak Republics are dismantling tariffs over a seven year period (like Poland, but somewhat less front-loaded). In addition to the speed of liberalization, another important difference relates to the fact that initial tariffs in Tunisia and the Mediterranean more generally are much higher than in the CEECs (Appendix Table 1). Average protection levels in the CEECs are in the 6 percent range, as compared to over 15 percent for many Mediterranean countries. For manufacturing, the differences are even greater, given that the average protection rate is in the 20-30 percent range.

A possible factor underlying the back-loaded nature of the tariff reduction process is that the government may have been concerned with the revenue implications of a more uniform move to free trade with the EU. The dependence on trade taxes in Tunisia – as is the case in the other countries of the region – is relatively high. Some 28 percent of government revenues are derived from trade taxes. The EU accounts for 68 percent of total imports, and generates 58 percent of total tariff revenue. Most of the tariff revenue generated from trade with the EU is currently collected on the imports of consumer goods (Annex 5) whose liberalization is back-loaded, as compared to intermediate and capital goods. Annex 5 accounts for 33 percent of total revenues, as compared to 12 and 9 percent, respectively, for Annexes 3 and 4 (Table 4). It is worth noting that the goods to be liberalized immediately generate only 3.6 percent of total revenue. While the approach taken minimizes revenue losses early in the program, the revenue constraint could have been addressed in a more uniform tariff reduction scenario. Alternative tax bases (excises, a value-added tax) are in effect in Tunisia.

Agriculture: A distinguishing feature of the EMA is that little will change in respect of agricultural trade. The objective of the EMA is to gradually liberalize trade in this sector. However, all it does in concrete terms is to largely confirm the status quo (existing preferential arrangements), while offering only limited improvements in access for specific products through expansion of tariff quotas and reduction/elimination of tariffs for specific quotas. Negotiations to improve on existing agricultural concessions are to be initiated after January 1, 2000. In this respect there is a substantial difference with the CEEC agreements. The latter, while also excluding agriculture from the reach of free trade, do provide detailed provisions granting CEECs' farmers preferential access to EU markets. Continued restrictions on exports to EU agricultural markets is a major factor that constrain the benefits of an EMA for Mediterranean countries. For a number of these countries, the potential of agricultural export is important. In the Moroccan case, for example, some 28 percent of exports to the EU are agricultural. The exclusion of this sector from liberalization seriously limits the potential welfare gains of an EMA. It is not that surprising therefore that the unwillingness (inability) of the EU Commission to significantly expand export opportunities was the stumbling block for Morocco to reaching agreement with the EU (Hamdouch, 1995).

Establishment: The right of establishment, that is., freedom to engage in FDI, is one of the objectives of the EMA. Modalities to achieve this objective are to be determined by the Association Council. No specific language is devoted to this subject; and in addition, no time path or target date is mentioned for the realization of the objective. In contrast, the right of establishment is a central element of the CEECs Agreements since the EU has granted since 1992 free entry and national treatment to all firms from the CEECs, except in air and

Table 4: Tariff Liberalization: Commitments by Tunisia (Industrial Products)

	Share of Trade		Share in Domestic Output	Share in Total Tariff Revenue	Import Weighted Average Tariff	Number of 6-digit Lines Total=5,019	% of Ttl	Share of Machinery & InterMediates	
	Exp	Imp						by line (%)	by import value (%)
ANNEX 3: 5 year transition	16	24	20	12.5	26.7	1,810	41	93	87
ANNEX 4: 12 year transition	7	29	22	9.2	30.4	1,127	26	94	89
ANNEX 5: 8 year transition starting in year 5	75	36	43	32.9	33.8	944	22	8	4
ANNEX 6: Exempted	1	1	1	n.a.	n.a.	37	1	0	0
Industrial goods not listed in an Annex:									
Immediate liberalization	1	10	14	3.6	21.6	470	10	100	100

Source: Calculations are based on COMEXT and World Bank data. All data are for 1994.

inland water transport and maritime cabotage. The CEECs also grant free entry and national treatment to EU firms, with transitional periods for certain sectors or activities.[13] This does not necessarily imply that FDI is restricted in Tunisia. However, it does signal that this was considered to be a "sensitive" issue, something that potential foreign investors may well take into account.

Capital movement: The EMA only requires that capital flows related to direct investment in Tunisia by EU firms in companies formed in accordance with current laws can move freely, and that income can be liquidated and repatriated. The CEECs Agreements again go further by requiring free mobility of capital and unrestricted repatriation of profits. Payment flows (current account transactions) resulting from liberalization commitments under the CEECs agreements are also unrestricted. Full convertibility and liberalization of capital account transactions are longer term objectives, although no time frame is mentioned for their realization.

Supply of service: Cross-border supply of services (that is, cross-border trade) has been excluded from both the EMA and the CEECs Agreements. The latter state that trade in services is to be liberalized progressively, taking into account the development of the services sector in each of the CEECs. This includes provisions relating to temporary movement of natural persons. No time frame is established for the liberalization of supply of services, nor is the achievement of freedom of supply of services mentioned explicitly as an ultimate objective. Separate disciplines are to be secured for air and inland water transport after the entry into force of each agreement. During the transitional period, the CEECs are to progressively adopt legislation consistent with that of the EU's in the field of air and land transport insofar as this serves to achieve the liberalization objectives of the agreement. International maritime services are to be liberalized through the signatories undertaking to apply effectively the principle of unrestricted access to the market and traffic on a commercial basis.

The EMA simply refers to the obligations of each country that were established under the General Agreement on Trade in Services (GATS). These obligations did not exist at the time the Europe Agreements were negotiated. Obligations under the GATS do not imply much, if any, liberalization (Hoekman, 1995b). MENA countries made very limited commitments under the GATS, subjecting less than 10 percent of their service sectors to the national treatment or market access principles (Hoekman, 1995a). No mention is made of maritime or air transport as in the CEEC agreements. The objective of the GATS is not "free trade" in services. In contrast, given the objective of accession to the EU, foreign investors know that, where CEECs are concerned, free trade and investment is the goal. Even in the absence of the accession issue, it can be argued that the non-reference to the GATS in the CEECs Agreements implies a stronger commitment to liberalization than is found in the EMA. While it may be understandable that possible labor movement associated with the provision of services is a sensitive issue for the EU – something that may also play a role in the FDI/capital movement context – "reciprocity" concerns are not a good rationale for Mediterranean countries to abstain from making commitments in these areas.

Competition policy: The EMA and Europe Agreements are similar with respect to the requirement to adopt the basic competition rules of the EU, in particular with respect to collusive behavior, abuse of dominant position, and competition-distorting state aid (respectively, Articles 85, 86, and 92 of the Treaty of Rome), insofar as they affect trade between the Community and each partner country. The implementation of the rules will proceed following their adoption by the Association Council within five years (as opposed to three years under the CEECs Agreements). Until then, GATT rules with respect to countervailing of subsidies will apply. State-aid, compatible with EU rules for disadvantaged regions (Article 92.3a Treaty of Rome), can be applied to the entire territory of Tunisia during the first five years. Such regional aid may be given by EU governments to regions in their countries with per capita incomes that are substantially below average, or to areas where there is significant unemployment. The low level of per capita incomes in the Mediterranean countries in comparison to those of EU states should ensure that non-industry specific state aids will be unconstrained in the medium term. The agreements also provide for enhanced transparency of state aids, each party agreeing to provide annual reports on the total amount and distribution of the aid given.

In both the Mediterranean and the CEECs cases, antidumping remains applicable to trade flows between partners. This despite the agreement by Tunisia (and the CEECs) to apply EU competition disciplines. One implication is that the security of market access rationale for regional integration was not met. At the very least, an analogue to Article 91:2 Treaty of Rome could have been included, under which it is required that as of the entry into force of the Treaty, products originating in one Member state and exported to another be free of duties, quotas and measures with similar effect if they are re-exported. That is, efforts are required to ensure that arbitrage is possible. That being said, it is certainly the case that the enforcement of competition laws in the MENA region is important, and could have major benefits in terms of ensuring that the benefits of trade liberalization are realized. Given existing market structures in these countries (in particular the prevalence of state-owned enterprises), anti-competitive business practices may be a problem.

The intra-Mediterranean dimension and rules of origin: An objective of the Tunisian agreement is to promote the integration of the Maghreb countries. More generally, the EU is in favor of greater integration of the economies of the Mediterranean countries. This is important, as the negotiation of bilateral agreements between the EU and each of the Mediterranean countries would otherwise lead to the so-called hub-and-spoke system. A problem with such an arrangement is that it creates incentives for firms to locate in the "hub", that is., the EU, as this gives them barrier-free access to all the "spokes". All other things equal, this creates forces against inward foreign direct investment by EU-based firms producing tradable goods. Partly for this reason the CEECs established a Central European Free Trade Agreement (CEFTA). To avoid a hub-and-spoke system from emerging, Mediterranean countries are well advised to pursue a similar strategy.

Intra-regional trade in MENA is limited. In part this reflects the similarity in endowments, in part the non-competitiveness of processed and manufactured goods that are produced. However, while currently small in absolute value (some $8.3 billion in 1990, or 8 percent of total exports), relative to the region's participation in world trade, intra-regional trade is already quite high (Yeats, 1994; Ekholm et al., 1995). Thus, the trade of Egypt, Jordan, Syria and Turkey with the region is four times more intensive than trade with the world as a whole. The only major economy in the region where intra-regional trade is clearly "too low" is Israel. Given the differences in the factor endowments and per capita income between Israel and some of its neighbors, intra-regional trade has the potential to grow substantially. More generally, intra-industry trade must expand if intra-regional trade is to grow substantially, as the endowments of many countries are quite similar. This has already been happening to some extent. Although most intra-regional trade was in oil and oil products a decade ago, the share of oil has fallen significantly, standing at only 35 percent in 1992 (as opposed to 80 percent in 1980). Existing intra-regional trade is to some (unknown) extent driven by barter deals and a web of preferential, commodity-specific "protocol trade" agreements. The latter involve preferential tariff rates on specific lists of goods of Arab origin. In conjunction with the finding that intra-regional trade is already quite high, this suggests that much of this trade may consist of the "wrong" goods, that is., those in which countries do not have a comparative advantage (see also Lawrence, et al. 1995 on this issue). Exports to non-regional partner countries may give a less biased view of potential trade inside the region. There appears to be little complementarity between exports of many of the countries in the region, in particular in the Middle East (for example, Egypt, Jordan, Israel, Syria – see Appendix Table 2).

The rules of origin that are included in an FTA with the EU and in possible intra-regional agreements are important since they may contribute to trade diversion. The Tunisian agreement allows for cumulation for rules of origin purposes for products produced in Algeria and Morocco as well as the EU and Tunisia. This may help create backward and forward linkages between the Maghreb countries and enhance the potential for intra-industry trade. The extension of cumulation to other Mediterranean countries, and the CEECs, would be more beneficial to participants. This requires that barriers to intra-regional trade are eliminated, and that existing commodity-specific preferential trade agreements are converted into full-fledged free trade agreements. As noted earlier, this will also ensure that the emerging hub-and-spoke nature of the EU's web of trade agreements is reduced.

There are various Articles in the EMA which mention the intra-regional dimension. Article 1, outlining the objectives of the EMA lists integration of the Maghreb countries as one of the Agreement's aims. Article 43 (on scope of economic cooperation) mentions that one objective of cooperation (that is, technical assistance) is to "foster economic integration within the Maghreb using any measures likely to further such relations within the region." Article 45 (Regional cooperation) states among other things that Parties will support activities that foster intra-regional trade within the Maghreb. Intra-regional integration is therefore defined rather narrowly (Maghreb, not Mediterranean).

Economic cooperation: One-third of the Articles of the Tunisian EMA deal with cooperation in economic, social and cultural matters. The prime objective underlying economic cooperation is to target "first and foremost" activities "suffering the effects of internal constraints and difficulties or affected by the process of liberalizing Tunisia's economy as a whole, and more particularly by the liberalization of trade between Tunisia and the Community" (Article 43). Methods of economic cooperation mentioned in the EMA include information exchange, provision of expert services (consultants), joint ventures (for example, the Euro-Partenariat program), and assistance with technical, administrative and regulatory matters. Specific areas mentioned in the EMA include regional cooperation, education and training, science and technology, the environment, modernization of industry (including agricultural processing), promotion and protection of investment (for example, negotiating investment protection and double taxation treaties), standardization and conformity assessment (introduction of EU procedures/rules, upgrading Tunisian testing labs), approximation of economic legislation, financial services (supporting restructuring; improving auditing and supervision), agriculture and fisheries (modernization, diversification), transport (modernization and restructuring; management; quality upgrading), telecommunications and information technology (standardization, introduction of electronic data interchange (EDI) and integrated service digital networks (ISDN)), energy, tourism, and statistics.

The various Articles listed above are largely oriented towards upgrading Tunisian infrastructure broadly defined (both physical and regulatory) and providing support for restructuring the economy. This support is not just reflected in technical assistance and advice, but is supported by financial assistance as well (see below). The specific mentioning of an issue area under the economic cooperation chapter presumably signals that this is a legitimate subject for using EU financial resources. One area of great importance for many countries in the region is cooperation on customs matters (Article 59). The aim of such cooperation is the simplification of procedures, the introduction of the EU' Single Administrative Document and linking EU and Tunisian transit systems. Active cooperation on these matters will be important for trade facilitation. Another issue area that is important is standardization and conformity assessment. The longer run objective of the EMA is to conclude agreements for the mutual recognition of certification (Article 40).

Social and cultural cooperation: This includes a number of Articles guaranteeing national treatment for Tunisian and EU nationals that have found legitimate employment in the partner country. As far as movement of workers is concerned, Parties are only committed to "dialogue" aimed at achieving progress in this area. Priority is to be given to projects and programs to reduce migratory pressure, inter alia by creating jobs and developing training in areas from which emigrants come; promoting the role of women through education; improving social protection and health cover systems; and by improving living conditions in poor, densely populated areas (Article 71).

Financial cooperation: As mentioned earlier, Mediterranean countries have received financial transfers from the EU under the auspices of the revolving 5-year Financial Protocols. The sums involved vary per country, and are significant. During the period of the Fourth Protocol (1991-96), Tunisia was allocated a total of ECU 284 million.[14] Under the EMA approach, financial protocols will not be renewed. Instead, the EU envisages earmarking a total amount of assistance – grants and loans – for all the Mediterranean countries. Individual allocations out of this total would not be pre-determined, but would in part be endogenous – depending on country performance, including the implementation of the EMA. Although not spelled out explicitly in the EMA, the Articles in the EMA on financial cooperation emphasize the link between EMA implementation and the provision of financial resources.

Article 75 of the Tunisian EMA states that:

> With a view to full attainment on the Agreement's objectives, financial cooperation ... shall entail:
> - facilitating reforms aimed at modernizing the economy;
> - updating economic infrastructure;
> - promoting private investment and job creation activities;
> - taking into account the effects of the progressive introduction of a free trade area on the Tunisian economy, in particular where the updating and restructuring of industry is concerned;
> - flanking measures for policies implemented in the social sectors.

Moreover, Article 76 goes on to state that the Community will examine ways to support structural adjustment policies needed to restore financial equilibrium, while Article 77 seeks to establish a basis for coordinated approaches to dealing with "exceptional macroeconomic and financial problems which could stem from the progressive implementation of the Agreement." However, the exact modalities of financial cooperation are vague, the relevant procedures to "be adopted by mutual agreement between the Parties by means of the most suitable instruments once the Agreement enters into force" (Article 75). How future financial transfers will compare to past flows remains to be seen, although the absolute value of transfers is expected to increase. Some ECU 4.7 billion has been earmarked to support Mediterranean countries, to be complemented by an equivalent amount of European Investment Bank resources.

Evaluation

To what extent will the EMA help MENA countries catch up with the CEECs? In principle, the liberalization of trade should do much to induce firms to upgrade their production capacity and improve their efficiency. In the long run, the EMA is likely to be beneficial to all of the countries involved. But it should be remembered that in principle the exercise may be economically welfare-reducing in the short-to medium-runs. Even if such proved not to be the case, there can easily be significant opportunity costs associated with preferential trading arrangements. The major potential advantage of the EMA is that it provides a commitment mechanism to MENA governments, allowing a gradual reform path to be more credible than otherwise. Credibility may be enhanced through the binding nature of the agreement, the implicit linkage that has been made between official financial transfers from the EU and implementation of the EMA, and the offer of wide-ranging technical assistance to help Mediterranean countries improve the administration of their regulatory regimes (for example, customs, certification of product standards).

However, the absence of binding commitments in the areas of direct investment and supply of services, and the maintenance of antidumping procedures, suggest that one potential justification for regional arrangements mentioned in Section II has not been met. That is, the EMA does not go significantly beyond existing multilateral (WTO) disciplines. Moreover, the transition path to free trade with the EU is a long one, with liberalization of goods competing with domestic production only starting five years after the entry into force of the agreements. This may well reduce the incentives to initiate rapid restructuring, and may create problems in implementing tariff reductions in the future (for example, through pressure for safeguard protection). The gradual liberalization may also be too slow in terms of maintaining existing export markets and capturing new ones in the face of increased competition from the CEECs and Asian economies, driven by the liberalization achieved in the Uruguay Round.

A potential rationale in favor of regional integration noted earlier is the existence of enforcement mechanisms that are more effective than those available under the WTO. In the EMA context, dispute settlement is dealt with by the Association Council. In the case of a dispute that cannot be addressed through consultations with the Council, one of the Parties may appoint an arbitrator. The other Party is then required to appoint a second arbitrator within two months, and the Association Council appoints a third one. Decisions by the three arbitrators will be taken by majority vote, with the Parties required to implement them. This goes beyond the WTO, where parties to a dispute are always free not to implement a recommendation by a WTO panel if they are willing to succumb to possible retaliation. Time will tell how this dispute settlement mechanism will work. It is important to note, however, that dispute settlement will only work if there are binding obligations. In a number of areas that are particularly relevant from a market access viewpoint such obligations have yet to be established, for example, regarding product standards. Disputes on such issues, for example, allegations that standards are used as non-tariff barriers, can only be dealt with by the WTO.

It is important that concurrently with the implementation of the EMA, external barriers to trade and foreign investment are reduced as well. A key issue in this context is related to the trade diversion question – the extent to which a shift away from efficient third country suppliers toward less efficient EU firms occurs, and the efficiency losses and implicit tariff revenue transfer that are associated with this. Given the lack of enhanced market access for Tunisian agricultural products, the extent for potential trade creation gains were limited. Much also depends on the value of the economic and financial cooperation that will flow from the EU to Tunisia (and the other Mediterranean partners). Another potential problem that may arise in this connection is the reliance on customs tariff for government revenue. As tariffs on

EU goods decline to zero, it may prove difficult to reduce MFN rates if alternative tax bases are not created.

Of course, these are all potential problems, and one can argue in favor of the liberalization strategy that was chosen. Thus, it may well be that by lowering tariffs on intermediate and capital goods, domestic industries are granted some up front compensation for the adjustment costs that must be incurred later, and are given time to restructure. It could also be argued that this strategy ensures that tariff revenues will gradually decline, again allowing more time to create alternative sources of funds for the Government. Nonetheless, the possible downside of the strategy should be recognized. It is clear that much will depend on the extent to which complementary actions are pursued to improve the functioning of the economy. An important point to raise in this connection is the fact that the EMA does little to ensure investors of national treatment or to grant the general right of establishment. This is a significant difference with the CEECs Agreements, which clearly spell out that right of establishment is a central part of the deal. Such establishment is permitted immediately for most activities, and a transition path is spelled out for the remainder. By signaling the fact that they are open to FDI and willing to lock in the commitment, the CEECs increased the incentives for foreign firms to establish and transfer much needed know-how by reducing political risk. FDI is especially important in the services area, where establishment often remains the best way to contest a market. Efficient services are crucial in terms of being able to participate in the global economy: telecommunications, information technology, port services, financial intermediation, and business support services are all key elements underlying the ability to compete on world markets. By limiting commitments to those made in the GATS, the EMA risks sending a signal that liberalization is not on the immediate agenda. It also puts the burden on unilateral efforts by Mediterranean countries to move forward.

An important factor underlying CEECs' export performance is the fact that firms are able to exploit sub-contracting of manufacturing products for export to the EU in a much greater degree than most MENA countries. Such OPT is important, as it greatly facilitates the penetration of EU markets. Foreign (EU) partners generally take care of distribution and quality control. OPT activities are frequently time-sensitive. Under just-in-time management practices, the availability of adequate services links (transport, harbor services, customs operations, telecommunications) plays a fundamental role in the decision on the location of outsourcing. Geography suggests that many Mediterranean countries could become competitive locations for outsourcing by European companies if access to efficient producer services is made available. Morocco and Tunisia illustrate this aspect as they are the only two

MENA countries to make use of OPT. However, in many countries in the region, significant changes in regulatory regimes and investment policies are required to improve the efficiency of services providers. Greater competition will do much to reduce price-cost margins and upgrade quality.

Actions to reduce the role of the state are particularly important. Indeed, the need to reform regulatory regimes affecting FDI and the operation of the services sector is part of a more general need to decrease the size of the public sector. Privatization of state-owned enterprises is a necessary condition for economic recovery and longer-run growth. Refraining from privatization will slow down the necessary adjustment process. Gradual implementation of free trade with the EU will put public sector enterprises under pressure to restructure, giving rise to pressure for assistance (subsidies, tax concessions, soft directed credit, capital infusions, and increase in import barriers). The net costs of an EMA without a significant privatization effort are likely to be much higher than if the implementation of the EMA is complemented by deregulation and privatization. At the very least, it would appear necessary that state firms confront hard budget constraints. Whether this is easier to achieve than privatization is an open question.[15]

Important political economy issues also arise in this context. Many MENA countries have a significant stock of educated workers that are either employed directly by the government's administration or by state-owned firms. They also have large pools of unskilled, under-employed labor. In addition, some countries such as Egypt have a substantial stock of unemployed university graduates (World Bank, 1995b). A necessary condition for the implementation of the EMA to be politically feasible is that increased job opportunities for the unskilled and the educated unemployed materialize, and that job losses in the state sector remain politically manageable. Greater employment opportunities for the unskilled may emerge through the creation of firms specializing in labor-intensive production (in part through exploiting the OPT option) and by improving access for agricultural exports. The latter has been excluded; a necessary condition for the former is the existence of adequate infrastructure and the absence of red tape (regulations, tax administration, customs). As far as the more highly educated are concerned, many of the potential job opportunities lie in the services sector. Realizing this potential requires deregulating services activities and allowing establishment by foreign providers. Even then, realism suggests that in countries where the existing labor force employed in services is already significant, net losses may well occur initially. FDI can do much to stimulate both labor-intensive and more skilled activities, be they in services or manufacturing. But these opportunities will materialize only if the regulatory and institutional environment is conducive to private sector investment. Indeed, in the absence of improvements in the legal and regulatory frameworks, opening up to trade with the EU may result in greater competition from imports without much in the way of new investment. If so, the political viability of EMA implementation will decline. Much will also depend in this connection on how EU financial assistance is used. A strong case can be made that there may be a high payoff for using EU grants to fund worker compensation schemes to facilitate downsizing of the public sector (World Bank, 1995b). The wording of the Articles in the EMA on the scope and priorities for financial and economic cooperation creates the presumption that such funding is possible.

Conclusions

There is increasing evidence that trade liberalization and integration into the global economy is associated with higher rates of economic growth (Sachs and Warner, 1995). A problem confronting any government seeking to shift from an inward-looking to an export-oriented trade regime is the need to offset resistance by interest groups that are likely to lose in the transition to a liberal environment. In the mid to the late 1980s, this political economy constraint was overcome by many countries in Latin America and Central and Eastern Europe as the result of external developments – the debt crisis, the fall of communism. In conjunction with the promise of large private financial inflows in the case of Latin America, and integration into Europe in the case of the CEECs, governments were able to "sell" broad-based economic reform (Rodrik, 1995). The MENA region did not participate in the "shock approach" to reform. It pursued a very gradual reform path. In part this was because governments were not convinced of the need for wide-ranging market opening – there was no external factor similar to the debt crisis in Latin America – but perhaps more importantly, because of the political costs that were expected from pursuing such a course.

The CEECs illustrate the case that far-reaching liberalization and a strategy of greater integration with the EU and the rest of the world will greatly expand trade and export-oriented production. Although the transition has been painful, the CEECs are now all experiencing real economic growth. The Europe Agreements are by no means the primary factor underlying CEECs' economic performance, but they probably have played an important role in anchoring expectations. The EMA option provides a unique opportunity to the Mediterranean countries to credibly pursue far-reaching liberalization of trade in a gradual fashion. In this respect they are therefore very beneficial. But in themselves the EMAs are not enough. They are limited to the liberalization of trade in manufactured products. They do little more than contain hortatory language as regards the liberalization of service markets and foreign investment, something that is required to help ensure a supply response and create new employment opportunities.

The absence of commitments in these areas may be related in part to the issue of privatization and the role of the State. Without public sector reform – at a minimum the introduction of hard budget constraints – the impact of trade liberalization will be both muted and possibly more intense. The impact may be muted because public enterprises are given preferential treatment and retain substantial market power. The impact may be exacerbated if public enterprises are forced to adjust, but new employment opportunities do not emerge because barriers to entry persist. The recent literature evaluating alternative explanations for the success of particular countries in attaining and sustaining high rates of economic growth concludes that while openness to the world economy is very important, in itself it is not enough. Equally important are efficient public institutions, domestic competition, a well-functioning services sector (finance, infrastructure, distribution, and so forth.), investment in human resources (education), high rates of private savings and investment, and a stable macro-economic environment. These factors cannot all be "imported" through an agreement with the EU. Some, however, could have been included in the EMA, thereby reducing the burden on Mediterranean countries to unilaterally pursue the reforms needed. As emphasized earlier, the policy regimes pertaining to FDI and the services sector are of particular importance in this connection. By not committing to a concrete transition path towards a liberal economic environment in the mentioned areas, an opportunity was missed. This is a matter of concern, especially when considering the magnitude of the capital (flight) owned by nationals of the region (World Bank, 1995a).

A similar conclusion can be drawn with respect to the issue of the long-term goal as regards the level of MFN tariffs that will be imposed on third countries. As noted earlier, one way for a regional agreement to be unambiguously welfare-improving is to use it as a deliberate strategy to offset existing political economy constraints on unilateral liberalization through the use of the financial and economic assistance that is on offer. Although this may indeed be the objective of Governments in the region, they have not publicized it. Without such an explicitly stated long-term perspective, it may prove more difficult than otherwise for Governments to reduce MFN tariffs substantially in the future. This is because incentives will be created for not only domestic firms to seek to continue to benefit from somewhat sheltered home markets, but EU firms fearing competition from third countries may also be induced to lobby for protection to be maintained. A clear time-table and transition path to be pursued concurrently with the implementation of the EMA would do much to avoid such problems, and would provide a strong signal to domestic producers that what ultimately counts is not the regional market, but the world market.

Notes

1   That is to say, the economic situation has never deteriorated to such an extent that "shock therapy" was unavoidable.
2   In what follows we abstract from the systemic or global welfare implications of regional integration. These are controversial and the subject of ongoing debate. See Bhagwati (1993) and the contributions in Anderson and Blackhurst (1993).
3   See Hoekman (1995b) for a detailed analysis of the GATS.
4   Enforcement of binding commitments may also be stronger under a RIA. In GATT, the ultimate enforcement is retaliation by "principal suppliers," the countries with whom a tariff concession was originally negotiated. Such retaliation, if it occurs, will take the form of increases in tariffs on exports of the country violating a binding. This may not constitute a sufficient deterrent threat. Alternatively, the country may offer to compensate principal suppliers by lowering other tariffs (on an MFN basis). These mechanisms may not exist in the RIA context. In the EU context, a FTA will not make allowances for the permanent re-imposition of tariffs. GATT does.
5   This section summarizes and updates material contained in Hoekman (1995).
6   Membership in the Council for Mutual Economic Assistance (CMEA), the now dissolvedtrading system of the former communist bloc, consisted in 1989 of Bulgaria, Cuba, Czechoslovakia, the German Democratic Republic, Hungary, Mongolia, Poland, Romania, the Soviet Union and Vietnam.
7   The welfare implications of OPT may be ambiguous, insofar as the policy regime induces EU sourcing of inputs that are more costly than what is available on the world market.
8   The RCA is defined as:

$$\frac{x_{ij}/X_j}{\Sigma_{i=1}^{N} x / \Sigma_{i=1}^{N} X}$$

where x_{ij} are exports of commodity i by country j, X_j are country j's total exports, and N is the number of countries.
9   Indeed, he also notes that the WTO was not considered a binding constraint by the Hungarian government; what counted was the commitment towards the EU.
10 "Strengthening the Mediterranean Policy of the European Union: Establishing a Euro-Mediterranean Partnership." Communication from the Commission to the Council and the Parliament, October 1994.
11 Trade data reported by EUROSTAT is either on a 6 or 8-digit level basis, making it impossible to relate exactly the tariff commitments (which use 7-digits) to publicly available tradestatistics. However, in most cases, a concordance from the 7 to the 6-digit level was straightforward.
12 This is because firms get access to cheaper inputs as input tariffs fall to zero, while continuing to benefit from tariffs on the goods they produce.
13 Poland, for example, granted immediate freedom of establishment and national treatment for construction and most manufacturing activities, with the exception of mining, processing of precious stones and metals, explosives, ammunition and

weaponry, pharmaceuticals, alcohol, high voltage power lines and pipeline trans-portation. All but the last two activities are to be liberalized by the end of 1997, at which time most service sectors will also be liberalized (financial, legal and real estate services excepted). By the end of the transitional period (10 years under the CEEC Agreements) all sectors are to be liberalized, except for acquisition and sale of natural resources and agricultural land and forests. The Czech and Slovak agree-ments liberalize FDI in all sectors immediately, except for the defense industry; steel; mining; acquisition of state-owned assets under privatization; ownership, use, sale and rent of real property; and the financial service industry. These activities are to be liberalized by the end of the ten year transition period. The Hungarian agreement is similar to the other CEEC agreements except that it adds legal services and gambling, lottery and similar services to the list of activities excluded indefinitely.

14 The amounts have been steadily increasing in nominal terms. During 1978-81, Tunisia obtained ECU 95 million. This rose to ECU 139 during 1981-86 and ECU 224 during 1986-91.

15 In general, the answer may well be yes if the Government desires to reduce resource flows to the public sector enterprises. By imposing an aggregate ceiling on the amount of such transfers, it may be able to insulate itself somewhat from individual claimants. Much depends here on the objective of the Government.

References

Anderson, Kym, and Richard Blackhurst (eds.), 1993. *Regional Integration and the Global Trading System*. London: Harvester-Wheatsheaf.

Bhagwati, Jagdish. 1993. "Regionalism and Multilateralism: An Overview" in J. de Melo and A. Panagariya (eds.), *New Dimensions in Regional Integration*. Cambridge: Cambridge University Press.

Csaba, Laszlo. 1995. "The Political Economy of Trade Regimes in Central Europe" in Alan Winters (ed.), *Foundations of an Open Economy: Trade Laws and Institutions for Eastern Europe*. London: Center for Economic Policy Research.

Ekholm, Karolina, Johan Torstensson and Rasha Torstensson. 1995. "Prospects for Trade in the Middle East: An Econometric Analysis" presented at the ERF confer-ence on Liberalization of Trade and Foreign Investment, Bogazici University, Istanbul, September 16-18.

Hamdouch, Bachir. 1995. "Perspective d'une Zone de Libre-Echange Entre Le Maroc et l'Union Europeene: Enjeux et Impacts" presented at the ERF conference on Liberalization of Trade and Foreign Investment, Bogazici University, Istanbul, September 16-18.

Hoekman, Bernard. 1995a. "The WTO, the EU and the Arab World: Trade Policy Priorities and Pitfalls." CEPR Discussion Paper No. 1226.

___. 1995b. "Tentative First Steps: An Assessment of the General Agreement on Trade in Services" in Will Martin and Alan Winters (eds.), *The Uruguay Round and the Developing Economies*. World Bank. Forthcoming.

Hoekman, Bernard, and Michael Leidy. 1993. "Holes and Loopholes in Integration Agreements: History and Prospects" in Kym Anderson and Richard Blackhurst (eds.), *Regional Integration and the Global Trading System*. London: Harvester-Wheatsheaf.

Lawrence, Robert, *et al*. 1995. *Towards Free Trade in the Middle East: The Triad and Beyond*. Cambridge: Harvard University, June

Panagariya, Arvind. 1995. "The Case Against Preferential Trading" presented at the

ERF conference on Liberalization of Trade and Foreign Investment, Bogazici University, Istanbul, 16-18 September.

Rodrik, Dani. 1995. "The Push Towards Free Trade in the Developing World: Why So Late? Why Now? Will It Last?" in S. Haggard and S. Webb (eds.), *Voting for Reform*. Oxford: Oxford University Press.

Sachs, Jeffrey, and Andrew Warner. 1995. "Economic Reform and the Process of Global Integration" in W. Brainard and G. Perry (eds.), *Brookings Papers on Economic Activity*, Vol. 1.

Sapir, André. 1995. "The Europe Agreements: Implications for Trade Laws and Institutions" in Alan Winters (ed.), *Foundations of an Open Economy: Trade Laws and Institutions for Eastern Europe*. London: Center for Economic Policy Research.

World Bank. 1994. "Kingdom of Morocco-Republic of Tunisia. Export Growth: Determinants and Prospects." Report No. 12947-MNA. World Bank, October.

___.1995a. *Claiming the Future: Choosing Prosperity in the Middle East and North Africa*. Washington DC: The World Bank.

___. 1995b. *Will Arab Workers Prosper or Be Left Out in the 21st Century?*. Washington DC: World Bank.

Yeats, Alexander. 1994. "Export Prospects of Middle Eastern Countries." World Bank. Mimeo.

Appendix Table I: Trade Taxes in MENA and East European Countries, 1993

	Share of Import Duties in Total Government Revenue	Share of "Other" Taxes in Total Import Tax Revenue	Average Collected Tariff (Revenue/Imports)
Morocco	17.7	52	17.5
Tunisia	28.3	46	18.7
Egypt	10.0	8	14.9
Jordan	35.9	40	17.8
Syria	10.0	25	16.4
Oman	3.2	--	3.0
UAE	--	--	--
Yemen	20.2	3	19.1[+]
Bahrain	9.2	--	4.0
Bulgaria	4.6	17	7.9
Czech Rep.	3.9	23	2.2
Hungary(1991)	5.8	--	8.6
Poland	6.5	--	5.9
Romania	3.8	--	7.0

Notes: -- *Zero or negligible;* +*Valued at the average parallel market exchange rate, the average collection rate was around 8 percent.*
Source: IMF Government Finance Statistics Yearbook, 1994: International Financial Statistics, 1994.

Appendix Table 2: Correlation of Regional Cooperation Agreement Indices of Exports to the EU, 1993

	JOR	LEB	SYR	ALG	SA	KUW	TUN	UAE	MOR	ISR	EGY
JORDAN	1.00										
LEBANON	-0.02	1.00									
SYRIA	0.01	0.44	1.00								
ALGERIA	-0.04	-0.04	0.25	1.00							
SAUDI ARABIA	0.01	-0.04	0.55	0.46	1.00						
KUWAIT	0.09	-0.01	0.56	0.46	0.95	1.00					
TUNISIA	0.16	0.01	-0.01	0.39	-0.04	-0.02	1.00				
UAE	0.10	0.07	0.14	0.02	0.17	0.22	0.12	1.00			
MOROCCO	0.17	0.00	-0.03	0.65	-0.05	-0.04	0.64	-0.00	1.00		
ISRAEL	0.21	-0.03	-0.07	-0.07	-0.05	-0.06	0.09	-0.04	0.14	1.00	
EGYPT	0.09	0.12	0.63	0.11	0.30	0.32	0.10	0.17	0.05	0.00	1.00

Source: Author's computations.

The Free-Trade Area
Between Morocco and the European Union

Introduction

The relations between Morocco and the European Union (EU) date back to the latter's establishment. These relations have faced growing difficulties over the past decade, mainly as a result of the enlargement of the EU to include those Mediterranean countries that compete directly with Morocco (Greece, Portugal, and especially Spain), the constraints imposed by the EU's Common Agricultural Policy (CAP), and the erosion of trade preferences in the wake of the Uruguay Round.

Along with its continental preoccupation and in parallel with its continued enlargement, the EU has developed a strategic interest in the Mediterranean Basin as a whole and, in particular, in those countries lying in the South Mediterranean, Morocco included. It is in this context that the EU has proposed a new mode of association with Morocco and other Southern Mediterranean countries. Central to this new mode of association is the creation of a free-trade area. But what are the issues at play and the likely consequences of such an agreement in the case of Morocco? These are the questions that this chapter will attempt to answer.

The Agreement was signed in February 1996 and it will come into force following ratification by all EU states. The issues underlying the EU-Morocco Association Agreement are both economic and geopolitical. This necessitates a retrospective review of the historical relations between Morocco and the EU and the difficulties encountered over time.

A Historical Overview of the EU-Morocco Relations

The EU-Morocco relations date back to the former's creation in its original form – the European Economic Community – in 1957. Indeed, particular provisions regarding relations with Morocco (and also with Tunisia) were already included in the Treaty of Rome. Two subsequent Agreements have regulated such relations: the 1969 Association Agreement and the 1976 Cooperation Agreement. However, neither Agreement resulted in improved EU-Morocco relations.

The Treaty of Rome

Two texts annexed to the Treaty of Rome made explicit reference to Morocco.

The first one was a Protocol. It stipulated that "the application of the treaty establishing the European Economic Community does not require any modification of the customs regime applied, at the outset of the implementation of the treaty, to France's imports originating in Morocco".[1] The customs regime referred to was that of customs exemptions applied to the vast majority of Morocco's exports to France.[2] Such exports consisted almost entirely of food products (cereals, fruits, vegetables, canned goods), raw materials, and semi-finished goods. Exports to France represented roughly 50 percent of Morocco's total exports.

The Protocol thus allowed the application of unilateral advantages that were being threatened by the establishment of the European Community (such as the common external tariff and the common agricultural policy). Therefore, the Protocol was meant to cover a transition period that would evolve quickly into an association regime with the Community.

The planned association regime was defined in the second text annexed to the Treaty of Rome – the "Declaration of Purpose" which stipulated that the six members of the European Community:

> Taking into account the Agreements and covenants of an economic, financial and monetary nature concluded between France and the other independent countries belonging to the Franc zone,
> Intent on maintaining and intensifying the traditional exchange links between the member states of the European Economic Community and the independent countries as well as contributing to the latter's social and economic development,
> Declare themselves ready, from the onset of implementation of the Treaty, to propose to these countries negotiations with a view to concluding economic association Agreements with the Community.[3]

The Association Agreement

The 1969 Association Agreement actually turned out to be a commercial Agreement and of a limited duration (5 years). It covered only partially the commercial exchanges between Morocco and the Community, and was concluded based on the principle of reciprocity, to the extent that it stipulated advantages for both parties. The major preferences that were granted by the Community to the Moroccan exports were the following:[4]

• Exemptions for industrial products and handicrafts, with the exception of agro-industrial products and cork products. Agro-industrial products – with the notable exception of wine, fruit juices, and certain fruit and vegetable-based canned products – were nonetheless granted some preferential access in respect of the applied customs duties (the fixed element of a common tariff duty).

• As for agricultural products, only citrus fruits benefited from an 80 percent reduction of the common tariff duty, provided their prices were higher than a given reference price.[5]

• Fish products, with the exception of canned goods, benefited from customs exemptions.[6] The preferences granted to fish-based canned goods varied among European countries, from exemption of customs duties without quantitative limits in the BENELUX (Belgium, the Netherlands and the Luxembourg) to partial exemption within the context of quantitative quotas in the other countries of the Community.

From Morocco's perspective, the main preferences granted to imports of European origin were as follows:

• Exemptions from customs duties for a list of products representing three percent of total imports from the Community.

• Tariff reductions in the order of 25 percent for another list of products representing seven percent of total imports from the Community.

• Given that such tariff advantages had been accorded *erga omnes* by the 1906 Algeciras Act,[7] the Community sought to obtain exclusive advantages, and that was accomplished by the adoption of global quotas in its own favor, representing 63 percent of all imports subject to tariff duties in Morocco.

Overall, this was an Agreement with limited impact that satisfied neither party. The advantages that were made available to Morocco were diluted by the proliferation of similar preferential agreements signed with other Mediterranean countries (Spain, Portugal, Greece, Turkey, Israel, and so forth.). Negotiations were scheduled for the third year of implementation of the Agreement. In 1976 – that is, two years after the expiration of the 1969 Association Agreement – they evolved into a larger agreement, the Cooperation Agreement.

The Cooperation Agreement

The Cooperation Agreement is part of a new type of more global Agreements comprising, in addition to the commercial track, other tracks including financial and technical cooperation as well as issues related to labor movement. These new aspects of the Agreement, albeit devoid of tangible and effective benefits, may be credited with initiating a new type of cooperation with a larger scope. The Agreement had unlimited duration, and the commercial track – which constituted a major portion thereof – no longer required reciprocity on the part of Morocco.

The trade preferences accorded to Moroccan exports by the nine member Market were as follows:[8]

• Maintenance of exemptions for industrial products and raw materials – again with the exception of cork products, which were subjected to a progressive ceiling.

• Agro-industrial products were still treated differently and less favorably than industrial products. They benefited generally from limited tariff reductions and were subjected to quantitative restrictions (quotas), minimum prices (reference prices) and quality conditions (as in the case of wine).

• Fish products continued to benefit from unlimited customs exemptions, with the exception of Morocco's main export product – sardines, which were subjected to minimum price conditions.

• As for agricultural products, an 80 percent tariff reduction was kept for citrus fruits, and a 40 to 60 percent preference was accorded to fruit and vegetable products although these were also subjected to seasonal restrictions (limited periods) and to minimum price conditions.

Finally, the Cooperation Agreement did not innovate as regards trade preferences. Indeed, the issues associated with Morocco's agricultural and agro-industrial exports to the European Community remained unresolved. These issues became more pressing following the accession of Greece, Portugal, and especially Spain to the Community.[9] The 1988 Adaptation Agreement – which was meant to address the issues that surfaced in the wake of the Community's second enlargement to include Morocco's trade rivals – hardly provided for new solutions.

The Erosion of Relations

EU-Morocco relations have been constrained by two aspects: asymmetry and erosion. Asymmetry stems from differences in size, level of development and bargaining power between the two parties. The second aspect has been the continued erosion of privileged relations between Morocco and the European Union. Such erosion has been in fact unavoidable in light of the internal and external policy objectives of the EU, as well as the continued drive towards liberalization on a world-wide scale.

The main objectives of the EU internal policies are to establish and deepen European integration. Two aspects of such a policy with particular impact on the relations with Morocco are "Green Europe" (the Common Agricultural Policy) and "Blue Europe" (the fishing policy). On the other hand, the EU's internal policy aims at enlarging the Union by extending membership to other countries. The EU has thus evolved from six to 15 member countries,[10] and the tendency is for the Union ultimately to cover the whole of continental Europe. The enlargement of the European Union has made relations with Morocco all the more difficult. By allowing some of Morocco's trade rivals to become full EU members, the Union has raised its own self-sufficiency rate – especially as regards agricultural products – and has thus accentuated the asymmetry between the two partners.

The EU's external policy has been increasingly marked by concerns over the intensification and harmonization of relations with its Mediterranean neighbors and those of Central and Eastern Europe. The proliferation of Association Agreements that were overtaken by Cooperation Agreements, and now by Free-Trade Agreements has in fact trivialized the advantages and privileges that had at first benefited only a limited number of "associated" countries, including Morocco.

The second element that has contributed to the erosion of the once-privileged EU-Morocco relations is the globalization and liberalization of the world economy, an achievement sealed by the Final Act of the Uruguay Round (UR). The UR Agreements have lead to the reduction of trade barriers and the extension of equal treatment in international exchanges, particularly concerning access to markets. What is of importance in as far as Morocco (and some other countries) is concerned is that the EU market will become more open and less preferential. Thus, any advantages the EU has extended to imports originating from Morocco and other associated countries – particularly those industrial products benefiting from customs exemptions – will gradually disappear, as the margin of preference accorded to products originating from on the one hand countries that have concluded an Association Agreement with the EU and, on the other, those that have not, most notably Southeast Asian countries, is eroded.

It is thus evident that the EU-Morocco Cooperation Agreement no longer fulfills Morocco's aspiration for privileged relations with the EU. The stakes at play are high, and they dictate the necessity to devise a new framework of cooperation between the two entities.

What are the Stakes?

The stakes underpinning negotiations with a view to the establishment of a new Association Agreement are very important at both the economic and geopolitical levels. What made the negotiations difficult is the fact that both parties differ in their assessment of these stakes. While for Morocco the aspirations are mostly economic in nature, for the European Union they are both geopolitical and economic.

The Stakes for Morocco

The economic stakes for Morocco from privileged commercial relations with the EU are enormous. The following indicators are revealing:[11] remittances from Moroccan nationals working in foreign countries represent the main source of income as recorded in the country's balance of payments account (roughly US$ 2 billion in 1993), and over 90 percent of those remittances originate from Moroccan nationals residing in the EU. In addition, revenues from tourism are the second most important item on Morocco's balance of payments account (US$ 1.2 billion in 1993), and 80 percent of such revenues are brought in by EU citizens. Furthermore, 70 percent of all foreign private investments made in Morocco originate in Europe.[12] In sum, the European Union is Morocco's single most important commercial partner, accounting for 54 percent of Moroccan imports and 63 percent of exports in 1994. The figures are even higher if we consider some of Morocco's key exports – 83 percent of finished products (representing over 29 percent of total exports), almost 94 percent of clothing and apparel products (corresponding to 17.6 percent of exports), and over 75 percent of fresh fruits and vegetables (Table 1).

Table 1: The Importance of Moroccan Exports to the EU by Major Product Group, 1994 (percentage)

	EU Share in Exports	Structure of Total Exports
Food Products	60.5	28.0
Fruits & Vegetables (not canned)	(75.2)	(5.7)
Energy and Raw Materials	55.0	16.9
Semi-Finished Products	49.2	25.7
Finished Products	82.8	29.4
Equipment	(81.1)	(3.5)
Consumption	(83.1)	(25.9)
Clothing & Apparel	(93.6)	(17.6)
Total	63.2	100.0
Share in Total Imports	54.0	--
Coverage Ratio (Exports/Imports) %	65.7	--

Source: BMCE (1995), Nos. 218-219.

The enhanced integration of the EU, its continued enlargement, and its evolving policy especially where it concerns the Mediterranean have posed formidable obstacles to Morocco's exports to the EU. The successful conclusion of the Uruguay Round has made this situation even worse. In fact, the EU's offer to the GATT/WTO has created even larger barriers to the entry of Moroccan fruits and vegetables. Paradoxically, the changes in the EU's Common Agricultural Policy that were undertaken to bring the latter into conformity with the Uruguay Round Agreements have made the EU agricultural market more closed than ever before. "Tariff equivalents" have replaced "compensatory taxes" and, above all, "entry prices" (minimum prices) to be applied all year round have replaced "reference prices," which were only in force for a specified season during the year. The setting of so-called "entry prices" at high levels approaching Europe's even most marginal production lines may effectively bar the entry of Moroccan products.[13] This is what happened in the beginning of 1995 in the case of certain Moroccan vegetable exports, particularly tomatoes.[14] The same may happen in the case of citrus fruits with the application of the new regulations concerning fruits in early 1996. Even agro-industrial products, which currently benefit from preferential conditions, will be subjected to customs duties at such high levels that they will no longer be competitive in the face of major competing products coming from Spain. That is what happened to Morocco's sardine exports starting in early May 1995.[15]

Over and above such immediate and tangible risks for a wide array of Moroccan exports to Europe, a much longer-term risk has started to take shape in a world economy marked by increased regionalization and globalization. That is the risk of marginalization faced by those small economies that fail to join the large dynamic regional blocs currently evolving in the world economy.[16] At stake here is a momentous strategic option. Morocco made its choice in 1984 by officially applying for membership in the European Union on the basis of economic and geopolitical reasons.[17] The same interests have permeated the proposed establishment of a permanent link with Europe through the Strait of Gibraltar (probably a tunnel), and the construction currently underway of the Maghreb-Europe gas pipeline.

The Stakes for the European Union

The stakes for the European Union are mostly geopolitical, since Morocco is only a small trading partner of the EU (indeed, the three main countries of the Maghreb – Morocco, Algeria and Tunisia – together account for less than one percent of the EU's total foreign trade). To be sure, some of Morocco's exports to the EU – most notably agricultural and fishing products – are far from negligible, but all of them could easily be replaced with imports from other countries without any significant impact on prices.

There are many other elements that shape EU's interests in Morocco. These relate to such issues as demography, culture, religion, strategic position, as well as the fact that Morocco belongs at once to the Maghreb, to the Mediterranean Basin, to Africa, and to the Arab and Muslim worlds. However, in addition to the geopolitical elements, Morocco and other Mediterranean countries have also increased the economic stakes for the EU.

In the wake of the first "oil shock," the Euro-Arab dialogue was marked by the economic concerns of the European Economic Community. No comprehensive Mediterranean policy framework was elaborated. Indeed, during the decades of the 1960s and 1970s, the dialogue was limited to similar Association Agreements, followed by Cooperation Agreements signed with certain Mediterranean countries. It was not until the 1990s that, in view of dramatic changes in the international context, the European Commission saw fit to design a "new Mediterranean policy," whereby it:

> ... reiterates its conviction that the geographical proximity and the intensity of myriad links have turned the stability and prosperity of DMCs (Developing Mediterranean Countries) into essential elements for the Community itself. The widening of social and economic gaps between the Community and the DMCs.would hardly be tolerable. Broadly speaking, the security of the Community is at stake.[18]

Likewise, the European Council of Heads of States and Governments convening in Essen in December 1994 stated that "the Mediterranean represents an area of strategic importance for the European Union."[19]

At the economic level, the goal is to "establish a vast economic space encompassing geographic Europe and the Mediterranean"[20] by means of a network of agreements between the European Union and over 30 countries in its immediate neighborhood. The objective is to promote the integration of these countries in the European economy to varying degrees. In descending order of integration, one should note the "European Association Agreements" with ten countries in Central Europe, the "Customs Union Agreement" signed with Turkey, the "Euro-Mediterranean Association Agreements" with eight Mediterranean countries, and the "Partnership and Cooperation Agreements" with 12 countries of the Commonwealth of Independent States. The economic space envisioned through such Agreements will be shaped notably as a Euro-Mediterranean Free-Trade Area.[21] In a similar vein, a free-trade agreement is currently being negotiated between the EU and the countries of the Gulf Cooperation Council (GCC). Prospects for peace in the Middle East have opened up vast horizons for Europe's strategy, which is now faced only with the US strategy, since Middle Eastern countries lack their own strategy. Was it just a coincidence that the Euro-Mediterranean Conference held in Barcelona and the Second Middle East and North Africa Economic Summit held in Amman took place at roughly the same time, that is, in the Fall of 1995?[22]

The Framework

Negotiations have been difficult, perhaps even harder than those that led to the signing of the Agreements of 1969 and 1976. Exploratory meetings were launched in 1992, followed by actual negotiations in early 1994. Morocco was the first country with which negotiations were started with a view to establishing the new "Euro-Mediterranean Association Agreements." Subsequently, similar negotiations were conducted with three other countries – Israel, Tunisia and Egypt, successively. Negotiations with Morocco were expected to be finalized by the end of 1995 in order to constitute the first series of such "Euro-Mediterranean Association Agreements".[23] A second series of Agreements will embrace four other countries (namely, Jordan, Algeria, Lebanon and Syria), but meetings remain at the exploratory stages.[24] This section will attempt to present the major features of the new Agreement.

A New Type of Agreement

The first thing one notices is the change in the title of the new generation of agreements. Indeed, the phrase "Association Agreements" dates back to the 1969 Agreement. Apart from reciprocal advantages, however, these two types of Agreements have very little in common. Given the new regional and international context, the "Euro-Mediterranean Association Agreements" belong to a new generation of agreements concluded in a spirit of reciprocity but also of partnership, and not exclusively of assistance.[25] Having unlimited duration, they aim at establishing a free-trade regime, and they are not limited to the commercial domain. They go beyond economic and financial issues to encompass technical, cultural, social, political, and even ecological matters. In fact, as far back as April 1992, the EU's Council of Ministers made the decision to negotiate a new Agreement with Morocco on the basis of "four main pillars:" political dialogue; economic, technical and cultural cooperation covering all fields of common interest to both parties; the progressive establishment of a free-trade area; and financial cooperation.[26] Moreover, this agreement was meant as the "first of a series of Euro-Maghreb Association Agreements"[27] as well as an example to other Maghreb countries.[28] However, due to the difficulties encountered in the negotiations with Morocco, the first such "Euro-Mediterranean Association Agreement" was signed with Tunisia on 17 July 1995 along the same principles.

What the EU had proposed to Morocco seems to be "analogous with and as comprehensive as the European Association Agreements signed between the EU and Poland or Hungary, the only exception being the prospects for accession," which is restricted to European countries exclusively.[29]

The general aspects of the agreement are similar to those to be found in the Agreement between the EU and Tunisia.[30] The Agreement includes commitments in respect of : political discipline; free circulation of goods; rights of establishment; payments, movement of capital, competition policy and other economic measures; economic and financial cooperation; and other general measures.

A Free-Trade Area

The commercial track represents the centerpiece of the Agreement, around which other aspects of economic and financial cooperation are woven. It anticipates the progressive establishment – over a 12-year period – of a free-trade area.

There are differences in the treatment accorded to industrial products (which exclude agro-industrial and fishing products) and agricultural products, as well as between the pace of liberalization of the European and Moroccan markets so as to take into account differences in the development levels between the two parties.

From the perspective of the EU, there has been confirmation of freedom of access in respect of industrial products – which already exists since the signing of the 1976 Cooperation Agreement – for Moroccan products through the exemption of customs duties and similar taxes.

As for Morocco, immediately following the implementation of the proposed Agreement, the country will no longer apply quantitative restrictions – or any other equivalent measure – to imports from the EU. There are four different lists of products, each of which will follow a specific time-frame for the elimination of the customs and taxes of equivalent effects that apply to the importation of products of EU origin. The products contained in the first list will be liberalized upon entry into force of the Agreement; those in the second list in three years (including the elimination of reference prices that are applied to certain products in this list, notably textiles and clothing products); those in the third list between three to twelve years; and at the expiration of the transition period for products that are in the fourth list.

Agricultural products and derivatives have been subjected to a lesser degree of liberalization. The label "agricultural products" encompasses agricultural goods per se, the products of agricultural industries, and fishing products. The achievement in this sector has been less ambitious than in the case of industrial products, mainly as a result of the EU's CAP. The schedule of concessions is partial and imprecise (indeed, vague), most strikingly in regard to its second phase.

During a first phase, the Agreement will uphold the advantages already extended by the EU within the framework of the previous agreements, but with some minor adjustments and improvements. It includes: limited increases in the volumes that are exempt of customs duties (three percent per year between 1997 and 2000) for certain fruits and vegetables (such as citrus fruits, tomatoes, potatoes, orange juice, flowers); the partial extension to the whole Community market – which has evolved into a single market without internal borders – of those advantages embodied in the France-Morocco Protocol (Protocol 1/7); and exemption from customs duties within the framework of quotas for certain products that would not otherwise benefit from it under the current regime (such as canned and frozen vegetables). On the eve of the second phase (that is, in the year 2000), the reciprocal liberalization of agricultural exchanges will be examined.

Financial, Economic and Technical Cooperation

In the near future, the aid instruments of the new Mediterranean Policy and the current budgetary guidelines of the European Commission are to be maintained.[31] Additional resources are made available in the medium term, particularly within the framework of the MEDA program.[32] A new balance in the policies of the EU – which has tilted excessively in favor of the countries of Central and Eastern Europe – will entail an increase in aid to Mediterranean countries.[33]

Together with financial cooperation, Morocco considers economic and technical cooperation as key elements for the success of the free-trade area. Such cooperation is already quite significant. It will become even more important within the framework of the Agreement, which calls for eighteen different programs of action. They include, inter alia, support for the private sector, support for structural adjustment, and support for socio-economic programs.[34]

Other Tracks

The provision of services by nationals from the countries of one party in the territory of the other is allowed in most sectors. Service providers will be allowed to open branches, subsidiaries, and so forth , as well as to benefit from "national treatment" and to employ their own citizens in the case of key personnel. However, the time frame for the implementation of these measures is not specified.[35]

The Agreement is limited mainly to the implementation of the social clauses embodied in the 1976 Cooperation Agreement, which have never been applied. Above all, they call for non-discriminatory treatment regarding work conditions, remuneration and social protection for Moroccan immigrants residing in the European Union (which hosts 80 percent of all Moroccan citizens living abroad). Further, a social and cultural dialogue – also tied to immigration issues – is expected to take place.

In addition, the Agreement includes systemic clauses which can be found in other free-trade agreements signed by the EU. These relate to norms and standards, protection of intellectual property rights, competition rules, smuggling, and narcotics. Lastly, political dialogue has been institutionalized and reinforced at the executive and legislative levels as well as in civil society.

Such is the current configuration of the future EU-Morocco Agreement. To be sure, obscure points, ambiguities and points of contention remain, but the negotiations currently underway are expected to settle them in due time.

Potential Impact

Some effects of the Agreement will be felt directly and in the near future, while others will take more time to materialize. Still, other effects – namely the dynamic ones, which are the most interesting and most promising for Morocco's future development – will depend not only on the liberalization of commercial exchanges, but also on a host of other factors, such as foreign investment and follow-up policies.

To date, no comprehensive studies have been undertaken in order to assess the ultimate impact of the Agreement. Hence, this section will limit itself to a tentative analysis of the likely effects. The latter are comprised of general effects; those bearing on public finance; and those related to the various sectors of economic activity.

Macroeconomic Effects

The establishment of a free-trade area with the EU is likely to add a great deal of dynamism to the Moroccan economy and raise its growth rate due to a combination of several factors, among which one should note:

• The creation of an atmosphere of confidence in the Moroccan economy, a sort of insurance, the consolidation of the achievements of structural adjustment and liberalization – such as accession to GATT in 1987, which led to the strengthening of the country's trade regime. In other words, it will act as a guarantee for the future of the Moroccan economy as it becomes tied to the largest market in the world.

• The growth of foreign private investment, notably from Europe, which already accounts for the bulk of investment in Morocco. The one and a half million Moroccans living in Europe would participate in this trend, and would thus be encouraged by the birth of a new economic space to help boost business links with Morocco by bringing in their savings and their expertise.

• The promotion of competition in the domestic market and, as a result, the creation of a more competitive economy for exports.

• The encouragement of technical progress, research and training, boosted by the new dynamics and by the strengthening of economic, technical and cultural cooperation within the framework of the new Association Agreement.

In conjunction with these clearly positive effects, other developments are likely to have mixed effects. First, by reducing and later eliminating tariff and non-tariff trade barriers as well as by enhancing competition, the free-trade area will exert downward pressure on domestic prices. That is only true for manufactured goods. For agricultural products, two other factors will act in an opposite direction: the high level of European prices and the reduction of subsidies, notably for exports, caused by the Uruguay Round will likely exert upward pressure on the prices of agricultural products.

The second impact will affect labor. By reinvigorating economic activity, particularly in labor-intensive sectors where Morocco has a comparative advantage, the free-trade agreement may help solve the country's unemployment problem, especially in the case of women, who constitute an economically active group with one of the highest unemployment rates in the economy.[36] By the same token, free trade may increase unemployment in other occupational categories, by creating difficulties in certain branches of economic activity or by leading to the bankruptcy of non-performing companies. The net global impact on Morocco's labor force – much like the regional impact – will depend on the respective intensity of these two opposite effects as well as on restructuring and retraining policies.

Impact on Public Finances

The implementation of a free-trade area will lead to immediate and significant losses in budget revenues. Such losses will increase progressively, reaching more than six percent at the end of the first five-year phase. By the end of the 12-year transitional period, these losses will have reached over two-thirds of customs revenues – that is, more than 13 percent of all budget revenues – and will represent over three percent of Morocco's GDP.[37] Likewise, the eventual increase in the prices of imported agricultural goods may lead to increases in budget expenditures earmarked for consumption subsidies.[38]

These two negative effects could be partially offset, in the medium term, by an increase in domestic fiscal revenues through the acceleration of economic growth. Nevertheless, the net effect will certainly be overwhelmingly negative for quite a long time. Hence, compensation mechanisms must be sought, notably through the sort of financial cooperation called for in the Association Agreement, in order to avoid jeopardizing the hard-won achievements of Morocco's structural adjustment program.[39]

Impact on Industry

Industry is the sector where the impact of the free-trade area will be felt from the very beginning. Also, it is the sector where the potential dynamic effects are the largest. Given the framework of Morocco's structural adjustment program, industry has undergone dramatic changes in the course of the past decade, mostly as a result of reforms in the incentive system and sharp reductions in tariff and non-tariff protection.[40] To be sure, these changes give Moroccan industry an edge in terms of its trading opportunities with Europe. Added to that is Morocco's commitment, within the framework of the Uruguay Round Agreements, to apply a tariff ceiling of 40 percent to manufactured goods.[41]

Table 2: Industrial Sector: Some Indicators of Size and Competitiveness, 1980-91

	1980	1991
Number of Enterprises	2,820	6,019
Value Added (1985 prices)[1]	9,825	22,702
Employment (thousand)	222	423
Value Added per Worker[2]	44	54
Real Wage Level[2]	24.7	20.3
Export/Output	0.13	0.22
Output/Absorption[3]	0.80	0.84
Imports/Absorption	0.30	0.34
Exports/Imports	0.33	0.55

[1] *Millions of 1985 Dirhams;*
[2] *Thousands of 1985 Dirhams:*
[3] *Absorption = Output + Imports - Exports*
Source: *CERAB (1994), pp. 5-7.*

Between 1980 and 1991 the number of industrial enterprises and their value added at constant prices have more than doubled, while employment has grown at a slower pace (Table 2). Thus, the value added per worker has increased. In addition, since real wages have declined, the unit cost of labor has declined even more, but that has not improved Morocco's competitiveness relative to countries with lower wage levels and/or higher productivity.[42]

By the same token, the ratio of exports to domestic production has risen. The same has happened to both the ratio of domestic production to absorption, and the coverage ratio of industrial imports by exports. These trends combined show a more focused orientation towards exports and higher competitiveness. At the same time, however, the domestic market has become more open to foreign goods due to increases in the ratio of imports to absorption.

The impact of the free-trade area on Morocco's industrial sector may be better understood through exports and imports of manufactured products. On the export front, Morocco's industrial goods[43] already benefit from customs exemptions in the European Union, which explains their concentration in this market even before the signing of the free-trade agreement. The distribution of Morocco's exports that are destined to the EU varies from sector to sector, anywhere between 36 percent and 94 percent (Table 3). However, Morocco's industrial goods seldom account for more than one percent of the European market.

Table 3: The Shares of Exports of Moroccan Industries to the EU Market (percentage)

Sector	Export/ Output (1990)	Share of to the EU (1988)	Morocco's Share of EU Market (1990)
Food Industries	1	78	1.2
Other Food Industries	25	38	0.5
Beverages & Tobacco	72	0.9	--
Textiles and Clothing	30	70	1.1
Clothing and Apparel	85	94	1.4
Leather/Leather Shoes	44	71	1.1
Wood/Wood Products	20	62	0.9
Paper/Cardboard	14	60	1.0
Mineral Products	2	36	0.6
Metallic Industries	16	62	1.0
Metal Works	2	46	0.7
Equipment Material	1	42	0.8
Transport Equipment	11	64	0.8
Electrical Equipment	16	78	1.3
Office Equip/Precision Inst.	5	51	0.8
Chemical Products	41	41	0.6
Rubber/Plastic Goods	5	58	0.9
Other Industries	9	73	1.1

Source: Ministry of Industry and Trade and World Bank. Cited in Jaidi (1995), p.151.

Does that mean that the prospects for Moroccan exports will be enhanced by the free-trade agreement? The actual situation is quite the opposite, mostly because of the Uruguay Round Agreements and the ensuing erosion of trade preferences previously enjoyed by Moroccan products. Textiles, which represent 40 percent of Morocco's industrial exports[44] and have a good sales performance in the European market, risk being adversely affected by the dismantling – over a period of ten years – of the Multi-Fiber Agreement and the gradual reduction of European tariff protection. That is what led analysts to estimate that GATT 1994 will spell losses for Morocco, in the order of one percent of its GDP. [45]

Hope is now centered around the export potential that could be mobilized due to increased competition and the actions undertaken by the Euro-Morocco partnership. Because of its potential for trade creation, the latter could compensate for the trade diversionary effects of the Uruguay Round.

As for imports, the freedom of access that European manufactured goods will enjoy in the Moroccan market as a result of the free-trade agreement, albeit gradual, will pose a formidable challenge to Morocco's industry. But the situation varies from sector to sector, as indicated by differences in tariff protection rates and import penetration ratios (Table 4).

The tariff protection rates vary from 24 percent for chemical and parachemical products to 57.5 percent for apparel, rubber and plastic goods. Added to that is the rate of quantitative protection. The fraction of production subject to quantitative restrictions shows a great deal of variance: 5 percent for non-electrical machinery; 12 percent for rubber products; 20 percent for transport materials; 46-47 percent for textiles and clothing; and 84 percent for shoes.[46]

The import penetration ratio also shows variation: 3 percent for clothing; 21 percent for leather and leather shoes; 38 percent for textiles and clothing products; 52 percent for transport materials; 66 percent for equipment material; and 87 percent for other manufacturing industries (Table 4).

The Ministry of Industry and Trade has divided Moroccan industrial sectors into four groups on the basis of their degree of protection and their competitiveness.[47] One could classify them in ascending order of responsiveness to free trade as such:

• Competitive industries enjoying little protection, such as the fertilizer industry and certain agro-industrial products (for instance, wine and canned citrus fruits). Free trade would not pose any problem for these products.

• Competitive industries enjoying a high degree of protection, such as yarns, shoes (both leather and plastic), electrical material, metal works, basic metallurgy, and beverages. In these cases, protection could be reduced with little damage.

- Non-competitive industries enjoying little protection, mostly those sectors that manufacture intermediate goods, such as iron, glass products, textiles for clothing products and fine wheat flour. The effects of free trade would be noticeable yet far from excessive.
- Non-competitive industries enjoying a high degree of protection, such as cheeses, paper and cardboard paper, skins, vehicle frames and assembly, and bolts and screws. Here, protection can hardly be justified. These industries would be the most adversely affected in the event of the creation of a free-trade area.

It is estimated in official circles that roughly 40 percent of Morocco's industries are competitive and export-oriented; about 20 percent have the potential to become competitive and need specific assistance in this regard; and the remaining 40 percent amount to non-competitive industries turned to the domestic market and highly protected. [48]

Table 4: Protection Rates and Import Penetration Ratios of Moroccan Industrial Sectors (percentage)

Sector	Tariff Rate	Penetration Ratio[1]
Food Industries	40.7	4
Other Food Industries	50.6	12
Beverages and Tobacco	49.5	8
Textiles and Clothing	50.0	38
Clothing and Apparel	57.5	3
Leather/Leather Shoes	46.5	21
Wood/Wood Products	na	42
Paper/Cardboard	50.5	17
Mineral Products	25.5	9
Metallic Industries	44.6	53
Metal Works	45.9	18
Equipment Material	44.4	66
Transport Equipment	49.2	52
Electrical Equipment	44.4	43
Office Equip./Precision Inst.	na	84
Chemical Products	24.0	30
Rubber/Plastic Goods	57.5	22
Other Industries	na	87

[1] *Imports/Absorption*
n.a: not available
Source: Ministry of Industry and Trade. Cited in Jaidi (1995), p. 156.

Impact on Agriculture

Agriculture is a much more vulnerable sector than industry. Progress towards free trade in agricultural goods has been very limited so far. Regarding imports, the impact of the free-trade area on agriculture is now only hypothetical. It is on the export front where problems arise.

Indeed, as regards exports, 28 percent of trade revenues are at stake (Table 1). In Morocco, agricultural activities directed towards the export market employ 500,000 people and provide for the livelihood of three million people concentrated in specific regions. The horticultural sector for export – which is under particular threat because of the EU proposal to GATT – employs over 25 percent of agricultural manpower and accounts – fresh and industrialized goods alike – for 80 percent of Morocco's agricultural exports, of which the main market is the EU (78 percent).[49]

On the import front, no significant liberalization is being expected during the first phase of the transitional period. Even though there has been a certain degree of rationalization of agricultural policies throughout the decade of structural adjustment, agriculture was less affected by liberalization than industry in Morocco. Indeed, the liberalization of imports and of prices of basic agricultural goods and their derivatives (such as sugar, cereals, oil seeds and oils) has been called off for the third time in 18 months. It was finally agreed in May 1996.[50] Negotiations on agricultural issues were more difficult owing to the complexity of the sector as well as important ramifications at the economic and social levels. Moreover, the consolidation of Morocco's tariff ceilings for agricultural products within the framework of the Uruguay Round took place at a very high level (289 percent), whereas the maximum tariff was much lower beforehand (45 percent). [51]

Future negotiations with the EU regarding free trade should take into account the degree of sensitivity of agricultural products. The latter could be subdivided into three categories. The first one – agricultural inputs – could be liberalized quite soon. The second category – products other than basic goods – could be the subject of a gradual liberalization of imports, after an initial transition phase. Lastly, the third category and the most vulnerable one – basic foodstuff – could conceivably be liberalized at the last stage, and after a transitional period.

Impact on Services

The establishment of a free-trade area between Morocco and the EU would also have a considerable impact on the development of services in Morocco, particularly tourism, international transport, financial services (banks, insurance companies, stock markets), and so forth. In this regard, it is important to note that Morocco has already proceeded, within its commitments in the Uruguay Round, to liberalize exchanges in a number of services, such as telecommunications, construction and engineering, environmental services, business, banking, insurance companies, tourism, as well as air and sea transport.[52]

Conclusions

Privileged relations between Morocco and the European Union date back to the latter's creation, in its original form, with the signing of the Treaty of Rome. Such relations have evolved and gone through various phases: "association," "cooperation," and in the present a new mode of association whose principal element is the establishment of a free-trade area. Negotiations have always been long and difficult, but they have also invariably been successfully concluded. This is explained by the stakes involved and the expected benefits. Apart from these, the last phases of negotiations are particularly important because of their strategic implications for the EU, for Morocco, and for the region as a whole.

In as far as the EU is concerned, the Agreement with Morocco falls within a strategic framework whose goal is to create a "vast economic space" covering Europe and the Mediterranean through a network of agreements that has the EU as its fulcrum. The Euro-Mediterranean free-trade area is expected to be established by the year 2010. In addition to its agreements with each individual country, the EU has encouraged Mediterranean countries to establish agreements with each other as well.[53]

For Morocco, the free-trade area with the EU is the capstone of a strategic choice – that of consolidating the country's ties with Europe.[54] In this regard, it is worth mentioning that the project revolving around a "medium-term strategic program" stipulated the application of the Agreement with the EU starting in 1996.[55]

For the region as a whole, the proliferation of Euro-Mediterranean association agreements – eight already signed, with four Agreements that were scheduled to be signed in 1995 and four others at a later stage, in addition to the Customs Union Agreement signed with Turkey – heralds the triumph of Europe's strategic vision. Even though the EU has encouraged horizontal cooperation, as exemplified by the South Mediterranean free-trade Agreements, future exchanges are likely to be dominated by vertical integration in view of two factors: the gaps in levels of development and the absence of a regional strategic vision on the part of Middle East and North African (MENA) countries. Indeed, the only limit to Europe's strategic vision would be the existence of another "vision" for the MENA region, one which has begun to surface at the MENA Economic Summits.

Notes

1 Cited in Mellah 1974, pp. 64-65.
2 The only products excluded, with some exceptions, were finished goods. See Hamdouch 1983, p. 198.
3 Cited in Mellah 1974, p. 61.
4 See Oualalou 1980, p. 60, and Mellah 1974, p. 164.
5 All other fruits and vegetables are thus excluded.
6 With the exception of tuna, which is subjected to quota restrictions in France.
7 The Algeciras Act of 1906 instituted the "open door" regime in Morocco. Above all, it stipulated equal treatment for imports coming from the major industrial powers Hamdouch 1983, p. 24.
8 Between the signing of the Association Agreement and that of the Cooperation Agreement, the European Community grew from six to nine members with the accession of Great Britain, Ireland and Denmark in 1973.
9 Greece in 1981, Spain and Portugal in 1986. This is refered to as the "second enlargement."
10 After the accession of Sweden, Finland and Austria in early 1995.
11 Office des Changes 1993, and the Moroccan Bank of Foreign Trade 1995.
12 For the first eleven months in 1994, see European Union 1995b. Total foreign private investments amounted to US$ 590 million in 1993. See Office des Changes 1993.
13 Sasson 1994, p. 55.
14 The situation was resolved by the adoption of a quota of 130,000 tons which was nonetheless clearly insufficient. See European Union 1995a, p. 4.
15 Because of the cancelling of negotiations towards the renewal of the Fishing Agreement between Morocco and the European Union. See *La Vie Economique*, 21 July 1995.
16 Hamdouch 1995.
17 The request was reiterated during the visit of the new French President to Morocco in July 1995.
18 *Le Monde Dossiers et Documents* 1995, p. 2.
19 European Union 1995a, p. 1.
20 European Union 1995b, p. 1 and supplement.
21 Ibid.
22 The Amman Summit in October 1995 and the Barcelona Conference in November 1995.
23 Negotiations were started with Morocco on 14 February 1994, with Israel on 21 February 1994, and with Tunisia on 23 January 1995. See European Union 1995b, supplement, and European Union 1995c, p.3.
24 Ibid.
25 The expression used in 1992 was "Partnership Agreement," but the European Union later changed it. See Alaoui 1994, pp. 79-83.
26 *Le Matin du Sahara*, 17 March 1994, pp. 1-3.
27 Project of negotiation guidelines adopted by the European Commission in December 1992. See Alaoui 1994, p. 83.
28 Ibid.
29 European Union 1995c, p. 1.
30 See *L'Economiste Maghrebin* 1995, No. 132, and Realites 1995, No. 498.
31 Memorandum presented by Morocco to the EU on 14 February 1994. In *Le Matin du Sahara*, 17 March 1994, p. 3.

32 European Union 1992.
33 *L'Economiste Maghrebin* 1995, No. 132, p. 18, and European Union 1995a, supplement 1996 and 1997: almost 5 billion ECUs (1 ECU = US$ 1.2) for the period 1995-1999 which are earmarked to 12 Mediterranean countries (of which 450 million ECUs for Morocco for the period 1996-1998) against 7 billion ECUs that have budgeted for East European countries.
34 European Union 1995d, 1996 and 1997.
35 With the exception of the transport sector. The right of establishment of natural persons and liberal professions was excluded.
36 The rate of female unemployment in Morocco's urban centers is 25 percent, compared to an overall rate of 16 percent for the total urban labor force. See *Direction de la Statistique* 1992.
37 Customs revenues represent nearly 20 percent of budget revenues, of which two-thirds (that is, roughly US$800 million, or 3.3 percent of Morocco's GDP) are accounted for by European product. Over 80 percent of these products are manufactured goods, of which 40 percent will be exempted from customs duties at the start of the first phase of the Agreement. See *Le Matin du Sahara*, 17 March 1994, BMCE 1995, No. 218, and *Direction de la Statistique* 1994.
38 Subsidies for consumption goods have declined considerably in the course of the structural adjustment program. They have gone from 3.2 percent of Morocco's GDP in 1982 to less than 0.7 percent in 1992. However, they have recently increased again, reaching 1.1 percent of GDP in 1994. See Bank Al-Maghrib 1993, 1994.
39 Hamdouch 1990, 1995.
40 Hamdouch 1990. Maximum import duties have decreased from 400 percent to 35 percent, and quantitative restrictions are now only applied to less than ten percent of Morocco's industrial production.
41 Zarrouk 1995, p. 32.
42 In 1991, Indonesia, China and Malaysia had lower salaries and, above all, much higher value added per worker in the sectors of textiles, clothing and shoes. Even countries with higher salaries, such as Tunisia and Turkey, have lower unit labor costs due to a greater differential in productivity. See Diwan 1995, Table 13.
43 With the exception of agro-industrial products, which are treated in conjunction with agricultural goods.
44 Ministry of Industry and Commerce 1994.
45 Fontagne and Peridy 1995, p. 711.
46 *World Bank Report on Industrial Development* 1992, cited in Jaidi 1995, p. 155.
47 Ministry of Industry and Commerce 1993.
48 Jaidi 1995, p. 157 and Ministry of Industry and Trade 1996, p. 33.
49 *Le Matin du Sahara*, 17 March 1994, p. 3. The agricultural sector is very important in Morocco, employing 40 percent of the economically active population and accounting for nearly 20 percent of the country's GDP.
50 *L'Economiste* 1995, No. 187; and 1996, No. 232, and *La Vie Economique* 1995, No. 3824; 1996, No. 3866; and 1996 No. 3898.
51 Zarrouk 1995, p. 32.
52 Ibid., p. 33.
53 European Union 1995a, 1995b, 1995c.
54 Hamdouch 1995.
55 *L'Economiste* 1995, No. 193, 17 August.

References

Alaoui, M. 1994. *La Cooperation entre l'Union Europeenne et les Pays du Maghre*b. Paris: Nathan.

Bank Al-Maghrib. 1993. *Annual Report.*

Bank Al-Maghrib. 1994. *Annual Report.*

Banque Marocaine du Commerce Exterieur (BMCE). 1995. *Bulletin d'Information.* No. 218, May.

CERAB, 1994, *Concurrence Interne et Competitivite Externe de l'Industrie Marocaine.* Summary Report (preliminary version), Rabat.

Direction de la Statistique. 1992. *Population Active Urbaine.*

Direction de la Statistique. 1994. *Annuaire Statistique du Maroc.*

Diwan, I. 1995. "A Human Capital Strategy for Integrating into World Markets." Paper presented at the ERF-sponsored workshop on Strategic Visions for the Middle East and North Africa. Gammarth, Tunisia, 9-11 June.

L'Economiste. 1995. Various issues. Casablanca.

___. 1996. Various issues. Casablanca.

L'Economiste Maghrebin. 1995. Various issues. Tunis.

European Union. 1995a. *Lettre d'Information de la Delegation de la Commission Europeenne au Royaume du Maroc,* No. 124, January.

___. 1995b. Ibid., No. 126, March.

___. 1995c. Ibid., No. 128, May.

___. 1995d. *Maroc/Union Europeenne, Bilan 1979-1995.* Edition No.4, June

___. 1996. Ibid., No. 144.

___. 1997. Ibid., No. 145.

Fontagne, L., and N. Peridy. 1995. "Uruguay Round et les Pays en Voie de Developpement." *Revue Economique,* Vol. 46, No. 3, May.

GERM, 1992. "Libre Echange: Quel Avenir pour les Relations Maroc-CEE?". Paper presented at the Journee d'Etude, 17 April 1992. Casablanca.

Hamdouch, B. 1983. *Specialisation Subie et Sous-Developpement du Maroc: Les Effects du Regime de la "Porte Ouverte" et de la Domination de Zone.* Casablanca: Editions Maghrebines.

___. 1990. *Politiques de Developpement et d'Ajustement au Maroc.* Casablanca: SMER.

___.1995. "Strategic Issues for Morocco." Paper presented at ERF-sponsored worshop on Strategic Visions for the Middle East and North Africa. Gammarth, Tunisia, 9-11 June.

Jaidi, L. 1995. "Le Projet de Zone de Libre Echange entre l'Union Europeenne et le Maroc." *Annales Marocaines d'Economie,* No. 11; Spring.

Mellah, M. F. 1974. *L'Association du Maroc a la Communaute Economique Europeenne: Aspects Politiques.* Casablanca: Editions Maghrebines.

Le Matin du Sahara. Various issues. Casablanca.

Ministry of Industry and Trade. 1993. *Les Incitations et la Protection dans le Secteur Industriel Marocain en 1991.* Rabat.

Ministry of Industry and Trade. 1994. *Situation des Industries de Transformation, Exercice 1993.* Rabat.

Ministry of Industry and Trade. 1996. *Strategie de Developpement Industriel a Moyen Terme 1996-2000.* Rabat.

Le Monde, Dossiers et Documents. 1995. No. 233, June.

Office des Changes, 1993. *Statistiques des Echanges Exterieurs du Maroc.* Rabat.

Oualalou, F. 1980. *Propos d'Economie Marocaine.* Rabat: SMER.

Realites. 1995. Various issues.

Sasson, A. 1994. "Le GATT Agricole et la Problematique des Relations Maroc-Union Europeenne." *Annales Marocaines d'Economie, GATT-Maroc: Enjeux et Implications.*

La Vie Economique. 1995. Various issues. Casablanca.

___. 1996. Various issues. Casablanca.

Zarrouk, J. 1995. "Policy Implications of the Uruguay Round Results for the Arab Countries." Paper presented at the conference on The Uruguay Round and the Arab Countries. Kuwait, January.

Central, East European, Baltic and Turkish Economies: A View to Future Membership in the EU[*]

Introduction

Major changes have affected the future of European Union (EU) during the last six years. Six years ago, the future of the EU seemed set: a gradual deepening towards real and monetary union. The breakdown of communism radically shifted the challenge from deepening to widening. First to come were the countries of the EFTA (Europe Free Trade Association). Their membership applications were a logical step. Since January 1, 1995 these countries have participated in the decision making process of the EU. Added to this list are the potential applicants from the Central European Economies: the Czech Republic, Hungary, Poland and the Slovak Republic. These countries may in fact have a solid claim to EU membership. All of them have signed Association Agreements with EU, but no timetable for accession has been offered. The next group of potential applicants consist of Bulgaria and Romania. These countries, which have also signed Association Agreements with the EU, have some way to go in policy reforms before becoming viable candidates. The third group of countries are the Baltic countries: Estonia, Latvia and Lithuania. In addition, there are countries such as Slovenia which has indicated its desire to accede to the EU, and Belarus, Moldova and Ukraine whose potential membership is highly uncertain. Finally, we have the Mediterranean applicants consisting of Cyprus, Malta and Turkey.

The chapter presents a comparative study of the countries in Central and Eastern Europe (CEE), the Baltics and Turkey, and analyses the implications of an enlarged EU that includes countries in CEE, the Baltic countries and Turkey. The next section compares these economies, particularly in relation to their trade policies and the trade agreements they have concluded with the EU. This is followed by aspects related to Turkey-EU Customs Union Decision (CUD) and the Europe Agreements (EA). The chapter then turns to consideration of the potential for trade creation between the EU, CEE, the Baltics and Turkey. The final section discusses the potential accession of these countries to the EU.

---

* I am grateful to Bernard Hoekman for comments on an earlier draft of this chapter. All errors are of course mine.

The Fundamentals

The economies of the EU, CEE, the Baltics and Turkey are at different stages of development. The EU countries are developed economies. Turkey is a middle income, free market economy with a relatively large public sector. On the other hand, the CEE and the Baltic economies are since 1989 in the process of transition from centrally planned to free market economies, and they face all of the associated difficulties.

Table 1 provides basic data on the economies under consideration. Per capita income is lowest in Romania, followed by Bulgaria, Lithuania, Slovak Republic, Latvia, Turkey, Poland, Czech Republic, Estonia, Hungary and Slovenia. Turkey's per capita income lies between that of Poland and Latvia, and is higher than that of the Slovak Republic, Lithuania, Bulgaria and Romania. This ordering changes if one examines per capita incomes calculated on the basis of purchasing power parity (PPP). The poorest country is again Romania, though now it is followed by Lithuania, Turkey, Bulgaria, Poland, Latvia, Hungary, Slovak Republic, Estonia and Czech Republic. No figures are reported for Slovenia. Thus, in PPP terms, the Czech Republic is the richest, and Turkish per capita income lies between that of Lithuania and Bulgaria.

In 1993, the exports (imports) of CEE-4 countries amounted to $ 41.3 (51.3) billion, those of the CEE-6 countries to $ 50.2 (61.9) billion, and those of Turkey to $ 18.1 (23.3) billion. Examination of the structure of production reveals that in Lithuania, the agricultural sector contributed 23 per cent to the country's 1993 gross domestic product (GDP) The share of agriculture in Turkey's GDP during the same year was 15 percent, 16 percent in Latvia, 13 percent in Bulgaria and 11 percent in Estonia. In all of the remaining countries excluding Greece, the share of agriculture was less than 8 percent. During the period since the implementation of market oriented economic reforms, output in the region has declined sharply. Recently, output has started to stabilize. During 1993, output increased in Poland and Slovenia, and during 1994 it increased in all of the transition economies. In all the countries under consideration, inflation in 1994 did not exceed two digit figures except in Turkey where inflation reached a high of 106 percent. Inflation during 1994 was running at an annual rate of 10 percent in the Czech Republic, 19 percent in Hungary and 32 percent in Poland (IMF, 1995a). By 1995 all countries under investigation were under stand-by agreements with the International Monetary Fund (IMF). Finally, it should be noted that the rate of population growth in all the countries under consideration is relatively low, save in the case of Turkey.

Table 1: Basic Data on CEE, EU and Turkish Economies

	1993 Population (million)	1993 GDP ($ billion)	Area (1000 Km2)	1993 GNP/Pop ($)	PPP Estimate of GNP/Pop (1993, $)	1993 Exports ($ billion)	1993 Imports ($ billion)	Share of Agricultural Value Added In GDP (%)	Average Real GDP Growth Rate 1991-94	Average Inflation Rate 1991-94	Estimated Population Growth Rate 1993-2000
CEE Countries											
Czech Republic	10.3	31.61	79	2,710	7,550	12.93	13.49	5.3	-5.7	25.2	0.1
Hungary	10.2	38.10	93	3,350	6,050	8.89	12.60	7.7	-3.4	24.6	-0.4
Poland	38.3	85.85	313	2,260	5,000	14.00	18.83	7.0	1.4	45.2	0.2
Slovak Republic	5.3	11.08	49	1,950	6,290	5.45	6.35	6.4	-5.9	26.6	0.4
CEE-4	64.1	166.64	534	2,574	5,810	41.26	51.26	6.8	-1.5	35.5	0.1
Bulgaria	8.9	10.37	111	1,140	4,100	4.07	4.24	12.8	-5.0	146.1	-0.5
Romania	22.8	25.97	238	1,140	2,800	4.89	6.40	20.9	-4.2	191.1	-0.1
CEE-6	95.8	202.98	883	2,317	5,337	50.23	61.91	8.9	-2.0	61.0	0.0
Former Yugoslavia											
Slovenia	1.9	10.34	20	6,490	--	6.09	6.50	5.1	3.2	26.1	0.1
Baltic Countries											
Estonia	1.6	5.09	45	3,080	6,502	0.46	0.62	11.1	-7.5	354.1	-0.5
Latvia	2.6	4.60	65	2,010	5,010	0.46	0.34	15.7	-14.8	305.1	-0.8
Lithuania	3.7	4.34	65	1,320	3,110	0.70	0.49	22.6	-23.1	431.9	-0.1
Baltic Countries	7.9	14.03	175	2,185	4,964	1.62	1.44	16.5	-14.7	362.1	-0.4
European Union											
Austria	7.9	182.07	84	23,510	19,430	40.17	48.58	2.7	1.9	--	0.5
Belgium	10.0	210.58	31	21,650	19,640	112.51	125.06	1.8	0.8	2.5	0.3
Denmark	5.2	117.59	43	26,730	19,560	35.91	29.52	3.1	1.8	2.0	0.1
Finland	5.1	74.12	338	19,300	15,530	23.45	18.03	2.4	-2.1	--	0.4
France	57.5	1,251.69	552	22,490	19,000	206.26	202.27	2.6	0.8	2.3	0.4
Germany	80.7	1,910.76	357	23,560	16,850	380.15	348.63	1.0	1.7	3.5	0.2
Greece	10.4	63.24	132	7,390	9,000	7.96	20.54	12.5	1.2	14.3	0.3
Ireland	3.5	42.96	70	13,000	13,490	28.61	21.39	6.6	3.5	2.4	0.3
Italy	57.1	991.39	301	19,840	17,830	168.46	146.79	3.2	0.7	5.3	0.0

Table 1: Continued

	1993 Population (million)	1993 GDP ($ billion)	Area (1000 Km2)	1993 GNP/Pop ($)	PPP Estimate of GNP/Pop (1993,$)	1993 Exports ($billion)	1993 Imports ($billion)	Share of Agricultural Value Added In GDP (%)	Average Real GDP Growth Rate 1991-94	Average Inflation Rate 1991-94	Estimate Population Growth Rate 1993-2000
Luxembourg	0.4	14.78	3	37,320	29,510	--	--	1.2	1.7	3.1	-
Netherlands	15.3	309.23	37	20,950	17,330	139.08	126.56	3.6	1.3	2.7	0.6
Portugal	9.8	85.67	92	9,130	10,710	15.43	24.60	3.5	0.8	8.3	0.0
Spain	39.5	478.58	505	13,590	13,510	62.87	78.63	3.5	0.8	5.7	0.1
Sweden	8.7	166.75	450	24,740	17,200	49.86	42.68	0.6	-0.8	--	0.5
United Kingdom	57.9	819.04	245	18,060	17,210	180.58	206.32	2.0	0.4	4.8	0.3
EU-12	369.0	6,718.43	3,240	19,685	17,276	1,451.30	1,439.59	2.4	1.1	4.1	0.2
Turkey	59.5	132.30	779	2,184	3,920	18.11	23.27	15.4	2.3	77.1	1.8

Source: World Development Report 1995, World Bank; various issues of the "Economist Intelligenc Unit Country Reports" on CEE economies; OECD in Figures, 1994 edition, OECD; various issues of European Economy, and World Economic Outlook, Oct 1995 IMF.
Note: Turkish data on GNP, per capita income, exports and imports refer to the year 1994.

During the last five years, all of the CEE and Baltic countries have made substantial progress in structural reform. In particular, prices in these countries are now largely determined by market forces. Privatization has proceeded rapidly in all of the countries except in the cases of Romania, Bulgaria and Slovenia. The share of the private sector in GDP in the Czech Republic has increased from 3 percent in 1989 to 65 percent in 1994 and from 3 percent in 1989 to 40 percent in 1994 in Bulgaria. By 1994, more than half of GDP was generated in most of the countries by the private sector. In comparison, one should note that the share of state owned enterprises in total value-added in the Turkish economy was 10.6 percent in 1990.[1]

The transition economies still need to achieve macroeconomic stability, reduce economic distortions and free resources for productive activity. The countries will then be on course for a sustainable economic growth. In the meantime, there is much to be done in order to make the economy more responsive to market forces. To this end, the countries have to foster competition. It is recognized that opening up to international trade would be the most effective mean to instill competition in the economy.

Table 2 shows the direction of trade of the countries under investigation during the years 1988 and 1994 and Table 3 presents the commodity composition. The following aspects are worth noting:

- The European Union has emerged to become the single most important trading partner for all of the CEE countries and Turkey during the period 1988-1994.
- Germany is the single most important trading partner within the EU for the CEE countries.
- Trade among the CEE countries has decreased during the period 1988-1994.
- Trade between CEE countries and the former Soviet Union has decreased substantially over the period 1988-1994.
- Textiles and clothing goods are the most important export items of Turkey, CEE and the Baltic countries to the EU.

Table 2: Territorial Composition of Trade of the CEE and Baltic Countries and of Turkey during 1988 and 1994

Partner Group	Bulgaria 1988	Bulgaria 1994	Czech 1988	Czech Rep. 1994	Estonia 1994	Hungary 1988	Hungary 1994	Latvia 1994	Lithuania 1994	Poland 1988	Poland 1994	Romania 1988	Romania 1994	Slovakia 1994	Slovenia 1994	Turkey 1988	Turkey 1994
TOTAL EXPORTS	100.00	100.00	100.00	100.00	100.00	100.00	100.00	100.00	100.00	100.00	100.00	100.00	100.00	100.00	100.00	100.00	100.00
EU-15	19.13	48.36	29.84	59.39	49.23	30.34	60.67	39.33	30.11	35.85	69.21	29.23	48.21	47.84	65.54	45.66	47.69
Germany	5.63	14.03	15.11	34.74	7.56	10.91	28.04	10.52	11.43	12.89	35.67	9.37	16.04	25.07	30.26	18.28	21.73
Austria	0.85	1.90	4.23	7.03	0.14	5.70	9.90	2.12	0.30	3.02	2.20	1.67	1.57	6.71	5.48	1.53	1.38
Finland	0.37	4.74	0.70	2.41	0.61	0.93	3.34	1.42	1.18	1.40	4.00	0.11	5.13	2.33	8.59	0.15	0.17
CEE & Baltic Countries and Slovenia	31.71	5.11	16.80	24.75	13.49	11.70	7.04	10.82	18.14	11.60	5.27	12.80	6.27	43.28	4.89	1.80	4.00
Former Soviet Union	na	10.79	34.20	4.90	29.35	27.70	14.63	36.80	46.67	24.30	8.27	24.40	6.25	3.83	4.63	2.30	7.80
Turkey	0.47	3.67	0.56	0.41	0.19	1.04	0.38	0.10	0.20	0.74	0.20	2.10	4.09	0.30	0.12	--	--
TOTAL IMPORTS	100.00	100.00	100.00	100.00	100.00	100.00	100.00	100.00	100.00	100.00	100.00	100.00	100.00	100.00	100.00	100.00	100.00
EU-15	36.42	45.35	33.30	63.99	63.62	34.67	56.35	40.66	32.21	33.89	65.31	7.08	48.18	43.14	68.42	42.88	46.91
Germany	16.75	14.24	17.70	35.09	9.64	13.90	23.56	13.61	13.75	13.00	27.47	2.50	17.96	21.43	23.55	14.30	15.67
Austria	3.69	2.50	5.30	7.40	0.54	7.20	10.51	0.72	0.62	4.30	2.57	0.80	2.74	6.70	10.27	1.50	0.91
Finland	0.60	3.05	0.54	4.25	1.43	0.81	3.05	1.53	1.78	1.05	4.52	0.04	5.09	2.16	8.17	--	0.61
CEE & Baltic Countries and Slovenia	19.33	5.30	16.80	17.73	5.48	12.30	6.03	12.88	11.66	12.00	4.39	17.60	5.12	33.04	6.79	2.80	3.10
Former Soviet Union	na	24.48	31.40	10.31	21.53	25.10	22.96	30.35	50.29	28.20	9.32	35.40	17.89	12.50	2.24	3.10	7.80
Turkey	0.53	1.80	0.34	0.28	0.03	0.32	0.24	0.16	0.08	0.44	0.43	0.44	2.12	0.08	0.29	--	--

Note: Trade during 1988 between each of the CEE countries and "CEE & Baltic Countries and Slovenia" refers only to trade between those countries and CEE countries.
Source: Direction of Trade Statistics, IMF, 1995.

Table 3: Commodity Composition Of Exports and Imports of CEE

Exports

SITC	COMMODITY	Bulgaria	Czech Republic	Estonia	Hungary	Latvia	Lithuania	Poland	Romania	Slovenia	Slovakia	Turkey
1 0-08+41+42	Food	8.35	2.67	5.67	12.71	1.22	3.76	8.52	3.16	1.64	2.02	17.45
2 1	Beverages and Tobacco	4.51	0.50	0.07	0.58	0.05	0.03	0.09	0.38	0.18	0.02	1.45
3 08+22 + 43	Other Food Items	1.10	0.64	0.78	1.73	0.05	0.63	0.43	0.23	0.13	0.51	0.18
4 2-22-27-28	Agricultural Raw Materials	4.36	4.30	14.18	2.93	16.79	6.22	3.78	1.68	2.07	3.01	2.37
5 27+28	Crude Fertilizers and Metallic Ferrous Ore	3.63	2.65	9.93	1.96	5.57	11.07	1.64	0.97	0.40	1.80	2.06
6 3	Energy	1.64	2.86	13.30	1.10	43.51	35.09	7.81	2.99	0.00	0.39	2.16
7 67+68	Iron and Steel and Non-Ferrous Metals	19.63	8.21	8.72	6.65	9.25	4.96	12.07	14.26	6.65	15.88	2.46
8 65+84	Textiles and Clothing	18.24	11.40	12.74	15.47	8.61	14.50	17.87	33.46	17.97	17.91	49.83
9 61+83+85	Hides and Leather	6.24	2.97	2.59	4.47	1.42	2.46	1.99	9.53	3.55	3.96	0.59
10 63+82	Wood Manufactures and Furniture	1.88	5.23	9.15	3.19	5.47	3.34	10.22	10.89	9.36	4.66	0.58
11 64	Paper	0.32	1.59	0.16	0.72	0.10	0.27	1.26	0.32	3.40	3.90	0.34
12 66	Non-Metallic Mineral Manufactures	1.90	5.95	2.64	1.79	0.44	0.63	3.46	2.88	2.24	5.63	2.44
13 5+62	Chemicals and Rubber Products	11.69	9.54	11.56	8.93	3.37	10.66	5.65	5.81	6.04	10.52	4.14
14 69	Metal Products	1.54	6.23	1.34	3.30	0.31	1.02	4.56	1.7	4.84	3.92	1.20
15 7	Machinery and Transportation Equipment	12.06	25.62	1.95	28.79	1.62	3.58	16.58	8.63	33.81	20.98	9.90
16 81+86+89+9	Miscellaneous Manufactured Articles	2.89	9.64	5.22	5.60	2.21	1.79	4.07	3.09	7.71	4.90	2.83
	First Three Sectors with Highest Shares	7, 8, 15	15, 8, 16	4, 6, 8	15, 8, 1	6, 4, 7	6, 8, 5	8, 15, 7	8, 7, 10	15, 8, 10	15, 8, 7	8, 1, 15

Table 3: Continued

Imports		Bulgaria	Czech Republic	Estonia	Hungary	Latvia	Lithuania	Poland	Romania	Slovenia	Slovakia	Turkey
SITC	COMMODITY											
1 0-08+41+42	Food	9.52	5.16	21.46	5.12	14.43	10.26	7.45	5.06	5.23	5.05	1.55
2 1	Beverages and Tobacco	3.47	0.78	5.07	0.49	10.74	11.5	0.51	0.74	1.30	0.63	0.57
3 08+22+43	Other Food Items	0.36	0.87	0.74	0.79	0.39	0.67	1.44	0.64	0.26	1.10	0.19
4 2-22-27-28	Agricultural Raw Materials	2.69	1.38	1.10	1.76	1.03	1.37	1.89	1.28	2.38	1.82	2.63
5 27+28	Crude Fertilizers and Metallic Ferrous Ore	0.39	0.43	8.08	0.22	0.03	0.03	0.38	0.67	0.98	0.22	4.66
6 3	Energy	3.39	0.82	1.44	0.58	2.01	0.49	1.84	2.52	2.02	0.48	1.70
7 67+68	Iron and Steel and Non-Ferrous Metals	2.00	3.85	1.03	2.78	0.69	1.23	2.69	1.60	4.88	4.61	5.27
8 65+84	Textiles and Clothing	10.75	6.99	6.38	10.75	8.77	9.60	12.92	21.35	12.29	9.87	5.26
9 61+83+85	Hides and Leather	3.13	1.76	1.94	3.58	2.47	1.45	1.28	6.28	2.71	2.69	1.27
10 63+82	Wood Manufactures and Furniture	1.63	1.78	1.27	1.89	2.07	1.87	1.00	1.06	2.01	1.75	0.63
11 64	Paper	1.80	1.49	0.86	1.90	1.10	0.89	2.27	1.10	1.80	1.10	1.26
12 66	Non-Metallic Minera Manufactures	1.56	2.07	1.28	1.96	1.46	1.06	1.95	1.22	1.80	1.82	1.22
13 5+62	Chemicals and Rubber Products	16.39	12.06	9.91	13.43	7.87	10.39	15.24	9.04	11.33	12.19	15.82
14 69	Metal Products	1.86	4.19	1.90	3.40	1.60	1.60	3.09	2.31	3.06	2.92	1.88
15 7	Machinery and Transportation Equipment	32.49	44.21	34.33	41.30	34.54	36.48	34.85	35.94	39.60	44.35	44.29
16 81+86+89+9	Miscellaneous Manufactured Articles	8.59	12.15	11.12	10.06	10.72	11.09	11.10	9.08	8.33	9.33	11.80
	First three sectors with highest shares	15, 13, 8	15, 16, 13	15, 1, 16	15, 13, 8	15, 1, 2	15, 2, 16	15,13,8	15, 8, 16	15, 8, 13	15, 13, 8	15, 13, 16

Source: Author's Calculations.

Table 4 shows the coefficient of similarity between the exports and imports of Turkey with those of the countries in transition. The index of similarity is calculated by comparing the export vector x with the import vector m using the formula for the cosine between two vectors:

$$\alpha = \frac{\Sigma x_i^j m_i^j}{\sqrt{\Sigma x_i^2 m_i^2}}$$

where X_i^j denotes country j's export of commodity i, X^j refers to total exports of country j, M_i^j j-th country's import of commodity i, M^j total imports of country j, $x_i^j = (X_i^j /X^j)$ is the share of commodity i in country j's total exports, $m_i^j = (M_i^j /M^j)$ share of commodity i in country j's total imports, $x_i^j = (x^j, .., x_n^j)$ country j's export share vector, and $m^j = (m_1^j, ..,m_n^j)$ country j's import share vector.

The coefficient of similarity varies between zero and one and has a straightforward interpretation. It is equal to one if the two (export and import) vectors are exactly the same. Conversely, the coefficient will equal zero in which case the two vectors are orthogonal if for each commodity exported the corresponding import of the same commodity equals zero, and for each commodity imported the export of commodity equals zero. Examination of the coefficient of similarity in the trading relationship between Turkey and the EU shows that:

- Turkish exports to the EU are similar to those of Romania, Poland, Bulgaria and Hungary to EU. The similarity between Turkish exports to the EU on the one hand, and the exports of the Baltic countries to the EU on the other hand is relatively low.
- Turkish exports to the EU are not similar to the imports of CEE countries from EU.
- Turkish imports from the EU are similar to the exports of Czech Republic to the EU. The similarity between Turkish imports from the EU and the exports of Latvia, Romania and Lithuania is relatively low.
- Turkish imports from the EU are similar to the imports of CEE and Baltic countries imports from the EU.

To analyze the sectors where countries have a comparative advantage, we calculate the index of revealed comparative advantage (RCA) which is given by:

$$RCA_i = \ln(\frac{(X_i / X)}{(X_i^{eu} / X^{eu})})$$

where X_i denotes export of commodity i by the country considered, X its total exports, X_i^{eu} refers to the total exports of commodity i to the EU from all

Table 4: Indexes of Similarity for Turkish Exports to and Turkish Imports from European Union with CEEC's Trade with European Union

	Turkish Exports	Turkish Imports
Bulgaria		
Exports	0.6896	0.3757
Imports	0.3768	0.7884
Czech Rep.		
Exports	0.4808	0.7157
Imports	0.2831	0.8769
Estonia		
Exports	0.3668	0.3247
Imports	0.2288	0.7143
Hungary		
Exports	0.6814	0.5442
Imports	0.3341	0.8595
Latvia		
Exports	0.1879	0.1768
Imports	0.3391	0.6542
Lithuania		
Exports	0.3512	0.2308
Imports	0.3096	0.7464
Poland		
Exports	0.7221	0.4004
Imports	0.3353	0.8442
Romania		
Exports	0.8221	0.2164
Imports	0.4073	0.7588
Slovakia		
Exports	0.5981	0.5728
Imports	0.2886	0.8923
Slovenia		
Exports	0.5993	0.5909
Imports	0.3178	0.7874

Level of Aggregation: 2-digit SITC
Source: Author's calculation.

sources excluding the exports of commodity i of the country under consideration; X^{eu} refers to the total exports to the EU from all sources excluding the total exports of the country under consideration. If this ratio is greater than one, then the country is said to have a comparative advantage in the production of that product relative to the rest of the world. Alternatively, if the RCA is less than unity, then the country is said to have a comparative disadvantage in the production of the said commodity vis-à-vis the rest of the world.

Table 5a shows the thirteen 2-digit SITC commodity groups (see the Appendix for a description of the 2-digit SITC groupings) with the highest RCA values in 1994. The table reveals the following aspects:

- the Czech Republic has a comparative advantage in the production of "sanitary, plumbing and heating" (SITC 81) materials, "coal" (SITC 32) and "cork and wood" (SITC 24).
- Hungary has a comparative advantage in the production of "live animals chiefly for food" (SITC 00), "meat and meat preparations" (SITC 01) and "footwear" (SITC 85).
- Poland has a comparative advantage in "coal" (SITC 32), "furniture" (SITC 82) and "cork and wood manufactures" (SITC 63).
- Bulgaria has a comparative advantage in "manufactured fertilizers" (SITC 56), "non-ferrous metals" (SITC 68) and "footwear" (SITC 85).
- Romania has a comparative advantage in "footwear" (SITC 85),"furniture" (SITC 82) and "clothing" (SITC 84).
- Turkey has a comparative advantage in "clothing" (SITC 84), "vegetables and fruit" (SITC 5) and "textiles" (SITC 65).
- Comparison of the sectors where the CEE countries enjoy a comparative advantage with those where Turkey has a comparative advantage reveals that both the Czech Republic and Turkey enjoy a comparative advantage in the production of the commodities "sanitary, plumbing and heating" (SITC 81), "non-metallic mineral manufactures" (SITC 66) and "manufactured fertilizers" (SITC 56); that Hungary and Turkey have a comparative advantage in "clothing" (SITC 84) and "sanitary, plumbing and heating" (SITC 81); that Poland and Turkey have a comparative advantage in "manufactured fertilizers" (SITC 56), "clothing" (SITC 84) and "crude fertilizers" (SITC 27); that Bulgaria and Turkey have a comparative advantage in "manufactured fertilizers" (SITC 56), "travel goods" (SITC 83), and "inorganic chemicals"; and that Romania and Turkey have a comparative advantage in the production of "clothing" (SITC 84), "manufactured fertilizers" (SITC 56), and "non-metallic mineral manufactures" (SITC 66).

Table 5a: Thirteen SITC Divisions with Highest RCA Values Computed for Trade with EU During 1994

Rank	Bulgaria		Czech Republic		Estonia		Hungary		Latvia		Lithuania		Poland		Romania		Slovakia		Slovenia		Turkey	
1	56	2.215	81	1.285	56	2.910	0	1.715	24	2.906	56	3.183	32	2.440	85	2.235	56	1.737	63	1.883	84	2.224
2	68	1.731	32	1.173	24	2.650	1	1.439	21	2.109	28	2.319	82	1.800	82	2.205	67	1.564	82	1.588	5	1.897
3	85	1.515	24	1.138	21	2.507	85	1.325	33	1.889	21	2.085	63	1.773	84	2.031	85	1.093	61	1.364	65	1.312
4	83	1.486	82	1.123	28	2.259	22	1.296	63	1.854	61	1.755	0	1.746	67	1.157	82	1.048	84	1.185	27	1.264
5	35	1.412	63	1.118	32	2.251	84	1.161	28	1.655	24	1.693	56	1.373	0	1.087	0	1.030	81	1.070	12	1.109
6	11	1.394	69	0.974	63	2.120	71	1.001	26	1.006	33	1.654	84	1.338	56	1.042	84	1.027	62	0.904	26	0.838
7	52	1.314	66	0.948	52	1.844	81	0.899	61	0.734	63	1.129	68	1.314	68	0.925	61	0.941	85	0.787	81	0.516
8	23	1.307	56	0.892	82	1.316	77	0.718	67	0.693	84	0.975	24	1.120	21	0.718	24	0.927	69	0.722	62	0.480
9	0	1.250	67	0.877	3	1.122	82	0.712	68	0.544	32	0.922	27	0.802	63	0.417	63	0.921	52	0.670	29	0.420
10	84	1.243	85	0.781	25	0.895	29	0.693	32	0.476	59	0.824	61	0.686	61	0.343	66	0.892	77	0.611	52	0.324
11	12	1.125	0	0.734	81	0.837	41	0.689	82	0.377	68	0.418	69	0.663	66	0.224	81	0.847	68	0.602	56	0.098
12	28	1.102	83	0.674	68	0.811	28	0.596	84	0.342	82	0.288	3	0.437	81	0.194	62	0.846	24	0.544	66	0.058
13	67	1.030	28	0.672	65	0.789	21	0.525	52	0.113	27	0.266	67	0.432	51	0.117	65	0.709	21	0.494	83	0.030
Turkish Comparative Advantage	56,83,52, 84,12		81,66,56, 83		56,52,81, 65		84,81,29		26,84,52		56,84,27		56,84,27		84,56,66, 81		56,84,66, 81,62,65		84,81,62, 52		--	

Source: Author's calculations using 2-digit SITC trade data from Eurostat.

Table 5b identifies the "winning" sectors in each of the countries under consideration. These winning sectors have been identified as those that have experienced the largest growth rates in any one country's exports during the period 1988-1994. From the table it follows that the winning sectors for Turkey are "coal" (SITC 32) and "paper" (SITC 64), for Hungary "power generating machinery" (SITC 71) and "office machines" (SITC 75), and for Bulgaria "non-ferrous metals" (SITC 68) and "other transport equipment" (SITC 79).

Table 6 shows the trade relations between CEE and Baltic countries on the one hand and Turkey on the other over the period 1985-1994. The table reveals that the exports of Turkey to the CEE and Baltic countries have increased from $ 107 million in 1985 to $ 723 million in 1994; even with this phenomenal increase of close to seven-fold, the trading relations between these countries and Turkey remain limited: in 1994 only 4 percent of Turkey's total exports found their way to the markets of the CEE and Baltic countries. Similarly, only 3 percent of Turkey's total import bill in 1994 were accounted for by exports from the CEE countries.

Table 7 gives the commodity composition of trade between CEE countries and Turkey during 1994. The table reveals that:

- The main export items from Turkey to Poland are "textiles and clothing", "hides and leather" and "chemicals and rubber products". These commodities account for 92 percent of all exports to Poland. On the otherhand, Turkey's main import items that originated from Poland were "machinery and transport equipment", "energy" and "textiles and clothing". These commodities account for 70 percent of all imports from Poland.

- The main export items from Turkey to Romania are "food", "machinery and transport equipment" and "chemicals and rubber products". These commodities accounted for 75 percent of Turkey's total exports to Romania. On the other hand, the main items that Turkey imported from Bulgaria in 1994 were "chemicals and rubber products", "energy" and "food". These commodities accounted for 38 percent of all imports from Romania.

- The main export items from Turkey to the Czech Republic in 1994 were "textiles and clothing", "food" and "hides and leather". These commodities accounted for 69 percent of total Turkish exports to the Czech Republic. On the other hand, Turkey's main import items from the Czech Republic were "machinery and transport equipment", "chemicals and rubber products" and "iron and steel and non-ferrous metals". These three commodities accounted for 86 percent of all imports from the Czech Republic.

Table 5b: Thirteen SITC Divisions with Highest Export Shares in 1994 to Export Shares in 1989 for Trade with EU

Rank	Bulgaria		Czech Republic		Hungary		Poland		Romania		Slovakia		Turkey	
1	68	8.896	96	16.656	71	5.808	61	7.091	21	777.746	79	17.544	32	21.796
2	79	7.616	75	9.601	75	5.533	9	5.730	32	766.878	61	9.087	64	13.782
3	9	7.432	77	5.367	43	4.912	63	2.649	25	124.935	56	7.584	79	6.254
4	85	5.954	61	4.850	78	3.741	81	2.439	8	109.572	68	6.757	42	5.981
5	61	5.624	79	4.363	25	3.536	89	2.224	43	34.989	42	4.271	25	5.517
6	42	4.911	68	4.061	81	3.354	55	2.222	79	19.283	77	3.805	59	4.354
7	88	3.727	69	3.873	76	2.691	82	2.215	61	6.681	76	2.697	77	3.744
8	52	3.348	81	3.531	77	2.401	54	2.053	85	6.392	84	2.552	22	2.967
9	43	2.643	56	3.258	88	2.275	56	1.851	42	5.360	69	2.436	24	2.543
10	81	2.447	8	2.914	21	2.236	84	1.810	0	5.007	81	2.279	81	2.374
11	71	2.379	87	2.535	91	1.699	66	1.797	93	4.954	64	2.082	54	2.304
12	53	2.358	42	2.439	64	1.626	26	1.761	28	4.671	8	2.021	82	2.001
13	84	2.017	88	2.292	69	1.540	78	1.701	27	4.390	85	1.927	62	1.979
Turkish Comparative Advantage	79, 42, 81		77, 79, 42		81, 77, 64		81, 82, 54		25, 79, 42		79, 42, 77 81, 64			

Source: Author's calculations using 2-digit SITC trade data from Eurostat.

Table 6: Trade Between Turkey and CEE and Baltic Countries During 1985-1994 (Million US $)

EXPORTS

	Bulgaria	Czech	Czech Rep.	Slovakia	Estonia	Hungary	Latvia	Lithuania	Poland	Romania	Slovenia	Total CEE and Baltic Trade	Total Turkish Exports	Share of Exports to CEE and Baltic Countries in Turkish Exports
1985	7.7	14.4	--	--	--	3.7	--	--	34.4	47.0	--	107.2	7958	1.3
1986	14.9	23.9	--	--	--	12.5	--	--	41.0	39.9	--	132.2	7457	1.8
1987	14.5	27.1	--	--	--	18.1	--	--	25.7	48.7	--	134.1	10,190	1.3
1988	28.1	35.3	--	--	--	24.8	--	--	77.6	76.0	--	241.8	11,662	2.1
1989	26.7	39.2	--	--	--	24.5	--	--	71.4	52.8	--	214.6	11,625	1.8
1990	10.4	64.4	--	--	--	30.6	--	--	103.4	83.2	--	292.0	12,959	2.3
1991	76.1	64.1	--	--	--	34.6	--	--	141.3	109.4	--	425.5	13,593	3.1
1992	72.2	52.3	--	--	--	27.0	--	--	186.3	173.1	--	510.9	14,715	3.5
1993	86.2	--	58.4	15.7	0.3	37.5	2.9	4.0	234.8	151.7	30.2	621.7	15,345	4.1
1994	133.7	--	62.2	12.8	0.8	58.3	2.1	8.3	249.5	175.3	19.9	723.0	18,106	4.0

IMPORTS

	Bulgaria	Czech	Czech Rep.	Slovakia	Estonia	Hungary	Latvia	Lithuania	Poland	Romania	Slovenia	Total CEE and Baltic Trade	Total Turkish Imports	Share of Imports to CEE and Baltic Countries in Turkish Imports
1985	98.7	39.0	--	--	--	53.6	--	--	49.3	63.6	--	304.2	11,343	2.7
1986	41.2	67.3	--	--	--	38.2	--	--	127.9	109.6	--	384.2	11,105	3.5
1987	9.4	45.9	--	--	--	70.6	--	--	62.5	229.4	--	417.8	14,158	3.0
1988	15.7	27.8	--	--	--	92.9	--	--	78.6	197.9	--	412.9	14,335	2.9
1989	3.3	72.1	--	--	--	87.2	--	--	98.1	238.5	--	499.2	15,792	3.2
1990	31.9	143.4	--	--	--	110.4	--	--	210.3	202.5	--	698.5	22,302	3.1
1991	139.9	155.4	--	--	--	133.6	--	--	150.6	198.6	--	778.1	21,047	3.7
1992	224.5	183.7	--	--	--	97.1	--	--	86.6	256.1	--	848.0	22,870	3.7
1993	243.2	--	223.0	21.9	3.4	86.7	2.7	13.8	91.1	300.8	45.9	1,032.6	29,429	3.5
1994	195.5	--	94.7	26.4	1.9	55.5	4.4	7.7	69.1	228.9	31.6	715.7	23,270	3.1

Source: Foreign Trade Statistics, State Institute of Statistics, Ankara.

Table 7: Commodity Composition of Turkish Exports to and Imports from CEE and Baltic Countries during 1994

			EXPORTS								
SITC	COMMODITY	Bulgaria	Czech Republic	Estonia	Hungary	Latvia	Lithuania	Poland	Romania	Slovakia	Slovenia
1	0-08+41+42	Food	29.96	13.49	19.23	9.02	13.97	41.38	2.36	43.36	22.05	20.57
2	1	Beverages and Tobacco	0.26	3.55	0.00	4.96	0.00	0.41	1.20	0.05	1.79	0.00
3	08+22+43	Other Food Items	1.56	0.12	0.00	0.05	0.00	0.71	0.08	1.53	0.00	0.00
4	2-22-27-28	Agricultural Raw Materials	1.14	0.70	0.00	0.24	0.00	0.02	0.37	0.08	0.00	2.65
5	27+28	Crude Fertilizers and Metallic Ferrous Ore	2.66	0.02	0.00	0.28	0.00	0.01	0.40	2.61	0.03	17.09
6	3	Energy	0.11	1.29	0.00	0.00	0.01	0.00	0.00	0.07	0.00	0.00
7	67+68	Iron and Steel and Non-Ferrous Metals	2.18	0.05	0.00	1.06	1.33	0.94	0.01	0.43	16.48	0.00
8	65+84	Textiles and Clothing	8.86	57.96	67.07	47.92	50.33	18.75	80.99	11.20	22.34	38.43
9	61+83+85	Hides and Leather	8.54	9.29	1.63	7.81	3.54	1.81	5.54	0.79	10.66	0.59
10	63+82	Wood Manufactures and Furniture	1.75	0.10	0.00	0.03	2.32	1.04	0.00	0.32	0.06	0.30
11	64	Paper	2.39	0.04	0.00	1.26	0.49	2.26	0.07	1.96	0.09	0.01
12	66	Non-Metallic Mineral Manufactures	5.51	0.28	0.83	1.07	5.71	1.16	0.28	1.11	0.34	0.01
13	5+62	Chemicals and Rubber Products	15.82	4.65	4.15	7.50	4.88	8.83	5.31	13.95	16.23	3.57
14	69	Metal Products	1.77	0.84	0.00	0.29	5.25	3.04	0.35	0.71	0.15	8.40
15	7	Machinery and Transportation Equipment	12.10	2.93	7.09	15.55	9.18	16.97	2.04	17.71	6.95	6.44
16	81+86+89+9	Miscellaneous Manufactured Articles	5.38	4.69	0.00	2.94	3.02	2.68	1.01	4.12	2.82	1.92
		First three sectors with highest shares	1, 13, 15	8, 1, 9	8, 1, 15	8, 15, 1	8, 1, 15	1, 8, 15	8, 9, 13	1, 15, 13	8, 1, 7	8, 1, 5

Table 7: Continued

SITC	COMMODITY		IMPORTS									
		Bulgaria	Czech Republic	Estonia	Hungary	Latvia	Lithuania	Poland	Romania	Slovakia	Slovenia
1 0-08+41+42	Food	3.15	3.65	17.22	16.71	0.00	11.37	1.66	17.48	3.97	9.91
2 1	Beverages and Tobacco	0.00	0.00	0.00	0.01	0.00	0.00	0.00	0.00	0.00	0.00
3 08+22+43	Other Food Items	5.33	0.00	0.00	0.33	0.00	0.00	0.01	0.04	0.00	0.02
4 2-22-27-28	Agricultural Raw Materials	9.44	2.93	81.78	2.42	54.77	33.67	5.88	6.22	0.57	0.17
5 27+28	Crude Fertilizers and Metallic Ferrous Ore	0.50	0.02	0.00	0.03	0.00	0.00	9.5	0.40	0.00	0.00
6 3	Energy	14.74	0.00	0.43	0.05	0.00	0.58	19.61	20.03	0.00	0.00
7 67+68	Iron and Steel and Non-Ferrous Metals	34.48	5.99	0.00	7.52	41.65	0.00	1.43	13.99	34.43	20.64
8 65+84	Textiles and Clothing	3.44	2.96	0.00	1.66	0.00	5.59	14.53	5.16	28.73	24.96
9 61+83+85	Hides and Leather	0.38	0.00	0.00	0.36	0.00	0.00	0.03	0.19	0.13	1.82
10 63+82	Wood Manufactures and Furniture	0.22	0.02	0.00	0.14	0.00	0.00	0.00	0.22	0.04	0.16
11 64	Paper	0.26	0.66	0.00	3.88	2.97	0.00	2.26	0.20	1.76	1.36
12 66	Non-Metallic Mineral Manufactures	1.37	2.14	0.00	1.09	0.00	2.10	1.57	2.69	0.87	0.07
13 5+62	Chemicals and Rubber Products	22.24	6.81	0.00	19.76	0.00	0.00	6.64	28.79	7.68	4.75
14 69	Metal Products	0.28	0.50	0.00	2.89	0.00	0.00	0.58	0.51	0.06	1.17
15 7	Machinery and Transportation Equipment	2.78	68.65	0.00	41.31	0.61	43.32	35.57	3.69	21.64	30.92
16 81+86+89+9	Miscellaneous Manufactured Articles	1.37	5.66	0.57	1.83	0.00	3.37	0.67	0.41	0.14	4.04
	First three sectors with highest shares	7, 13, 6	15, 13, 7	4, 1, 16	15, 13, 1	4, 7, 11	15, 4, 1	15, 6, 8	13, 6, 1	7, 8, 15	15, 8, 7

Source: Author's calculations using 2-digit SITC trade data from State Institute of Statistics, Ankara.

Turkey-EU Customs Union Decision and the Europe Agreements

The Turkey-EU Customs Union Decision (CUD) and the EA represent major contributions to the integration process of CEE and Turkish economies within Europe. The implications of these Agreements are far reaching, going beyond trade-related aspects to include such aspects as the progressive adaptation of the legal framework in the CEE and Baltic countries and Turkey to EU legislation.

Turkey-EU Customs Union

Turkey's application to join the European Economic Community (EEC) was made on July 31, 1959. Following difficult and protracted negotiations, the application ultimately resulted in the signing in Ankara on September 12, 1963 of the Association Treaty. The stated objective of the Agreement is to promote the continuous and balanced strengthening of trade and economic relations between the parties, while taking full account of the need to ensure accelerated development of the Turkish economy and the need to improve the level of employment and living conditions of the Turkish people. According to the Ankara Treaty, the association was to be implemented in three phases: a preparatory phase, a transition phase and a final phase.

During the preparatory period, the EEC granted unilateral concessions to Turkey in the form of financial assistance and preferential tariffs against Turkey's traditional exports. In the meantime, Turkey did not have to alter its trade regime. On May 16, 1967, Turkey lodged in Brussels its application for negotiations to enter the transition phase. The Additional Protocol to the Ankara Treaty was signed on November 23, 1970, and became effective on January 1, 1973. The basic aim of the Additional Protocol was the eventual establishment of a customs union which was eventually concluded on March 6, 1995. Henceforth, the final phase of the association process became effective following ratification by the European Parliament on January 1, 1996.

As of January 1, 1996, goods started to circulate freely between the territories of the parties. In addition, Turkey has adopted of January 1, 1996 the Community's common external tariff (CET) on goods from third parties and it will embrace by the year 2001 all of the preferential trade agreements the EU has concluded over time.

Table 8 provides estimates of the nominal protection rates for the years 1994 and 2001, by which time all the adjustments required by the CUD have been completed. The economy-wide nominal protection rate (NPR) against imports from the EU was 10 percent in 1994 when weighted by the sectoral import values, against 22 percent against imports from third countries. Detailed examination of the structure of protection against goods originating from the EU during 1994 reveals that the highest Turkish NPRs were in the sectors of "fruits and vegetables" (72 percent), "alcoholic beverages" (72 percent) and "non-alcoholic beverages" (57 percent). In the case of trade with third countries we note that during 1994 the highest NPRs were in the sectors "processed tobacco" (100 percent), "alcoholic beverages" (94 percent) and "fruits and vegetables" (73 percent).

Table 8: Turkish Nominal Protection Rates before and after the Customs Union with EU

I-O CODE	SECTOR	NPR with EU in 1994	NPR with EU After Customs Union	NPR with Third Countries in 1994	Average MFN Tariff Rates after Customs Union	Average Tariff Rates for GSP Beneficiaries after Customs Union
1	Agriculture	41.27	41.26	41.65	41.26	41.26
2	Animal Husbandry	3.48	1.37	4.18	1.37	1.37
3	Forestry	0.01	0.01	0.01	0.01	0.01
4	Fishery	47.92	47.84	54.08	47.84	47.84
5	Coal Mining	3.33	0.00	3.33	4.00	0.00
6	Crude Petroleum	0.00	0.00	0.00	0.00	0.00
7	Iron Ore Mining	0.00	0.00	2.22	0.00	0.00
8	Other Metallic Ore Mining	0.13	0.00	1.21	0.00	0.00
9	Non-Metallic Mining	9.09	0.00	11.02	0.95	0.95
10	Stone Quarrying	1.95	0.00	2.18	0.02	0.00
11	Slaughtering and Meat	10.21	10.21	10.21	10.21	10.21
12	Fruits and Vegetables	72.49	68.01	72.62	68.01	68.01
13	Vegetable and Animal Oil	16.31	16.31	16.38	16.29	16.29
14	Grain Mill Products	41.33	41.02	41.33	41.02	41.02
15	Sugar Refining	28.79	28.79	28.79	28.79	28.79
16	Other Food Processing	26.47	18.31	28.99	18.31	18.31
17	Alcoholic Beverages	72.10	5.25	94.28	11.28	7.35
18	Non-Alcholic Beverages	56.92	0.00	69.81	14.83	0.00
19	Processed Tobacco	44.40	0.00	99.91	9.40	0.00
20	Ginning	0.00	0.00	2.22	0.72	0.72
21	Textiles	21.19	0.00	27.10	17.30	7.60
22	Clothing	14.75	0.00	20.65	19.90	9.30
23	Leather and Fur Production	7.85	0.00	12.57	10.20	2.80
24	Footwear	24.40	0.00	35.70	22.50	9.10
25	Wood Products	15.25	0.00	18.97	2.00	0.05
26	Wood Furniture	26.22	0.00	32.64	5.50	0.00
27	Paper and Paper Products	13.59	0.00	17.58	2.70	0.00
28	Printing and Publishing	8.23	0.00	10.79	4.52	0.00
29	Fertilizers	8.22	0.00	16.38	8.10	0.00
30	Pharmaceutical Production	3.33	0.00	8.99	5.30	0.00
31	Other Chemical Production	10.79	0.00	17.62	8.71	0.04
32	Petroleum Refining	22.54	0.00	24.35	2.70	0.00
33	Petroleum and Coal Products	5.62	0.00	7.52	2.15	0.00

Table 8: Continued

I-O CODE	SECTOR	NPR with EU in 1994	NPR with EU After Customs Union	NPR with Third Countries in 1994	Average MFN Tariff Rates after Customs Union	Average Tariff Rates for GSP Beneficiaries after Customs Union
34	Rubber Products	19.57	0.00	23.91	5.60	0.03
35	Plastic Products	24.61	0.00	31.68	9.90	0.00
36	Glass and Glass Production	16.85	0.00	21.94	5.76	0.00
37	Cement	30.45	0.00	32.88	3.14	0.00
38	Non-Metallic Mineral	18.33	0.00	23.21	5.47	0.00
39	Iron and Steel	8.00	0.00	10.70	5.50	3.30
40	Non-Ferrous Metals	4.52	0.00	8.43	3.20	0.50
41	Fabricated Metal Products	18.36	0.00	25.29	6.00	0.11
42	Non-Electrical Machinery	7.36	0.00	12.50	4.40	0.00
43	Agricultural Machinery	6.98	0.00	12.18	3.50	0.00
44	Electrical Machinery	9.69	0.00	16.64	8.30	0.00
45	Shipbuilding and Repairing	6.13	0.00	12.89	0.50	0.00
46	Railroad Equipment	0.00	0.00	4.61	4.04	0.00
47	Motor Vehicles	27.33	0.00	33.10	9.40	0.00
48	Other Transport Equipment	0.01	0.00	1.76	1.60	0.00
49	Other Manufacturing Industries	2.92	0.00	8.19	2.95	0.00
MEAN		10.22	1.34	22.14	6.92	2.71
STANDARD DEVIATION		17.68	14.48	15.36	13.79	14.51

Source: Author's calculations.
Own calculations for all sectors in columns 1, 2 and 3.
NPRs for sectors 21, 22, 23, 24, 39 and 40 in column 4 have been obtained from Laird and Yeats
(1990); for sectors 25, 26, 27, 30, 34, 35, 42, 44, 45 and 47 from GATT (1993) ; and author's cal-
culations for remaining sectors.

The Additional Protocol to the Ankara Treaty divided up the imports of Turkey between two lists. Those industrial products in which it was thought that Turkey could achieve international competitiveness relatively early were placed on the "12-year list." Other manufactured products were put on a 22-year list, for which a customs union (CU) would not be achieved until 1995. With the formation of the CU with the EU, Turkey has reduced the NPRs to zero on all the commodities that were included in the 12-year and 22-year lists.

Two other sets of products were treated separately: (i) agricultural products and (ii) products falling within the mandate of the "European Coal and Steel Community" (ECSC). In order to establish freedom of movement of agricultural products, Turkey will have to adjust its policy in such a way as to adopt the EU common agricultural policy (CAP). But as will be explained in more detail, it is most unlikely that the freedom of movement of agricultural products will be achieved in the near future. Therefore we expect the NPR's on agricultural products to remain unchanged over the next few years. As for the products falling under the ECSC, these were subsequently treated under a "Free Trade Agreement" (FTA) which was signed in December 1995. The FTA envisions the gradual liberalization of trade in ECSC products over a period of three years. Therefore by the year 2001, the NPR's for products included in the 12 and 22-year lists and the ECSC products are projected to be zero. Referring back to Table 8, 38 industries will enjoy zero NPR. After the formation of the customs union, the average nominal protection rate in trade with EU will be reduced to 1.34 percent. Furthermore, we note that the highest NPR in trade with the EU will affect the following sectors: "fruits and vegetables" (68 percent), "fishery" (48 percent) and "agriculture" (41 percent).

In the case of trade with third parties, a distinction has to be made in respect of trade with member countries of the EFTA, the Mediterranean countries, the Central and Eastern European countries, the Baltic countries, developing countries having the Generalized System of Preferences (GSP) treatment and the Lomé Convention countries. With each of these country groups, EU has concluded preferential trade agreements. Since Turkey after the formation of the CU will have to apply the Community's CET and accept all of the preferential agreements the EU has concluded over time, at the latest by 2001, Turkey in five years will be faced with different sets of tariff rates for different groups of countries. In the case of EFTA countries, CEE countries, the Baltic countries and Israel, which have free trade agreements with the EU, the nominal tariff rates that will be applied by Turkey in the year 2001 on imports from these countries will be identical to those applied on imports from the EU. Thus the NPR's given in column 2 of Table 8 will have to apply to about 54 percent of imports, which is the average share of Turkish imports from EU, EFTA, CEE and Baltic countries and Israel in total imports during the 1991-1993 period. For these countries, the average tariff will decrease from 22 percent to 1 percent. The share of developing countries that enjoy preferential access to the Turkish market (through the GSP) is around 28 percent. Finally the share of countries like the USA, Japan and Canada, – whose exports to the EU face the CET, in Turkish imports is 19 percent. Columns 4 of Table 8 shows the average most favored nation (MFN) tariff rates obtained under the assumption that Turkey does not change the NPR's on agricultural commodities. Similarly column 5 of Table 8 shows under the same assumptions the average tariff rates for GSP beneficiaries. Thus we assume that the tariff rates Turkey will apply by 2001 will be as shown in columns 2, 4 and 5 of Table 8. Note that the average NPR for EU countries and for countries that enjoy free trade agreements with the EU will be 1 percent, for countries like

USA, Japan and Canada 7 percent and for GSP beneficiaries 3 percent.

Table 9 shows the average share of imports from different country groups in total Turkish imports as well as the corresponding Turkish NPR's applicable on imports from these country groups before and after the formation of the customs union with the EU. The table makes it clear that all of Turkey's trading partners stand to benefit from the formation of the CU.

Table 9: Share of Country Groups' Imports in Total Turkish Imports

	Share in Imports (1991-1993 Average)	NPR 1994 (Before CU)	NPR 2001 (After CU)
EU Countries	46.02	10.22	1.34
Countries EU has FTA with	7.75	22.14	1.34
GSP Countries	27.54	22.14	2.71
Countries EU Applies the MFN Tariffs	18.46	22.14	6.92
Mediterranean Countries	1.60	22.14	2.71

Source: Author's calculations based on Foreign Trade Statistics, State Institute of Statistics, Ankara.

Regarding market access for Turkish exports to the EU, we note that the latter had abolished the nominal tariff rates on imports of industrial goods from Turkey on September 1, 1971. However, certain exceptions were made. The Community retained the right to charge import duties on some oil products over a fixed quota, and to implement a phased reduction of duties on imports of particular textile products originating in Turkey. In addition, trade of ECSC products have been protected by the Community through application of non-tariff barriers (NTBs) and anti-dumping measures. After the year 2001, the NPR applied by the EU on imports of all industrial goods from Turkey including textiles and steel products will be reduced to zero as long as Turkey will fulfill all of its obligations stated in the CUD. This means that Turkey needs to effectively implement the measures regarding "intellectual, industrial and commercial property rights" and "competition policy" including measures regarding "public aid". Furthermore, Turkey has to adopt EU garments and textile agreements with third countries. As emphasized above, the market access conditions of the Agreement will not cover the agricultural commodities. Finally one should note that in the event of non-fulfillment of obligations by Turkey by the year 2001, the country will still be faced with anti-dumping and countervailing duty measures. In this case market access restrictions by 2001 would extend from the agricultural commodities to sensitive products such as textiles, clothing, iron and steel products.

The CUD offers rapid liberalization of trade. But there are some drawbacks in the liberalization provided through countervailing duties, anti-dumping procedures and safeguard measures which are mentioned in Articles 36, 42, 61 of the CUD. Article 36 specifies that as long as a particular practice is incompatible with the competition rules of the CU as specified in Articles 30-32 of the CUD and "in the absence of such rules if such practice causes or threatens to cause serious prejudice to the interest of the other Party or material injury to its domestic industry" the Community or Turkey may take the appropriate measures. Article 42 allows anti-dumping actions as long as Turkey fails to implement effectively the competition rules of the CU and other relevant parts of the acquis communautaire. In those cases, Article 47 of the Additional Protocol signed in 1970 between Turkey and the EC will remain in force. Finally, Article 61 is about safeguards which offer another drawback in the liberalization. The Article states that safeguard clauses as specified in Article 60 of the Additional Protocol will remain in effect. According to Article 60 the Community may take necessary protective measures if serious disturbances occur in a sector of the economy of the Community or prejudice the external financial stability of one or more Member States, or if difficulties arise which adversely affect the economic situation in a region of the Community.

The Europe Agreements

During the 1990s, the CEE and Baltic countries introduced sweeping reforms which changed the nature of their trading regime, and set the stage for their enhanced integration into the world economy. The trade reforms comprised three elements. First, the system of compulsory import and export licenses of the period before 1990 was abolished and with it the state monopoly over foreign trade. Second, current account convertibility of the currencies was introduced. Finally, nearly all quantitative restrictions on exports and imports were lifted. As a result, the customs tariff has become the primary instrument of foreign trade policy. There were frequent tariff adjustments during the period. Table 10 summarizes the developments in the trade regimes of the countries in transition.

The CEE countries sought support from the EU immediately following the political upheaval in their countries in the late 1980s. Support came in the form of Trade and Co-operation Agreements that were signed during the period 1988-1990. Negotiations for the Association Agreements called the "Europe Agreements" (EA) between the EU on the one side and the Czech, Slovak Federal Republic, Hungary and Poland on the other side started in

December 1990 and were signed on December 16, 1991. The Interim Agreements which cover the trade aspects of the Europe Agreements entered into force on March 1, 1992. Similar Agreements with Romania and Bulgaria have been signed during 1993 and the Interim Agreement with Romania became effective starting May 1, 1993 and in the case of Bulgaria starting with February 1, 1994. In the meantime all of the above Agreements have been ratified by national parliaments and the European Parliament. In 1995, negotiations with the Baltic countries (Estonia, Latvia, Lithuania) were concluded and the Agreements were signed, and in 1996 Slovenia followed suit. The last four agreements have not, as of January 1997, been ratified.

All of the EAs have similar structure and contain between 122 and 124 Articles. Articles 1-6 deal with political dialogue and general principles. Articles 7-36 refer to the movement of goods, and Articles 37-58 to the movement of workers and establishment and supply of services. Articles 59-69 cover issues related to movement of capital, competition and approximation of laws. Articles 70-103 refer to economic, cultural and financial co-operation. Articles 104-124 contain institutional, general and final provisions. Each EA is accompanied by a set of Annexes and Protocols.

According to the stipulations of the Interim Agreements, a free trade area is to be established at the end of a transitional period of a maximum duration of ten years, divided into two successive stages of five years each, starting from the entry into force of the Agreement (March 1992). Thus by March 2002 the countries consisting of the Czech Republic, Hungary, Poland, the Slovak Republic and the EU Member States will form a free trade area. On the Community side, the Association Agreements consolidate all the previous unilateral trade concessions, while laying the ground for the complete removal of all trade obstacles by the end of the transitional period. The trade provisions involve the immediate removal of all quotas on industrial commodities except for textiles and ESCS products, while import tariffs will be progressively eliminated over a period ranging between 2 and 5 years. The CEE countries will reciprocate more slowly by phasing out tariffs and quotas over 4 to 9 years. To qualify for concessions under the EA, products must originate in CEE countries. The EAs recognize the mineral and agricultural products exported from the CEE countries as commodities originating in CEE countries. For all other commodities the rules of origin require that imported materials from outside of the CEE countries do not exceed 40 percent or 50 percent of the value of the output. In other words, this is a 60 percent local content requirement, which is rather strict. Finally, it should be stressed that the provisions of the EAs provide for a cumulation of origin among the CEE countries.

Table 10: Regimes of the Countries in Transition

	Trade Tariff and Non-Tariff Import Barriers	Export Quotas and other Export Barriers	Exchange Regime
CEE Countries			
Czech Republic	Average weighted tariff 5.7 % in 1993. Quantitative import restrictions on some agricultural products, textiles, clothing, steel and coal; licences for oil, gas and weapons.	20 percent of exports required licensing in 1992. Export tax of 100 %, applies only to antiques and art works. Export licensing for livestock and plants, some natural resources, and products such as textiles and steel which are subject to quotas in other countries.	Current account convertibility for enterprises, some capital controls. Peg to DM/USD basket.
Slovak Republic	A 10 % surcharge on imports established in March 1994 was removed in August. Average weighted tariff in 1993 was 5.7 %. Quantitative import restrictions on some agricultural products, textiles, clothing, steel and coal; import licenses for oil, gas and weapons.	Export licensing for livestock and plants, some natural resources, and products such as textiles and steel which are subject to quotas in other countries.	Current account convertibility for enterprises, some capital controls. Peg to DM/USD basket.
Hungary	About 10 % of imports subject to quota or licensing restrictions, with number increasing in 1994. Average unweighted tariff changed from 13 % (1989) to 11 % (1991) to 16 % (1992); further increase in 1994.	Export of fuels, wheat and industrial raw materials subject to licences (a little less than 25 % of exports). 80 % of the agricultural budget in 1993 devoted to export subsidies. In 1992 these amounted to an estimated 13 % of export value.	Current account convertibility (except tourism). Some restrictions remain on capital account. Peg to USD/ECU basket.
Poland	Average weighted tariff 11 % on industrial products and 18 % on agricultural products (1993). Most quantitative restrictions eliminated in 1990. Quotas on wheat, cars, alcohol, cigars, cigarettes, engine oil and petrol.	Minimal export restrictions. Most export subsidies were eliminated in 1990.	Largely current account convertibility, limits on resident capital account transactions. Preannounced crawling peg regime.
Romania	Most licensing requirements eliminated in May 1992. Weighted average tariff 11.7 % (1993). Restrictions only for arms, drugs and items affecting national health. 30 % anti-dumping duty on alcohol, vehicles, TVs and video-recorders imposed between May-Oct. 1993.	Export quotas on raw materials for conservation reasons and drugs for price support reasons. Occasional export bans on food, fruits and wood products. Reduced export licensing requirements since June 1993.	Virtual current account convertibility (except tourism), but capital controls. Floating exchange rate.
Bulgaria	Average tariff from 13 % (1989) to 11 % (1991) to 16 % (1992). 22 % average tariff on industrial goods reported in 1994. Minimum prices for tyres and steel pipes. Restrictive import licences for a limited number of products. Some tariff quotas on processed foods and agricultural products.	Export taxes on 30 items, mainly foodstuffs, have replaced most export quotas. Export quotas on six primary commodities. Occasional export bans on agricultural products. Registration and licensing restrictions still operative.	Few restrictions on current account, heavy controls on capital account. Floating rate.
Former Yugoslavia			
Slovenia	Generally tariff free. Where tariffs are applied rates range up to a maximum of 25 %. Customs formalities tax of 1%. Some quotas on agricultural and textile products (96 % of products free of quotas).	Temporary export duties of 10-25 % on raw materials. Permit for export of susceptible goods.	Full current account convertibility, some restrictions on capital account. Floating exchange rate.
Baltic Countries			
Estonia	Only 14 % of imports are subject to duties (10 % for furs, sea and road vehicles), average weighted tariff 1.4 % (1993). Licences for alcohol and tobacco. No quantitative restrictions. Import subsidies abolished beginning of 1992.	Minimal export barriers. 100 % export tax on antiques and art works. Quotas removed except for export ban on gravel and specialised clay. Most licensing requirements removed Oct. 1991. No export subsidies.	Full current account, virtual capital account convertibility. Currency board with rate fixed to DM.
Latvia	Basic tariff 15 % (as of March 1994), but many exceptions at 0.5 %(raw materials, food products); some high agricultural tariffs. Import licensing and quotas for military products and tobacco. No import subsidies.	Export taxes on raw materials, precious metals and antiques. Few quantitative restrictions, mostly for health and national security reasons. No export subsidies.	Full current and capital account convertibility. Informal peg to SDR.
Lithuania	Import tariffs 5-15 %: higher for food products, alcohol, tobacco and about a dozen manufactured goods (carrying tariffs up to 25 %). No quotas since Oct. 1993 except for health and safety reasons.	Some export taxes on raw materials and foodstuffs. No export subsidies. Some quantitative restrictions. Export licensing system abolished in July 1993.	Full current and (virtually) capital account convertibility. Currency board, with rate fixed to USD.

Source: European Bank for Reconstruction and Development. Transition Report, October 1994

The critical issue considered in the Agreements is access to the EU market that is granted to countries in transition. Most products defined in the international trade classifications, with the notable exclusion of agricultural products, are offered access to the EU markets free of tariffs and quantitative restrictions (QR) within one year. In the case of agricultural products, the Agreements affect five main product groups: meat, live animals, fruit, vegetables and processed agricultural commodities. Trade in grain is not covered by the Agreements. Agricultural exports from CEE countries will be permitted to increase by 10 percent in each of the next five years. Variable levies will decrease by 30-60 percent over a three-year period. Quantities exported by CEE countries above the quota limits will be subject to full tariffs and levies.

Kaminski (1994) examined in depth the industrial commodities covered by the EAs. He found that these commodities account for more than three quarters of EC imports from the CEE countries. Only Bulgaria and Hungary, with strong specialization in agricultural products, have relatively low shares as shown in Table 11. The table shows the average tariff rates applied by the EU on industrial imports from CEE countries during the pre-Agreement period. The average tariff rate was 0.1 percent for Poland, a GSP beneficiary country, and 6.9 percent for Bulgaria, a country that did not have GSP status. However, in addition to tariff barriers, the CEE countries faced (NTBs), which had become the major instrument of protection in the EU. NTB coverage ratios, as measured by the share of imports subject to NTBs in total, has varied among the CEE countries. It is highest in the case of Romania and lowest in the case of Bulgaria.

Kaminski (1994) divides the industrial commodities into six groups: immediate free trade group, textiles and clothing group, ECSC group, the quota/five year delayed group, the one-year delayed free trade group, and the four-year delayed free trade group. The "quota/five year delayed" group (includes organic and inorganic chemicals, some leather products, cork and wood products, glass, electric machinery, optical goods, plastics, footwear, furniture, motor vehicles and toys) is quite large in terms of CEE exports to the EU. This group accounts between one fourth and one third of CEE's industrial exports. The trade liberalizing measures for this group are a mixture of cuts in custom duties and increases in tariff quotas and ceilings. Custom duties are suspended within the limits of tariff quotas which will be increased annually by about 20 percent. Custom duties on imports in excess of quotas are to be reduced progressively to zero by the end of the fifth year. By 1997 there will no longer be either quotas or tariffs.

Table 11: Importance of Industrial Products in CEE Exports to EU and Pre-Agreement Market Access for Different Industrial Commodity Groups

	Share of Industrial Commodities in Total Exports to EU during 1991	Simple Average Tariff Rate		NTB Coverage Ratio	
		Industrial	Other	Industrial	Other
Bulgaria	73.0	6.9	11.6	22.5	48.3
Czechoslovakia	92.0	7.0	11.7	24.0	52.5
Hungary	73.0	0.1	9.4	24.2	57.7
Poland	81.0	0.1	10.5	23.6	48.6
Romania	94.0	0.0	8.6	28.4	59.8

Immediate Free Trade Group

	Share in Industrial Exports	Simple Average Tariff Rate	NTB Coverage Ratio
Bulgaria	43.0	5.6	3.6
Czechoslovakia	44.0	5.7	3.8
Hungary	50.0	0.0	3.7
Poland	41.0	0.1	3.8
Romania	32.0	0.0	3.4

Textiles and Clothing Group

	Share in Industrial Exports	Simple Average Tariff Rate	NTB Coverage Ratio
Bulgaria	20.9	10.8	90.6
Czechoslovakia	13.6	10.7	87.6
Hungary	21.4	0.1	85.1
Poland	17.6	0.0	88.8
Romania	28.2	0.1	86.2

The Steel ECSC Sub-Group

	Share in Industrial Exports	Simple Average Tariff Rate	NTB Coverage Ratio
Bulgaria	11.4	5.4	74.6
Czechoslovakia	10.5	5.6	64.4
Hungary	4.2	0.0	58.2
Poland	4.5	0.1	57.4
Romania	3.6	0.0	68.2

The Quota/Five Year Delayed Free Trade Group

	Share in Industrial Exports	Simple Average Tariff Rate	NTB Coverage Ratio
Bulgaria	16.3	8.6	18.8
Czechoslovakia	26.5	8.7	20.6
Hungary	24.3	0.0	21.0
Poland	23.6	0.0	21.7
Romania	31.4	0.0	23.7

Source: Kaminski (1994).

For ECSC products, specific provisions will apply. In particular, customs duties on imports applicable in the EC on steel products will be completely eliminated by the beginning of the fifth year. Quantitative restrictions on iron and steel products were eliminated with the entry into force of the Interim Agreements. In the case of coal products the time required for liberalization of trade is four years. The Community will abolish quantitative restrictions in one year. Certain imports will be liberalized by Spain and Germany within four years. Kaminski (1994) estimates that in the case of "steel ECSC subgroup" the MFN tariffs are in the range of 5.4-5.6 percent, and the GSP tariffs 0.-0.1 percent. The NTB coverage ratios vary between 57.4 and 74.6 percent. The share of this group in industrial exports was 11.4 percent in the case of Bulgaria and 3.6 percent in the case of Romania. On the other hand, import duties on textiles and clothing by the EC will be abolished over five years and those on outward processing trade immediately. Quantitative restrictions will be removed in not less than five years. Finally, one should note that in accordance with the asymmetry principle, custom duties on most industrial products originating in the EC are to be progressively reduced to zero. The time schedule for Poland is five years and for the Czech Republic, Hungary and Slovak Republic it is nine years.

The above considerations reveal that by the end of the century the NTB coverage ratios, the average tariff rates and their standard deviation will be reduced to zero for all the groups of EU industrial imports originating from CEE countries. Similarly, in the case of EU industrial exports to CEE countries, the NTB coverage ratios, the average tariff rates and their standard deviation will be reduced to zero by the year 2002. Thus the EAs offer rapid liberalization of trade. But there are as in the case of CUD some drawbacks in the liberalization provided through anti-dumping procedures, countervailing duties and safeguard measures which are mentioned in Articles 29-31, 33 and 62-64 of the EAs. Article 29 allows anti-dumping actions. It is well known that EU anti-dumping practices create another form of NTBs. The Agreements specify that anti-dumping actions must accord with Article VI of the GATT, but most EU practice is GATT-consistent. Hence there is little comfort for CEE exporters. However, the EU has given a major concession in this field. Immediately after signing the European Agreements, the EU committed itself to treating the CEE countries as "market" rather than "non-market" economies. This is of prime importance for these countries as the manner in which anti-dumping investigations are carried out depend on whether a country is considered of one or the other type. The "state trading country" arrangements which the Community applied in respect of dumping practices were replaced on March 1, 1992 by the normal GATT arrangements.

Countervailing duties are dealt with in Article 62-63 of the EA with Hungary, and again these can only applied in a GATT-consistent manner. Safeguards offer another drawback to the drive towards trade liberalization. The general safeguard clause contained in the Agreements ties in perfectly with GATT rules. The Community has allowed the CEE countries to protect their incipient industries during the transition period. Another derogation enables them to deal with balance of payments difficulties. From the point of view of the EU, the Agreements allow for unspecified safeguard measures. Following Article 30, safeguard measures are permitted if imports from CEE countries cause either "serious injury to domestic producers of like or directly competitive products" or "serious disturbances ... or difficulties which could bring about serious deterioration in the economic situation of a region." Article 21 is a special safeguard provision for agricultural goods allowing discretionary contingent protection when imports originating from one party cause serious disturbance to the markets of the other party. Following the bilateral consultation procedures provided for in the agreements, greater importance is attached to consultations and conciliation than to unilateral actions.

In respect of movement of workers, establishment and services, the Agreements do not guarantee any access to workers from CEE countries to the Community's labor market beyond what is guaranteed bilaterally by the member states. They guarantee CEE countries workers non-discrimination and certain rights in the EC so long as they are "legally employed." In general, each party agrees to grant treatment to the other party's enterprises and workers no less favorably than that granted to its own companies or nationals. Freedom of establishment is, however, limited by restrictions on the Community side which affect the free movement of labor, for example, a Hungarian firm can be established in the Community but must employ, with only few exceptions, staff recruited within the Community.

The Impact of Turkey-EU Customs Union and of the Europe Agreements

When Turkey signed the Customs Union Decision, and when the CEE countries signed the EAs, they all committed themselves to undertaking some drastic tasks that include, inter alia, harmonization of commercial legislation as regards competition policy, state aids, intellectual and industrial property rights, and adoption of new rules on customs classification, valuation, rules of origin, technical regulations, standards and government procurements, and so forth.

Historically, Turkey has been using intensively during the past two decades three different tools of industrial policy: investment incentives, export incentives and the overall policy framework affecting state-owned enterprises. In addition, subsidies were also prevalent, though they are no longer compatible with the rules of the Turkey-EU CUD. Articles 30-41 of the CUD require that Turkey adopts the EU competition rules, including measures regarding public aid within two years, that Turkey's legislation in the field of competition rules is made comparable with that of the Community and that the legislation is applied effectively.

Since 1967 Turkey has also granted production incentives in order to promote investment in activities and areas which the government regarded as desirable. The incentives, regulated by laws and decrees, aimed at reducing the cost of investment and the need for external financing as well as increasing profitability. The various types of investment incentives used until lately included: customs exemptions; low interest credit for investment; tax exemptions and exemptions from some fees and duties; contributions from the Resource Utilization Support Fund; postponement of the value-added tax and exemption from construction fee; allocation of foreign exchange for investment purposes; investment incentive allowance; support from the Investment Finance Fund; real estate tax exemption; accelerated deprecation and re-evaluation; incentive premium; land allocation; incentive for additional employment; and special incentives for scientific research and development (R&D). Through the use of these measures, the Turkish government has been able to increase the profitability of investments. According to a study by the Commission of the European Communities (1989), the investment incentives in Turkey can lead to very high aid levels. It has been estimated that the aid level may reach a high of 77 percent of the investment cost of a project in developed regions, and to even higher levels in regions enjoying priority in development.

On the export side, the various types of export incentives provided by the government during the 1980s and 1990s included: export tax rebates; foreign exchange allocations; payments from the "Support and Price Stabilization Fund"; duty free imports of intermediate inputs; exemption from corporate income tax; payments from the Resource Utilization Support Fund; rebates on freight charges; exemptions from various taxes; fuel oil and electricity subsidy; and a deduction system. Togan (1994) shows that the average economy wide export subsidy rate has decreased from 32 percent in 1983 to 13 percent in 1990. Finally, in respect of the policy on state-owned enterprises in Turkey, we note that the Turkish public enterprise sector is very large. The state had for a long time monopolies in the following sectors: tobacco, war weapons, railways, air-transport, air and sea-port administration, post and telecommunication and sugar production; and in the manufacturing sector the state-owned enterprises were heavily concentrated in basic metals, chemicals, petrochemicals, fertilizers, newsprint, paper, oil refineries, cement and textile production. The state-owned enterprises have shown in general poor economic performance due to the soft-budget constraint they faced. These firms are not submitted to commercial code and as such they escape bankruptcy laws. The state-owned enterprises receive subsidies from the government in the form of direct transfers, equity injections and debt consolidation. There are also barriers to exit in Turkey. Public firms are often not allowed to go bankrupt.

The investment incentive schemes in Turkey sought to encourage investment, rather than to increase competition. The credit incentives, which were supposed to promote entry, have often turned into instruments that reinforced the position of the large incumbents. Furthermore, the government with its large share of the banking system has exercised direct control over the allocation of credit, and credit from public banks has often been extended not on the basis of commercial considerations. For a long time, neither a specific competition legislation was enacted nor a competition policy was in fact enforced. To promote competition within the country, Turkey during the 1980s has eliminated quantitative restrictions in foreign trade and decreased substantially the levels of nominal and effective protection rates. However, these reductions were not sufficient to ensure the proper functioning of the markets. There was an urgent need for competition policies which would relax barriers to entry and exit. Thus, in December 1994, Turkey adopted its own competition policy (the "Law on the Protection of Competition"), which was largely modeled on EU practice.

In respect of the export regime, Turkey had subscribed to the GATT Subsidies Code in 1985, thus agreeing to eliminate export subsidies by 1989. And since Turkey's status in the GATT has become that of a member of the World Trade Organization, it had signed the GATT 1994 Agreement on Subsidies and Countervailing Measures (SCM) which prohibits governments from granting subsidies contingent upon either export performance or domestic content requirements. Recently, Turkey has eliminated most of the investment and export incentives. Within this context, GATT-legal subsidies, such as those earmarked for (R&D) and those that are intended to facilitate the adaptation of plants to new environmental regulations, have been introduced in 1995. It has been emphasized that export subsidies will be restricted to those provided to R&D activities, to environmental projects, and to export promotion activities that involve participation in trade fairs, conducting market research and organization of educational activities such as seminars and conferences.

Although considerable progress has been achieved in the fields of investment and export incentives, such was not the case in the area of public enterprises. Notwithstanding the fact that privatization had become a prominent part of the Turkish structural adjustment program since 1983, many difficulties made it hard to move forward on this front.

Thus, in order to comply with the rules of the CUD, Turkey will have to stop subsidizing its public enterprises at the prevailing rates, align its state aid policies to those of the EU, and it will have to apply the same competition policies to all firms, private or public. This adjustment will certainly be costly, but unless it is undertaken and the rules applied effectively to all private and public firms, the EU may resort to commercial defense instruments (antidumping and countervailing duties) against Turkey.

The CUD's rules on subsidies will have a positive impact on competition in the economy. When faced with intensified competition, domestic industries, which may have reaped monopolistic profits in a relatively protected domestic market, will be forced to act competitively. The relatively high concentration ratios in Turkey are expected to decline over time. Furthermore, the markups between prices and marginal costs will tend to decline in the private sector following the effective implementation of competition policies, and firms in the public sector will be expected to act more competitively.

Similar considerations apply in the cases of the EAs. For example, the competition provisions of the EA that were signed between Hungary and the EU are contained in Articles 62-67. Articles 62.1, 62.2 , 62.4 (a) and 64 which read as follows:

> 62.1: The following are incompatible with the proper functioning of the Agreement, in so far as they may affect trade between the Community and Hungary:
>
> (i) all agreements between undertakings, decisions by associations of undertakings and concerted practices between undertakings which have as their object or effect the prevention, restriction or distortion of competition;
>
> (ii) abuse by one or more undertakings of a dominant position in the territories of the Community or of Hungary as a whole or in substantial part thereof;
>
> (iii) any public aid which distorts or threaten to distort competition by favoring certain undertakings or the production of certain goods;
>
> 62.2: Any practices contrary to this Article shall be assessed on the basis of criteria arising from the application of the rules of Articles 85, 86 and 92 of the Treaty establishing European Economic Community.
>
> 62.4 (a): For the purposes of applying the provisions of paragraph 1 (iii), the Parties recognize that during the first five years after the entry into force of this Agreement, any public aid granted by Hungary shall be assessed taking into account the fact that Hungary shall be regarded as an area identical to those areas of the Community described in Article 92 (3) of the Treaty establishing the European Economic Community. The Association Council shall, taking into account the economic situation of Hungary, decide whether that period should be extended by a further period of five years.

64: With regard to public undertakings, and undertakings to which special or exclusive rights have been granted, the Association Council shall ensure that as from the third year following the date of entry into force of this Agreement, the principles of the Treaty establishing the European Economic Community, in particular Article 90, and the principles of the concluding document of the April 1990 Bonn meeting of the Conference on Security and Co-operation in Europe, in particular entrepreneurs' freedom of decision, are upheld.

Thus, the EAs' rules on competition relate to agreements between firms restricting competition, abuse of dominant power, the behavior of public undertakings and competition-distorting state aids. The rules are concerned with the behavior of governments as well as firms. According to Article 64, public undertakings and undertakings to which special or exclusive rights have been granted are to be subject to the principles of Article 90 EEC within three years of the entry into force of the association agreement. Article 62.4 (a) states that state aid, compatible with the EU rules for disadvantaged regions (Article 92.3 (a) of the Treaty of Rome) can be applied to entire territories during the first five years. Since the EA competition rules are similar to those specified in Articles 30.1, 31.1, 32.1 and 33 of the Turkey-EU CUD, considerations similar to those expressed in the case of Turkey will apply. In the meantime, all of the CEE countries have introduced competition legislation. The CEE laws have also been modeled on the EU approach to competition policy.

The success of the transition from an environment where anti-dumping measures are used as in the cases of Turkey-EU and CEE-EU trade, to a situation where commercial relations are governed by competition rules, depends on the evolution of the level of integration between States. This integration will be accelerated as stressed by Marceu (1995) as long as markets are harmonized through stronger competition enforcement and the phasing-out of anti-dumping measures. Thus, the success depends on the effective implementation of competition policies by the national governments in Turkey and CEE countries.

In addition to competition policy, the CUD contains commitments on intellectual, industrial and commercial property rights. The Agreement requires that Turkey insures adequate and effective protection and enforcement of intellectual property rights and that it will implement the Uruguay Round Agreement on "Trade-Related Aspects of Intellectual Property Rights" (TRIPS) by 1999. Furthermore, Turkey will have to adopt by January 1, 1998 legislation to secure the patentability of pharmaceutical products and production processes. Regarding copyright, the Agreement requires that piracy such as counterfeiting or boot-legging be effectively banned and that the terms of protection in cases of translation, should not be inferior to fifty years in those cases in which the term is calculated on a basis other than the life of the person. Turkey by now has a new Copyright Law and a new Patent Law which are in conformity with the EU conditions. Similar considerations apply in the context of the EAs. Articles 63-64 of the EA with Hungary states that the latter will provide in five years a level of protection of intellectual, industrial and commercial property rights similar to that that exists in the Community, including comparable means of enforcing such rights.

The economic rationale for the protection of intellectual property rights is framed in terms of costs and benefits (Hoekman, 1995). The costs include increase in payments for proprietary knowledge, price increases associated with greater market power for knowledge producers, the costs associated with the displacement of pirate activities, the costs of additional R&D and those related to administrative and enforcement of intellectual property rights protection. Potential benefits include new inventions fostered by higher levels of R&D, greater technology, increased foreign trade, increased foreign direct investment flows and hence increases in per capita income of the country. Within this context, the main task facing Turkey and the CEE countries is the transformation of their intellectual property rights regime into an effective instrument for the promotion of innovation, and hence increases in income.

Article 26 of the CUD requires Turkey to adopt the EU's customs provisions in the fields of (i) origin of goods, (ii) customs value of goods, (iii) the introduction of goods into the territory of the customs union, (iv) customs declaration, (v) release for free circulation, (vi) movement of goods, (vii) customs debt, and (viii) right of appeal. Article 8 of the CUD states that Turkey shall incorporate within five years into its internal legal order the Community's instruments relating to the removal of technical barriers to trade. Furthermore, Article 46 of the Customs Union Decision specifies that negotiations aiming at the mutual opening of Contracting Parties' respective government procurement markets be initiated as soon as possible after January 1, 1996. In addition, effective functioning of the customs union requires the modernization of the customs system in Turkey. A new draft customs law has been prepared replacing the current customs law. The new draft customs law aims for speedy customs release, simplified procedures and full automation of customs procedures. Recently, the customs administration has been going through extensive training programs. Turkish customs will begin to use computer systems and will introduce on-line declaration procedures. The computer will make it possible to have at each customs point not only the relevant information for the collection of customs duties, but also the necessary information on preferential agreements and anti-dumping regulations needed to determine the correct amount of taxes to be collected.

The above provides a welcome opportunity to improve the functioning of the markets in the economies under consideration. During the transition period until about 2002, each of the economies under consideration can be considered as moving from an inefficient production point located inside the society's production possibility frontier (PPF) towards an efficient production point on the PPF. Furthermore, the new rules and disciplines, such as the rules on intellectual property rights, will over time shift the PPF outward as a result of technical progress that will be achieved during the adjustment period.

We now turn to consider the impact of changes in tariffs on the allocation of resources. As nominal protection rates change, so will domestic prices. These changes will affect different sectors in different ways, and we will aim to identifying those sectors that would potentially lose from these changes, and those that may gain. This necessitates an in-depth calculation of effective protection rates (EPR) for the years 1994 and 2001. The results are reported in Table 12. From the table it follows that the formation of the customs union will lead to an increase in the value-added of the following sectors: "grain mill products", "sugar refining" and "clothing". On the other hand, the following sectors will experience a decline in value-added: "processed tobacco", "petroleum refining" and "non-alcoholic beverages". The table indicates that the most sensitive ten sectors in the Turkish economy are the following: processed tobacco, petroleum refining, non-alcoholic beverages, alcoholic beverages, wood furniture, footwear, plastic products, cement, motor vehicles and wood products.

Potential for Trade between EU, CEE and Baltic Countries and Turkey

As the CEE and Baltic countries complete their transition to market-based economies and enhance their market access opportunities to the EU markets, the geographic distribution of trade will change. A critical question is: what is the potential for trade between EU, CEE and Baltic countries and Turkey. This question has been answered by various economists including Winters and Wang (1994) and Baldwin (1994) for the CEE and Baltic countries. They show that the potential trade with the EU is much larger than the actual. Thus, once the CEE and Baltic countries complete their transition to market economies, become further integrated into the world economy, and reap the benefits of the Europe Agreements and Free Trade Agreements, trade between CEE and Baltic countries on the one hand and EU on the other will increase. Baldwin estimated how much trade would have occurred in 1989 if the CEE and Baltic countries had never been under communist regime, but did enjoy the same level of income as they did in 1989 and if the countries did not face

Table 12: Turkish Effective Protection Rates Before and After the Customs Union with EU and Sensitive Sectors in the Turkish Economy

I-O CODE	SECTOR	EPR 1994	EPR 2001	Effects of the Customs Union
19	Processed Tobacco	159.71	-84.25	-243.96
32	Petroleum Refining	180.44	3.75	-176.69
18	Non-Alcholic Beverages	128.03	-40.69	-168.72
17	Alcoholic Beverages	145.43	-13.57	-159.00
26	Wood Furniture	62.67	1.67	-61.00
24	Footwear	67.17	15.12	-52.05
35	Plastic Products	48.45	2.22	-46.24
37	Cement	46.02	0.65	-45.37
47	Motor Vehicles	46.21	1.97	-44.24
25	Wood Products	37.28	0.67	-36.61
41	Fabricated Metal Products	35.90	0.66	-35.24
34	Rubber Products	33.95	1.29	-32.66
21	Textiles	28.79	2.68	-26.11
38	Non-Metallic Mineral	26.79	1.30	-25.49
36	Glass and Glass Production	25.54	1.26	-24.28
16	Other Food Processing	29.37	5.33	-24.04
27	Paper and Paper Products	19.20	-0.04	-19.24
44	Electrical Machinery	16.83	1.97	-14.87
29	Fertilizers	13.63	1.78	-11.85
31	Other Chemical Production	12.61	1.45	-11.16
23	Leather and Fur Production	10.73	0.43	-10.30
9	Non-Metallic Mining	9.91	0.47	-9.45
39	Iron and Steel	11.10	2.88	-8.22
42	Non-Electrical Machinery	8.37	0.45	-7.92
45	Shipbuilding and Repairing	6.51	-0.83	-7.34
43	Agricultural Machinery	6.82	0.03	-6.79
12	Fruits and Vegetables	291.43	285.80	-5.63
40	Non-Ferrous Metals	6.11	0.85	-5.27
30	Pharmaceutical Production	4.52	0.50	-4.02
28	Printing and Publishing	4.42	1.04	-3.39
2	Animal Husbandry	-18.61	-21.65	-3.04
49	Other Manufacturing Industries	1.91	-0.04	-1.95
20	Ginning	-138.12	-139.98	-1.86
5	Coal Mining	1.81	0.71	-1.10
10	Stone Quarrying	0.29	-0.09	-0.37
3	Forestry	-0.28	-0.01	0.26
6	Crude Petroleum	-0.78	-0.06	0.72
46	Railroad Equipment	-0.21	0.57	0.78
48	Other Transport Equipment	-0.84	0.23	1.07
1	Agriculture	44.41	45.60	1.19
4	Fishery	56.58	58.10	1.52
8	Other Metalic Ore Mining	-1.68	-0.13	1.54
13	Vegetable and Animal Oil	6.62	8.76	2.14
7	Iron Ore Mining	-2.74	-0.21	2.53
11	Slaughtering and Meat	16.82	21.36	4.55
33	Petroleum and Coal Products	-6.14	0.08	6.23
22	Clothing	7.44	17.35	9.91
15	Sugar Refining	-54.25	-35.98	18.27
14	Grain Mill Products	281.46	301.45	19.99
MEAN		18.44	1.12	
STANDARD DEVIATION		72.32	65.39	

Source: Author's calculations.

any market access restrictions. The ratio of potential to actual trade of the EU(12) to the CEE countries would have been twice as large as the actual figures. Similarly, the ratio of potential to actual exports of CEE countries to EU(12) varies from 1.2 for Romania to 5.2 for Bulgaria. But these estimates ignore an important point. The old planning regime depressed trade as well as incomes. As trading partners get richer, bilateral trade flows will tend to rise. The reason for this is straightforward. As a country grows richer, it buys and sells more abroad.

In an attempt to assess the magnitude of new market opportunities between Turkey on the one hand and the CEE and Baltic countries on the other, a gravity model of trade flows can be utilized. Gravity models have been successfully applied to different types of flows, such as migration, commuting, recreational traffic, and interregional and international trade. Typically, the log-linear equation used specifies that a flow from origin a to destination b can be explained by supply conditions at the origin, demand conditions at the destination, and economic forces either assisting or resisting the flow's movement.[2]

In its basic form, the equation is written as:

$$\ln X_{ab} = \alpha + \alpha_1 \ln(GNP_a / POP_a) + \alpha_2 \ln(GNP_b / POP_b) + \alpha_3 \ln POP_a + \alpha_4 \ln POP_b + \alpha_5 \ln DIST_{ab}$$

where X_{ab} is the US dollar value of exports from country (a) to country (b), GNP_a, and GNP_b are, respectively, income in country a and country b expressed in US dollar, POP_a and POP_b are, respectively, the population of country (a) and (b), and $DIST_{ab}$ denotes the distance from the economic center of a to that of b in kilometers.

Deflated GNP data were obtained from various issues of the "World Development Report" prepared by the World Bank for the period 1990-1992. The data on bilateral trade flows between 20 industrial countries over the period 1990-92 were extracted from the "Direction of Trade Statistics" and have been converted to real value using the export unit values reported in the "International Financial Statistics" of the IMF. The estimated equation is given by:

$$\ln X_{ab} = -27.881 + 1.051 \ln(GNP_a / POP_a) + 0.422 \ln(GNP_b / POP_b) - 0.839 \ln DIST_{ab}$$
$$(-33.875)\ (18.633) \qquad\qquad (8.894) \qquad\qquad (-47.457)$$

$$+ 0.824 \ln POP_a + 0.812 \ln POP_b$$
$$(41.75) \qquad (50.207)$$

$$n = 1200,\ R^2 = 0.8772;\ r = 0.183;\ DW = 2.067$$
$$(6.411)$$

where n refers to number of observations, and the t-statistics are reported in parenthesis for each estimated coefficient.

The gravity model, which was estimated on data that do not include the CEE and Baltic countries and Turkey, gives a relationship between GNP, distance and bilateral trade flows for a "normal" pair of countries, that is countries that are integrated into the world trading system. Applying the estimated coefficients to the actual data on the countries under investigation, we can predict the trade flows between Turkey and CEE and Baltic countries once the latter set of countries become "normal" countries. That is to say, once they complete their transition to market economies, are fully integrated into the world trading system and face no major market access problems. The mechanics of the projection is simple. Estimates for the relevant countries' per capita GNP, population and distance are plugged into the equation which generates the import and export pattern for trade between concerned countries.

Table 13 shows the potential values of exports and imports for trade between Turkey and CEE and Baltic countries for the year 1992. It is clear from Table 13 that the potential trade with CEE and Baltic countries is much larger than the actual. The data reveal that Turkey's exports to CEE and Baltic countries could increase by about 150 percent above their 1993 level and that Turkish imports from CEE and Baltic countries would increase by 45 percent.

Chances of EU Membership

To study the chances of EU membership of the CEE and Baltic countries and of Turkey we consider the evidence from previous EU enlargements. The results are reported in Table 14. The table reveals that the EU has shown more concern in respect of the following parameters: the prospects of functioning democracies in applicant countries, the level of per capita incomes in those countries, the size of the population and the share of the agricultural sector in a country's GNP. In all of the previous cases of successful applications, the applicant country had to prove that it had functioning democracies for a period of at least seven years (Greece). In no previous case the successful applicant country (Portugal) had a per capita income which was less than 61 percent of the poorest EC member (Greece), and a population that was larger than 27 percent at the accession (UK). Finally, in no case had the share of agriculture in GDP exceeded 18 percent (Ireland). Table 15 gives basic data on the actual and potential applicant countries consisting of CEE countries, Baltic countries, Slovenia and Turkey. All of the transition economies started to have functioning democracies only during the early 1990s. Turkey on the other hand has moved back to an open, liberal political system since 1983. In respect of population, we note that the EU population consisting of 15 countries would increase by 16 percent in case Turkey accedes and by 10 percent if Poland becomes a member. The size of the population of all the remaining

Table 13: Actual and Potential Trade Between EU, CEE and Baltic Countries and Turkey During 1992

Country	Actual Exports from Turkey	Potential Exports from Turkey	Ratio of Potential to Actual Exports	Actual Imports into Turkey	Potential Imports into Turkey	Ratio of Potential to Actual Exports
	(US$ million)	(US$ million)		(US$ million)	(US$ million)	
Bulgaria	86.22	235.23	2.73	243.24	178.98	0.74
Czech Republic	58.45	134.01	2.29	222.99	150.13	0.67
Estonia	0.30	20.58	69.29	3.44	24.29	7.07
Hungary	37.51	196.40	5.24	86.68	248.35	2.87
Latvia	2.89	29.45	10.18	2.75	27.93	10.16
Lithuania	3.95	35.25	8.92	13.82	26.31	1.90
Poland	234.80	342.83	1.46	91.10	333.48	3.66
Romania	151.65	408.19	2.69	300.78	283.59	0.94
Slovak Republic	15.74	82.46	5.24	21.91	78.87	3.60
Slovenia	30.21	70.54	2.34	45.88	143.79	3.13
	621.72	1,554.94	2.50	1,032.57	1,495.72	1.45

Note: The actual trade figures refer to the year 1993.
Source: Author's calculations and Foreign Trade Statistics, State Institute of Statistics, Ankara

countries is relatively small. The share of agriculture in GDP is 23 percent in the case of Lithuania, 21 percent in Romania, 16 percent in Latvia, 15 percent in Turkey, 13 percent in Bulgaria and 11 percent in Estonia.

Since the CEE countries have not yet produced national accounts that are up to Western standards, various sources have estimated national incomes for these countries and those estimates vary enormously thus giving rise to difficulties in providing a realistic assessment of the development level of the countries. Table 15 is based on two sets of estimates of per capita incomes as reported in the "World Development Report 1995" of the World Bank. The first estimate is per capita income measured in current US dollars and the second takes into account the purchasing power parities of national currencies (PPP). Examining the per capita income levels measured in current US dollars we note that per capita income in Romania during 1993 is 15 percent of the per capita income of the poorest EU member, namely Greece. The per capita income of Bulgaria is also 15 percent of the income level in Greece, that of Lithuania is 18 percent, the Slovak Republic 26 percent, Latvia 27 percent, Turkey 29 percent and Poland 31 percent. The situation looks different if one examines these figures using PPP. Thus per capita income in Romania reaches 31 percent of that of Greece; Lithuania's is 35 percent; Bulgaria's is 46 percent and so on. If the EU were to apply the 61 percent threshold to the applicant countries, then only Slovenia would satisfy the criteria if per capita incomes are measured in current US dollars. On the other hand, if the EU were to base its opinion on the PPP, then Bulgaria, Romania, Latvia, Lithuania, Poland and Turkey would fail the test. All of the other countries would satisfy the 61 percent threshold.

A related question is how incomes are expected to evolve over time, and whether the CEE countries, the Baltic countries and Turkey would be able to catch up to the 61 percent per capita income level of the poorest EU member in the near future. Table 16 contains data on the growth rates of population projected by the World Bank for the period 1992-2000 and reported in the "World Development Report 1994". During the period 1970-1992, Greece's GNP has grown at an annual rate of 3 percent and that of Turkey at 5 percent. In what follows, we shall consider the potential developments in CEE, Baltic countries' and Turkey's per capita GNP in comparison to the potential developments in Greece's per capita GNP. We assume that Greece's GNP will grow in the future at the same growth rate that has been achieved over the period 1970-1992 (that is, 3 percent). Furthermore, we assume that the population of Greece will grow at the annual rate of 0.5 percent. Table 16 has been prepared for different values of the growth rate of real GNP for the CEE, the Baltics and Turkey. We assume following Sheehy (1994) that the CEE and the Baltics can grow at either the pessimistic rate of 3 percent, or at the probable rate of 5

Table 14: Previous EC Enlargements

	UK	Ireland	Denmark	Greece	Spain	Portugal	Austria	Finland	Sweden
Democracy Restored				1974	1977	1974			
EC Accession	1973	1973	1973	1981	1986	1986	1995	1995	1995
Per Capita Income at Accession									
% of EC Average	82.0	53.5	122.9	40.7	49.5	22.8	118.6	97.3	127.4
% of Poorest EC Member	113.4	74.1	170.2	75.7	133.5	61.4	312.9	256.7	336.0
Population at Accession									
% of EC Total at Accession	26.9	1.5	2.4	3.5	13.3	3.5	2.3	1.5	2.5
Share of Agricultural Value Added in GDP at Accession	3.0	18.3	7.1	16.1	5.6	7.4	2.7	2.4	0.6

Source: Author's calculations using data from various issues of European Economy.

percent or at the optimistic rate of 6 percent. Regarding Turkish GNP the pessimistic rate is assumed to be 4 percent, the probable rate 5 percent and the optimistic rate 7 percent. Table 16 which is based on current US dollar values of per capita incomes reveals the following aspects:

• If the GNP of the CEE and the Baltic countries grows at the pessimistic growth rate of 3 percent and Turkish GNP at the rate of 4 percent, none of the countries except Slovenia will reach 61 percent of the Greek per capita income level over the next 25 years.

• If the CEE and Baltic countries' GNP grows at the probable rate of 5 percent and Turkish GNP at the rate of 5 percent, Hungary will reach the 61 percent threshold value after 15 years and Estonia after 21 years. With the exception of Slovenia, the remaining countries will fail to satisfy this threshold.

• If the GNP of the CEE and the Baltic countries grows at the rate of 6 percent and Turkey's GNP at the rate of 7 percent, the Czech Republic will satisfy the threshold value after 19 years, Hungary after 12 years, Poland after 25 years, Estonia after 14 and Turkey after 19 years. This will however not be the case in the Slovak Republic, Romania, Latvia and Lithuania.

Baldwin (1994) summarizes the conditions for EU membership under eight headings:

1. free movement of goods, services and factors of productions within the Union;
2. adoption of EU's common external tariff and trade policy vis-à-vis the third countries;
3. harmonization of commercial legislation;
4. participation in the European Monetary System and future monetary system;
5. adoption of EU's Common Agricultural Policy (CAP);
6. supranational appellate system to enforce consistent application of Community law throughout the Union;
7. open government procurement; and,
8. common policy promoting the disadvantaged regions by structural spending.

As emphasized above, Turkey, by forming the CU with the EU will satisfy the first condition partially, the second and third components of membership will only be satisfied by the year 2001. It is worth noting that the CUD does not cover the free movement of services or labor. The Agreement is also silent on movement of capital. The fourth component (participation in EMU)

Table 15: Basic Data on Actual and Potential Applicants for Membership in EU

	Bulgaria	Czech R.	Estonia	Hungary	Latvia	Lithuania	Poland	Romania	Slovak R.	Slovenia	Turkey
Democracy Restored	1990	1990	1992	1990	1993	1992	1990	1990	1990	1992	1983
Per Capita Income Relative to EU Income in 1993											
% of EC Average	5.8	13.7	15.6	16.9	10.2	6.7	11.4	5.8	9.9	32.8	11.0
% of Poorest EC Member	15.4	36.7	41.7	45.3	27.2	17.9	30.6	15.4	26.4	87.8	29.6
Per Capita PPP Income Relative to PPP EU Income in 1993											
% of EC Average	24.4	44.9	38.7	36.0	29.8	18.5	29.8	16.7	37.4	--	23.3
% of Poorest EC Member	45.6	83.9	72.2	67.2	55.7	34.6	55.6	31.1	69.9	--	43.6
Population Relative to EU Population in 1993											
% of EC Total	2.3	2.8	0.4	2.8	0.7	1.0	10.4	6.2	1.5	0.5	16.1
Share of Agricultural Value Added in GDP during 1993 (%)	13.2	5.5	15.2	8.2	15.0	24.8	7.4	21.6	6.6	5.0	15.4
Share of Agricultural Labor in Total Civilian Employment 1(%)	17.4	6.5	15.4	8.1	18.4	19.0	26.9	32.2	10.3	--	42.8

Source: Author's calculations using data from various issues of World Development Report and European Economy.

Table 16: Expected Developments in CEE, Baltic Countries and Turkey's Per Capita GNP

	Per Capita Income	Assumed Annual Growth of GNP	Assumed Annual Growth of Population	YEARS ELAPSED				
				5	10	15	20	25
PESSIMISTIC SCENARIO								
CEE Countries								
Czech Republic	2,710	3.0	0.2	36.49	36.32	36.14	35.97	35.79
Slovak Republic	1,950	3.0	0.6	26.26	26.13	26.01	25.88	25.75
Hungary	3,350	3.0	-0.4	45.11	44.89	44.68	44.46	44.25
Poland	2,260	3.0	0.2	30.43	30.29	30.14	29.99	29.85
Romania	1,140	3.0	0.0	15.35	15.28	15.20	15.13	15.06
Bulgaria	1,140	3.0	-0.4	15.35	15.28	15.20	15.13	15.06
Baltic Countries								
Estonia	3,080	3.0	-0.3	41.48	41.28	41.08	40.88	40.68
Latvia	2,010	3.0	-0.4	27.07	26.94	26.81	26.68	26.55
Lithuania	1,320	3.0	0.0	17.78	17.69	17.60	17.52	17.43
Slovenia	6,490	3.0	0.1	87.40	86.97	86.55	86.13	85.72
Turkey	2,184	4.4	1.9	31.46	33.50	35.66	37.97	40.43
Greece	7,390	3.1	0.5					
PROBABLE CASE								
CEE Countries								
Czech Republic	2,710	5.0	0.2	40.18	44.02	48.23	52.84	57.89
Slovak Republic	1,950	5.0	0.6	28.91	31.67	34.70	38.02	41.65
Hungary	3,350	5.0	-0.4	49.67	54.41	59.62	65.32	71.56
Poland	2,260	5.0	0.2	33.51	36.71	40.22	44.06	48.28
Romania	1,140	5.0	0.0	16.90	18.52	20.29	22.23	24.35
Bulgaria	1,140	5.0	-0.4	16.90	18.52	20.29	22.23	24.35
Baltic Countries								
Estonia	3,080	5.0	-0.3	45.66	50.03	54.81	60.05	65.79
Latvia	2,010	5.0	-0.4	29.80	32.65	35.77	39.19	42.94
Lithuania	1,320	5.0	0.0	19.57	21.44	23.49	25.74	28.20
Slovenia	6,490	5.0	0.1	96.22	105.42	115.49	126.54	138.63
Turkey	2,184	5.4	1.9	33.00	36.85	41.15	45.95	51.30
OPTIMISTIC SCENARIO								
CEE Countries								
Czech Republic	2,710	6.0	0.2	42.13	48.39	55.59	63.87	73.37
Slovak Repulic	1,950	6.0	0.6	30.31	34.82	40.00	45.96	52.79
Hungary	3,350	6.0	-0.4	52.08	59.82	68.72	78.95	90.69
Poland	2,260	6.0	0.2	35.13	40.36	46.36	53.26	61.18
Romania	1,140	6.0	0.0	17.72	20.36	23.39	26.87	30.86
Bulgaria	1,140	6.0	-0.4	17.72	20.36	23.39	26.87	30.86
Baltic Countries								
Estonia	3,080	6.0	-0.3	47.88	55.00	63.19	72.59	83.38
Latvia	2,010	6.0	-0.4	31.25	35.89	41.23	47.37	54.42
Lithuania	1,320	6.0	0.0	20.52	23.57	27.08	31.11	35.74
Slovenia	6,490	6.0	0.1	100.89	115.90	133.14	152.95	175.70
Turkey	2,184	7.0	1.9	35.58	42.84	51.58	62.10	74.77

Source: Author's calculations

is not a requirement for membership. The CUD addresses condition 5, but it does not seem to be possible for Turkey to adopt the CAP in the near future. External assistance would be essential for the implementation of this condition. In the case of CEE countries, they will satisfy in the near future the third condition of membership completely. The first condition will be satisfied partially as the EAs do not cover the free movement of labor. The Europe Agreements contain sections on services and on capital movements. Since the EAs are free trade agreements, the CEE countries will not satisfy condition 2 of membership. The countries are free to determine the level of tariffs against third countries. Regarding the CAP, similar considerations as in the case of Turkey apply. Again, as in the case of Turkey, the fourth component (participation in the European Monetary Union) is not a requirement for membership.

The components that are of real concern to the EU are the fifth (CAP) and eighth (structural funds), especially since both involve transfer of resources from the EU to the acceding member. The net cost to the EU should not threaten the prospect of receiving more transfers than the richer EU countries can reasonably be expected to finance. To determine the net costs associated with the membership of the CEE and Baltic countries and of Turkey we make use of the results obtained and of the approach developed by the Center for Economic Policy Research (CEPR, 1992) and Baldwin (1994), where the net cost is defined as the difference of between on the one hand the structural funds and the Common Agricultural Policy price support received by the countries, and of the national budgetary contribution to the EU on the other.

Consider first the problems associated with the adoption of CAP by the countries concerned using the example of Turkey, where agriculture has economy-wide implications. During 1994, agriculture accounted for about 15 percent of GDP and 44 percent of total employment in the economy. Although these shares have been falling over time, they do not compare favorably with those found in the EU countries. According to the Organisation for Economic Cooperation and Development (OECD) (1994), the value-added per agricultural worker in Turkish agriculture amounts to only 21 percent of the value-added per non-agricultural worker in Turkish non-agricultural sector. The low productivity in agriculture is associated with a farm structure characterised by small, fragmented holdings, a poor level of education and training of farmers leading to low farm household incomes. Furthermore, nearly half of the population of Turkey still lives in rural areas. In Turkey, population growth rates have exceeded 2 percent annually. The highest fertility rates are found in rural areas, with out-migration from these areas also tending to be high. Although emigration has slowed down, internal migration towards urban areas continues at a fast pace.

The objectives of Turkey's agricultural policy are to:

- ensure adequate levels of nutrition and food supplies at reasonable prices to consumers;
- raise production levels and yields while reducing the vulnerability of production to adverse weather conditions;
- move towards self-sufficiency, increase farm incomes and improve income stability;
- increase exports; and,
- to develop rural areas.

In pursuit of these objectives, the government has implemented a set of measures that provide support to producers prices, complemented by trade-related measures, the subsidization of farm inputs, and transfers related to investments in infrastructural projects. The OECD (1994b) cumulated all these support measures into the Producer Subsidy Equivalents (PSE) which measure the value of monetary transfers to producers from consumers of agricultural products and from taxpayers resulting from a given set of agricultural policies in a given year. According to the OECD study, total support as measured by the PSE is estimated to have risen during the period 1991-93 to around 40 percent – double the rate in the period 1979-81, and the share of total agricultural transfers in total GDP has amounted to 14 percent in 1991, 12 percent in 1992 and 11 percent in 1993. Thus, the average annual amount of total transfers to agriculture over the 1991-1993 period was about $14 billion. At this point, it should be noted that agriculture besides being subsidized has also been heavily protected as is evident from inspection of columns 1 and 3 of Table 8.

During the last few decades, Europe has been experiencing a dramatic decline in agriculture. The gradual but massive transfer of labor from farms in Europe has created severe economic and social problems especially for uprooted families and their dependents. This is the prime justification for ambitious agricultural policies introduced under the name "Common Agricultural Policy" which is intended to alleviate the burden of relocation from farm to city. According to the Treaty of Rome, the major goals of the CAP are to increase agricultural productivity, insure a fair standard of living for farm community, stabilize farm product markets, provide food security and secure supplies to consumers at reasonable prices.

The CAP is based on three guiding principles: (i) unity of the market, (ii) Community preference, and (iii) financial solidarity. According to the first principle, free movement of agricultural commodities is achieved through the common market order; the second principle provides agricultural markets with protection from foreign competition through market interventions; the third principle guarantees the financing of agricultural support programs from the EU budget mainly through the European Agricultural Guidance and Guarantee Fund (FEOGA). Kirmani (1994) reports that high levels of support are provided to agriculture in the EU where the PSE ratio was 46 percent in 1990, 47 percent in 1992 and 48 percent in 1993. The support has significantly reduced the EU's net food imports since the 1970s, and has substantially increased self-sufficiency ratios in the EU. But the CAP has been under great pressure to reduce the drain on the EU budget. The 1992 MacSharry reform of the CAP aimed at curbing excess production of cereals by means of set-asides of arable land and reductions in guaranteed prices, with compensation to farmers in the form of a fixed payment per hectare under cultivation. The reforms are an important step towards the market-oriented system. It was expected that by the end of the 1995/96 marketing season, intervention prices would have been reduced to world prices (European Economy, 1994). Had such a plan been implemented, there would have been no need for export subsidies or import taxes starting from 1996 onwards. Even if such a policy was in fact implemented, it should be stressed that it would not imply that the PSE ratio in the EU would decline to zero. The system of regionally calculated "compensatory" area payments tied to set-aside schemes will insure that the decline in agricultural incomes is reduced over time. Thus, in the EU, the "market price support" would decline to zero but positive amounts of "direct payments" would still be paid. As a result, the PSE ratio could be held at its present levels.

According to Articles 22-25 of the CUD, Turkey, in order to establish the freedom of movement of agricultural products, will have to adjust its agricultural policy in such a way as to adopt the CAP measures. But is this possible? What does the adoption of CAP measures mean for Turkey?

At current domestic prices, Turkey is a net exporter of some and net importer of some other farm products. But those domestic prices when converted at equilibrium exchange rates are below the EU domestic prices. Should Turkey be given preferential, tariff-free access to the EU agricultural markets at existing EU prices, then overall supply could be expected to increase in Turkey. The output of all farm products in Turkey will be higher. The aggregate level of food self-sufficiency will rise. Turkish consumers would face higher prices. Anderson and Tyers (1993) have determined that Visegrad farmers would be better off by $ 52.5 billion annually. Thus, allowing Visegrad countries into the CAP would involve a massive transfer from the EU taxpayers and Visegrad consumers to Visegrad farmers. Anderson and Tyers estimate that the total extra cost to the EU budget would amount to $ 47 billion each year. This cost would bankrupt the CAP. Since similar results would be obtained in the Turkish case, the problem faced by Turkey is who is going to provide the necessary funds? Since Turkey cannot devote an amount similar to the figures given above from its own resources for the support of Turkish agricultural sector, and since the EU would be unwilling to bear the cost, the idea of establishing a fund similar to FEOGA in Turkey would have to be abandoned. As a result, it seems that freedom of movement of agricultural products between Turkey and the EU cannot be achieved in the near future.

Furthermore, the adoption of the CAP might also involve the equalization of PSE ratios and also the equalization of farm incomes. Can Turkey raise the standard of living of Turkish farm population to that of the EU? At this point, it should be noted that the average yields of wheat and Barley in Turkey are 2 tons/hectare, whereas the same yields in France are 6.4 and 5.9 tons/hectare respectively (OECD, 1994a). Thus, even if in Turkey and in the EU commodity prices were equalized and all kinds of subsidies in the form of direct payments to producers, subsidies to capital and other inputs, subsidies in the form of general services, regional subsidies and tax concessions were eliminated, agricultural incomes in Turkey would be lower than those in France because of the large productivity differential. In order for Turkey to increase its agricultural income levels to those in France, it would in addition have to increase agricultural productivity through additional investments in agriculture, which will probably take a long time. All these arguments lead to the conclusion that the freedom of movement of agricultural products between Turkey and the EU cannot be achieved in the near future. Similar arguments hold in the case of the CEE and the Baltic countries.

Consider next the issues related to structural funds. These are transfers from Brussels to poorer member states and regions. The funds are aimed at encouraging greater economic and social cohesion. About half of structural funds is channeled into low income regions defined as the regions with per capita incomes less than 75 percent of the EU average. The funds are used to improve infrastructure in the low income regions and to provide local training. A recent study by the EC Commission (European Economy, 1993) asserts that Portugal and Greece are likely to receive ECU 400 per capita in the future. Using this approach the Visegrad-4 would receive 32.5 billion US dollars.

The budget revenue of the EU consists of receipts based on national value-added taxes (VAT) receipts, tariff revenues, variable duties and GNP contributions. Currently, the EU budget amounts to about 1.2 percent of the Union's total GDP. This fraction is set to go up to 1.3 percent by the year 2000. Using the 1.3 percent figure, the contribution of the Visegrad countries is determined as US $ 6.9 billion. Hence, the net budgetary cost to the EU of admitting Visegrad-4 as members would amount to US $ 72.6 (47 + 32.5 - 6.9) billion. Baldwin admits that the figure is too large. His own estimates of the net cost of membership are shown in Table 17. From the table it follows that admitting the Czech Republic, Hungary and Slovenia as new member states of the Union would cost EU US $ 5.63 billion. Admitting in addition Poland as a new member would increase the cost to US $ 13.75 billion. Admitting in addition the Baltic countries, the Slovak Republic, Bulgaria and Romania would increase the annual cost to US $ 33.38 billion.

Table 17: Total Budget Cost of EU Membership (billion US $)

	Czech Republic	2.50
	Hungary	2.88
	Slovenia	0.25
Sub-Total		5.63
	Poland	8.13
Sub-Total		13.75
	Estonia	0.75
	Latvia	1.50
	Lithuania	1.75
Sub-Total		17.75
	Bulgaria	2.88
	Romania	11.63
	Slovak Republic	1.13
Sub-Total		33.38

Source: R.E. Baldwin, (1994).

The estimates presented are rather rough. But one aspect is clear. The CEE and the Baltic countries and Turkey would impose a large burden on the EU taxpayers if they would accede to the EU, and the latter were to apply its current rules of the CAP and the structural funds. Note that the 1994 EU budget has amounted to ECU 72.3565 billion ECU. Hence the burden of admitting the Czech Republic, Hungary, Poland and Slovenia into the EU would constitute about 15.2 percent of the EU budget. Admitting the remaining CEE and the Baltic countries to the Community would increase the cost to 36.9 percent. These figures are indeed large for the Community. If the EU intends to admit these countries as new members, then either the budget has to be increased considerably or the rules on "structural funds" and "price support under CAP" have to change.

The budgetary outlays to the EU have to be evaluated relative to potential gains which would come in terms of increased trade and political stability. Estimates of potential EU trade with the CEE and the Baltic countries and with Turkey using the Gravity model reveals that the trade of the CEE, the Baltics and Turkey with the EU would increase considerably over the coming decades. Politically, there are gains to be derived from a future stable central and eastern Europe and Asia Minor. It seems that sustainable high growth of GNP by potential candidates is a prerequisite for membership to the EU. But the whole question boils down to how much the EU would be willing to spend to integrate these countries into its own economy.

Notes

1 *OECD Economic Surveys: Turkey 1992-1993.* Paris: OECD.
2 The gravity equation has been justified theoretically by Bergstrand (1985) among others.

References

Anderson, K., and R. Tyers. 1993. "Implications of EC Expansion for European Agricultural Polices, Trade and Welfare." Discussion Paper Series No. 829. London: Center for Economic Policy Research.

Baldwin, R.E. 1994. *Towards an Integrated Europe.* London: Center for Economic Policy Research.

Bergstrandt, J.H. 1985. "The Gravity Equation in International Trade: Some Microeconomics Foundations and Empirical Evidence." *Review of Economic Studies*: 474-478.

Center for Economic Policy Research. 1992. *Is Bigger Better? The Economics of EC Enlargement.* London.

Commission of the European Communities. 1991. *The Community Budget: The Facts in Figures.* Brussels: Office for Official Publications of the European Communities.

Commission of the European Communities. Statistical Office, *Trade Statistics* (on diskettes). Luxembourg.

Commission of the European Communities. 1993. "Stable Money - Sound Finances: Community Public Finance in the Perspective of EMU." *European Economy*, No 53.

Economist Intelligence Unit. *Country Reports and Country Profiles on CEE Countries, Baltic Countries and on Former Yugoslavia.* Various Issues.

European Bank for Reconstruction and Development. 1994. *Transition Report.* London:EBRD.

Hoekman, B.M., and P.C. Mavroidis. 1994. "Linking Competition and Trade Policies in Central and Eastern European Countries." World Bank Policy Research Working Paper 1346. Washington, D.C.

International Monetary Fund. 1995a. *World Economic Outlook*, Washington, D.C.:IMF. May.

International Monetary Fund. 1995b. *Direction of Trade Statistics Yearbook,* Washington, D.C.:IMF

Kaminski, B. 1994. "The Significance of the "Europe Agreements" for Central European Industrial Exports." World Bank Policy Research Paper 1314. Washington, D.C.

Kirmani, N., N. Calika, *et.al.* 1994. *International Trade Policies: The Uruguay Round and Beyond: Volume I. Principal Issues.* Washington, D.C.:International Monetary Fund.

Marceu, G. 1995. "The Full Potential of the Europe Agreements: Trade and Competition Issues: The Case of Poland." *World Competition:* 35-69.

Mastropasqua, C., and V. Rolli. 1994. "Industrial Countries' Protectionism with Respect to Eastern Europe: The Impact of the Association Agreements Concluded with the EC on the Exports of Poland, Czech Republic and Hungary." *World Economy:* 151-169.

Organization for Economic Cooperation and Development. 1992. *Economic Surveys: Turkey 1991-1992.* Paris:OECD.

Organization for Economic Cooperation and Development. 1994. "National Policies and Agricultural Trade." *Country Study Turkey.* Paris:OECD.

Togan, S. 1994. *Foreign Trade Regime and Trade Liberalization in Turkey during 1980s.* London: Avebury Press.

Winters, L.A., and Z. K. Wang. 1994. *Eastern Europe's International Trade.* Manchester and New York: Manchester University Press.

World Bank. 1995. *World Development Report 1995.* Washington, D.C.

Appendix
Classification Scheme for Revised SITC, Revision 2

SITC COMMODITY

Food and Live Animals Chiefly for Food

00	Live Animals Chiefly for Food
01	Meat and Meat Preparations
02	Dairy Products
03	Fish and Fish Preparations
04	Cereals and Cereals Preparations
05	Vegetables and Fruits
06	Sugar and Sugar Preparations
07	Coffee, Tea, Cocoa, Spices
08	Feeding Stuff for Animals
09	Miscellaneous Edible Products

Beverages and Tobacco

11	Beverages
12	Tobacco and Tobacco Manufactures

Crude Materials, Inedible, Except Fuels

21	Hides, Skins and Furskins, Raw
22	Oil Seeds and Oleaginous Fruit
23	Crude Rubber
24	Cork and Wood
25	Pulp and Waste Paper
26	Textile Fibres and their Wastes
27	Crude Fertilizers and Crude Minerals
28	Metalliferrous Ores and Metal Scrap
29	Crude Animal and Vegetable Materials

Mineral Fuels, Lubricants and Related Materials

32	Coal
33	Petroleum & Petroleum Products
34	Gas, Natural and Manufactured
35	Electric Current

Animal and Vegetable Oils, Fats, and Waxes

41	Animal Oils and Fats
42	Fixed Vegetable Oils and Fats
43	Animal and Vegetable Oils and Fats, Proc.

Chemicals and Related Product

51	Organic Chemicals
52	Inorganic Chemicals
53	Dyeing ,Tanning and Colouring Materials
54	Medicinal and Pharmaceutical Products
55	Essential Oils and Perfume Materials
56	Fertilizers, Manufactured
57	Explosives
58	Plastic Materials
59	Chemical Materials and Products, N.E.S.

SITC COMMODITY

Manufactured Goods Classified Chiefly by Material

61	Leather Manufactures
62	Rubber Manufactures
63	Cork and Wood Manufactures
64	Paper
65	Textiles
66	Non-metallic Mineral Manufactures
67	Iron and Steel
68	Non-ferrous Metals
69	Manufactures of Metal

Machinery and Transport Equipment

71	Power Generating Machinery and Equipment
72	Machinery Specialized for Particular Industries
73	Metalworking Machinery
74	General Industrial Machinery and Equipment
75	Office Machines
76	Telecommunications Apparatus
77	Electrical Machinery
78	Road Vehicles
79	Other Transport Equipment

Miscellaneous Manufactured Articles

81	Sanitary, Plumbing, Heating
82	Furniture
83	Travel Goods
84	Clothing
85	Footwear
87	Scientific Instruments and Optical Goods
88	Photographic Apparatus and Optical Goods
89	Miscellaneous Manufactured Articles

Commodities and transactions not classified elsewhere in the SITC

91	Postal Packages
93	Special Transactions
94	Animals, Live
95	Armoured Fighting Vehicles
96	Coin
97	Gold, Non-Monetary

Contributors

Mohamad Amerah is the senior economic advisor with the ministry of Economy and Commerce in Abu Dhabi. His fields of specialization are international trade and growth, and labor economics. He has published extensively on issues of trade, industrial development and labor markets with an emphasis on Jordan and the Occupied Palestinian Territories.

Ishac Diwan is with the World Bank in Washington, DC and is the regional coordinator of the Economic Development Institute. He has numerous publications in the areas of international finance and trade. His current research focuses on labor and Middle East-related issues.

Simeon Djankov is currently a Consultant with the World Bank in Washington, DC He has published widely in the areas of corporate governance, privatization, and trade policy. His areas of interest also include financial sector reform and regional disintegration.

Bachir Hamdouch is Professor and Head of the Economics Department of the National Institute of Statistics and Applied Economics in Rabat, Morocco, as well as a consultant for Moroccan commercial banks. His publications are in the areas of labor migration, macroeconomics, international trade and development, with an emphasis on Morocco.

Bernard Hoekman is a senior economist with the Development Economics Research Group of the World Bank in Washington, DC. His current research is on trade-related issues of economies in transition in the Middle East, North Africa and Europe. His publications focus on world trade issues and agreements.

Hans Löfgren is currently Research Fellow in the Trade and Macroeconomics Division of the International Food Policy Research Institute in Washington, DC. His research and publications focus on the development and application of general equilibrium and sector models to analyze the impact of macro and micro policies on agriculture and the poor in the Middle East.

Mahmoud Mohieldin is Assistant Professor of Economics at the Faculty of Economics and Political Science of Cairo University, as well as Economic Advisor to Egypt's Minister of State for Economic Affairs. He specializes in the economics of finance with an emphasis on developing countries and applied macroeconomics. His publications have included issues relating to informal credit transactions, financial reform, trade in services and regional integration.

David Nygaard is the Director of Country Programs with the International Food Policy Research Institute (IFPRI) in Washington, D.C and was the coordinator for the IFPRI's global initiative "A 2020 Vision for Food, Agriculture, and the Environment". He also serves as Vice Chair of the Middle East Research and Information Project and Board member of the Near East Foundation

Sherman Robinson is Division Director of the Trade and Macroeconomics Division at the International Food Policy Research Institute in Washington, DC His numerous publications are on international trade policy, the economics of developing countries and the methodology of multisector modeling.

Raed Safadi is currently Senior Economist with the Organization for Economic Cooperation and Development (OECD) in Paris, where he is working on trade and trade-related issues of concern to developing economies. His fields of specialization are international trade, international finance, and environmental economics.

Sübidey Togan is currently Professor of Economics and Chairman of the Department of Economics at Bilkent University in Ankara, Turkey. His publications focus on the Turkish economy with an emphasis on liberalization and international trade.

Ercan Uygur is Professor and Head of the Department of Economics at the Faculty of Political Science at Ankara University in Ankara, Turkey, as well as a consultant to the Turkish Central Bank. His publications focus on the Turkish economy in the areas of macroeconomics, econometrics and foreign trade

Jackline Wahba is a Lecturer in the Economics Department of Southampton University in the United Kingdom. Her research has focused on migration, remittances, international trade, and labor markets in developing countries

Michael Walton is the Director of the Poverty Reduction and Economic Management Network at the World Bank in Washington, DC He served as Staff Director for the 1995 World Development Report on Labor and has been the World Bank country economist in various Pacific and African locales.

Alexander Yeats is the Principal Economist with the World Bank's Development Research Group in Washington, DC. His research focuses on trade and development issues. He has written six books and published numerous articles in leading academic journals on these subjects.

Index